Imagining Marketing

T0358468

Why do museum visitors prefer the fake to the real?

Imagination is a word that is widely used by marketing practitioners, advertisers especially, but rarely examined by marketing academics. This neglect is largely due to the imagination's 'artistic' connotations, which run counter to the 'scientific' mindset that dominates marketing scholarship.

Of late, however, an artistic 'turn' has taken place in marketing research and *Imagining Marketing* accentuates this turn by arguing that the mantle of imagination has now passed from the artist to the marketer. It contends, moreover, that the tools and techniques of artistic appreciation can be successfully applied to all manner of marketplace phenomena.

Key features include:

*   The treatment of artistic artefacts as a source of marketing understanding
*   a detailed discussion surrounding the argument that marketers should adopt more imaginative modes of academic expression
*   an analysis of the kind of art that marketing is, and the place of imagination in marketing's artistic palette.

Imagining Marketing: Art, Aesthetics and the Avant-Garde provokes a new way of thinking about marketing, and will prove invaluable to marketing academics, researchers and practitioners.

Stephen Brown is Professor of Marketing Research at the University of Ulster. He has written or co-edited ten books and has been published in a wide variety of prominent academic journals.

Anthony Patterson is a Research Assistant at the University of Ulster, and has written several papers on the interface between art and marketing.

Routledge Interpretive Marketing Research

Edited by Stephen Brown
University of Ulster, Northern Ireland
and Barbara B. Stern
Rutgers, the State University of New Jersey, USA

Recent years have witnessed an 'interpretative turn' in marketing and consumer research. Methodologists from the humanities are taking their place alongside those drawn from the traditional social sciences.

Qualitative and literary modes of marketing discourse are growing in popularity. Art and aesthetics are increasingly firing the marketing imagination.

This series brings together the most innovative work in the burgeoning interpretative marketing research tradition. It ranges across the methodological spectrum from grounded theory to personal introspection, covers all aspects of the postmodern marketing 'mix', from advertising to product development, and embraces marketing's principal sub-disciplines.

Imagining Marketing

Art, aesthetics and the avant-garde

Edited by Stephen Brown and Anthony Patterson

London and New York.

First published 2000
by Routledge
2 Park Square, Milton Park, Abingdon, Oxon, OX14 4RN

Simultaneously published in the USA and Canada
by Routledge
270 Madison Ave, New York NY 10016

Reprinted 2002

Transferred to Digital Printing 2007

Routledge is an imprint of the Taylor & Francis Group

© 2000 Stephen Brown & Anthony Patterson

Typeset in Perpetua by RefineCatch Limited, Bungay, Suffolk

British Library Cataloguing in Publication Data
A catalogue record for this book is available from the British Library

Library of Congress Cataloging in Publication Data
Brown, Stephen
        Imagining marketing : art, aesthetics, and the avant-garde / Stephen
Brown & Anthony Patterson.
            p. cm. – (Routledge interpretive marketing research)
        Includes index.
ISBN 0–415–23486–7
        1. Arts – Marketing.   2. Creation (Literary, artistic, etc.)   I.
Patterson, Anthony.   II. Title.
    III. Routledge interpretive marketing research series.
    NX634 .B765   2000
    700′ 68′8 – dc21   00–055226

ISBN10: 0–415–23486–7 (hbk)
ISBN10: 0–415–43968–X (pbk)

ISBN13: 978–0–415–23486–3 (hbk)
ISBN13: 978–0–415–43968–8 (pbk)

Printed and bound by CPI Antony Rowe, Eastbourne

Publisher's Note

The publisher has gone to great lengths to ensure the quality of this reprint
but points out that some imperfections in the original may be apparent

Contents

Contributors

Søren Askegaard was born in 1961. He is Associate Professor of Marketing at SDU Odense University, Denmark and Professor of Marketing at Lund University, Sweden. He has a Masters degree in Social Sciences from Odense University, a post-graduate Diploma in Communication Studies from the Sorbonne University, Paris and a PhD in Business Studies from Odense University. His research interests are generally stuck in the field of consumer behaviour analysis from a cultural perspective, although he finds it difficult to concentrate very long on one particular topic. He has received two well-deserved (if you ask his wife) Danish research awards. His work does not appear in most major journals, although he once contributed to 'The Flag Bulletin'.

Russell W. Belk is the N. Eldon Tanner Professor of Business Administration and Professor of Marketing at the David Eccles School of Business, University of Utah. He received his PhD at the University of Minnesota and has been at DESB for the past 20 years. He previously had appointments at the University of Illinois and Temple University, and has had visiting appointments at the University of British Columbia (Canada), Craiova University (Romania), and Africa University (Zimbabwe) as well as honorary appointments at Hong Kong City University (Hong Kong), Edith Cowan University (Australia), and the University of Michigan (USA). His areas of expertise are consumer behaviour, qualitative research, and marketing and development. He is past president of the Association for Consumer Research and president-elect of the Society of Marketing and Development. He has received two Fulbright grants (1991–2 and 1998–9), is a fellow in the Association for Consumer Research and the American Psychological Association, and has received several awards for best journal articles, best journal reviewer, and best instructor. He is also a recipient of the University of Utah Distinguished Research Award and has published more than 250 books, articles, and videotapes.

Stephen Brown is an academic installation artist. He made his reputation with the infamous *Double Blind Review*, a tent embroidered with the titles of all the manuscripts he's trashed under the protection of the peer review system. It was more like a marquee, actually. The subversion continued with *Desk*, a provocative exhibit comprising the artist's actual two-drawer university desk, plus modesty board, strewn with empty coffee cups, Post-It notes, overdue library books, journal rejection letters and a mound of unanswered memoranda. So outrageous did *Desk* prove, that the installation was attacked by two deranged marketing scientists, who proceeded to tidy it up and almost got as far as sharpening the pencils before they were physically restrained by security guards. Undaunted, Stephen is currently working on *Nix the Mix*, a series of four monumental sculptures in the shape of giant pea pods. Constructed from discarded copies of Kotler, the works are due to be installed outside the Marketing Science Institute (Boston), the American Marketing Association (Chicago), the Chartered Institute of Marketing (Cranfield) and the European Marketing Academy (Brussels). Unless the Tate gets in touch first . . .

Fabian Faurholt Csaba was born in London in 1966. He has an MA in Languages and International Commerce and received his PhD in Marketing and Consumer Theory from University of Southern Denmark, Odense University in 1999. His dissertation analysed the commercial and cultural significance of shopping malls. He currently does most of his shopping and research in Ankara, Turkey, where he is Assistant Professor of Marketing at Bilkent University's Department of Management. He is a founding member of the Center for Research in Transitional Societies at Bilkent University.

Ian Fillis is Lecturer in Marketing in the Faculty of Management at the University of Stirling, Scotland. He holds a BSc in Civil Engineering from the University of Glasgow, an MA in Marketing from the University of Ulster and a PhD on the internationalisation process of the smaller firm from the University of Stirling. His main research interests focus on issues at the marketing and entrepreneurship interface such as creativity and innovation, in addition to exploring international marketing and export related phenomena. As well as attempting to follow a creative approach to his research, he also enjoys investigating the world of art history, visiting galleries, and supporting Liverpool Football Club.

Robert Grafton Small. Prematurely retired after posts in Marketing at Strathclyde and Organisational Symbolism at St Andrews, Robert Grafton Small has been damned with high praise and a meagre pension. Currently an honorary associate of Keele University, he maintains an active interest in original research, publishing and the occasional academic adventure.

Matthew Higgins is an alumnus of the Dudley Local Education Authority. Having graduated in Sociology from Staffordshire Polytechnic, Matthew temporarily escaped the dole queue by pursuing a career in Marketing. Matthew is currently a Research Associate in the Management Centre at the University of Leicester. He is still studying for his PhD at Keele University where he is examining representations of ethics in marketing.

Elizabeth C. Hirschman is Professor of Marketing in the Faculty of Management at Rutgers, the State University of New Jersey. She has published articles in a wide variety of social science and business journals. She is past president and treasurer of the Association for Consumer Research and past vice president of the American Marketing Association. Her primary research interests are philosophy of science, interpretive research methods and the semiotic analysis of cultural media.

Morris B. Holbrook is W.T. Dillard Professor of Marketing, Graduate School of Business, Columbia University, New York, where he teaches courses in communication and in consumer behaviour. Besides his articles in various marketing journals, his research has appeared in publications devoted to research on consumer behaviour, semiotics, cultural economics, the arts, aesthetics, psychology, organisational behaviour, communication, leisure and related topics. Recent books include *Daytime Television Shows and the Celebration of Merchandise: The Price is Right*; *The Semiotics of Consumption: Interpreting Symbolic Consumer Behavior in Popular Culture and Works of Art* (with Elizabeth C. Hirschman); *Postmodern Consumer Research: The Study of Consumption as Text* (with Elizabeth C. Hirschman); and *Consumer Research: Introspective Essays on the Study of Consumption*.

Pauline Maclaran is Reader in Marketing at De Montfort University, Leicester. Prior to becoming an academic she worked in industry for many years, initially in marketing positions and then as a founder partner in her own business, a design and marketing consultancy. Her main research interests are feminist perspectives and gender issues in marketing; and the utopian dimensions of contemporary consumption, particularly in relation to the festival marketplace.

Andrew McAuley (cover design) is an unemployed artist who works as an academic in the University of Stirling where he is a Senior Lecturer in Marketing. He has just been appointed as Vice Dean Teaching in the Faculty of Management where he intends to slay dragons and right wrongs. His artistic bent originates from being awarded a Brooke Bond National School Award for Infants Art in 1967. He would love to hear from any other winners of said award. Only very cruel people would say his style has not moved on much. Instead a Canadian friend said, 'You have some nice art stuff McAuley. You could actually become a starving artist instead of a starving academic. Instead you have become both – is that good?'

Stephanie O'Donohoe is a Senior Lecturer in Marketing at the University of Edinburgh. A graduate of Trinity College, Dublin and the College of Marketing and Design, Dublin, she completed a PhD at Edinburgh exploring young adults' experiences of advertising. Her research addresses consumers' experiences of advertising, the implications of treating ads as texts to be read, and marketplace dealings with death, dying and bereavement. Her work has been published in a range of journals, edited volumes and conference proceedings.

Anthony Patterson was born in 1973 on a beautiful summer's day in a little town called Ballymoney. As a young child when asked, 'what do you want to be when you grow up?', he would reply, 'a cement mixer'. Sadly, mechanisation has since rendered this career option obsolete and so he had to settle for a job working alongside Stephen Brown in the University of Ulster, Coleraine. He has made the most of it, though, having registered for a PhD on the consumption and production of Irish theme pubs. He looks forward to the day when he will be able to sign his name as Dr Patterson and plans to celebrate this momentous occasion by driving across America in a convertible.

Simone Pettigrew is Senior Lecturer in Marketing at Edith Cowan University, Perth, Western Australia. Her current research areas include the negative outcomes of consumer behaviour, culture and consumption, alcohol studies, grounded theory, and Internet marketing. Simone has previously held several marketing roles in both private and public organisations, particularly within the Australian energy sector.

David Pickton is Principal Lecturer in Marketing and Deputy Head of the Marketing Department at De Montfort University. He has worked in marketing and advertising in client and agency organisations and is a CIM Chartered Marketer. His academic interests lie in the areas of marketing communications, competitive marketing intelligence and the management of marketing. Non-academic interests include writing poetry.

Hope J. Schau is an Assistant Professor of Marketing at Temple University, Philadelphia. She completed her degree at the University of California, Irvine in 2000. Her dissertation, 'Consumer Imagination, Identity, and Self-expression in Computer Mediated Environments', traces the Western philosophical notion of imagination and applies it to consumer-brand relationships in personal websites. She has an undergraduate degree in English (Creative Writing) and is the author of several short stories and poems that have found their way to publication.

Jonathan E. Schroeder is a Visiting Researcher at the Swedish Royal Institute of Technology, in the Department of Industrial Economics and Management. He is also a research affiliate at the European Center for Art and Management in Stockholm. His book *Visual Consumption* is forthcoming from Routledge. His research is focused on articulating how images work – clarification, communication, and conceptualization of brand image, corporate image, product image, and identity image. He is particularly sensitive to ethical issues surrounding identity, images, and corporate communication.

John F. Sherry, Jr., Professor of Marketing at the Kellogg School, is an anthropologist who studies both the sociocultural and symbolic dimensions of consumption and the cultural ecology of marketing. He is a Fellow of the American Anthropological Association, as well as the Society for Applied Anthropology. He is a past President of the Association for Consumer Research, and a former Associate Editor of the *Journal of Consumer Research*. He enjoys wandering the world as a researcher, teacher, and consultant. He writes poetry in his spare time and is an avid flatwater paddler.

Warren Smith is a graduate of Warwick, Lancaster and Keele Universities. He dislikes so called 'funny', 'ironic' or 'self-deprecating' biographies. He lives alone.

Craig J. Thompson was not born a coalminer's daughter. Rather, he is the son of a fallen Southern Baptist woman but that's all right mama. His daddy's identity has always been a matter of public dispute but rumour has it that a Pentecostal evangelist cum professional wrestler cum Elvis impersonator with a reputation for courtin' did the deed. Thompson's uncertain connection to this simulacra of the magical aura of Elvis has none the less conferred certain professional advantages. Illegitimacy is the discursive subtext of Thompson's oeuvre. He uses illegitimate methods to study illegitimate topics. Amazingly, much of this misbegotten work has been published in formerly legitimate journals much to the stupefaction of befuddled editors who found themselves powerless to stop these recurrent travesties and who could only muddle the words 'I am all shook up' when pressed for an explanation by the angry hordes of righteously indignant marketing scholars. All in all, Thompson ain't done too bad for a Southern White Trash bastard. Thankyouverymuch.

Darach Turley is Senior Lecturer in Consumer Behaviour and a former Director of the MBA programme at Dublin City University. His first degree is in psychology, and he also has a Masters degree in philosophy and a PhD in consumer behaviour. His research interests include the senior market, advertising and older viewers, and the relationship between bereavement and consumer behaviour. His work has been published in the *Irish Marketing Review*, in conference proceedings of the Association for Consumer Research and the Academy of Marketing, and in various edited volumes on marketing. He is co-editor, with Stephen Brown, of *Consumer Research:Postcards from the Edge*. (Routledge)

Joel Watson is currently working on his PhD in Marketing and MFA in Film at the University of Utah. He has a degree in business from the University of Virginia, and a degree in Philosophy of Science from the University of Maryland. After a long stint as an entrepreneur the lure of the family business (both parents were college professors) drew him to academia where he has found room to explore. Explorations thus far include: creating, arranging and consuming of space; the meaning behind the symbol and placement of tattoos; the diffusion of hit records, and the changing world of art, media and popular culture. He has also written and directed eight short films, and is currently at work on a feature length screenplay. More than anything he hopes his further studies will illuminate the complex emotion that is present in all that we do. Whether it is love, lust, hate or anger, emotion is powerful and it is where he would like to be 'Must I dream and always see your face' – Jeff Buckley.

Preface: *Ceci n'est pas une préface*

For my sins of omission, commission and postmodernism, I receive a lot of very strange letters. Most of these, as you might expect, come from dyed-in-the-wool Kotlerites, who accuse me of heinous crimes against marketing, consider me the spawn of the Devil, and invariably conclude with the intimation that I need a damn good thrashing (I do, *I do!*). Others come from the representatives of disillusioned publishing conglomerates, who express disappointment at my latest sales figures, reluctantly pass on my proposal for a two-volume study of *Analogy and Anadiplosis in Alderson* and wonder if they could possibly have their advance back, please (or, failing that, the pound of flesh I unwisely used as collateral). Yet others come from the Dean and assorted university apparatchiks, who are keen to know why the nation's blue-chip companies aren't clamouring for my short courses, consultancy services and anything else, basically, that they can top-slice (yeah, it's a mystery to me too). And yet other communiqués come from bemused marketing students, who have been assigned my texts – as a cruel and unusual punishment, presumably – and wish to express their, er, heartfelt thanks, eternal gratitude and ever so kind regards (my duty, as they say, is to serve).

By far the craziest correspondents, however, are those who inquire if I write poetry as a sideline and, working on the assumption that I do, they thought-fully enclose a stanza or several of their own. To be perfectly honest, I'm never quite sure how to respond to these letters, since artistic types can be a tad testy. Saying the wrong thing might be taken very badly and, before you know it, I'd have all sorts of abusive phone calls, death threats and flaming e-mails. I get enough of those from my colleagues. But the truth is, I don't write poetry and I never have, not even as a lovelorn adolescent. I was much too busy reading *The Code of the Woosters*, learning the chords of *Sheena is a Punk Rocker* and playing in goal for an amateur, very amateur, double-digit-defeats-a-speciality, football team. The only 'poems' I've ever penned are entombed in the perma-sealed leaves of my less than best-selling texts. Doggerel fanciers aside, these odes, lays and epics appeal to a very limited constituency of connoisseurs, those with cloth ears, no taste and chronic learning difficulties.

In my more egocentric moments, admittedly, I consider myself the William McGonagall of the marketing academy. Nevertheless, the bottom line – literally rather than figuratively – is that I'm not a poet and I know it. (No, don't encourage me . . .)

Yet, despite my dreadful ditties, profound philistinism and autodidactic aesthetic, I firmly believe that marketing is an art; that art can provide significant insights into marketing matters; and that marketing has much to learn from the arts, broadly defined. As a sometime consumer researcher, I am convinced that the comic routines of (say) Eddie Izzard are an important source of information on recalcitrant shopping trolleys and the longueurs of standing in line at the checkout. His observations are just as meaningful, if not moreso, than those derived from questionnaire surveys, focus groups or depth interviews. Likewise, there may be a better description of the phenomenology of ice-cream eating than that proffered by Philippe Delerm in *La première gorgée de bière et autres plaisirs minuscules*, but it won't be found in the academic marketing literature, I suspect. I'm absolutely certain, furthermore, that Guinness's *Gallery* – a television ad where the protagonist makes his way through postmodern tableaux vivant of timeless masterpieces, including Rembrandt's *Night Watch*, Renoir's *Luncheon of the Boating Party* and van Gogh's *Vincent's Chair* – is a work of art in and of itself. I feel the same way about the current cinema commercial for Nike Football, which not only amalgamates elements of *The Matrix*, *Mission:Impossible*, *Star Wars*, *Terminator 2* and *Entrapment* into a mini museum heist movie, but its production values are so high that it deserves to go on permanent display in the Museum of Modern Art. Just donate it.

Vulgarian I may well be, but at least I'm not the only one. For more than fifty years marketing academics have debated the artistic and/or scientific status of the subject – after a fashion. As I've discussed at interminable length elsewhere, the bulk of this debate – if it can be described as such – centred on marketing's scientific credentials (science/not science), as opposed to its artistic merits (art/ not art), let alone the interpenetration of the two (the art of science/the science of art). To this day, indeed, it is unusual to find a chapter on Design in mainstream marketing textbooks, and as for Aesthetics – forget it! Marketing regards itself as a proto-science and, while this has considerable political utility ('hard facts' and 'the market says' can always be used to good effect in intra-organisational power struggles), the fruits of this pseudo-scientific labour have been slow to materialise. Sadly, we are still awaiting our *Principia Martematica*, *Descent of Mammon* or, for that matter, *A Brief History of Timex*. The DNA of consumption continues to elude us; marketing's theory of everything is nowhere to be found; and, when it comes to genetically modified market segments, don't hold your breath. Meanwhile, the hole in the owe-zone layer just keeps getting bigger and bigger.

Although the rocket scientists of the marketing academy have been reluctant to abandon their Mission to Mars Bar ambitions – they've been promising us major breakthroughs since Sputnik, at least – there is growing evidence of an emerging artistic imperative. This aesthetic orientation is partly attributable to widespread postmodern scepticism towards science as such, but it is also due to the realisation that Art is a massive and extremely important industry. The recent millennium commemorations, for example, have placed public art high on the political agenda. The world is witnessing a spate of museum building, the like of which hasn't been seen for one hundred years (Tate Modern, the MoMA extension, Pompidou's refurbishment, the East River Guggenheim, Seattle's Experience Music Project, the Jewish Museum in Berlin, Leibeskind's V&A 'spiral', etc., etc., etc.). Movies, moreover, are America's biggest export; Pokémon holds out similar possibilities for Japan – or perhaps it just seems that way – and the arts are a central plank of Tony Blair's five-year plans for Cool Britannia. (The British beef industry may be bereft, but its artists are singularly adept at slicing livestock in half.) As the headline-grabbing antics of YBAs aptly demonstrate, art is hot, science is not. Granted, this distinction is not clear-cut, since scientific accomplishments continue to provide fodder for artists' febrile imaginations (quarks, charms, chaos and so on) and there is much debate on the work of art in an age of cybernetic reproduction. Nevertheless, it is also true to say that the hottest scientists nowadays are not necessarily Nobel Prize winners, but those who have written best-selling books about their research – Steven Pinker, Stephen Hawking, Stephen J. Gould *et alia*.

These developments, as one might expect, are forcing an academic marketing re-think, albeit a hesitant marketing rethink. The old science-or-bust mindset is gradually breaking down. There is a growing realisation that marketing needs to be imagined anew for the twenty-first century and that the arts may assist in this challenging task. The aim of the present book, then, is to assemble a collection, a display, an exhibition – who said rogues' gallery? – of some of the most interesting academic research at the arts/marketing interface. It is based on a conference held in Belfast, Northern Ireland, the third and last in a pre-millennial series. *Imagining Marketing* is thus a companion volume to *Romancing the Market* and *Marketing Apocalypse*, both published by Routledge. As before, the book would not have been possible without the unstinting support of the University of Ulster, the incredible staff at St Clement's Retreat House and the prodigious professionalism of the contributors, who revised and returned their chapters in record time. Thank you all. The Marketing Paradiso Conclave was ably organised by my colleague and co-editor, Anthony Patterson, for which I am very grateful. I am no less grateful to Michelle Gallagher of Routledge, who has 'kept the faith' with this somewhat unorthodox series. May your rewards in Heaven be manifold and bounteous (they certainly won't be worldly!). My old friend Toshiba Tecra helped with the difficult task of assembling the final manuscript – I have to say that, otherwise he crashes on me – and my wife and daughters made themselves scarce when the air got too blue to be breathable. Many, in sum, had to suffer for the art of marketing. Now it's your turn. Enjoin.

Stephen Brown
April 2000

Introduction

Imago, Iago, A-go-go

Imagine there's no Kotler
It's easy if you try
No dearth below us
If only they would buy
Imagine all the P-eople
Looking for the way
A.P.I.C.
You may say that I'm a schemer
But I'm not the only one
I hope some day you will join us
And marketing will be as one.

1 Figments for sale: marketing, imagination and the artistic imperative

Stephen Brown and Anthony Patterson

> Art is adventurous, marketing safe; art seeks the unexpected, marketing yearns for the predictable; art wants the amazing, marketing the comfortable; art is orgasmic, marketing anal. Yet we need both, and we both want to make money; we both want the biggest audiences. We have no alternative but to live together in a constructive way, learning from and understanding one another.
>
> Tusa (1999: 120)

Untitled # 1 (imagine no possessions)

In a recent BBC poll, John Lennon's *Imagine* was voted 'the song lyric of the twentieth century'. Immediately re-released by Parlophone, the 1971 mega-hit shot to the top of the charts once again, where it occupied the No. 1 slot at the time of the millennial transition. The eponymous album was subsequently re-issued, in digitally remastered format, along with the usual paraphernalia of limited edition memorabilia – explanatory booklet, never-seen-before photographs, tie-in television programme about the making of the record, etc. What's more, the piano on which Lennon composed his masterwork (complete with cigarette burns!) was put up for auction on the Internet, with an estimated reserve price of between $1.5 and $3 million.

An everyday story of modern marketing, one might think. An exemplary instance of marketing campaign co-ordination. An object lesson in striking while the marketing iron is hot. Or is it? Closer examination reveals that the whole episode is riven with ambivalence. A multi-millionaire rock star sings about a possessionless world. The recorded product is possessed by millions of people worldwide, making more millions for the would-be possessionless muso, who eventually pays a very heavy price for his popularity. Thirty years later, the single is re-released into a consumption-obsessed society, where possessions are nine-tenths of the law, and it precipitates yet another round of passionate posses-sionlessness.[1] Only this time, the person in the re-broadcast video is no longer in possession of his possessions, having departed to the possession-free paradise he once sang about so eloquently. The re-issued, premium-priced commemorative album clocks in at 39 minutes, an egregious rip-off at a time when hour-long CDs are the norm and often contain hidden tracks, enhanced capabilities or analogous add-ons. And, the piano being auctioned is not the white baby-grand in the famous *Imagine* video, but a battered upright, currently on display in Liverpool's 'Cavern Experience', an ersatz, tourist-trinket-filled replica of the original Cavern Club, where the Beatles plied their trade before they were famous and possessions possessed them.

O tempora. O mores. O marketing

The *Imagine* imbroglio can be dismissed as an artefact of the *fin de siècle*, a time when past regrets and future hopes are on particularly prominent display (Brown 1999a). Alternatively, it can be regarded as an examplar of today's retro-marketing mindset, where dead celebrities are involuntarily exhumed to endorse 'classic' products – Gordon's gin (Clark Gable), Ford motors (Steve McQueen), KFC (Colonel Saunders) and so on – or used to add lustre to not so classic goods and services (Brown 1999b). Then again, conspiracy theorists, anti-capitalists and the No-Logo contingent (see Klein 2000) might consider Lennon's re-animation to be yet another example of marketers' duplicitous misappropriation of people's utopian aspirations for mendacious, money-grubbing ends.[2] As if! Regardless of the rationale, the *Imagine* occurrence raises interesting issues concerning the relationship between art and commerce, truth and falsity, past and present, dreams and reality. In short, the marketing imagination, the subject matter of this book.

Imagination, to be sure, is one of those words that is widely used – often in association with 'creative' – but rarely examined in detail. As Kearney rightly observes in his magisterial genealogy of the construct:

> imagination lies at the very heart of our existence. So much so, that we would not be human without it. But precisely because imagining is such an immediate and inextricable feature of our experience it is easy to take it for granted, to assume it as given. As a result, we usually lapse into an attitude of inattentiveness, ceasing to worry about the everyday ins and outs of imagination, forgetting to ask about its origins and ends.
>
> (Kearney 1998: 1)

Nowadays, imagination is usually regarded as a good thing, a universal verity, something that everyone has or ought to develop. Who, after all, would not wish to be (well) endowed with 'the creative or constructive faculty of the mind', as the *OED* has it? Some of the more straight-laced amongst us might balk at the associated dictionary definitions concerning 'fantasy', 'contrivance' and 'unjustified beliefs'. These are the 'figments' our mothers warned us about, the vivid imaginings that will 'run away with you' if you're not careful. But most people consider imagination to be a possession worth possessing. This is particularly true of practising managers, who are routinely exhorted to kick-start their stalled or seized imaginations (Morgan 1993); to break out of the red tape tied box of bureaucratic convention (O'Keeffe 1999); and 'to imagine their future the way good novelists imagine their stories' (Jensen 1999). Marketers, moreover, are regularly encouraged to exercise their imaginations on the multi-gym of customer orientation (Gabay 1998; Postma 1998); Ted Levitt (1986: 127), no less, considers imagination to be 'the starting point of success in marketing'; and leading sociologist Colin Campbell (1987, 1998) maintains that the advent of modern consumer society is attributable to the over-active imaginations of nineteenth-century Romantics.' Indeed, a recent *tour d'horizon* of the emergent 'entertainment economy' – the mega-media forces, from the Internet to MTV, that are radically re-shaping our lives – concludes that the most valued commodity of all is *the human imagination* (Wolf 1999: 296, emphasis in original).

Just as marketers are expected to be imaginative, so too they require nothing less from their customers (see Schau 2000). 'Imagine yourself in a Mercury', intones the television ad for Ford. 'Fire your imagination', British Gas recommends. 'Follow your imagination' to Cannock Beds Direct. 'Riches beyond imagination', await subscribers to *Analyse*, a magazine for day traders. 'Imagine a Northern Personal Loan', the ATM screen intimates. Barbados, after all, is 'just beyond your imagination'; Orlando is 'destination imagination'; or, if the imaginary personal loan is burning an imaginary hole in your imaginary pocket, London's Millennium Dome offers 'an extraordinary journey of the imagination'. (Book now to avoid disappointment.) Hi-fi makers Bose, meanwhile, ask us to 'imagine an entire system'. 'Let your imagination run riot', observes *The Observer*. The Honda HRV 'has always captured the imagination'. Suzuki simply invite us to 'imagine' their Vitara V8 4x4. 'Imagine', alternatively, 'what you could do with £60,000 when you enter the McCord Free Prize Draw'. And, while some might wonder about Camper Shoes ('walk more, imagine more!') when they claim that 'imagination can change the world', it can certainly help defeat fatal diseases, or so the recent 'Imagination for Cancer' art exhibition attests. Imagination, Eagleton (2000: 45) assures us, is the most 'unreservedly positive' term in the literary-critical lexicon; it is 'one of those words of which everyone approves'; nothing less than a synonym for 'the global reach of the mind'.

It was not always thus, however. The genealogy of imagination is long and tortuous, dating back to the doubts expressed by Plato and the denunciatory diatribes of the Judeo-Christian elders (e.g. Scruton 1974, 1994; Tuan 1989; Warnock 1976). The ancient Greeks, according to Kearney (1994), associated imagination with the Promethean theft of fire. This transgressive and ungodly act prompted Plato to dismiss imagination as a pernicious strategy of simulation, a misjudged attempt to fabricate fake copies of reality. Aristotle, admittedly, was much less censorious, since the act of imagining – recalling past experiences and anticipating future ones – could serve as an aid to practical reasoning. However, he was careful not to endorse it unequivocally. 'Imagination,' he concluded, 'is for the most part false' (quoted in Kearney 1998: 3).

Aristotle's 'for the most part', however, was too much for biblical exegetes – for the most part – who dated imagination to humankind's primal scene in the Garden of Eden, when Adam was tempted to envisage alternative Edenic arrangements and was expelled for his impudence. Consequently, a long line of Christian thinkers, from Augustine to Aquinas, warned against the dangers of imagination – graven images, carnal thoughts, idolatrous activities and demonic possession, to name but the least pernicious. Imagination, of course, had some practical value, insofar as it helped the faithful envisage the hosannas of Heaven and the horrors of Hell, but it was a double-edged instrument, one that had to be used sparingly and at all times under the watchful eye of reason, dispassion and faith (Kearney 1994, 1998).

The principal reason for pre-modern philosophers' suspicion of imagination was the latent threat it posed to the existing order. Its ability to transcend the here and now, by simultaneously recovering the past and projecting a future, inevitably invited seditious thoughts about doing things differently. It opened the door to other options, new ways of looking at, reflecting on, or actively organising the world. These premonitions-cum-admonitions came to fruition in Kant's 'Copernican Revolution' in thought, which placed imagination at the centre of the intellectual universe, and reached their apogee in the imagination-driven ruminations of the Romantic Movement. Schelling, for instance, considered it to be the 'unconscious poetry of being'. Samuel Taylor Coleridge distinguished between primary and secondary imagination, arguing that the former represented a 'repetition in the finite mind of the eternal act of creation'. And, Charles Baudelaire, clearly a Camper Shoes celebrity spokesperson *avant la lettre*, concluded that imagination was 'the queen of faculties . . . which decomposes all creation and creates a new world' (see Hill 1977). Imagination, to be fair, was not the only distinguishing feature of the Romantic Movement, but a host of commentators concur that it was of paramount importance (e.g. Bowra 1961; Day 1996; Drabble 1995). Romanticism, in Bloom's (1970: 19) resonant phrase, was nothing less than an 'apocalypse of the imagination'.

Apocalypse notwithstanding, the Romantic Movement is still very much with us, late and soon, albeit it operates under a 'postmodern' *nom de plume* (e.g. Brown *et al*. 1998; Elam 1992; Livingstone 1997). Imagination, moreover, has sired the sorts of mutant intellectual offspring you wouldn't want to meet in a dark alley, late at night, without a canister of Mace close to hand. One thinks, for example, of Jacques Lacan's 'imaginary', Carl Jung's 'active imagination', and the 'poetical imagination' of Gaston Bachelard, to say nothing of Allan Bloom's late lamented 'liberal imagination', the only thing that can save higher education from the inferno of relativism (Bachelard 1969; Bloom 1987; Chodorow 1997; Lacan 1977). Kearney (1998), in fact, has identified seven distinct schools of imagination in twentieth-century Continental philosophy. Brann's (1991) magisterial summa notes six separate intellectual approaches to the imaginative manifold (philosophical, psychological, literary, etc.) whilst choosing to ignore non-Western traditions and the occult imagination, which has served as a compelling counterpoint to the Judeo-Christian mainstream. What's more, there has been much debate amongst post-structuralists concerning the status of human imagination in relation to the purportedly decentred subject positions of postmodernity (Kearney 1994). Some consider it a solipsistic anachronism, others argue that imagination can be re-imagined for a postmodern age, and yet others cleave to the old-fashioned view that imagination is 'a prelude to action, an incitement to reflection, and an intimation of paradise' (Brann 1991: 798).

From the perspective of the present text, the minutiae of these debates are immaterial. The important point is that the standing of imagination is and always has been ambivalent, paradoxical, uncertain, betwixt-and-between. Just like John Lennon. Just like marketing. For every Baudelairian encomium to imagination, there is an admonition about imagination's dark side, its inclination to 'run wild' or 'leap' in an 'overactive' way. Imagination is potentially dangerous, threatening, uncontrollable, something that has to be captured, tamed, fed, exercised, stirred, stretched and strictly supervised, lest it leads us astray. Even when imagination attained its socio-cultural zenith, in the mid- to late-nineteenth century, the then revered personal traits were 'respectability', 'solidity', 'character' and 'reputation'. Imagination was considered dangerously subversive, a threat to society, the preserve of disreputable individuals like poets, playwrights, artists and aesthetes (Lears 1981). As Oscar Wilde cogently observed, 'society often forgives the criminal; it never forgives the dreamer'.

Installation # 2 (art for mart's sake)

The ambivalence at the heart of imagination is nowhere better illustrated than at the arts/marketing interface. Art, the quintessentially imaginative activity,[4] has traditionally been positioned in opposition to the degraded and degrading values of the marketplace. Art's task, according to received wisdom, is to unsettle, undermine and, ideally, usurp the trading classes, the mendacious middlemen, the fat cats of industry, the uncultivated 'till-fumblers' (as Yeats tellingly described them). True, the very idea that art is capable of toppling Western capitalism is one of the most imaginative figments of the artistic imaginary, but ever since Arnold, Ruskin, Pound, Leavis, Eliot, Greenberg, Adorno and all the rest posited art as a potential weapon against bourgeois barbarians, profit-fixated philistines and value-for-money vulgarians, the market has been subject to periodic outpourings of artistic invective (see Conrad 1998; Edwards 1999; Fineberg 2000; Tusa 1999).

Even Pop Art operators like Andy Warhol, Claes Oldenburg and Roy Lichten-stein, who ostentatiously absorbed and refracted commodity culture, only did so as an ironic comment on the commodification process, as a slap in the face of capital and the art world's complicity with its maleficent machinations (Stangos 1994). The fact that they made a fortune from doing so is neither here nor there.

If marketing, advertising, commodification and capitalism were once the four-letter words of artspeak, so to speak, they are now epithets of approbation. Almost. One of the most striking things about the contemporary artistic scene is the advent of market mindedness (Collings 1997, 1998, 1999; Haden-Guest 1996; Hughes 1997; Stallabrass 1996, 1999). These days, the distinction between art and marketing has all but dissolved; 'selling out' is less a term of disparage-ment than an indication that stocks need replenishing; and art-for-mart's-sake is the rallying cry of choice. Or so it seems. Certainly, there is no shortage of corroborative evidence. Aside from the marketing *brouhaha* that surrounds today's blockbuster exhibitions – ticket receipts, television specials, tasteful catalogues, T-shirts, tea-towels, tote bags and the traditional array of tie-in merchandise – marketing artefacts frequently turn up in, or form the focus of, cutting edge artworks. One thinks, for example, of Ashley Bickerton's *Tormented Self Portrait*, which consists of a collage of corporate logos, from Citibank to Samsung; Michael Landy's *Closing Down Sale*, an installation of shopping trolleys, surmounted by day-glo, everything-must-go posters; Jake and Dinos Chapman's *Tragic Anatomies*, erogenously enhanced manikins with nothing on but brand name trainers; Henry Bond's *Cult of the Street*, a photographic paean to the fashion victims of South Kensington; Martin Maloney's homage to today's ad-bombarded, brand-fixated, blank generation, *Sony Levi*; Masaaki Sato's super-realist newspaper stands with mysteriously transposed magazine titles; Jac Leirner's *Que sais-je*, an assemblage of plastic carrier bags from prominent artworks vendors; and, Xavier Veilhan's striking portrait of a giant penguin doing its grocery shopping in *The Supermarket* (see Lucie-Smith 1995; Stallabrass 1999).

Artists, analogously, increasingly employ the apparatus of marketing in their attempts to move the merchandise. Komar & Melamid conduct detailed cross-cultural marketing research before painting their parodic 'most wanted' and 'least wanted' canvasses (Wypijewski 1999). Jenny Holzer uses billboards, LED dis-plays, till receipts and commercial breaks to broadcast her award-winning artistic aphorisms (Waldman 1997; Joselit *et al.* 1998). Matthew Barney's much-vaunted cycle of video art, *Cremaster*, features the Goodyear blimp in a leading role. Adam Chodzko advertises for contributors to his *God Look-Alike Contest* and reproduces the submissions without comment (Stallabrass 1999). Telephone-engineer-turned-artist John Hayvend has developed art vending machines that are installed in public toilets alongside contraceptives dispensers (Cook 2000). Chris Ofili famously commandeered a market stall to sell his infamous elephant-dung, impasto-to-get-your-teeth-into mosaics (Collings 1999). And, the recent renaissance of British art has been attributed to the artist-led establishment of alternative channels of distribution. In essence, this involved self-curated exhibitions in disused warehouses and factories, thereby cutting out the middleman and circumventing the impossible-to-break-into gallery circuit (Burn 2000a).

Contemporary artistic discourse, what is more, is replete with admittedly backhanded endorsements of marketing orientation. Art, according to Whitford (1999: 9) is 'a branch of marketing'. Success in the artworld is 'all about cocky self confidence, presentation and marketing wizardry', says Pitman (2000: 44). Salesmen, realtors and advertisers are today's great artists, contends supermartist extraordinaire, Jeff Koons (Haden-Guest 1996). Bell (1999) concludes his cogent summary of the current artistic scene by comparing it to a full-line department store, situated in the middle of a boisterous Saturday morning market. TAG Sales is revolutionizing the retailing of original artworks with its pile-em-high-sell-em-cheap policy (and with nary a squeak from affronted aesthetes). Turner Prize nominee, Tracey Emin – she of the notorious unmade bed – has not only acknowledged that 'it is impossible to make it in art without an understanding of commerce', but is also perfectly happy to appear in advertisements for Sapphire Dry Gin (on the basis, presumably, that if it's good enough for Andy Warhol . . .). At one stage, moreover, she actually operated a retail store, in partnership with fellow artist Sarah Lucas, that sold all sorts of kitschy artistic artefacts, most notably its Damien Hirst-emblazoned ashtrays (Stallabrass 1999).

Damien Hirst, in many ways, exemplifies the marketing mindedness of modern artists. The ageing *enfant terrible* of BritArt, he is a nothing if not brilliant self-publicist, as might be expected from the son of a second-hand car dealer. His grisly installations, from the pickled tiger shark of 1991, through the bisected cow and calf of 1993, to the lost sheep of 1994, are designed to attract the attention of the tabloids and keep his name in the public eye. Like *haute couture* fashion houses, these extravagant creations act as a loss leader for his money-spinning Spin Art (buckets of paint thrown on to rapidly spinning discs) and Dot Art (regular grids of multi-coloured spots, made out of household emulsion), which are produced in factory-like conditions by squads of assistants. What's more, he has variously run a theme restaurant with celebrity chef Marco Pierre White; made a much-derided experimental video, *Hanging Around*; had a hit record, *Vindaloo*, with members of the rock band Blur; wrote a door-stop, crush-the-coffee-table, self-indulgent-to-the-point-of-narcissistic autobiography, *I Want to Spend the Rest of My Life Everywhere with Everyone, One to One, Always, Forever, Now*; and, at all times, worked on his trouser-dropping, cheeky-chappie, give-us-a-fag, gutter-press pleasing artistic persona. Even the affronted critiques of fellow artists, such as the attack on his work by an ink-wielding rival, have merely added to the Turner Prize winner's marketing mystique (see Barber 2000; Burn 2000b; Collings 1997, 1999; Haden-Guest 1996; Meecham and Sheldon 2000).

Although Hirst epitomises the 'high visibility' that Kotler once espoused (Rein *et al.* 1997), he is a mere amateur beside Mark Kostabi, former scourge of the New York art scene (Chalmers 1993). A marketing graduate of the University of Southern California, Kostabi is renowned for his garish oil paintings of faceless mannequins – sort of Spiderman meets Keith Haring – albeit he is probably best known for album cover art (Guns n' Roses, The Ramones and many more). He is no less famous for his marketing shock tactics, which put Jeff Koons, Julian Schnabel, Andy Warhol, Salvador Dali, Marcel Duchamp and Édouard Manet to shame (Lucie-Smith 1995). Naturally, he doesn't actually paint his own pictures, since such trivialities are left to dragoons of dogsbodies and screeds of anonymous associates (McEvilley 1996). In fairness, this is not exactly uncommon in the post-Pop world, nor was it particularly unusual amongst old masters, but Kostabi is unique insofar as he actually advertises for ideas and concepts (at one stage, he ran an 'ideas contest' in the trade magazine, *Flash Art*); he treats his employees abominably (minimum wage, clock in and out, no job security, etc.); and he adds insult to injury by plastering the walls of his studio – Kostabi World – with marketing mantras and 'Kostabisms' ('faster pieces are masterpieces', 'a picture is worth a thousand dollars', 'there's a collector born every fifteen minutes'). What's more, as a regular subscriber to the no-such-thing-as-bad-publicity credo, he revels in his reputation as the art world's most hated person and con artist supreme (Kostabi 1996). Thus he boasts of stealing other people's ideas; paints parodies of the purported slave-like conditions in Kostabi World; considers his selling skills more important than his artistic abilities; and, believe it or not, runs courses on self-marketing for wannabe Kostabis. Likewise, he plays the artist–rebel role to the hilt by variously criticising his credulous customers, insulting the curatorial community, double dealing on his dealers, picking fights on talk shows, posing for photographs in a suit made out of money and shamelessly exploiting the (extremely lucrative) market for corporate kitsch (Chalmers 1993). Hence the frequency with which business- and management-related material appears in his paintings – boardrooms, cash registers, pocket calculators, computer screens, office equipment and, above all, dollar bills. Such is Kostabi's effrontery that he successfully sued two ex-employees for forgery when they tried to pass off their own paintings as Kostabi originals. The fact that Kostabi didn't actually paint the 'originals' (whereas the defendants did) and that the great man is not averse to stealing ideas (to say nothing of his borrowings from art history), is simply by-the-by, a mere bagatelle. The Kostabi brand name was being compromised by copycats and, in a marketing-orientated art world, that kind of outrageous behaviour could not be tolerated. Whatever next?!

Work # 3 (lifesavers imitates art)

Just as recent years have witnessed the marketisation of art, so too it has seen the 'artification' of marketing. Never reluctant to exploit a fad, passing or otherwise, marketers have been quick to wrap themselves in the increasingly fashionable raiment of art. Absolut Vodka is perhaps the most celebrated exponent of the art/ advertising amalgam – its much-lauded series includes Absolut Warhol, Absolut Haring, Absolut Hirst and Absolut Ofili (see Lewis 1996) – but it is not alone. Silk Cut, BMW, Selfridges and JMC Holidays, to name but four, have found inspiration in the wrappings of Christo, his 'umbrellas' installation especially. Ford famously sliced an Escort in half, in homage to Damien Hirst's family background. Miró, Mondrian, Rothko and Picasso have done their bit for the Spanish Tourist Board, L'Oréal, Harvey Nichols and Perrier respectively. Matisse, Mucha and Munch have been pressed into service for Levi's, Moët and, of all things, *Marketing Week* magazine. Grant Wood's *American Gothic* has been appropriated on countless occasions, as have the works of Norman Rockwell, Georgia O'Keeffe and Maxfield Parrish (the less said about *The Mona Lisa*, *The Last Supper* and Botticelli's *The Birth of Venus*, the better – see Dorfles 1969; Ward 1991; Williamson 1978). Beck's Bier, meantime, produces limited edition bottle labels designed by the leading lights of BritArt, such as Rachel Whiteread, Gilbert & George and, inevitably, Damien Hirst. Habitat regularly mounts in-store exhibitions; Monsoon occasionally displays artworks in its show-windows; Tower Records has been known to give Hirst's Spin Art a spin; Swatch makes 'art specials', post-industrial timepieces designed by Keith Haring, Mark Kostabi, Yoko Ono and many more; and, no discussion of the art/marketing interface would be complete without reference to the immortal Magritte-inspired surrealism of Benson & Hedges' longrunning, award-winning, gone-but-not-forgotten cigarette advertising campaign (Brown 1995a).

B&H, of course, is now safely ensconced in the V&A; British Airways' advertising is part of MoMA's permanent collection; the Louvre's *Musée de la Publicité* possesses an archive of approximately 100,000 advertisements; and, let's be honest, the recent display of Dyson vacuum cleaners, Logitech computer mice and Alessi kitchen implements in Glasgow's Lighthouse (Redhead 2000) is as nothing compared to the touring exhibition of Barbie Dolls (coming soon to a gallery near you), *The Art of Star Wars* (currently showing at the Barbican for a limited run) and the Domaine de Bagatelle's landmark installation of antique garden gnomes (the horror, the horror!). The traffic, moreover, is not one-way, because museums are emerging as a model for twenty-first-century place-marketing. In addition to the manifold museum stores that line the malls of America – let alone museumified marketscapes like NikeTown, Sony Metreon and Ralph Lauren's flagship store to end all flagship stores at 72nd and Madison – it seems that every self-respecting mega-brand (and many not so mega-brands) have 'museums' devoted to their illustrious heritage. There's the World of Coca-Cola in Atlanta, the Volkswagen Museum in Wolfsburg, Cadbury's Chocolate Museum in Bourneville, Kellogg's Cereal City in Battle Creek, Colman's Mustard Museum in Norwich and Bewley's Coffee Museum in Dublin. The list is endless.

In this regard, it is noteworthy that one of the most influential art galleries in London is controlled by a marketing man, Charles Saatchi. Feared and fawned upon in equal measure, the advertising guru's collecting habit, opinion leadership and touring exhibitions, such as 1997's *Sensation*, are paradigmatic of today's art for mart's sake mentality (Burn 2000c).

Some martistic *aficionados*, indeed, have actually asserted that the mantle of modern art has descended upon the marketer (Brown 1995a). Modern art's licence to disturb, unsettle and confront the viewer with uncomfortable images is less the preserve of the artist than the hallmark of the advertiser. The antics of Benetton, whose latest prank adds photographs of condemned prisoners to extant depictions of AIDS victims, terrorist attacks, blood-drenched fatigues, etc., is by far the most egregious example of advertising's avant-garde attempt to *épater les bourgeois*. But there's lots more where Benetton's coming from. As exemplified by the provocative promotional tactics of FCUK, Diesel, Haägen Dazs and, lately, a slough of desperate-for-an-image dot-com companies, aesthetic shock is increasingly induced by the marketing rather than the artistic community (Marconi 1997; Saunders 1996; Wheeler and Day 2000). Now, this is not to suggest that contemporary art has lost its confrontational edge. The public outrage precipitated by Saatchi's *Sensation* show, Marcus Harvey's portrait of mass murderer Myra Hindley in particular, indicates that art can still disrupt, dismay, disgust and disconcert as it has done in the past (Warner 2000). At the same time, however, the shock tactics of marketers have much greater impact than those of artists, if only by dint of their wider circulation, constant repetition and, most importantly, 'not art' status. That is to say, whereas we *expect* to be shocked by art, advertising is *supposed* to sell, albeit this distinction is becoming difficult to sustain in the light of marketing's gross-is-good mindset (Brown 2000). More to the point, it is evident that aesthetically induced outrage is a marketing tactic in itself, a legitimate if somewhat clichéd move in today's highly competitive marketplace. Shock tactics are part of the arts marketing armoury and, as such, Charles Saatchi's *Sensation* must be considered a brilliantly executed marketing manoeuvre. Art is war.

Although the interpenetration of arts and marketing is undeniable, it is not indisputable. Some forty years after Jasper Johns bronzed two Ballentine beer cans and Andy Warhol displayed his 'Lifesavers' Marilyns,[5] some twenty-five years after Duane Hansen sculpted super-realist shopping trolleys and Richard Prince re-photographed Marlboro ads, and some ten years after Jeff Koons shocked the seen-it-all artworld with his larger-than-life-size kitsch collectibles (Yorkshire terriers, Michael Jackson and Bubbles, stainless steel inflatable bunny, etc.), the relationship between art and commerce is still uneasy. Aside from the avant-garde achievements of Adbusting aesthetes, those who deface posters with anti-capitalist sentiments (Klein 2000), several artists have complained bitterly about advertisers' appropriation of their handiwork. A plagiarism suit was instituted against Guinness by the video artist Mehdi Norowzian, who claimed that the company's television ad, *Anticipation*, featuring a man idiot dancing around a settling pint, was stolen from his experimental short, *Joy*. Turner Prize winner Gillian Wearing got extremely upset when Volkswagen appropriated her trademark 'signs', where street-people hold up hand-written placards expressing sentiments contradicted by their physical appearance. Damien Hirst threatened legal action against British Airways' subsidiary, Go, when it suddenly sprouted Spot Art,[6] Bridget Riley did likewise when Harrods' ads went suspiciously Op-Art; and, advertising agencies' latter-day attempts to avoid exorbitant reproduction fees by 'reshooting' the classic photographs of Helmut Newton and Richard Avedon amongst others, have also ended up in court.

Standing trial, however, is too good for abominable marketing men, according to the French artistic establishment, many of whom are deeply upset by Citroën's latest addition to its fleet, *The Picasso*. As prominent art critic Jean Clair contemptuously observed, 'His name has been sullied and when you sully a painter's name, you pollute his whole work. Youngsters will soon be asking why this man was named after the car. They won't see his paintings in the same light' (Sage 2000: 31). Citroën's marketing department, naturally, remains unmoved, not least because it has benefited from £2 million worth of free shock-horror publicity and more than 10,000 people have placed orders for the vehicle.

Such huffings and puffings are pretty much par for the course and one would have to be pretty naïve to believe it was anything other than a Citroën-stoked publicity stunt from the outset.[7] In the early- to mid-1990s, admittedly, there was much earnest discussion in the weekend supplements and glossy lifestyle magazines about the artistic status of advertising (as part of the perennial postmodern conversation piece pertaining to the elision of the elite/popular cultural divide). The high-water mark was Tony Kaye's one-man protest outside the Tate Gallery, which had refused to support the adman's assertion that his 1993 television commercial for Dunlop Tyres was worthy of inclusion in its hallowed halls. The controversy rumbles on, furthermore, in the anarchistic activities of Bank, an artistic collective dedicated to counter-commodification guerrilla tactics. To this end, it produces parodic brochures, churns out corporate-speak mission statements, issues bogus PR material, mounts ersatz advertising campaigns ('you can bank on us'), parades pseudo-celebrity endorsements ('"A better investment than the Franklin Mint Diana Doll" – Sadie Coles, art dealer') and runs a free Fax-Back service commenting on the press releases of leading galleries, giving them marks out of ten for pomposity, obscurantism and all-round pretension (Collings 1999; Stallabrass 1999).

Entertaining though they are, the principal problem with such anti-commercial critiques is that they have already been done – and done much better – by the marketing community itself (e.g. 'image is nothing', 'FCUK advertising', Death brand cigarettes, etc.). Working artists may complain when their big idea is quoted, co-opted, appropriated, plagiarised, stolen or whatever by horrid marketing men, but when one compares Guinness's idiot dancer to Norowzian's, or Volkwagen's placards to Wearing's or, indeed, the apercus of advertising (Beanz, Meanz, Heinz; Just Do It) to the haikus of Holzer (Abuse of Power Comes as No Surprise; Protect Me From What I Want), it is clear that the marketers don't come off second best. The artists, in fact, probably benefit from the increased exposure. At a time, moreover, when the world's most august auction houses have been exposed as price-fixing fraudsters, many old masters have been revealed as camera obscura toting charlatans, Damien Hirst freely admits that his Spin Art was 'borrowed' from *Blue Peter*, a children's television programme, and the Russian émigré pranksters Komar & Melamid sell neo-expressionist canvases painted by Indian elephants (a joint venture with Ofili can't be far away!), contemporary art is hardly in a position to call the marketing kettle black.

Exhibit # 4 (marketing is everything)

Regardless of these minor martistic differences, the fact of the matter is that marketing is central to twenty-first-century artistic endeavour. Indeed, such is its omnipresence in aesthetic circles that art critics are engaging in what can only be described as a retrofit operation. The received wisdom of romanticism, modernism and the avant-garde, which equated commercialism with selling out, inauthenticity and pandering to the *hoi polloi*, is being challenged – and to some extent replaced – by a new set of convictions. Namely, *that artists have been marketers all along*. Bogart (1995), for example, has published an intimate history of the relationship between art and advertising (see also Jardine 1996; Lears 1994; Sivulka 1998) and the merits of mass marketed kitsch are being re-assessed by art historians (Kulka 1996; Olalquiaga 1999; Wollen 2000). The work of once reviled commercial artists – Norman Rockwell, Maxfield Parrish, Alphonse Mucha, Elbert Hubbard – is being rescued from the limbo of worthlessness and the degree of their detestation deconstructed (Warhol and Johns have been outed as collectors of Rockwell, for instance). The marketing background of many leading artists and critics, such as Barbara *Shop-til-you-Drop* Kruger, Andreas *Piss Christ* Serrano, Jeff 'kitschy, kitschy' Koons, Andy 'nice shoes' Warhol, Rene 'This is not a P' Magritte, Kurt 'Dada's prodigal son' Schwitters, and Clement 'art or kitsch' Greenberg, is being openly acknowledged (Collings 1999; Storr 1990; Varnedoe and Gopnik 1990a, 1990b). The commission-caging stunts of the old masters, and their apparent willingness to accommodate clients' demands, are increasingly regarded as right and proper rather than an impediment to free expression (Lavin 1990). Even the anti-market posturing of the avant-garde has been re-interpreted as an astute marketing ploy:

> The Romantic concept of culture held that what real artists and writers produced was a superior reality – a kind of work that, being imaginative,

transcended the workaday world of ordinary cultural production. The artists themselves were thought to be exceptional, gifted beings whose talents were extraordinary – impassioned geniuses who created not for the market but some higher ideal . . . In fact, the idea of 'culture' was always in part a clever marketing concept.

(Seabrook 2000: 68)

Now, if marketing were vaingloriously minded, its ever-mounting credibility in artistic circles might be interpreted as the ultimate triumph. Once considered completely beyond the pale – unspeakable, untouchable, unthinkable, unimaginable – marketing has captured the crown jewels of the cerebral firmament. The barbarians have sacked the citadel. The arrivistes have finally arrived. The bourgeoisie has bested the avant-garde. According to Seabrook (2000), indeed, we have entered a whole new cultural dispensation where marketing has *subsumed* art. Long gone are the days when elite culture stood aloof, spouting eternal verities about the state of the world, whilst refusing to truck with the hucksters of popular culture. Long gone are the days when art reluctantly accepted that marketing is necessary, only as an unwelcome add-on. Long gone, even, are the days when de-differentiation held sway, as artists showed their work in supermarkets and museums filled with television screens (Brown 1995a). These days, marketing calls the shots, marketing rules the roost, marketing says what goes. Marketing maketh Manet.

Marketing, in other words, hasn't so much merged with art as acquired it as an (admittedly dodgy) going concern. Before breaking out the bunting, however, or constructing a larger-than-life-size effigy of Kotler, to be carried shoulder high around the Getty Museum on designated saints' days – or should that be sales' days? – several significant caveats must be introduced. In the first instance, the latter-day triumph of marketing is not exactly of its own making, nor is it an admission by the arts establishment that you-wuz-right, we-wuz-wrong. Reduced government subsidies, rather, increased reliance on corporate sponsorship, and additional competition from alternative leisure activities, such as theme parks, heritage centres and suburban shopping malls, have forced the arts to pander to popular taste, speak the management Esperanto and hustle for every column inch in the Sunday supplements. Second, the liberal arts' willingness to interrogate marketing matters is totally unrelated to the intellectual accomplishments of their business school brethren. Sociologists, anthropologists, art historians and all the rest may well be discussing marketing concerns, but they are legitimising these studies by re-inventing their own traditions, not building on the foundations laid by management science. Sad, but true. Third and most importantly perhaps, marketing means different things in the artistic and corporate spheres. Marketing for marketers means what it says in the BFBAM (big fat books about marketing). It means careful consumer research; it means segmentation, targeting, positioning; it means marketing plans; it means product portfolios and life cycles; it means break-even points; it means brand management; it means meaningful relationships. In the artistic sphere, by contrast, marketing means promotional gimmicks, stunts, affronts and stand-out-from-the-crowd hyperbole. It means excessive, exaggerated, eye-catching activities, the more outrageous the better. It means roll up, roll up; it means the greatest show on earth; it means to infinity and beyond. It means Mark Kostabi, Jeff Koons and Komar & Melamid. It means Damien Hirst, Andy Warhol and Julian Schnabel. It means that there is more than a phonic relationship between Barney and Barnum.[8]

It is, of course, entirely fitting that marketing's success is predicated on false premises. Not only is this singularly ironic in the light of marketing's smug, know-it-all, we-have-the-technology mindset, but it is doubly ironic in the light of marketing's post-war academic pretensions. Forty something years ago, marketing suppressed its artistic side and set off in pursuit of Scientific Status, an implausible not to say impossible dream (see Brown 1996).[9] As the twenty-first century dawns, however, scientific recognition seems as far away as ever, since those pesky laws of the marketplace still refuse to reveal themselves (come out, come out, wherever you are). Meantime, the artworld has clutched marketing to its bosom, albeit less than wholeheartedly, albeit out of necessity rather than choice, albeit in a form that most fully-paid-up marketers wouldn't recognise. This return of the marketing repressed may be embarrassing for some hard-core advocates of 'the scientific method', whatever that is, but one suspects that the majority of marketers will consider it more of an opportunity than a threat. After all, it affords endless opportunities to explain how to do it 'properly'; it gives us a chance to steer those irresponsible artistic types onto the marketing straight-and-narrow; and it allows marketers to challenge their sadly mistaken misconceptions, misrepresentations, miscalculations, misinterpretations. Certainly, there is no shortage of marketing-made-easy books for the arts community, broadly defined (Diggle 1994; Hill *et al.* 1995; McLean 1997). Kotler and his collaborators have been particularly active in this area, as one might expect (e.g. Kotler 1982; Kotler and Kotler 1998; Kotler and Scheff 1997).

There is, however, another way to look at it. Rather than study *the market for arts*, as many consumer researchers do (audience research, segmentation analyses, etc.), or *marketing for the arts*, as the catalogue of Kotler-clone textbooks attests (ace strategy with nice art attached), it might be better to consider *the arts for marketing*. That is, work on the assumption that marketing has much to learn from the arts, not the other way around. The presumption that 'marketers know best' is astonishing, to say the least, even when it is confined to marketing 'territory'. (We don't know much about art but we know what we like in a marketing plan, or research report, or SWOT analysis.) Not only does the 'mid-life crisis' literature suggest that we don't actually know what we like in a marketing plan or whatever (Brown 1995b), but it can also be contended that the arts community has a better understanding of marketing than marketing does. Maybe Matthew Barney, Damien Hirst, Jeff Koons and Mark Kostabi know more about marketing than Kotler and his cookie-cutter cronies. Maybe marketing should swallow its pride and try to learn from the arts. Maybe the greatest act of marketing imagination is to accept that imagining marketing is necessary, that marketing science has had its day, that the APIC fast breeder is bereft, as is its RM runt.

Or, to be more charitable, maybe it's time to recognise that APIC can only take us so far and it's taken us about as far as it can go. Ever more marketing science is *not* the way forward; nor is hyper-happy-clappy-customer-hugging; nor, for that matter, is increased 'professionalism' with its royal warrants, codes of conduct and gold stars for good behaviour. It is time to imagine marketing anew: new century, new concept, new challenge, new conviction, new course, new courses, new curriculum, new constitution. This may sound subversive and it's meant to. Imagining always is. Indeed, it is our contention that the arts, as the principal repository of humankind's imaginative prowess, can help us posit future possibilities, future prospects, future perfects, future pasts (Brown 2000). To paraphrase a past futurist – with a passing nod to Holbrook (1993) – ask not what marketing can do for art, but what art can do for marketing.

This artistic imperative, it must be stressed, does not mean that marketers have miched art lessons hitherto. Apart from countless practitioner-orientated publications – learn from great literature, Shakespeare for managers, win with Winnie the Pooh and what have you (Brawer 1998; Corrigan 1999; Williams 1995) – there have been innumerable academic attempts to interrogate the arts in the fifteen years since Russell Belk's (1986) stentorian reveille for consumer researchers. As discussed at length elsewhere (see Brown 1997), the *Arts for Marketing* movement can be divided into three broad schools pertaining to Art, Aesthetics and the Avant-Garde.[10] The Art school, in essence, engages with the marketing content of artistic artefacts; that is to say, it culls the canon for representations of marketing and consumption-related phenomena. To this end, studies of films, television programmes, novels, poems, songs, dance, drama, comic books, the fine arts – in short, the entire spectrum of artistic endeavour – have been undertaken by marketing academics, with varying degrees of success (e.g. Belk 1986; Belk and Bryce 1993; Brown 1995c, 1997; Hirschman 1998; Holbrook 1995; Holbrook and Grayson 1989; Stern and Schroeder 1994; Thompson 1998). The Aesthetics school applies the tools and techniques of artistic appreciation to marketing institutions and ephemera – advertising campaigns, shopping centres, products and brands, service encounters and so forth. Barbara Stern, a consumer researcher trained in literary criticism, has been especially active in this area and where she has led several others have followed (see Heilbrunn 1996, 1998; Maclaran and Stevens 1998; McQuarrie and Mick 1996; Mick and Politi 1989; Scott 1990, 1994; Stern 1989, 1995, 1996). The Avant-Garde school, on the other hand, argues for radically different forms of marketing discourse and representation. The standardised research report or formulaic academic paper – introduction, literature review, methodology, findings, discussion, conclusion – could and should make way for poetry, photography, painting, performance and all manner of 'unconventional' modes of marketing discourse (Belk 1998; Brown 1998b, 1999c; Holbrook 1995, 1998; Mead 1994; Sherry 1991, 1998; Stern 1998). These modes may be different from those that typify the mainstream, but that doesn't make them uninsightful, or unconvincing, or unworthy of serious consideration. Quite the reverse.

Although relatively few researchers are actively engaged in the *Arts for Marketing* movement, they have been energetic in pursuit of their aims. An impressive body of publications now exists. Yet, despite these achievements, the extant literature is somewhat limited in scope, both at the intra-school and at the inter-school levels. Thus the Art school focuses on movies and television, the Aesthetes tend to concentrate on advertising and promotion, and the Avant-Gardists are poets, first and foremost. Aesthetics, what is more, is the biggest single category, by far, with the Art group some way behind and the Avant-Garde a distant third. These imbalances, admittedly, are relative rather than absolute – since most 'artistic' domains have been explored to some degree – and are largely attributable to the personal preferences-cum-proclivities of individual researchers. The existing channels of academic distribution, which are not really geared to accommodate avant-garde experiments, are another important factor, as is the 'critical' function of manuscript reviewers and scholarly gatekeepers generally.[11] There is, nevertheless, ample opportunity for additional academic research in each of the Art, Aesthetics and Avant-Garde arenas.

The present book aims to do just that and more besides. It spans a wide spectrum of artistic forms – fine art, performance art, tattoo art, poetry, literature, music, museums, photography – and at the same time contributes to each of the *Arts for Marketing* schools of thought. It deals with a diversity of marketplace phenomena – consumer behaviour, competitive strategies, branding, internationalisation, retailing, servicescapes, advertising, SMEs, external environment, etc. – in a variety of representational styles. It includes chapters written in traditional scholarly prose; both hyperbolic and low-key creative writing exercises; and several fascinating hybrids of academese and free expression, truth and lies, insight and imagination. And then, of course, there's the poetry, which ranges from (very) blank verse to a pastiche of Samuel Taylor Coleridge's finest hour.

In addition to offering a reasonable cross-section – we hesitate to describe it as a representative sample – of imaginative marketing scholarship from the Art, Aesthetics and Avant-Garde schoolyards, the book seeks to address some of the aforementioned imbalances. Thus the Art section concentrates on fine art and literature rather than film and television. The Aesthetics section consists of a single chapter (on account of the abundance of extant publications) and moves the discussion away from advertising and promotion to museums and heritage centres. The Avant-Garde component, finally, contains chapters by some of the leading exponents of creative writing in the marketing academy (editor excepted). *Imagining Marketing*, then, seeks to serve as a useful point of departure, inasmuch as it is the first texhibition of the *Arts for Marketing* movement, as well as a provocative, occasionally outrageous, volume in its own write. If not quite an academic *Armory*, certainly a scholarly *Sensation*.

Ambivalence # 5 (*l'imagination au pouvoir*)

Appropriately enough, the first chapter in the Art section takes sensationalism as its starting point. According to Jonathan Schroeder, the controversy surrounding Calvin Klein's CK One campaign, which was accused of trafficking in kiddy porn and generally corrupting the innocent youth of America the Beautiful, is analogous to the outrage that accompanied Édouard Manet's *Olympia* of 1863. Nowadays, Manet is widely regarded as a reactionary renegade, who once claimed that the sole purpose of art is to help calm the nerves of stressed-out businessmen,[12] to say nothing of his blatant product placement for Bass in *A Bar at the Folies Bergère*. However, he was the shock-horror marketer of his time, the Luciano Benetton of La Belle Epoch. Manet's intention, as Schroeder notes, was to establish his name and reputation – by hook or by crook – and, although he was genuinely upset by the *scandal d'estime* surrounding *Olympia*, he benefited enormously from the accompanying publicity. Thus, when it comes to the strategic use of outrage, Calvin Klein is just the latest in a long line of sensationalists. If not exactly a Johnny-come-lately, CK One is standing on the (Gargantuan) shoulders of giants.

Scandal-mongers also figure prominently in Chapters 3 and 4. Taking his cue from the sensationalists' sensationalists, Salvador Dali and Andy Warhol (albeit with a respectful nod to Vincent van Gogh and Frank Lloyd Wright), Ian Fillis reflects on the relationship between artistic and marketing creativity. He examines the situation of SMEs in the arts-and-crafts sector and shows how entrepreneurs are forced, on account of their lack of resources, to rely on imagination, risk-taking and rule-bending. Barnumarketing, in other words (Brown 1998a). The same, Fillis contends, should be the case in the marketing academy, which remains deeply immired in me-too methodologies, hackneyed publication formats and 'so-what?', 'who cares?', tell-us-something-we-don't-know scholarship. A *salon de refuse* is called for and, to this end, the author posits a Proclamation of Marketing Artistry. A marketing manifesto, no less! This sixteen-point academic agenda ranges from an emphasis on innovative thought, through rejection of traditional marketing approaches, to a desire to work with change rather than against it. The choice, as Fillis rightly concludes, is ours to make.

Chapter 4, by contrast, comprises a straightforward summary of the career of Ireland's most successful marketing man (Tony O'Reilly, Feargal Quinn and

Harry Ferguson, notwithstanding). James Joyce, to be sure, is rarely held up as a master of the ignoble marketing arts. If anything, he is regarded as an unfortunate casualty of the commodification process, a great artist whose reputation has been hijacked by cheap-jack marketing types, with their tourist trails, kitsch collectibles and ersatz Bloomsday celebrations. There is more than a grain of truth in this perception – a veritable bushel – as Anthony Patterson and Stephen Brown show in their case study of the James Joyce theme pub in Paris. At the same time, however, the great man was complicit in his own commodification; his work is replete with marketing allusions; and he was not averse to exploiting commercial opportunities when they came his way. Like Édouard Manet, Salvadore Dali, Calvin Klein and Luciano Benetton, James Joyce revelled in his outrageousness and used it to brilliant self-publicising effect. Were he alive today, or so the cliché goes, one suspects that he would consider mainstream marketing to be an abomination – unimaginative, unthreatening, uninspired, unconscionable. Marketers wake!

Wakes of another kind feature in Chapter 5 by Stephanie O'Donohoe and Darach Turley. Drawing upon two literary engagements with bereavement, *Jesus and the Adman* and *Way to Go*, they explore the space where marketing and mortality meet, a space that the research community has been reluctant to reconnoitre hitherto. Death is not only a taboo subject, but it is almost beyond representation, which makes engagement with it particularly problematic for positivistic marketing academics (since tick-box questionnaires are hardly up to the task). Art, however, offers a way of interrogating what Mark Rothko famously termed The Void. Taking Durkheim's distinction between sacred and profane as their necromarketing starting point, Turley and O'Donohoe propose *kratophany* as a useful means of conceptualising the thanatic encounter. This is then used to frame a detailed study of dealing in death and consumers' complaints about the way mortality is represented in print advertising. Despite the morbidity of the subject matter, the chapter repays close attention, not least because it is beautifully written. The author may be mouldering in his grave, as Barthes contends, but his soul goes marketing on.

Death, dying, expiration, the void, the beyond, the outer limits and other equally profound concerns are also the domain of science fiction. Indeed, it is one of the chestnuts of the hoary 'art versus science' debate that artists have a better record of predicting the future – Jules Verne, H.G. Wells, A.C. Clarke, etc. – than their scientific associates. Irrespective of the accuracy of this assertion (futurologists are inclined to count the 'hits' and ignore the 'misses'), the very existence of a literary category like science fiction calls the traditional science/art dichotomy into question. SF, of course, is a massively popular genre, with manifold modes of delivery. These include books, movies, TV series, video games, Trekkie conventions, theme park rides, *Art of Star Wars* exhibitions, etc., all of which are heavily marketed. Marketing, however, is not just something that is done *to* science fiction, it is often the subject *of* science fiction. As Warren Smith and Matthew Higgins explain in Chapter 6, SF has addressed marketing matters from its earliest days (over-consumption, shopping addiction, subliminal embeds *et al.*). Like so many artistic forms, science fiction offers a critique of, yet remains beholden to, the commercial system. Co-option is unavoidable. Assimilation is art's fate. Trust no one.

The intellectual standing of SF is, and always has been, profoundly ambiguous. On the one hand, it is promoted as a form of quasi-scientific extrapolation and social comment. On the other hand, it is regarded as low-brow trash, formulaic fairy stories for the fully grown. Fairy stories are no less ambivalent, since they too are variously accused of corrupting young minds – violent, androcentric, politically incorrect, and so on – and acting as a repository of ancient wisdom. Yet, irrespective of their psycho-social integrity, fairy stories are an integral part of marketing practice, as advertising's cavalcade of cartoon characters, impossible situations, just-so occurrences and mini-morality tales bears eloquent witness (Brown 1998c). Fairy stories, admittedly, have very few supporters in the market- ing academy, that pristine place of white-coated workers, hush-hush laboratories and exciting breakthroughs just around the corner. However, it is all change in Chapter 7, where Søren Askegaard and Fabian Csaba employ the archetypal fairy tale framework of good versus evil to explain the post-war cola wars in Denmark. Indeed, it is entirely appropriate that this totemic tale – big bad multinational devours little local brand – is set in Denmark, the domicile of Hans Christian Andersen. Unlike most of Andersen's fabrications, unfortunately, this story does not end happily, despite the disconcertingly jolly brand name of the local cola.

Marketing, to be sure, is the Hans Christian Andersen of scholarship. It is renowned for its imaginative tall tales – The Princess on the Ps, for starters – yet remains a bit of an outsider, an academic arriviste with an outsized scholarly chip on its shoulder. Just as the great Dane was regarded as a rustic, as a social climber, as someone who desperately tried to disguise his low-born background (Prince 1998), so too marketing aspires to gentility, desires to be taken seriously and at all times tries to hide its hucksterish origins (hence the perennial pontification about propriety, ethics, morality, customer care, marketing science and suchlike). For all his unattractive airs and graces, however, Hans Christian Andersen remains one of the crowning glories of Danish culture, as a beautifully appointed museum in Odense attests. Museums, in point of fact, are the cockpit, the crucible, the crux of martistry, insofar as they are the place where the aspirations of art and practicalities of marketing meet, merge and mesh. At least in theory. In practice, the relationship between museums and marketing has always been fraught. It is appropriate, therefore, that the Aesthetics section of the book should be given over to an extended treatment of the museum/marketing amalgam. In Chapter 8, Stephen Brown, Elizabeth Hirschman and Pauline Maclaran combine the theories of prominent postmodern philosopher Fredric Jameson with an in-depth empirical study of three heritage parks to show that, far from being a necessary evil, marketing is an integral part of the museum experience.

Now, it may be some time before a museum of marketing scholarship is established – its construction will doubtless coincide with the creation of a Nobel Prize in the subject – but when that happy day dawns the work of Morris B. Holbrook will undoubtedly be amongst the first exhibits. One of the pioneers of *Arts for Marketing*, Holbrook believes in practising what he preaches. His elegant essays on everything from Jazz to Joyce, Freud to Furbies, and *Paradise Lost* to *The Price is Right*, represent the nearest thing to out-and-out artistry in the marketing academy. It is fitting, then, that the Avant-Garde section is initiated by the Sage of Riverside Drive, the Oracle of the Ponocos, the Maharishi of Montauk. Chapter 9 consists of an empyrean excursus on entelechic entitulation (for the lexically challenged amongst us – thesaurustics? – he's referring to the significance of titles). Titillating and titivating by turns, Holbrook's surreal verging on sublime essay assays Tupperware, Tommy Moore, Teddy Bears and Tipper Gore, taking in movies and music, photography and politics, literature and legalese, and memories and marketing, along the way. Harold Bloom, the leading literary theorist, also gets a mention in Morris's impossible to summarise, sufficient to experience, certain to astonish, introspective adventure. Read it and whelp.

Interestingly, Harold Bloom looms large in Chapter 10 as well, as does Morris Holbrook, as indeed do whelps. The runaway winner of the *Imagining Marketing* award for the longest title in the text – entelechic entitulation in excelsis – Craig Thompson's 'tour de farce' is a *tour de force* of creative writing, an irruption of his deeply repressed desire to deconstruct the primordial phallic premises of patriarchy that remain ineradicably inscribed in the intellectual institutions and academic intercourse of marketing and consumer research. Yes, as the author notes at one point, that is a damn long sentence. A custodial sentence, no less. As, indeed, is everything we write in our attempts to entrap, interrogate and reform the marketing jurisdiction. Disciplining the discipline is Thompson's theme and, in order to cast off marketing's cerebral shackles, he takes us on a trailer-trash trail of toil, tears, testaments and testicles. Tasteless, some might say, but then you haven't tasted mine, says the Matthew Barney of marketing research. Accordingly, Thompson's oneiric onanism embraces Elvis Presley, Hank Williams (I, II and III) and the one and only Whitey Caldwell, a magnificently (entitularly) endowed Pentecostal preacher of the author's adolescent imaginings. 'Arse longa vita Beavis', as Butt-head almost said.

If Tommy gunning and Holbrookian hitmanship epitomise the heavy artillery end of academic avant-gardism, the secret service makes a brief but low-key appearance in Chapters 11 and 12. Hyperbole, hyperactivity and hypermarketing are conspicuous by their absence, comparatively speaking, though there are lessons to be learned from these pared-down, cite-lite short stories. In Chapter 11, Hope Schau proffers a bitter-sweet tale set in a postmodern marketing milieu.

'Suburban Soundtracks' describes a difficult encounter with a former lover, where the ersatz magic of the setting – a theme shopping centre in Southern California – belies the awkwardness of the interchange. Vestiges of personal chemistry and the aftershock of painful memories collide to inconclusive effect amid the potted plants, *al fresco* seating arrangements and empty coffee cups of latte capitalism. *Pace* Marx, capitalists fake history but not under circumstances of the consumer's choosing. Be that as it may, a lighter note is introduced in Chapter 12, when Stephen Brown bites into and instantly regurgitates a less than appetising slice of American Pie. Autophobia, 'the authorities' and our author's all-too apparent airheadedness, combine to provide the Candide of consumer research with an unforgettable encounter in the land of the free gift. Keep on (tow-)truckin.

Unforgettability is again on the agenda in Chapter 13. Russell Belk, the inadvertent hero of Candide's hapless collision with the forces of law and order, opens the drawer of his desk and pulls out a mask. However, this is no ordinary mask, the mask of dispassionate scholarship, the mask that marketers hide behind in their hopeless attempts to become respectable members of the community of scholars, the academy with a capital 'A'. Russ's mask, rather, is a battered relic of family life, a precious possession, a private joke. It is an irreplaceable memento that makes unannounced – yet unforgettable – appearances at salient moments in the Belks' existential arc, from early struggles, through teenage trauma, to eerily empty nest. But the mask is more even than a repository of happy memories, an evocative reminder of days gone by. It is a precious possession that can never be discarded, a worthless piece of plastic that is beyond price, a sacred object that means more than words can say. Like William Blake's grain of sand, Belk's broken-down mask transacts, transcribes, transfixes, transmits and transcends the trials and tribulations of existence. It is a symbol of the indescribable, the unnameable, the eternal, the something rather than nothing. What's more, it bespeaks Russell Belk to anyone who knows him, or has sat at his feet, amazed by his energy, enthusiasm and erudition.

Just as Russ Belk is encapsulated by his Groucho glasses, so are tattoos an embodiment of self for Joel Watson. Chapter 14 elaborates on his interstitial poem, *The Spiral*, by spinning a symbol-rich short story of self-discovery around an empirical investigation of body art. The meanings that such decorative indulgences have for the individuals concerned – corporeal memorabilia, sub-cultural affiliations, icons of personal identity, markers of life transitions – are absorbed into and refracted through Watson's incredible aesthetic sensibility. The outcome is an atmospheric artwork that remains true to traditional marketing and consumer research, inasmuch as it comprises a cogent empirical study of an important marketplace phenomenon. But, at the same time, Joel's hyper-real tale possesses an inescapable power of its own. Subjective and objective are combined and surmounted, leaving the author and his readers in a postmodern limbo, a spiral of self-absorption and self-abnegation, of selfishness and selflessness, an ambivalent place of hope and fear, love and hate, knowledge and superstition, magic and marketing, art and artifice. Strangely strange but oddly normal.

Normality, happily, is not a word that springs to mind where Bob Grafton Small is concerned. The magic realist of the marketing academy, Grafton Small brings *Imagining Marketing* to a close with a marvellous meditation on representation, reputation and reportage. He commences with a misquotation of his work in a mainstream marketing anthology and takes off on a twisting, turning, textual trajectory of recollection, reconception, reflection and reflexivity. Research and the research game – publish, perish, profess, procure – are the author's targets, though his purpose is more poetic than prosaic, more phantasmagoric than pragmatic, more prospective than performative (in the Lyotardian sense). The journey, so they say, is more important than the destination – though Virgin Rail ticket-holders might beg to differ – and there are few travelling companions in the marketing academy more eloquent, elegant, engaging and entertaining than Bob Grafton Small.

Grafton Small's chapter, then, encapsulates the overall intention of this text. Despite its catholicism, *Imagining Marketing* does not claim to be the final word on *the arts for marketing* movement. Final words, after all, are anathema to the imaginative. There's always more to be said and more who wish to say it. Like the Duracell bunny, the postmodern conversation keeps on going, even though the contributors constantly change. Unlike our scientifically orientated colleagues – who form the majority, admittedly – the aesthetes of the marketing academy have no desire to discover the truth, unearth the facts, find an explanation, or establish a theory of everything. Our aims, rather, are ambiguity, uncertainty, interminability, in perpetuity and ad infinitum. We undertake research in a spirit of eternal openness (reimagining is all) instead of eventual closure (now we know). As such, the purpose of the present text is to provide a quick sketch of the martistic landscape, in the full knowledge that our pen and ink outline of this prodigious panorama will be filled in or overpainted in the fullness of time. A wide range of techniques is on show, from aquatint to zoophorus, as it were, and all sorts of approaches are employed – realism, impressionism, expressionism, etc. However, if there is one expression that captures our intention, it is *L'Imagination au Pouvoir*. Coined by the proto-postmodern protesters of Paris 1968, just as John Lennon was composing his peerless possessionless masterpiece, 'Imagination to Power' is the pith of marketing's artistic imperative. And, if that doesn't work, we'll stage a sin-in at the Marketing Science Institute . . .

Notes

1 *Imagine*, of course, was successfully re-issued in the aftermath of Lennon's assassination, thereby proving Marx's dictum that history repeats itself, the first time as tragedy (1980), the second time as farce (1999).

2 They'll be doubting the veracity of the BBC poll next. Manipulated by the record company? Surely not!

3 Some consumer researchers claim that Campbell suffers from an overactive socio-logical imagination (Holbrook 1996), but he is one of the few to examine imagination in detail. Most marketing and consumer researchers use 'imagination' in a fairly colloquial sense (e.g. Bocock 1993; Elliott 1997; Murray and Ozanne 1991). An important exception is Schau (2000).

4 This statement should not be taken to mean that scientists are unimaginative. Far from it. The processes of scientific and artistic discovery are analogous in many respects (Brown 1996). One of the greatest follies of the literary-critical elite, according to leading luvvie Lord Bragg (1999: 2), 'has been the ascription of the imagination to the arts only, leaving science as the PC Plod of dull thought'.

5 'Lifesavers' Marilyns refers to the colour scheme of Warhol's earliest representation of Monroe, which was based on the eponymous count-line candies sold at almost every checkout and kiosk in the United States (Polo would perhaps be the closest UK equivalent). As for the Ballantine beer cans, there is a famous story that Jasper Johns' 1960 sculpture was motivated by Robert Rauschenberg's chance remark that the wheeling-dealing gallery owner, Leo Castelli, could sell virtually anything as art, even beer cans. Rauschenberg, incidentally, had engaged with commodity culture a couple of years earlier, when he incorporated empty Coke bottles into his *Coca-Cola Plan* of 1958 (Varnedoe and Gopnik 1990a). Pop-Art, moreover, had important British ante-cedents in the work of Richard Hamilton, Eduardo Paolozzi, Peter Blake and Richard Smith (Britt, 1989; Burn 2000d; Spalding 1986). In art history, however, antecedents are always ready to hand and infinite regress soon rears its ugly head. On this basis, it could be – and has been – argued that the first 'advertisements' were the cave paintings of Neolithic man (Sivulka 1998), though Neanderthal niche marketing and Cro-Magnon mail shots doubtless pre-dated the copy-writers of Lascaux and the art directors of Altamira.

6 Given Damien's 'borrowings', the BA injunction is a bit much. One can only surmise that it was done for the publicity value. Plagarism, clearly, is the fifth P of arts marketing, as Hirst's latest kafuffle testifies. His 20ft bronze statue of a cross-sectioned human body, *Hymn*, is a scaled up replica of a child's toy. Charles Saatchi, however, has paid £1 million for the artwork; the toy manufacturers, Halbro, have complained about the artist's misappropriation; Damien Hirst says he expects to be sued by the incensed organisation; and, naturally, everyone involved has benefited enormously from the free publicity (Burn 2000b). Thus does an imaginative artwork of a scientific object become a marketing bonanza for all concerned. Art, science and marketing in perfect harmony!

7 Any self-respecting art historian should know that Picasso pillaged commercial culture in his early collages (e.g. *Landscape with Posters* (1912), *Pipe, Glass and Bottle of Rum* (1914), *Bottle of Bass, Wineglass, Packet of Tobacco and Calling Card* (1914)). Therefore, we can safely infer that the whole *Picasso* controversy is a Citroën set-up.

8 This is a fairly bold assertion, admittedly, since the relationship between art and marketing is much more complex than these crude dichotomies suggest. These days, the principles of marketing are taught in art schools; masters degrees in arts marketing are available; and arts administrators can plan a marketing campaign with the best of them. (They can also use the terminology to browbeat recalcitrant artists and in their negotiations with potential corporate sponsors or funding agencies.) The basic stereotype still holds good, however.

9 C.P. Snow and Shelby Hunt notwithstanding, the distinctions between art, science and marketing have *never* been clear-cut. Just as working artists have always kept a weather eye on the machinations of the market and found inspiration in the scientific wonders of their time, marketers have also consistently pillaged the artistic canon when it suited their nefarious purposes and adopted the mantle of science if it helped sell the product category or service offering concerned. Just think of all those white-coated laboratory workers endorsing improbable but impressively named shampoo, tooth-paste and washing powder additives. For a review of the relationship between art, science and marketing see Conrad's (1998) superlative cultural history, *Modern Times, Modern Places*.

10 The scholarly thought police will doubtless complain that we haven't defined our terms properly. This is true, but as in the case of 'imagination', terms like 'art', 'aesthetics' and 'avant-garde' have been subject to extensive and ultimately inconclu-sive debate. Useful summaries of these (centuries long) controversies are contained in Meecham and Selden (2000), Bredin and Santoro-Brienza (2000) and Wood (1999). Enjoy.

11 The internet, admittedly, offers great potential in this particular regard. At present, sadly, web-based publications are held in very low esteem, largely because almost anything – good, bad, indifferent – can be posted thereon. No tenure, in short, for internet installation artists.

12 This statement has also been attributed to Claude Monet and Henri Matisse, though the original source is irrelevant. The important point is that the once-shocking images produced by Manet and his fellow impressionists (like Monet), or Matisse and his Fauvist followers are now regarded as affable, unthreatening, ersatz. Cheap and cheerful corporate wallpaper, in effect.

References

Bachelard, G. (1969 [1957]) *The Poetics of Space*, trans. M. Jolas, Boston: Beacon Press.

Barber, L. (2000) 'Art struck. How I fell in love with Britart', *Life: The Observer Magazine*, Sunday 19 March, 4–6.

Belk, R.W. (1986) 'Art versus science as ways of generating knowledge about material-ism', in D. Brinberg and R.J. Lutz (eds) *Perspectives on Methodology in Consumer Research*, New York: Springer-Verlag, 3–36.

—— (1998) 'Multimedia approaches to data and representations', in B.B. Stern (ed.) *Representing Consumers: Voices, Views and Visions*, London: Routledge, 308–38.

—— and Bryce, G. (1993) 'Christmas shopping scenes: from modern miracle to postmodern mall', *International Journal of Research in Marketing* 10, 3: 277–96.

Bell, J. (1999) *What is Painting?: Representation and Modern Art*, London: Thames & Hudson.

Bloom, A. (1987) *The Closing of the American Mind*, Harmondsworth: Penguin.

Bloom, H. (1970) 'The internalization of the quest romance', in *The Ringers in the Tower: Studies in Romantic Tradition*, Chicago: University of Chicago Press, 12–35.

Bocock, R. (1993) *Consumption*, London: Routledge.

Bogart, M.H. (1995) *Artists, Advertising and the Borders of Art*, Chicago: University of Chicago Press.

Bowra, M. (1961) *The Romantic Imagination*, Oxford: Oxford University Press.

Bragg, M. (1999), 'Whose side are you on?', *The Observer Review*, Sunday 7 March, 1–2.

Brann, E.T.H. (1991) *The World of the Imagination: Sum and Substance*, Lanham: Rowman & Littlefield.

Brawer, R.A. (1998) *Fictions of Business: Insights on Management from Great Literature*, New York: John Wiley.

Bredin, H. and Santoro-Brienza, L. (2000) *Philosophies of Art and Beauty: Introducing Aesthetics*, Edinburgh: Edinburgh University Press.

Britt, D. (1989) *Modern Art: Impressionism to Post-modernism*, London: Thames & Hudson.

Brown S. (1995a) *Postmodern Marketing*, London: Routledge.

—— (1995b) 'Life begins at 40?: further thoughts on marketing's mid-life crisis', *Marketing Intelligence and Planning* 13, 1: 4–17.

—— (1995c) 'Sex 'n' shopping: a "novel" approach to consumer research', *Journal of Marketing Management* 11, 8: 769–83.

—— (1996) 'Art or science?: fifty years of marketing debate', *Journal of Marketing Management* 12, 4: 243–67.

—— (1997) *Postmodern Marketing Two: Telling Tales*, London: ITBP.

—— (1998a) 'The unbearable lightness of marketing: a neo-romantic, counter-revolutionary recapitulation', in S. Brown *et al.* (eds) *Romancing the Market*, London: Routledge, 255–77.

—— (1998b) 'Unlucky for some: slacker scholarship and the well wrought turn', in B.B. Stern (ed.) *Representing Consumers: Voices, Views and Visions*, London: Routledge, 365–83.

—— (1998c) 'Tore down à la Rimbaud: illuminating the marketing imaginary' in S. Brown *et al.* (eds) *Romancing the Market*, London: Routledge, 22–40.

—— (1999a) 'Premonitions of Paradiso: millennial madness, *fin de siècle* fever and the end of the end of marketing', in S. Brown and A. Patterson (eds) *Proceedings of the Marketing Paradiso Conclave*, Belfast: University of Ulster, 1–13.

—— (1999b) 'Retro-marketing: yesterday's tomorrows, today!', *Marketing Intelligence and Planning* 17, 7: 363–76.

—— (1999c) 'Devaluing value: the apophatic ethic and the spirit of postmodern consumption', in M.B. Holbrook (ed.) *Consumer Value: A Framework for Analaysis and Research*, London: Routledge, 159–82.

—— (2000) *Marketing: The Retro Revolution*, London: Sage.

——, Doherty, A.M. and Clarke, W. (1998) 'Stoning the romance: on marketing's mind forg'd manacles', in S. Brown *et al.* (eds) *Romancing the Market*, London: Routledge, 1–21.

Burn, G. (2000a) 'Off the scrapheap', *The Guardian G2*, Thursday 13 April, 6–7.

—— (2000b) 'What Damien did next', *The Guardian G2*, Monday 10 April, 1–5.

—— (2000c) 'The godfather', *The Guardian G2*, Friday 14 April, 4–5.

—— (2000d) 'The invisible man', *The Guardian G2*, Tuesday 11 April, 2–3.

Campbell, C. (1987) *The Romantic Ethic and the Spirit of Modern Consumerism*, Oxford: Blackwell.

—— (1998) 'Shopping, pleasure and the sex war', in C. Campbell and P. Falk (eds) *The Shopping Experience*, London: Sage, 166–76.

Chalmers, R. (1993) 'Con artist?', *The Observer Magazine*, Sunday 20 June, 18–26.

Chodorow, J. (1997) *Jung on Active Imagination*, Princeton: Princeton University Press.

Collings, M. (1997) *Blimey! From Bohemia to Britpop: The London Artworld from Francis Bacon to Damien Hirst*, London: 21 Publishing.

—— (1998) *It Hurts! New York Art from Warhol to Now*, London: 21 Publishing.

—— (1999) *This is Modern Art*, London: Weidenfeld & Nicolson.

Conrad, P. (1998) *Modern Times, Modern Places: Life & Art in the 20th Century*, London: Thames & Hudson.

Cook, R. (2000) 'When art is pants: your chance to own a very limited edition', *The Business*, Saturday 4 March, 8.

Corrigan, P. (1999) *Shakespeare on Management: Leadership Lessons for Today's Managers*, London: Kogan Page.

Day, A. (1996) *Romanticism*, London: Routledge.

Diggle, K. (1994) *Arts Marketing*, London: Reingold.

Dorfles, G. (1969) *Kitsch: An Anthology of Bad Taste*, London: Studio Vista.

Drabble, M. (ed.) (1995) *The Oxford Companion to English Literature*, Oxford: Oxford University Press.

Eagleton, T. (2000) *The Meaning of Culture*, Oxford: Blackwell.

Edwards, S. (ed.) (1999) *Art and its Histories: A Reader*, New Haven: Yale University Press.

Elam, D. (1992) *Romancing the Postmodern*, London: Routledge.

Elliott, R. (1997) 'Existential consumption and irrational desire', *European Journal of Marketing* 31, 3/4: 283–94.

Fineberg, J. (2000) *Art Since 1940: Strategies of Being*, London: Laurence King.

Gabay, J. (1998) *Imaginative Marketing*, London: Teach Yourself Books.

Haden-Guest, A. (1996) *True Colors: The Real Life of the Art World*, New York: Atlantic Monthly Press.

Heilbrunn, B. (1996) 'In search of the hidden go(o)d: a philosophical deconstruction and narratological revisitation of the eschatological metaphor in marketing', in S. Brown *et al.* (eds) *Marketing Apocalypse: Eschatology, Escapology and the Illusion of the End*, London: Routledge, 111–32.

—— (1998) 'In search of the lost aura: the object in the age of marketing romanticism', in S. Brown *et al.* (eds) *Romancing the Market*, London: Routledge, 187–201.

Hill, E., O'Sullivan, C. and O'Sullivan, T. (1995) *Creative Arts Marketing*, Oxford: Butterworth-Heinemann.

Hill, J.S. (ed.) (1977) *The Romantic Imagination: A Casebook*, Basingstoke: Macmillan.

Hirschman, E.C. (1998) 'When expert consumers interpret textual products: applying reader-response theory to television programs', *Consumption, Markets and Culture* 2, 3: 259–309.

Holbrook, M.B. (1993) 'The role of semiotics in research on consumer esthetics', in M.B. Holbrook and E.C. Hirschman (eds) *The Semiotics of Consumption: Interpreting Symbolic Consumer Behavior in Popular Culture and Works of Art*, Berlin: de Gruyter, 1–60.

—— (1995) *Consumer Research: Introspective Essays on the Study of Consumption*, Thousand Oaks: Sage.

—— (1996) 'Romanticism, introspection and the roots of experiential consumption: Morris the Epicurean', in R.W. Belk, N. Dholakia and A. Venkatesh (eds) *Consumption and Marketing: Macro Dimensions*, Cincinnati: South-Western, 20–82.

—— (1998) 'Journey to Kroywen: an ethnoscopic auto-auto-auto-driven stereographic photo essay', in B.B. Stern (ed.) *Representing Consumers: Voices, Views and Visions*, London: Routledge, 231–63.

—— and Grayson, M.W. (1989) 'The role of the humanities in consumer research: close encounters and coastal disturbances', in E.C. Hirschman (ed.) *Interpretive Consumer Research*, Provo: Association for Consumer Research, 29–47.

Hughes, R. (1997) *American Visions: The Epic History of Art in America*, London: Harvill Press.

Jardine, L. (1996) *Worldly Goods: A New History of the Renaissance*, Basingstoke: Macmillan.

Jensen, R. (1999) *The Dream Society: How the Coming Shift from Information to Imagination will Transform your Business*, New York: McGraw-Hill.

Joselit, D., Simon, J. and Salecl, R. (1998) *Jenny Holzer*, London: Phaidon.

Kearney, R. (1994) *The Wake of Imagination*, London: Routledge.

—— (1998) *Poetics of Imagining: Modern to Postmodern*, New York: Fordham University Press.

Klein, M. (2000) *No Logo*, London: Flamingo.

Kostabi, M. (1996) *Conversations with Kostabi*, Boston: Journey Editions.

Kotler, N. and Kotler, P. (1998) *Museum Strategy and Marketing: Designing Missions, Building Audiences, Generating Revenue and Resources*, San Francisco: Jossey-Bass.

Kotler, P. (1982) *Marketing for Non-profit Organisations*, Englewood Cliffs: Prentice-Hall.

—— and Scheff, J. (1997) *Standing Room Only: Strategies for Marketing the Performing Arts*, Cambridge: Harvard Business School Press.

Kulka, T. (1996) *Kitsch and Art*, University Park: Penn State Press.

Lacan, J. (1977 [1966]) *Ecrits: A Selection*, trans. A. Sheridan, London: Routledge.

Lavin, I. (1990) 'High and low before their time: Bernini and the art of social satire', in K. Varnedoe and A. Gopnik (eds) *Modern Art and Popular Culture: Readings in High and Low*, New York: Abrams, 18–50.

Lears, J. (1981) *No Place of Grace: Antimodernism and the Transformation of American Culture, 1880–1920*, Chicago: Chicago University Press.

—— (1994) *Fables of Abundance: A Cultural History of Advertising in America*, New York: Basic Books.

Levitt, T. (1986) *The Marketing Imagination*, New York: Free Press.

Lewis, R.W. (1996) *Absolut Book. The Absolut Vodka Advertising Story*, Boston: Journey Editions.

Livingstone, I. (1997) *Arrow of Chaos: Romanticism and Postmodernity*, Minneapolis: University of Minnesota Press.

Lucie-Smith, E. (1995) *Art Today*, London: Phaidon.

Maclaran, P. and Stevens, L. (1998) 'Romancing the utopian marketplace: dallying with Bakhtin in the Powerscourt Townhouse Centre', in S. Brown *et al.* (eds) *Romancing the Market*, London: Routledge, 172–86.

Marconi, J. (1997) *Shock Marketing: Advertising, Influence, and Family Values*, Chicago: Bonus Books.

McEvilley, M. (1996) 'Foreword', in M. Kostabi *Conversations with Kostabi*, Boston: Journey Editions, xi-xiii.

McLean, F. (1997) *Marketing the Museum*, London: Routledge.

McQuarrie, E.F. and Mick, D.G. (1996) 'Figures of advertising rhetoric', *Journal of Consumer Research* 22, March: 424–38.

Mead, R. (1994) 'Where is the culture of Thailand?', *International Journal of Research in Marketing* 11, 4: 401–04.

Meecham, P. and Sheldon, J. (2000) *Modern Art: A Critical Introduction*, London: Routledge.

Mick, D.G. and Politi, L.G. (1989) 'Consumers' interpretations of advertising imagery: a visit to the hell of connotation', in E.C. Hirschman (ed.) *Interpretive Consumer Research*, Provo: Association for Consumer Research, 85–96.

Morgan, G. (1993) *Imaginization*, Thousand Oaks: Sage.

Murray, J.B. and Ozanne, J. (1991) 'The critical imagination: emancipatory interests in consumer research', *Journal of Consumer Research* 18, September: 129–44.

O'Keeffe, J. (1999) *Business Beyond the Box*, London: Nicholas Brealey.

Olalquiaga, C. (1999) *The Artificial Kingdom: A Treasury of the Kitsch Experience*, London: Bloomsbury.

Pitman, J. (2000) 'One man show', *The Times Magazine*, Saturday 15 April, 38–44.

Postma, P. (1998) *The New Marketing Era: Marketing to the Imagination in a Technology Driven World*, New York: McGraw-Hill.

Prince, A. (1998) *Hans Christian Andersen: The Fan Dancer*, London: Allison & Busby.

Redhead, D. (2000) *Products of our Time*, London: Birkhäuser.

Rein, I.J., Kotler, P. and Stoller, M. (1997) *High Visibility: The Making and Marketing of Professionals into Celebrities*, Chicago: NTC Publishing.

Sage, A. (2000) 'Art world fumes as the car in front is a Picasso', *The Times*, Saturday 15 January, 6.

Saunders, D. (1996) *Shock in Advertising*, London: Batsford.

Schau, H.J. (2000) *Consumer Imagination, Identity, and Self-expression in Computer Mediated Environments*, unpublished PhD dissertation, Irvine: University of California at Irvine.

Scott, L.M. (1990) 'Understanding jingles and needledrop: a rhetorical approach to music in advertising', *Journal of Consumer Research* 17, September: 223–36.

—— (1994) 'The bridge from text to mind: adapting reader-response theory to consumer research', *Journal of Consumer Research* 21, December: 461–80.

Scruton, R. (1974) *Art and Imagination: A Study in the Philosophy of Mind*, London: Methuen.

—— (1994) 'Imagination', in R. Scruton (ed.) *Modern Philosophy: An Introduction and Survey*, London: Sinclair-Stevenson, 341–54.

Seabrook, J. (2000) *Nobrow: The Culture of Marketing – The Marketing of Culture*, New York: Knopf.

Sherry, J.F., Jr. (1991) 'Postmodern alternatives: the interpretive turn in consumer research', in T.S. Robertson and H.H. Kassarjian (eds) *Handbook of Consumer Research*, Englewood Cliffs: Prentice Hall, 548–91.

—— (1998) 'The soul of the company store: Nike Town Chicago and the emplaced brandscape', in J.F. Sherry, Jr. (ed.) *Servicescapes: The Concept of Place in Contemporary Markets*, Chicago: NTC Business Books, 109–46.

Sivulka, J. (1998) *Soap, Sex and Cigarettes: A Cultural History of American Advertising*, Belmont: Wadsworth.

Spalding, F. (1986) *British Art Since 1900*, London: Thames & Hudson.

Stallabrass, J. (1996) *Gargantua: Manufactured Mass Culture*, London: Verso.

—— (1999) *High Art Lite*, London: Verso.

Stangos, N. (1994) *Concepts of Modern Art: From Fauvism to Postmodernism*, London: Thames & Hudson.

Stern, B.B. (1989) 'Literary criticism and consumer research: overview and illustrative example', *Journal of Consumer Research* 16, December: 322–34.

—— (1995) 'Consumer myths: Frye's taxonomy and the structural analysis of consumption text', *Journal of Consumer Research* 22, September: 165–85.

—— (1996) 'Deconstructive strategy and consumer research: concepts and illustrative exemplar', *Journal of Consumer Research* 23, September: 136–47.

—— (1998) 'Poetry and representation in consumer research: the art of science', in B.B. Stern (ed.) *Representing Consumers: Voices, Views and Visions*, London: Routledge, 290–307.

—— and Schroeder, J. (1994) 'Interpretive methodology from art and literary criticism: a humanistic approach to advertising imagery', *European Journal of Marketing* 28, September: 114–32.

Storr, R. (1990) 'No joy in Mudville: Greenberg's modernism, then and now', in K. Varnedoe and A. Gopnik (eds) *Modern Art and Popular Culture: Readings in High and Low*, New York: Abrams, 160–90.

Thompson, C.J. (1998) 'Show me the deep masculinity: Jerry McGuire's postmodernised identity crisis and the romantic revitalization of patriarchy (or the mythopoetic subtext of relationship marketing)', in S. Brown *et al.* (eds) *Romancing the Market*, London: Routledge, 56–73.

Tuan, Y-F. (1989) *Morality and Imagination: Paradoxes of Progress*, Madison: University of Wisconsin Press.

Tusa, J. (1999) *Art Matters: Reflecting on Culture*, London: Methuen.

Varnedoe, K. and Gopnik, A. (1990a) *High and Low: Modern Art and Popular Culture*, New York: Museum of Modern Art.

—— (1990b) *Modern Art and Popular Culture: Readings in High and Low*, New York: Abrams.

Waldman, D. (1997) *Jenny Holzer*, New York: Guggenheim Museum.

Ward, P. (1991) *Kitsch in Sync: A Consumer's Guide to Bad Taste*, London: Plexus.

Warner, M. (2000) 'A new twist in the long tradition of the grotesque', *London Review of Books* 22, 8: 24–5.

Warnock, M. (1976) *Imagination*, London: Faber & Faber.

Wheeler, B. and Day, J. (2000) 'Shock tacticians', *Marketing Week*, 23 March, 30–31.

Whitford, F. (1999) 'Back to the futurists', *The Culture*, Sunday, 24 February, 9.

Williams, J. (1995) *Pooh and the Philosophers*, London: Methuen.

Williamson, J. (1978) *Decoding Advertisements: Ideology and Meaning in Advertising*, London: Marion Boyers.

Wolf, M. J. (1999) *The Entertainment Economy*, London: Penguin.

Wollen, P. (2000) 'Say hello to Rodney', *London Review of Books* 22, 4: 3–7.

Wood, P. (ed.) (1999) *The Challenge of the Avant-Garde*, New Haven: Yale University Press.

Wypijewski, J. (1999) *Painting by Numbers: Komar and Melamid's Scientific Guide to Art*, Berkeley: University of California Press.

Section 1
Art

awakening one day

to discover
       my own longing
embodied here
       in giving touch
to you
       roused rudely
from a lover's lethargy
       to learn it
was myself that sought
       to summon back
those cuppings and claspings
       traces and kneads
that you were not
       a conduit of grace
has fixed me

John F. Sherry, Jr.

2   Édouard Manet, Calvin Klein and the strategic use of scandal

Jonathan E. Schroeder

To exhibit is for the artist the vital concern, the sine qua non, for it happens that after looking at something you become used to what was surprising or, if you wish, shocking.

(Édouard Manet 1867, quoted in Cachin 1995)

Wasn't the controversy a blessing in disguise? You mean, did we sell more jeans? Yes, of course!

(Calvin Klein, quoted in Plaskin 1984)

The intellectual, cultural and conceptual separation of art and commerce is strong. When I mentioned the topic of this chapter to a colleague who had just finished her dissertation on Manet, she was shocked (shocked!) that I would make such a comparison between the master painter and a mere businessman. She insisted that the socio-historical context of Manet and Klein were sufficiently distinct to make simple comparisons facile, and that the intentions of the two men were, of course, completely at odds with each other. Yes, I agree that there are clear differences between the two figures. But I am interested in the connections between Manet the artist and Klein the designer and businessmen. Both were masters in turning diversity into publicity. Both were creative men driven by commercial success aided by strategic marketing techniques. Both gained early success utilising images of women representing prostitutes – Manet with his 1863 nude *Olympia*, Klein with his use of Brooke Shields who was well known for playing a child prostitute in the movie *Pretty Baby*. Both are celebrated for bringing concerns with 'real life' into their work. If we begin to see the connections between these two exemplars, we gain insight into the permeable boundaries between art and commerce, as well as the role of the image and how it functions within culture. Furthermore, we gain insight into the strategic use of scandal to attract attention, and gain recognition in the effort to create powerful brand images, whether in fashion or art.

This chapter will use Manet and Klein to discuss brand strategy, from a perspective that breaks down the traditional boundaries between art and commerce. I am interested in drawing connections between these two well-known scandalmongers, whose work is based on images, both visual and brand images. I will argue that Manet, much like Klein, was concerned with getting his name and image known, and although first dejected by the reception of his controversial work, he ultimately benefited from publicity. Calvin Klein has consistently produced marketing images that have caused uproar, and the image of his clothing and cosmetics is largely based on a sexuality bordering on the fringe.

I will first discuss the image in consumption and marketing strategy. Then I will briefly discuss the careers of Manet and Klein, with a focus on the well-known scandals their images caused. Manet's *Olympia* and Calvin Klein's CK One campaign will be of particular concern. Next, I will meditate a bit on the strategic use of scandal. I will close with a consideration of the problems and possibilities of turning to art within consumer and marketing research, for the art–commerce dichotomy referred to above seems to be alive and well within marketing scholarship.

The image

A key characteristic of the economy of the twenty-first century is the image. Brands are developed based on images, products are advertised via images, corporate image is critical for managerial success. If we understand that the market is based on images – brand images, corporate images, national images, and images of identity, then we realise that vision is central to understanding management in the information society. As consumer theorist Susan Willis puts it:

> In advanced consumer society, the act of consumption need not involve economic exchange. We consume with our eyes, taking in commodities every time we push a grocery cart up and down the aisles in a supermarket, or watch TV, or drive down a logo-studded highway. The visual consumption of the commodity form is so much a part of our daily landscape that we do not consciously remark on such acts of consumption.
>
> (Willis 1991: 31)

Marketing is the institution that handles most of the roles that religion, the state and the family once held: providing meaning in a myth-like way that helps us make sense of our world. Firms attach meaning to the product through images and then attempt to connect this image to the identity of the person who perceives the ad. Even if we as individual consumers purchase very few of the products advertised, the ads still function as meaning producers. Often, we define ourselves by what we do not buy – 'I would never wear a Rolex', or 'I will boycott Nike', or 'You wouldn't catch me wearing those polyester skirts'.

Advertising techniques and metaphors have crept into almost every area of life. Political candidates are packaged, their image carefully constructed with marketing and political experts. Singles advertise in personal advertisements, marketing and selling themselves as a bundle of attributes, much like product marketing. We sell our ideas, make a case for our arguments, and so forth. Brands are bought and sold for their image value over and above a firm's physical, intellectual or organisational assets. Internet companies are traded for enormous sums based on their image, rather than sales or profits.

The world of imagery in ads is directly connected to the visual past – art history (cf. Aumont 1997; Leppert 1997). Advertising creates a dream world of images where anything seems possible. Except, that is, advertising places limits on the imagination due to its very purpose. Its cultivation of images is designed with one thing in mind: purchase. Advertising sells the past to the future via a sophisticated and often misunderstood information technological system (Berger 1972).

I contend that advertising is the dominant global communication force. As sociologists Goldman and Papson declare: 'The power of advertising lies in its ability to photographically frame and redefine our meanings and our experiences and then turn them into meanings that are consonant with corporate interests' (1996: 216). For advertising is no longer a means of merely communicating information about products, it is the engine of the economy and a major player in the political sphere. Goldman and Papson continue: 'This power to recontexualize and reframe photographic images has put advertising at the center of contemporary redefinitions of individuality, freedom, and democracy in relation to corporate symbols' (1996: 216).

The importance of the image places a premium on understanding how images function, what they do, how people respond to them and why they are so important. Manet and Klein are exemplars of image creators, yet they are rarely discussed together, as they belong to the different worlds of art and commerce. To more fully investigate images, we turn to art history, a discipline that has been looking at images for a while now.

Links between art and commerce

Art – like marketing – is an important cultural institution that transmits and reflects values, meaning and beliefs. In the words of an art historian, 'social history and art history are continuous, each offering necessary insights into the other' (Baxandall 1987: 12). Studying art historical trends that shaped art and the society that produced it reveals a different perspective on consumer culture. By scrutinising subtle changes in art, their eventual ramifications, and the rise of art as a commodity, a unique insight is gained into the history of market economies. Art, of course, is part of culture and is a complex institution. There are many, many connections between art and consumption. I am suggesting that by turning to art, and focusing attention on the use of images within the art system, we gain an appreciation of how images function within consumption processes.

Although the use of art history and criticism is still comparatively rare in consumer and marketing research (though see Hupfer 1997; Schroeder 1992, 1997a, 1997b, 1998a, 1998b; Schroeder and Borgerson 1998; Stern and Schroeder 1994; Watson 1992; Witkowski 1996, 1999), the converse is not true. Several art historians have discussed broad issues of consumer behaviour. For example, Simon Schama discusses many aspects central to consumer research – such as collecting, demand, luxury goods – in his monumental study of Dutch art (Schama 1988). Other art historians take a market-oriented approach to the art market, demonstrating that art is governed by market forces similar to manu-factured goods (e.g. Goldthwaite 1993; Jensen 1994; Watson 1992). Historical scholarship investigating societal trends often invokes art history in discussing consumption or marketing issues (Jardine 1996; Jensen 1994; Schama 1988; Watson 1992). While art historians are surveying the marketing of art, consumer researchers have been slow to turn to art to analyse consumer processes – a central feature of the culture that art depicts, packages, comments on, and is marketed within. A notable exception is Joy's paper on the art market's influence in corporate strategy, which dubbed corporate sponsors of art 'the Modern Medicis' (1993).

Art, like advertising, often celebrates wealth, power and the status quo. Indeed, art is a product in many respects, to be consumed through auction and gallery sales, museum patronage, reproductions, commercial art and so forth. The line between art and commerce is a blurry one; many artists specifically produce things to be sold, artist's letters from the past are full of references to monetary matters, and advertising has incorporated the techniques, look and producers of art (see Schroeder 1995). Advertising agencies, photography studios and design firms are full of people with art history training (Bogart 1995; Lears 1994). Furthermore, the world of advertising represents a popular art form that is often represented in fine art museums (Schroeder 1997b). Thus, it seems reasonable to turn to art history – a field that has been analysing images for hundreds of years – to expand our knowledge of consumption.

Art critic John Berger described important correspondences between the his-tory of art and advertising, and he showed how advertising depends heavily on the techniques, symbols and history of paintings. Advertising depends on the language of painting that celebrates wealth and private property and is often nostalgic, referring back to a golden age. Specifically, advertising uses art conventions of form – genre, poses, symbols – as well as techniques borrowed from painting and photography. Advertising often invokes the world of art, for example, Leonardo Da Vinci's *Mona Lisa* appears often in ads as an icon of portraiture, fine art, value and as a vehicle for humour. Ads often call products masterpieces, or a work of art, and so forth. Direct connections to painting, such as the image itself, the ad frame, and 'quoting' art historical sources give a certain presence to ads, linking them to taste, prestige and affluence. Manet's *Olympia*, for example has been parodied hundreds of times, and often serves as a theme for advertisements. In general, art is a sign of affluence, it belongs to the good life. Artistic references also suggest a cultural authority, superior to crass material interests. Thus, by referring to art, advertising can denote both wealth and spirituality; luxury and transcendent cultural value. In opening up this dialogue between art and marketing, I hope to add to the enterprise of research that takes images seriously, both for their power to persuade and for their pervasive role in visual culture (see O'Donohoe 1997). My framework views advertising as a powerful representational system that produces knowledge through discursive practices. I draw on diverse fields of knowledge, spanning the traditional boundaries between them, opening up a space to encounter the contemporary visual landscape, filled with manufactured images (see Schroeder 2001).

In a previous paper, I argued that the Pop artist Andy Warhol might be viewed as a consumer researcher. His output – paintings, prints, films, books and designs – offer insights into consumption and marketing outright. Moreover, Warhol was adept at building his own image into a brand – the Andy Warhol brand, which lives on today more than a decade after his death. I pointed out five areas of concern to marketing that a close study of Warhol might contribute to: brand equity, fashion, imagery, packaging and identity (Schroeder 1997a). I have also argued that Renaissance art and the patronage system is a useful place to investigate consumer behaviour. I concluded that during the period in history known as the Italian Renaissance the consumption of art began to resemble affluent society's basic consumer habits. Market conditions arose to generate a dazzling array of consumer goods – including art, architecture, clothing and furniture. An art historical approach identifies a major shift in consumer desire – signaling the privatisation and personalisation of art. Works of art that reflected the values, influence and wealth of Renaissance capitalists are now honoured historically as great and valuable cultural artefacts, kept in elaborate museums, and form the basis of a thriving tourist industry (Schroeder 1997b).

We can also look at the content of art and advertising to gain knowledge of the interactions between these two image-based cultural communications systems. For example, Stern and Schroeder combined literary and art historical techniques to gain semiotic understanding of advertising (1994). Schroeder and Borgerson looked at the way gender has been represented in the history of art and advertising (1998). Schroeder and Zwick contend that the representational history of the male body is being influenced by current trends in advertising (2000). However, the image itself is not the whole picture. Here, I am more interested in how images – in art and marketing – become tools in gaining attention and building brand awareness and recognition.

Édouard Manet, painter of modern life

Manet was born in Paris in 1832. His father wanted him to become a lawyer, but settled on a career in the navy. However, Manet failed the entrance examinations, joined the merchant marines and, upon his return, convinced his father to let him enrol in art school. He began exhibiting his work in the early 1860s, and became notorious for his painting *Déjeuner sur l'Herbe*, first shown with his religious work *Jesus Mocked* in 1863.

After exhibiting *Déjeuner sur l'Herbe* at the Salon des refusés Manet became famous overnight. The central subject of *Déjeuner* was two men and a naked woman picnicking near a pastoral river (see Tucker 1998). The composition was based on classical motifs: 'Manet here took up a theme already exploited by Raphael and Titian but, arriving in his own fashion at Courbet's realism, he executed a work which is more coarse than sensual, with a very novel vision for painting' (Savy 1998). Rather than deal with classical or mythological motifs, Manet's work dwelled in the here and now. His subjects were recognisable, the symbolic overtones were not emphasised and the public reaction to the painting was intense. The former title of *Déjeuner* was *La Partie carrée*, which refers to 'a fourway debauch, involving two men and two girls, who sleep together, go for walks together, eat together, and kiss' (Krell 1996: 33). Racy stuff, for the 1860s, and a perfect pretext for Manet to represent a nude woman. Several years later, Manet showed *Olympia*, which secured his place among controversial image-makers and divided the critics as to his reputation. However, it made him more famous and a household word in France: 'The clamour set off by the *Olympia* and the *Jesus Mocked* added to the previous noise made by the *Déjeuner sur l'Herbe*, gave to Manet the kind of notoriety that no other painter had had before' (Théodore Duret, quoted in Cachin 1995).

Critical reaction focused on Manet's subjects as well as his style of painting, which has become celebrated as realism – a distinct break from the academic traditions of historical themed painting with hidden brushwork. Manet's handling of paint was coarse, thick and seen as crude by many contemporary critics. Furthermore, Manet's use of scandal was recognised early, 'Manet will have taste the day he gives up choosing subjects solely for their ability to create a scandal' (art critic Ernest Chesneau, in Cachin 1995: 49). His intentions were interpreted, too: painting scandalous subjects was seen as 'more or less a conscious strategy that Manet pursued throughout his entire career . . . [Manet was] no doubt fully aware of the provocativeness of the canvas' (Cachin 1995: 50–1).

The attention that Manet gained through his paintings became central to his career and fame as an artist. As we shall see, Calvin Klein has been consistently criticised for his advertising imagery, yet his fame, his sales and his brand image remain excellent. Most art historians focus on the dejection Manet experienced, yet it was his negative attention that fuelled his supporters, among them

Zola and Baudelaire (Clark 1985: Fredrich 1991). Zola's first article on Manet gushed:

> It appears that I am the first to praise Manet without reservation . . . I am so sure Manet will be one of the masters of tomorrow that I should believe I had made a good bargain, had I the money, in buying all his canvases today. In 50 years they will sell for fifteen or twenty times more.
>
> (quoted in Krell 1996: 72).

Zola's emphasis on the investment value of Manet's paintings is clear.

On the other hand, most critics roundly dismissed *Olympia*. The painting shows a nude woman reclining on a bed, being waited on by a black woman. The criticism centred on the way the nude woman was represented and painted: 'Manet wants to become famous by shocking the bourgeoisie' (Cachin 1995: 50). Nudity, it seems, was acceptable in allegorical paintings, but Manet appeared to show 'just' a prostitute. Once again, writers noted the use of scandal:

> *Olympia* can be understood from no point of view, even if you take it for what it is, a puny model stretched out on a sheet. The colour of the flesh is dirty, the shadows are indicated by more or less large smears of blacking . . . here is nothing, we are sorry to say, but the desire to attract attention at any price.
>
> (Théophile Gautier, quoted in Cachin 1995)

Both Manet and Klein exploited images of women to build their names. The history of art is replete with dubious uses of the female body, which has been discussed at length elsewhere (Schroeder and Borgerson 1998, for a review). Suffice it to say that these two men did little to advance the cause of women or gender equality in their appropriation of gender poses and stereotypes. We may protest that it is the society that is hypocritical or repressive, but I would argue that Manet and Klein only seized opportunities to exploit sexist tendencies in the image use. In this chapter, I am more concerned with strategic use of images, but I do want to include a warning from an innovative feminist art historian:

> Women in the history of Art have traditionally been the objects of desire and the gaze . . . To recognize this is not to diminish the accomplishment of these artworks . . . these images are important for many reasons, some of which involve their revelations regarding the particular historical moments of their creation. These works of Art, therefore, act as lenses of our culture, making more clearly visible what we see and what it is presumed we want to see.
>
> (Staniszewski 1995: 151).

Manet entered the canon of important artists, and his works hang in museums worldwide. His reputation rests on his way of painting real-life scenes, which represented an important break with the academic tradition. He died fairly young in 1883 of complications from a long bout with syphilis.

Calvin Klein, promoter of modern life

Klein was born in New York in 1942. He attended the Fashion Institute of Technology in Manhattan and began producing clothing designs in the early 1960s. His first break came from Bonwit Teller, a major department store and clothing buyer. He was successful in selling his fashions lines, but his real fame began in the 1970s when he was part of the decadent disco crowd of Studio 54 in New York City (Churcher and Gaines 1994). In 1979, he hired the photographer Richard Avedon to shoot Brooke Shields in a series of designer blue jeans advertisements, which became some of the most celebrated and criticised images of the twentieth century. Shields has gained notoriety by portraying a 12-year-old prostitute in the movies, and she was given advertising copy 'Nothing comes between me and my Calvins'. For those of us who were adolescents around this time, the ads were sensationally titillating – *double entendres*, revealing poses, incredibly tight designer jeans! I remember the campaign well, and my freshman room-mate in college taped one of the ads to our dorm room wall. The campaign skyrocketed Calvin Klein to huge fame, and sales of his 'designer' jeans took off.

Calvin Klein's campaigns sparked controversy and comment for the next twenty years (e.g. Lippert 1996; Miller 1992; Seo 1998; Sullivan 1995). Sex appeal is usually invoked by Klein's ads and provides much of the equity in his products that cover the gamut from blue jeans to evening wear. Klein perfected his media response to criticism during the firestorm over the Brooke Shields campaign. He insisted that people are reading into the ads, that he is only celebrating sex and beauty and that he uses professional models, who are paid to act: 'Actually, we were using Brooke as an actress, she was playing different roles: a liberated woman, a teenager, a vamp. . . . People read things into my commercials that didn't even exist' (in Plaskin 1984). This set of defences has pretty much stayed the same for his entire career. In 1995, he had his most serious problems with a campaign 'in which young people appear in provocative positions that critics have blasted as child pornography' (Agins 1995: A1). The FBI began an investigation into Klein's alleged use of underage models in an attempt to press charges under child pornography laws. The offending ads were pulled, but after they achieved a place in the Klein pantheon of provocative images (Goldman 1995). He seems to enjoy his role of scandalous image maker, 'I drive down Broadway every day to my studio, and I purposely have the Calvin Klein billboards arranged in Times Square so that I can see them' (in Plaskin 1984).

Klein and many other advertisers have been criticised for not showing the product, not discussing the product's attributes. For those of us in marketing, this is, of course, nothing new, for we know that images are what move products off the shelves. In Klein's words, 'If you want to sell jeans, don't talk about them' (in Plaskin 1984). Klein also has been able to promote a 'face' of the Calvin Klein brand, from Brooke Shields through Kate Moss: 'His ability to pick girls is astounding. It's a miracle, it's foolproof' (Isaac Mizrahi, quoted in Singer 2000).

The CK One campaign

One of Calvin Klein's most successful recent campaigns is for CK One. Introduced in 1994, CK One is a fragrance marketed to both sexes *'for a man or a woman'* reads the ad copy – noteworthy in today's targeted environment, especially in a product category that is closely linked with gender identity and sexual allure. CK One is marketed through unusual channels, as well. It is sold in Tower Records music stores, and its packaging resembles an aluminum military type water bottle (Sloan 1996). The fragrance is successful and the ad is well known among teenagers and twenty-somethings, and Calvin Klein has introduced a second gender neutral fragrance campaign, CK be (Sloan 1996). The multi-million dollar CK One campaign was the first to garner the Fragrance Foundation's top awards in both men and women's fragrance categories (Campbell 1995).

The CK One images seem to play and subvert gender norms, and they have generated much attention and controversy (e.g. Elliot 1994). They have become an icon of 1990s advertising, and have been copied, emulated and parodied by other campaigns. The CK One ad has caught the attention of many, and has greatly influenced the world of advertising photography (e.g. Seo 1998). It was displayed in the Whitney Museum of American Art in New York as part of the art exhibition 'The Warhol Look' (Francis and King 1997). As an advertising exemplar, CK One provides a compelling image to subject to visual analysis. Much like Manet's *Olympia*, they seem to depict a different sort of subject than the traditional advertising milieus had dealt with. Furthermore, as in *Olympia*, we have themes of race, identity, sexuality, and nudity circulating through the image, adding to its allure and attraction (see Lipton 1999). It is therefore useful to spend some time with the CK One ads in order to compare them with Manet's much earlier image. (As there is a lack of description of most advertising images and a wealth of material on Manet, I will devote more time to CK One.)

It is significant that the ads make no mention of the product's physical attributes, but instead promote a highly abstract connection between the models and using the brand (Stern and Schroeder 1994). We are asked to transfer meaning from the look of the people in the ad – their image, lifestyle, physical appearance – onto the product (Goldman 1992; Williamson 1978). Therefore, it is critical to understand how meaning is constructed in this ad. Important contributors to meaning are art historical referents that inform and influence the creation and reception of the ad. This not to imply that all viewers see the art historical antecedents in images such as the CK One ad, or that all viewers would make the same connections. However, the traditions of art history have informed how we relate to the visual world, have profoundly affected advertising imagery and are a part of the training of advertising image producers.

There are several versions of the basic ad, all consisting of a stark black and white image of several people standing, most facing the camera. In certain CK One images, several separate photographs seem to be joined together, resulting in a jarring, disjointed look.

One focal subject of the ad is Kate Moss, the famous British supermodel, who dominates the scene through her fame. Moss got her start towards supermodel stardom after being photographed by Corrine Day for the July 1990 cover of *The Face* magazine (see Moss 1997). She gives the viewer a hook into the ad and guides its interpretation (Berger 1972). Kate Moss 'hails' us, the viewer, by her fame, her roles in other Calvin Klein ads and her image as a white, heterosexual woman informed by her well-publicised romantic liaisons with male stars. Moss's status overwhelms the other figures in the ad, rendering them supporting players in the icon-driven world of celebrity.

The CK One ad features stark black and white photographs of people who seem out of place in the advertising pantheon. Skinheads mingle incongruously with tough looking black women. Feminine men are posed next to Kate Moss. Men with long hair pose next to a short-haired woman with large tattoos on her arm. In the first image, there is clearly a sexual element.

The CK One ads were photographed by Steven Meisel in the style of Richard Avedon, arguably the world's most influential modern fashion photographer. Meisel, known for 'striking, highly art-directed portraits of celebrities and androgynes of both sexes . . . routinely "samples" [other] photographers' work (Daly and Wice 1995: 146). Avedon is known for his stark, icon-making black and white portraits of the famous and not-so-famous as well as his technique of breaking away from still fashion poses to favour more naturalistic shots of people moving about, gesticulating, talking and generally not appearing posed (Solomon 1994). Avedon also photographed one of Calvin Klein's most enduring images, Brooke Shields proclaiming that nothing comes between her and her Calvins (Sullivan 1995).

Specifically, the CK One ad is 'reminiscent of Richard Avedon's 1969 photograph of the factory crowd' (Francis and King 1997: 177). This photograph of Andy Warhol and various friends and assistants comprises four separate images placed together, and is strikingly similar to the CK One ad. Men and women in various states of dress and undress pose for Avedon's camera, staring blankly forward. The background is white, the black and white contrast is harsh, and the subjects look a bit unkempt and tough. Warhol was well known for his entourage of 'downtown' models, artists and hangers-on, and the Factory came to represent a way of life outside the mainstream uptown world of established art galleries and museums. By photographing the CK One ad in the style of Avedon's Warhol gang photograph, Meisel superimposed one icon – Andy Warhol – onto another, CK One.

Like many Avedon photographs, the CK One image is photographed against a plain white background that serves to de-centre the subjects, de-contextualise them and help to undefine the portrait. That is, it is unclear where this group is or where they might come together. Kate Moss's presence serves to ground us, and her vacant bored expression serves as a signifier – instructing us how to make sense of the image.

In the CK One ad, Kate Moss serves as a visual anchor. She is well known, non-threatening (especially when compared to others in the ad), her image is that of a famous supermodel. In other words, she represents the world of cosmetics, fashion and glamour. As Calvin Klein said of his famous model: 'there's an air of reality about Kate that sets her apart. She represents the generation that is now coming along, and she appeals to them – her attitude, her look and her style is very easy, natural and unaffected' (quoted in White 1994: 90). She can fit in anywhere. She has entered this world of difference for us, and is able to maintain her identity in the midst of difference. Thus, we are unchanged by the experience of this ad. We don't risk actually becoming different, racially or sexually. It is unclear why white skinheads – who are associated with intolerance in popular discourse – are lumped in with others, especially black women. What are they were doing in this group, and why are they so angry?

The CK One image struck a responsive chord among consumers, but also started a wave of criticism regarding what was dubbed 'heroin chic' – a glorification of drug use via using models who appeared to be on heroin – the use of underweight models, particularly Kate Moss, and the general grungy appearance of the ads (Elliot 1994). There is a remarkable similarity to the outrage of the ad critics in the mid-1990s and the art critics of the 1860s (see Smith 1999). To fully understand why images like this leave such a mark, it is crucial to bring diverse tools to bear on the problem. In particular, art historical theories of identity construction and representation seem particularly relevant for understanding how brands and products fit into consumer identity. Furthermore, we gain insight into the strategic use of scandal via a turn to the past and a look at Manet's spectacular rise based largely on provoking publicity.

Art, branding, controversy

The similarities between Manet and Klein are compelling. Each employed images of women infused with sexuality to attain fame. Each professed to celebrate beauty, and both used models that became famous in their own right. (Klein's models made much more money, however.) Each garnered both praise and criticism. Klein, of course, seems somewhat more sophisticated in his techniques, and he is able to make more money because he needn't sell 'originals'. Although Manet was adept at marketing his image and building up the Manet 'brand', Andy Warhol is the artist that was able to capitalise on publicity and printing technology to achieve marketing success on a much grander scale (Schroeder 1997a). My colleague may still quibble that Manet was an Artist, whereas Klein is only interested in selling things. However, I contend that that is exactly what Manet intended, and that he was very good at selling – both his art and himself.

Manet and Klein demonstrate that scandal may not always be negative. Publicity serves to alert the public of one's existence and fan the fuel of fame. In image-based businesses, fame – or brand recognition – is of central concern. Several contemporary advertising campaigns have honed the strategic use of scandal – Benetton and Diesel come to mind. Benetton is notorious for utilising real life images of war, death and mayhem to promote their line of Italian clothing. In many ways, it is a strategy that owes a deep debt to Manet and Klein. Of course, these two are not the only figures to benefit from scandal, but I think due to the content and concepts in their images, and how they were criticised, they merit comparison.

I, of course, am not suggesting that strategic thinking expands to include scandal. I'm shocked that one might think so! Rather, in calling attention to the strategic use of scandal, I seek to broaden the concept of branding and strategy to include artists and others who work in image-based businesses (see Guillet de Monthoux 1993). I am interested in paying attention to how images work in the cultural systems of art and advertising, and I think that the connections between the two are growing.

Conclusion

This chapter is part of a larger call for inclusion of art historical issues within the marketing research canon. The work, career and critical reception of the artist Manet and the businessman Calvin Klein were used as cases to illustrate what I call the strategic use of scandal. That is, how controversial publicity surrounding images can be useful in building brand recognition. Two streams of thought were developed: 1) The connections between art and advertising via a focus on the image, and 2) links between branding strategy via the image. Although the art historical background of advertising would seem to be a natural subject for marketing researchers, it remains poorly developed within marketing and consumer research. I contend that that greater awareness of the connections between the traditions and conventions of visual culture and the production and consumption of images leads to enhanced ability to understand how advertising works as a representational system and signifying practice. However, this represents only a small fraction of the potential for work from a visual frame. The traditional separation of art and business, carefully cultivated and maintained by those whose interest it serves, has obscured the potential of studying the art market as *the* exemplar of consumer culture. For it is art that is based on images, value and identity above all other sectors of the market. Art represents the highest goals of humans, and also the most crass commercialism and speculation. With the rise of the artist as the acknowledged producer of artwork, the art market has also been an extreme example of branding strategy. Consumption is inherently visual, yet consumer researchers have seemed reluctant to embrace art history and visual studies as critical fields for study.

Art-centred approaches offer a means of developing unique insights into advertising imagery's prominence within visual culture. Art historical techniques help articulate a grammar of visual representation that producers and consumers use to decode advertising's messages (see Scott 1994). Regardless of intention, ads often invoke art historical themes, settings and references that contribute to their meaning – as an advertisement for a particular product as well as a cultural artefact. As discussed here, meaning in ads is not wholly contained within the image itself. Furthermore, advertising's success has depended on a way of seeing ads as connected to the larger worlds of art museums, movies and lived experience. Increased sensitivity to visual elements and their social, historical and cultural contexts is critical to appreciating the power of advertising imagery.

Although photography is the most pervasive form of communication in the world, most of us have had little formal training in the historical background of photography, the processes of photographic production or the function of pictorial conventions. Advertising, like photography, seems to present a world that just is, even though photographic images are cropped, selected and edited for consumption. A fully developed art-centred research programme will include issues of film theory and criticism, graphic design, prints and artistic production, to name a few.

Connecting advertising to the world of art history helps us to understand advertising as a global representational system. Further research might investigate specific art historical references in advertising, the gaze, and representing gender and culture. In addition, advertising research can take advantage of useful tools developed in art history and cultural studies to investigate the poetics and politics of advertising as a representational system. Finally, art-centered analyses often generate novel concepts and theories for researchers. The world of marketing intersects with the art world in numerous ways. The separation of art and business – into high and low forms of communication and culture – has had a profound influence on how art is viewed by researchers, cultural critics, and consumers alike. An art-centred approach suggests re-framing this research tradition to acknowledge both commercial mechanisms inherent in the art market and advertising's prominent place in visual culture. Art historians seldom discuss the cultural power of advertising imagery; marketing researchers rarely apply art criticism. This state of affairs can be largely explained by these respective scholars' training and interests. However, framing advertising within a long tradition of persuasive image making impels us to bring art historical methods to bear on images. Via this interdisciplinary enterprise, marketing researchers gain an enormous body of accumulated knowledge, techniques, and perspectives to explore meaning construction in contemporary consumer society.

References

Agins, T. (1995) 'FBI has designs on Calvin Klein in child-porn probe', *Wall Street Journal*, 9 September, 1, 4.

Aumont, J. (1997) *The Image* (trans. C. Pajackowska), London: British Film Institute.

Baxandall, M. (1987) *Patterns of Intention: On the Historical Explanation of Pictures*, New Haven, CT: Yale University Press.

Berger, J. (1972) *Ways of Seeing*, London: Penguin/BBC.

Bogart, M.H. (1995) *Artists, Advertising, and the Borders of Art*, Chicago: University of Chicago Press.

Cachin, F. (1995) *Manet: Painter of Modern Life* (trans. R. Kaplan), London: Thames & Hudson.

Campbell, R.H. (1995) 'CK One takes top awards', *Houston Chronicle*, 29 June, Fashion Section, 8.

Churcher, S. and Gaines, S.S. (1994) *Obsession: The Lives and Times of Calvin Klein*, New York: Carol Publishing Group.

Clark, T.J. (1985) *The Painting of Modern Life: Paris in the Age of Manet and his Followers*, London: Thames & Hudson.

Daly, S. and Wice, N. (1995) *alt.culture: an a-to-z guide to the '90s — underground, online, and over-the-counter*, New York: HarperPerennial.

Elliot, S. (1994) 'Ultrathin models in Coca-Cola and Calvin Klein campaigns draw fire and a boycott call', *New York Times*, 26 April, D18.

Francis, M. and Kings, M.(1997) *The Warhol Look: Glamour, Style, Fashion*, Boston: Bulfinch Press.

Friedrich, O. (1991) *Olympia: Paris in the Age of Manet*, New York: Morrow.

Goldman, K. (1995) 'Calvin Klein halts jeans ad campaign', *Wall Street Journal*, 29 August, B6.

Goldman , R. (1992) *Reading Ads Socially*, London and New York: Routledge.

Goldman, R. and Papson, S. (1996) *Sign Wars: The Cluttered Landscape of Advertising*, New York: Guilford.

Goldthwaite, R.A. (1993) *Wealth and the Demand for Art in Italy 1300–1600*, Baltimore: Johns Hopkins University Press.

Guillet de Monthoux, P. (1993) 'The spiritual in organizations: on Kandinsky and the aesthetics of organizational work', in S. Lakse and S. Gorbach (eds) *Spannungsfeld Personal Entwicklung*, Wein: Manzshe Verlags.

Hupfer, M. (1997) 'A pluralistic approach to visual communication: reviewing rhetoric and representation in World War I posters', in D. Maclinnis and M. Brucks (eds) *Advances in Consumer Research*, 24, Provo: Association for Consumer Research, 322–7.

Jardine, L. (1996) *Worldly Goods: A New History of the Renaissance*, New York: Doubleday.

Jensen, R. (1994) *Marketing Modernism in Fin-de-Siècle Europe*, Princeton, NJ: Princeton University Press.

Johnston, P. (1997) *Real Fantasies: Edward Steichen's Advertising Photography*, Berkeley: University of California Press.

Joy, A. (1993) 'The Modern Medicis: corporations as consumers of art', in R.W. Belk (ed.) *Research in Consumer Behavior*, New York: JAI Press.

Krell, A. (1996) *Manet and the Painters of Contemporary Life*, London: Thames & Hudson.

Lears, T.J. (1994) *Fables of Abundance: A Cultural History of Advertising in America*, New York: Basic Books.

Leppert, R. (1997) *Art and the Committed Eye: The Cultural Functions of Imagery*, Boulder, CO: Westview/HarperCollins.

Lippert, B. (1996) 'Sex: both sides now', *Adweek* , 18 March, 26–8.

Lipton, E. (1999) *Alias Olympia: A Woman's Search for Manet's Notorious Model and Her Own Desire*, Ithaca, NY: Cornell University Press.

Miller, C. (1992) 'Publisher says sexy ads are OK, but sexist ones will sink sales', *Marketing News*, 23 November, 8–9.

Moss, K. (1997) *Kate*, London: Pavilion Books.

O'Donohoe, S. (1997) 'Leaky boundaries: intertextuality and young adult experiences of advertising', in M. Nava, A. Blake, I. MacRury and B. Richards (eds) *Buy This Book: Studies in Advertising and Consumption*, London: Routledge, 257–75.

Plaskin, G. (1984) 'Calvin Klein interview', *Playboy*, May.

Savy, N. (1998) *Musée d'Orsay Pocket Guide*, Paris: Réunion des Musées Nationaux.

Schama, S. (1988) *The Embarrassment of Riches: An Interpretation of Dutch Culture in the Golden Age*, Berkeley: University of California Press.

Schroeder, J.E. (1992) 'Materialism and modern art', in F. Rudmin and M. Richins (eds) *Meaning, Measure, and Morality of Materialism*, Provo, UT: Association for Consumer Research, 10–14.

—— (1995) Essay Review: *Fables of Abundance: A Cultural History of Advertising in America* by Jackson Lears, *Marketing Modernism in Fin-de-Siècle Europe* by Robert Jensen, and *Privacy and Publicity: Modern Architecture as Mass Media* by Beatriz Colomina, *Design Issues* 11: 76–81.

—— (1997a) 'Andy Warhol: consumer researcher', in D. MacInnis and M. Brucks (eds) *Advances in Consumer Research*, Vol. 24, Provo: Association for Consumer Research, 476–82.

—— (1997b) 'Roots of modern marketing in Italian Renaissance art', in A. Falkenberg and T. Rittenberg (eds) *Proceedings of the Macromarketing Seminar*, Bergen, Norway: Norwegian School of Economics and Business Administration.

—— (1998a) 'Purchasing persona: consumption, representation, and identity', in E. Traube (ed.) *Culture and Visual Representation*, Wesleyan University Center for the Humanities Paper Series.

—— (1998b) 'Consuming representation: a visual approach to consumer research', in B.B. Stern (ed.) *Representing Consumers: Voices, Views, and Visions*, New York: Routledge, 193–230.

—— (2001) *Visual Consumption*, London: Routledge forthcoming.

—— and Borgerson, J.L. (1998) 'Marketing images of gender: a visual analysis', *Consumption, Markets, and Culture* 2: 161–201.

—— and Zwick, D. (2000) 'Consuming masculinity: advertising, the gaze, and male bodies', in R. Meyer and S. Hoch (eds) *Advances in Consumer Research*, 27, Provo, UT: Association for Consumer Research.

Scott, L.A. (1994) 'Images of advertising; the need for a theory of visual rhetoric', *Journal of Consumer Research* 21, September: 252–73.

Seo, D. (1998) 'A new obsession: Calvin Klein ads with a wholesome bent? yes, he says but critics unsure', *Los Angeles Times*, February D4, 5.

Singer, S. (2000) 'Calvin's sixth sense', *Vogue* [US edition], March, 488–91.

Sloan, P. (1996) 'Real people suit Calvin Klein in CK B, jeans and boxers ads', *Advertising Age*, 19 August: 3, 30.

Smith, L. (1999) Talkin' trash website, *http://www.talkintrash.com/adv/CK/index.html*

Soloman, D. (1994) 'A career behind the camera', *Wall Street Journal*, 25 March, 31.

Staniszewski, M.A. (1995) *Believing is Seeing: Creating the Culture of Art*, New York: Penguin.

Stern, B.B. and Schroeder, J.E. (1994) 'Interpretive methodology from art and literary criticism: a humanistic approach to advertising imagery', *European Journal of Marketing* 28, September: 114–32.

Sullivan, R. (1995) 'Denim and desire', *Vogue* [US edition], November: 166, 168, 170.

Tucker, P.H. (ed.) (1998) *Manet's Le Dejeuner Sur L'Herbe*, Cambridge: Cambridge University Press.

Watson, P. (1992) *From Manet to Manhattan: The Rise of the Modern Art Market*, New York: Random House.

White, L. (1994) 'Small wonder: the Kate Moss phenomenon', *Vogue* [British edition], August: 90–5.

Williamson, J. (1978) *Decoding Advertisements*, New York: Marion Boyers.

Willis, S. (1991) *A Primer for Everyday Life*, New York: Routledge.

Witkowski, T.H. (1996) 'Farmers bargaining: buying and selling as a subject in American genre painting, 1835–1868', *Journal of Macromarketing* 17, Fall: 84–101.

—— (1999) 'The Art of consumption', in E. Arnould and L. Scott (eds) *Advances in Consumer Research* Vol 26, Provo, UT: Association for Consumer Research.

3   The endless enigma or the last self-portrait (or, what the marketer can learn from the artist)

Ian Fillis

A preliminary sketch

Given that we have now reached the new millennium, there may be hope for the future of both marketing and art. Imagine the impact artists such as Caravaggio, Rembrandt and Michelangelo (Gombrich 1996) could have achieved in their own lifetime if they had at their disposal the vast media machine that now seems to dominate our daily lives. An example of the successful merging of marketing and art can be seen in the coverage of the annual Turner Prize (Button and Searle 1997), resulting in increasing visitor numbers at the Tate Gallery (Wilson 1990) and in enhanced reputations for the artists concerned. I recently attended a poetry reading in Glasgow given by Billy Childish (Childish 1999), erstwhile boyfriend of Tracey Emin (Brown 1998), the seemingly ubiquitous Turner Prize nominee. Apart from being a poet, Billy Childish is also a songwriter, independent record label songster and artist. Mr Childish has spent a number of years revelling in his niche market position of punkish anarchy but now that he has co-authored the 'Stuckist Manifesto' (Alberge 1999), he is in danger of becoming popular among a wider audience. This manifesto was written partly as a reaction to the current state of play in British art, and was also named in honour of the views held by Tracey Emin concerning her one time boyfriend and his paintings. It remains to be seen if the 'Stuckist Manifesto' will have the same impact as those developed by the Surrealists (Breton 1966) and the Futurists (Tisdall and Bozzolla 1977) but it is encouraging that at least one creative group sees fit to challenge the status quo in their industry.

Although from both an academic and a business perspective, marketing is sometimes perceived to be a relatively new development, I argue that examples of marketing, and especially creative marketing, have existed for centuries. I have succeeded in tracing entrepreneurial marketing as far back as the period of the Italian Renaissance (Fillis 1999) and Hellenistic Greece (Nevett and Nevett 1987) and believe that other commentators are equally able to suggest precedent behaviour. Given the development of artistic behaviour over the past five centuries, and the sometimes relatively quick succession from one generally acceptable viewpoint and practice to another, there are lessons to be learned from examining creative behaviour among individuals and groups who are intent upon proactively challenging the status quo.

A recent example of art meeting marketing and the subsequent challenging of established practices can be seen in Charles Saatchi's *Sensation* show, first exhibited in London, and then the Brooklyn Museum in New York (Barnbrook 1998). Not only did the amount of attention generated as a consequence of both media and mayoral outcry act to heighten awareness of the exhibition, but it also served to raise the status of the artists being exhibited. Charles Saatchi could be described as an entrepreneurial risk taker, identifier of opportunities and promoter of British creativity. He has certainly endeavoured to bring together the disciplines of marketing and art, greatly assisted by his years of experience working in the advertising industry. Although little has been written in an academic sense in terms of the relationship between marketing and art, there is at least some literature on corporate sponsorship of events such as art exhibitions (Meenaghan 1983), art and advertising imagery (Stern and Schroeder 1994) and the applicability of the marketing concept to the art industry (Hirschman 1983). However, marketing is of course much more than just a method of promotion and communication and the issues raised in this work need further discussion elsewhere in a range of forums.

The outcry against 'BritArt' mirrors much of the displays of angst and amazement generated when the Impressionists first attempted to exhibit their work (Rewald 1973). Initially gaining loud condemnation from the visitors to the annual Salon exhibition, their attempts to shape future thinking eventually swayed opinion as their work became accepted. In terms of risk-taking behaviour, members of artistic schools such as that at Barbizon (Adams 1997) certainly displayed large amounts of self-belief and confidence, if not the arrogance shown by the master liar, painter and designer, one Salvador Dali. One of the most successful marketing successes in recent times was the Monet exhibition at the Royal Academy in 1999. Originally castigated by the both the art establishment and the public alike, Monet is now lauded as one of the finest artists of all time. Jones describes the event as:

> a prophecy of what art will become in the 21st century: less an art exhibition than an anthropology of class and taste in contemporary Britain as it exploded into a must-see event that systematically filtered through as many people as possible.
>
> (Jones 2000: 14)

A useful question to pose at this juncture might be: have we reached the end of meaningful marketing, is continual referral to past fads and fashions enough to sustain its advance or can we learn from past masters in creativity to ensure that the future of marketing is secured? The link between marketing, creativity and art needs exploring further in order to enhance this understanding. Early examples of this interaction during the period of the Italian Renaissance included the development of a thriving market for second-hand altar pieces, doors in the style of craftsmen such as Lorenzo Ghiberti, readily available paintings of the Madonna and Child and the ability to manufacture personalised coats of arms to order (Welch 1997). At this time, the artist and mastercraftsman gained a large degree of respect and notoriety, but it was really the wealthy merchant families and patrons who controlled much of the artistic market. Evidence of similar entrepreneurial endeavour can be seen in recent research at the marketing and entrepreneurship interface examining the growth of the arts-and-craft firm and the export development of the textile firm (McAuley 1998; Watson *et al.* 1998). Many of the creative activities carried out by artists, designers and others in the cultural industries can be compared similarly with that found in some smaller firms across a range of other sectors. Given that many microenterprises suffer from an inherent lack of resources (Storey 1994), I believe that creative activity acts to drive the individual and the organisation forward. Hackley and Mumby-Croft comment on the usefulness of the interface between marketing and entrepreneurship in helping to understand creativity:

> marketing and entrepreneurship share common conceptual and practical ground and that this commonality can be made sense of in the context of a conceptual framework which emphasises the applied creative problem solving dimension of each field. Thus to the extent that creative (or innovative) behaviour is a significant feature of radical marketing success, it might also be said to lie at the heart of much successful entrepreneurial endeavour.
>
> (Hackley and Mumby-Croft 1998: 505)

So by adopting a creative approach in tandem with an alternative visualisation of the problem itself, the smaller firm can aim to resolve the issue in a more artistic and free thinking way than that offered by following a structured path. The arts and crafts discipline offers some worthy lessons in originality of thought and deed, where the personnel concerned are driven to succeed because of their limited resources:

> Creativity does not come out of the void. It is the impulse to search out the possibilities and varieties of solutions offered by the craft tradition which will produce novelty and originality, because what the craftsman learns is not only to copy but also to vary, to exploit his resources to the full and push his skill to the very limits of what a task will allow and suggest.
>
> (Gombrich 1996: 363)

It is debatable whether any marketer, either academic or practitioner, can honestly say that they have followed this practice to the full extent of their capabilities. The typical craft firm suffers from severe resource limitations in terms of finance, personnel, management and marketing competencies but a number of these firms survive because of their entrepreneurial orientation, creativity and sheer will and determination to succeed. There are lessons for us all here: instead of concentrating solely on gathering a set of recognised formal marketing skills, we should also focus on enhancing creative approaches in whatever we do. Rampley (1998) believes that creativity results from the ability to reach beyond learned formulae and procedures. This suggests that those willing to take creative risks in both marketing and art should deviate from given practices. The example of the microenterprise owner/manager adapting marketing planning procedures to suit the situation specific (Carson *et al.* 1995; Macdonald 1995) may be viewed as such a practice, while the artist who breaks new ground by utilising new media can also be perceived as creative. It is the degree of innovation and creativity that differs, according to the industry and the particular situation. Although marketing and art can be taught to a certain degree, it can be argued that the creative approach to both may be more of an intuitive nature than anything else. Also, when it comes to analysing the processes involved, problems can arise in their measurement as Kant remarks:

> where an author owes a product to his genius he does not himself know how the ideas for it have entered his head, nor has he it in his power to invent the like at pleasure or methodically.

(Kant 1952: 168)

By examining published biographies and other accounts of creative behaviour and personality (Cox 1926; Galton 1870; Guilford 1950; Rose 1975), a framework of creative marketing metaphors and proclamations for future success can be constructed. An example of a useful outcome within marketing includes the possibility of encouraging creative approaches in the small firm in both domestic and international marketing contexts. Ultimately it is hoped that more visionary methodologies will also be willingly embraced within marketing academia as the creative few reject existing modes of interpreting marketing in order to reach a more imaginative state of understanding. Ehrenzweig paints an interesting picture of what might happen if we make the wrong choice:

> There was another tree in the paradise garden apart from the tree of knowledge; it was the tree of life. Had the first human pair eaten from the tree of life they would have become immortal. It seems only logical that the second tree in the garden was the tree of death, the fruit of which would

have given instant death. It was not a forbidden tree; the choice was voluntary.

(Ehrenzweig 1970: 247)

In order to reach the ecstatic heights achieved by some creative individuals, the path taken by the tree of life should be followed. This path should follow a new direction, not previously followed by those willing to take risks; for example, artists frustrated by popular taste and lack of purpose have always sought to change direction by creating a different genre and then stimulating demand for the new work they produce. There are some within marketing who are equally capable of challenging the status quo by developing an alternative agenda. If this is not done, then we all face a future clinging to the branches of the tree of death, with no clear direction. New methodologies and alternative conceptualisations are needed in order to drive the discipline forward. The danger is, of course, that by creating an alternative, this new option will at some stage become popular and direction will again be lost.

Personal picture perspective

I am a big fan of all things artistic and exploring the link between marketing and creative practice seems a natural bridge between my research interests and my extra-curricular activities. At one time I attempted to eke out a living by selling my own paintings in such wonderful spots as Ballintoy Harbour and the picturesque Portstewart in Northern Ireland. Admittedly, marketing my work was frustrating at times, with word of mouth communication and the gallery being the main marketing mechanisms. Still a frustrated artist, I now attempt to paint on a different canvas, focusing on researching issues at the marketing and entrepreneurship interface such as creativity, as well as exploring small firm exporting. Critical analysis of existing theory has uncovered inadequacies in its ability to explain successfully the behaviour of both the smaller and the owner/manager at domestic and international level (Bell 1995; Coviello and Munro 1995). Instead, factors such as creativity and innovation act as a driving catalyst in spurring both the individual and the organisation forward. By examining innovative behaviour from an artistic perspective, partly through the use of the metaphor, a clearer picture of successful creativity can be gained. The investigation of creative characters such as Vincent Van Gogh and Salvador Dali has long been of personal interest. I recently attended an exhibition of the pioneering modernist architect Frank Lloyd Wright and was struck by his creative imagination. I then considered that there may be some merit in profiling the characteristics of these creative practitioners and then to encourage the application of the metaphors and descriptors subsequently developed as an aid to understanding behaviour of the owner/manager of the smaller firm, as well as stimulating similar behaviour within the academic community.

The use of the metaphor has been adopted in certain areas of marketing and entrepreneurship (Arndt 1986; Carney and Williams 1997; Goodwin 1996; Hunt and Menon 1993; Rindfleisch 1996) but, in line with Day (1998), I believe that creativity and innovation issues located at the marketing and entrepreneurship interface deserve particular attention (Hills 1987; Hulbert *et al.* 1998). Ennew and Binks (1999: 475) see the interface as possessing characteristics associated with individuals involved in entrepreneurial marketing in terms of their creativity, innovation, alertness, risk taking and flexibility. Recent work has centred on the examination of the marketing and entrepreneurship interface through the investigation of various issues outside the traditional boundaries of SME research (Fillis 1998; McAuley and Fillis 1999). One of the central themes has been the exploration of the concept of creativity and how this can help to explain the behaviour of the more entrepreneurially-minded owner/managers of the smaller firm. More specifically, the examination of those working in the arts and crafts sector has spurred me on to looking at some additional creative metaphors within the artistic world. Small business research has attempted to discuss the virtues of creative practice (Bridge *et al.* 1998) but I believe it has not, as yet, been developed into a more meaningful construct and explanation for thought-provoking marketing theory and practice.

Method or madness?

In order to better understand the central issues of the meeting of marketing and art, I have followed an approach identified within the social psychology literature that appears to fit comfortably with the purposes of this investigation, instead of espousing the merits of adopting various humanist or positivist perspectives (Gabriel 1990; Gill and Johnson 1991; Smircich 1983). The focus within creative research has tended to concentrate on the study of the personality of the creative individual, mainly drawing on the pioneering work of Guilford (1950). The study of entrepreneurial traits has certainly received much attention within the entrepreneurial literature; the characteristics of the marketing-oriented firm and its owner/manager have also been researched almost *ad nauseam* (Johnston and Czinkota 1982; Smart and Conant 1994). Within applied areas of marketing, such as exporting and other modes of internationalisation behaviour, various attempts to profile firms and individual managers have also been carried out (Burton and Schlegelmilch 1987; Cavusgil *et al.* 1979). However, I believe that we have not really achieved an improved understanding of the central issues, given that many of these studies are essentially self-replicating in nature, with no fresh methodological approach.

Research on creativity has tended to follow one of three approaches (Amabile 1983): the classical laboratory experiment where variables can be controlled as the subjects are manipulated (Roethlisberger and Dickson 1939); the use of personality, intelligence and creativity tests in order to identify those individuals from a population with higher than average scores (Rose 1975; Wallach and Kogan 1965); and the study of biographies and autobiographies of popular creative individuals in order to identify particular intellectual and personality characteristics (Cox 1926; Galton 1870). As an example, artists such as Van Gogh and Salvador Dali provide us with some remarkable insights into their weird and wonderful personalities through their various correspondence with their peer groups and, in the case of Dali, with his own creative imagination in justifiably unbelievable works such as *The Secret Life of Salvador Dali* (Dali 1942).

It is this final approach that I have chosen to follow in order to better understand the link between marketing and art. Amabile (1983) believes that social factors impinge greatly on creativity. Certainly within the artistic community, social issues have a large part to play in the motivation of individuals who may spend large periods of time working alone but who cling to the ideals of such groups as the Surrealists, Realists, Modernists, Postmodernists, Structuralists and Poststructuralists, to name but a few (Adams 1996; Fernie 1996). Marketing is also a largely social phenomenon, given that we are constantly reminded of the power and worth of the consumer and that various other publics are involved from time to time. Amabile offers some reasons why first-person accounts should serve as meaningful research material in order to grasp the essence of creativity. The individual concerned tends to refer to a number of socially embedded factors that have affected the work that has subsequently been produced. These issues should not be used to test hypotheses but be used more as an aid to their formation and if a number of common issues from a number of sources are repeatedly identified, then these could serve to identify particular creative phenomena. There are, of course, criticisms of pursuing research on creativity: Rampley (1998), for example, believes that since creativity has links with the humanist notions of genius, imagination and subjectivity, there are inherent conceptual difficulties. There are also criticisms from Marxists, Feminists and Poststructuralists (Frascina and Harris 1997). Hauser (1982) does not accept the concept of the spontaneous creative person but does, however, acknowledge that creativity exists at the conceptual level. Kant (1952) concentrates on the idea of genius, rather than creativity, but Rampley believes that they are strongly related and argues that creative practice does not follow a set of predetermined rules based on concrete concepts. Rather, these rules are more loosely developed and cannot therefore be copied as best practice for future endeavours. However, the products of genius can serve to provide a set of rules for future imitation. Rampley accepts that these criticisms of creativity have fundamentally failed to explain the underlying cause of innovation, and why certain rules and procedures are periodically broken in order to achieve creative goals.

The artist as marketer

I have identified partly through accident, partly through my own enthusiasm for wandering around art galleries and museums, a number of particularly interesting creative practitioners within the discipline of art. However, before focusing on notions of artistic genius and groundbreaking creative shifts found in the work of Van Gogh, Dali and Warhol, I feel that mention must be made of the contribution of the related discipline of architecture.

Frank Lloyd Wright: a 'living' legend

Architects may not usually fall under the label of artist, but because of the sense of vision, creativity and innovative approaches adopted by some within the discipline, such as Frank Lloyd Wright (De Long 1998), the division between art and architecture becomes blurred. I recently attended an exhibition of Frank Lloyd Wright's work at the Kelvingrove Art Gallery and Museum in Glasgow (Glasgow Museums 1994). The exhibition presented his wonderfully creative concept of the *Living City*, originally conceptualised as *The Disappearing City* (Wright 1932). Although chiefly an architect, Wright also had interests in applied art and town planning. He saw himself as 'the world's greatest architect', which compares similarly to the grandeur expressed by the world's greatest artist, performer and liar, Salvador Dali (Gibson 1997). It is generally accepted that Wright was the chief initiator of modern Western architecture, described by De Long as comparable to the innovatory influence of Brunelleschi (Welch 1997) on Italian Renaissance architecture. Wright had no formal architectural training, but instead served a formative apprenticeship under the auspices of another pioneering architect, Louis H. Sullivan (Morrison 1998). Wright's creative output was influenced both by the English Arts and Crafts Movement and by the vocabulary of Japanese artistic forms and techniques (Dormer 1997), much like Van Gogh and the Impressionists (Denvir 1993). He also had an affinity with all things natural, believing that business life and private life were inextricably linked via natural forces (Kaufmann 1978). These natural forces can also be identified in various biographies and paintings by Dali and Van Gogh, where the surrounding landscape serves to provide some sort of motivational propulsion for creative output. Much like the clientele surrounding Dali as he became more and more established as a leading Surrealist figure, Wright was courted by some of America's most wealthy and powerful business people. One of his philosophies was that instead of resisting change, it was better to work with it. De Long cloaks him in biblical imagery: 'Like those of most prophets, his visions outdistanced immediate reality' (1998: 22). Examples of his visions included the concept of the Aerotor, a type of helicopter that had no need for landing fields. With his perception of Broadacre City, there would be redistribution of land ownership with each family having at least one acre and one automobile apiece, rent would be eliminated, and individual productivity would be promoted instead of the ogre of big business. He was really a visionary, proactive identifier of changing lifestyle and human behaviour, and embraced these issues within his own work. What is this, if it is not marketing?

Vincent's last self-portrait

There are a number of lessons to be learned from Vincent Van Gogh's tempestuous life, one of which must be his never-ceasing drive and self belief. An in-depth appreciation of the artist's daily thoughts and deeds can be readily gained from the incredible amount of communication by letter between himself and his brother Theo (Hanson and Hanson 1955; Roskill 1967; Sweetman 1990). Tracing his short life, dedication to several causes can be identified, including the relationship with his younger brother Theo, to religion and to painting. Given that Van Gogh did make many mistakes and was unsuccessful within his own lifetime, some may argue that meaningful lessons cannot possibly be extracted from his life. I argue otherwise in that many talented contemporary inventors, creators and potential marketers exist today but are not given the correct type and level of support in order to become successful. More encouragement and mentoring of creative individuals is needed. Sweetman describes Van Gogh as 'an isolated, rejected prophet of modern art', ironic given his family's link with religion. Vincent's father Theodorus was one of twelve children fathered by Pastor Vincent Van Gogh. This religiously Protestant background may help to explain Van Gogh's willingness to suffer through his dedication for a cause many others would have happily surrendered. An early artistic influence must have been his mother, who was a reasonably accomplished amateur artist, although there tended to be an ever-present desire that Vincent should become part of the Van Gogh 'solid Dutch bourgeois family' through the pursuit of a respectable trade. As a young boy, Vincent demonstrated his intense curiosity through his love of nature and study of insects. In a similar vein to Salvador Dali, Van Gogh was from a reasonably wealthy family but grew up in a community subjected to rural poverty. As Van Gogh developed his interest in painting, initially through working for his Uncle Cent and then under the artist Anton Mauve (Alley 1981:504), he became aware of an avant-garde movement of artists working in the Barbizon community outside Paris, one of several emerging artistic movements at that time (Adams 1997). They had a particular fascination for nature and painting *en plein air*, which proved to be a particularly inviting prospect for Van Gogh. Sweetman notes that, 'What all the different groups of nature painters had in common was a rejection of the tired classical and religious subjects perpetuated by the academies and displayed in the various annual salons'(1990: 18).

Van Gogh willingly embraced this philosophy, although he was never able to realise his potential financially or in terms of artistic success within his own lifetime, unlike some of his contemporaries. His Uncle Cent, however, owned several galleries specialising in this new wave painting and could be described as a gallery manager with extreme foresight. He was able to anticipate future artistic taste and exploit the developing market, much in the same manner as Charles Saatchi today. One crucial factor that shaped Van Gogh's life was that, although he appeared reasonably happy to pursue a career as a clerk in his uncle's art dealership, he felt that he was continually being pushed into situations that were not of his own volition and as a result he rebelled. Both Van Gogh and Dali were heavily influenced by a number of people in terms of their artistic practice and philosophical rebellion. Van Gogh's influencers included Jean Francois Millet (Murphy 1999) and Anton Mauve, while Vermeer (Ades 1988; Snow 1994) is constantly cited as a major influence on Dali. Entrepreneurs and marketers are also subjected to various influences, be they directly aware of the influencing effect or whether a more intangible process is involved. Van Gogh, according to Sweetman, was always willing to embrace new concepts, new ways of seeing since 'his attitude throughout his life remained catholic and celebratory rather than exclusive and judgemental' (1990: 41). As marketers we can attempt to follow a similar path in that we should attempt to shun some existing practices and embrace 'new' ideas and fresh perspectives outside our traditional disciplinary boundaries in order to move marketing forward.

The enigmatic Salvador Dali

Salvador Dali was one of the greatest self-publicising marketers of all time, allowing him to grow into a commercial success through his art and other related forms of production. Analysing Dali's characteristics unveils the notion of acute observation, seeing what others cannot see, thus differentiating him from the masses. Being able to identify and recognise new opportunities resulted in him gaining competitive advantage. Through the ability to direct his own future, he saw himself as the salvation of art:

> I was destined, as my name indicates, for nothing less than to rescue painting from the void of modern art, and to do so in this abominable epoch of mechanical and mediocre catastrophes in which we have the distress and the honour to live.
>
> (Dali 1993: 4)

In marketing, we need to carry out more creative approaches to research, to rescue it from the replicative, highly structured method found in many quantitative pieces of work. Another parallel can be drawn from Dali's food preference for runny Camembert rather than spinach. In marketing research this can be compared to the more fluid qualitative paradigm, rather than the sometimes tasteless quantitative method. Dali was prone to certain actions undertaken for no apparent reason, such as deliberately falling down the stairs in order to elicit the desired reaction from others. As marketers we should think less about the consequences of certain actions and focus on experimentation, taking risks, observing any reactions and capitalising on any opportunities created as the result of the action. Another interesting insight into Dali's character was his ability to visualise things in unconventional ways; for example, when eating some snails he perceived Sigmund Freud's cranium to be in the form of a snail, containing a spiral-shaped brain that could be extracted using a needle. Another example of this unconventionalism can be seen in the artist's early interest in the practice of automatic expression, later adopted by the Surrealists:

> My speeches would succeed one another in a purely automatic fashion and often my words would in no way correspond to the stream of my thoughts. The latter would seem to me to attain the summit of the sublime and I had the impression of discovering each second, in a more and more inspired and unerring fashion, the enigma, the origin and the destiny of each thing.
>
> (Dali 1993: 73)

Again, this is yet more evidence to suggest that we try to adopt alternative approaches to research and that, by doing so, clearer visualisation and understanding of the issues can be gained. Dali believed in the paradisal state achieved by being in the womb before birth. This could also refer to the protected state of being cocooned within current marketing practice but in order to flourish we need to suffer anguish through the process of rebirth by pursuing alternative paths. We should shrug off the need to be surrounded by protective membranes such as established marketing institutions and try to be more adventurous. This spirit is continually referred to by Dali in his recollections of childhood memories and experiences of his environment, which he then incorporated in his art. A wider perspective should also be encouraged within marketing where there is a danger of adopting too narrow a focus. Appreciation of the surrounding environment seemed to spur Dali on to a greater level of ambition than most:

> My whole life has been determined by . . . two antagonistic ideas, the top and the bottom. Since my earliest childhood I have desperately striven to be at the 'top'. I have reached it and now that I am there I shall remain there till I die.
>
> (Dali 1993: 72)

As marketers, our ambition may be to learn what others have done and then copy their procedures, or adapt these methods to suit our own needs, or invent new methods and derive new needs. Also, by reaching new heights in marketing, some individuals will achieve immense satisfaction and the kudos that results from that position. There are a number of lessons to take from Salvador Dali's sense of ambition, wonderfully demonstrated when he announced, 'At the age of six I wanted to be a cook. At seven I wanted to be Napoleon. And my ambition has been growing steadily ever since' (Dali 1993: 1). Dali's ambition to be a cook and then Napoleon can be viewed as a metaphor for proactive, assertive marketing. The question is, do we want the rest of society to view us as cooks using trad-itional recipes, as super-cooks adapting and improvising with the limited resources at their disposal, or as leaders such as Napoleon or as something even greater, more immortal, more omnipotent? Perhaps we should take a leaf out of Dali's thoughts and focus on the notion of promoting marketing intellect:

> Since 1929 I have had a very clear consciousness of my genius, and I confess that this conviction, ever more deeply rooted in my mind, has never excited in me emotions of the kind called sublime; nevertheless, I must admit that it occasionally affords me an extremely pleasurable feeling.
>
> (Dali 1993: 2)

Here Dali discusses the almost erotic effect of the notion of being a genius. It may then be feasible to extend the concept to the world of marketing where there are already a number of publicly acclaimed business geniuses, but this does not appear to be the case within marketing academia. Perhaps the real issue to be addressed is that we should be comfortable in the way in which we research, whether in academia or in industry, and that by hopefully uncovering some marketing secrets previously untold through the stringent chains of quantitative approaches we can at least experience some level of pleasure. Brandon (1999) uncovers some of these secrets by providing one of the latest accounts of the Surrealist movement, of which Dali was a main protagonist. Surrealism as a movement was formed and given momentum following a performance of a play by Guillaume Apollinaire (Little 1976) in Paris in the summer of 1917. The drama *Les Mamelles de Tiresias* (involving an overweight woman removing her clothing to reveal two gas filled balloons serving as her breasts that were then released into the audience) was interrupted by an attempt by Jacques Vaché to fire his revolver into the audience (Vache 1995). After the performance, his friend André Breton defined the simplest surrealist act as 'going into the street, revolver in hand, and shooting at random into the crowd' (Brandon 1999: 11), suggesting that disregard for convention through the use of some sort of powerful weapon can result in creative, ground-breaking action. Interestingly, Apollinaire willingly embraced the Italian Futurist Manifesto (Edwards 1999) as one of the guiding factors in the development of Surrealism. The Futurists aspired to a love of danger and fearlessness, as well as courage, audacity and revolt (Marinetti 1909). From a marketing context, the gun acts as a metaphor for the elimination of existing marketing practice and as a revolt mechanism in order to embrace novel approaches. Breton's Surrealist declaration (Bureau of Surrealist Research 1925) echoes some of the Futurist doctrine. The group rejected the value of literature but made it clear that they would use it when necessary to convey their message, describing Surrealism as 'not a new means of expression, or an easier one, nor even a metaphysic of poetry. It is a means of total liberation of the mind and of all that resembles it' (Edwards 1999: 210–11). For Surrealists, revolution was a key theme through the promotion of disinterest and detachment from current practices, believing that existing thought had inadequate foundations and that they were prepared to embark on physical means in order to achieve their wishes. It is doubtful that there will ever be a true marketing revolution. Perhaps the best we can hope for is the evolution of theory and practice over time with no great paradigm shifts (Desphande 1983).

Andy Warhol's New York marketing diet

Another example of marketing converging with art is through the establishment and promotion of museums solely dedicated to one artist, such as the Dali Museum (Wach 1996) and the Andy Warhol Museum (Angell 1994). McClarence describes the Warhol museum as:

> the world's biggest single-artist museum – a sweeping celebration of celebrity, consumerism and Campbell's soup cans in an eight-storey former warehouse. It devotes 35,000 square feet to one man's preoccupation with publicity-as-art.
>
> (McClarence 1999: 28)

Among the objects being marketed are his collection of cookie jars and his Oxidation series of paintings produced using synthetic polymer paint and urine. As long as there is a demand for the artist as product, it seems irrelevant in what medium the product manifests itself, sometimes the more bizarre the better. Warhol describes his belief in the benefits of encouraging the interaction of artistic creativity and sound business practice:

> Business art is the step that comes after art. I started as a commercial artist, and I want to finish as a business artist . . . Being good in business is the most fascinating kind of art . . . making money is art and working is art and good business is the best art.
>
> (Warhol 1975: 92)

By believing in the merits of adopting multiple approaches to marketing we can use creative thinking to stimulate future achievements. Artistic and scientific methods should be jointly encouraged, not pilloried by opposing combatants. Warhol seemed not to mind too much being labelled as a 'loner' as this served to differentiate him from others and subsequently pull certain individuals towards him and his philosophies (Warhol 1975: 23). The essence of Warhol's work and the philosophy of the Pop Art movement is summarised by Sontag who believed that 'Pop Art (uses) a content so blatant, so "what it is", it . . . ends up being uninterpretable' (1964: 220). Warhol sought to use this naked, overt imagery in order to convey his message, which he successfully differentiated from other artistic messages at that time. Although some marketing practitioners have adopted this 'up front' marketing, academic marketers have not been so quick to follow.

Pop Art developed as a counter culture, a deliberate attempt to deviate from established codes of practice. The same could be said of Van Gogh's Impressionism and Dali's Surrealism. Warhol rejected the concept of visualising a piece of art as involving craftsmanship, hand-produced for a *cognoscente* who values the personality of the artist. Instead, he encouraged the mass production of art, mainly through the silk screen process and was able to use his persuasive powers developed from his days in advertising in order to generate self-publicity. Warhol exhibited an intense jealousy if he could not have first choice on 'absolutely everything', afraid that someone else might get to do it first even though he may have had no real wish to do it or have it himself. His eccentric nature can be seen in his eating habits: for example, when he ate out in New York, he adopted the 'Andy Warhol New York City Diet'. This comprised of ordering everything on the menu, not actually eating anything of real substance, having the food wrapped up to go, and then leaving it on some street corner or windowledge for a homeless person to discover. This attitude serves as an example of his creative and eccentric personality, which at one time attracted the interest of a company that wanted to buy his 'aura', rather than his products (Warhol 1975: 77).

A further insight into Warhol's philosophy is shown in the way in which he existed while working on shoe drawings for magazines. Since payment was based on each drawing, he counted up each individual drawing, working out how much he would then get paid. This suggests that, at least during this period, he was living on a day-to-day, down-to-earth basis with not much security. He prescribes this practice for every creative practitioner where 'an artist should count up his pictures so you always know exactly what you're worth, and you don't get stuck thinking your product is you and your fame, and your aura' (Warhol 1975: 86). The issue for marketers, then, is how we can measure our own worth: by the products that we sell, by the advertisements recalled by the viewer, by the number of papers we publish, by the books we write, by our reputation, or by some other measure.

When he was shot, Warhol was working at his place of business, Andy Warhol Enterprises. He attempts no precise definition of what was actually produced there, or who was employed or what their true function was. He described the personnel as consisting of freelancers who worked on special projects as well as a number of what he termed 'superstars' or 'hyperstars' with hard to define talents and whose work was difficult to market. There are merits for adopting this approach both within the marketing academic community and within the marketing industry in general. By obtaining a 'superstar' status, the once difficult to market product then acquires a status unachievable by the majority of the competition. Even when Warhol was wounded, the dynamism of his business helped work to progress through a creative kinetic process. Warhol developed an interesting marketing philosophy that he utilised to great effect. Derived from his distaste of the avant-garde, one-off pieces produced for the connoisseur of the period, he comments that given the result of popular taste, there are particular instances of bad taste found among the leftovers. The trick is then to utilise this bad taste in order to turn the work into something interesting. This results in an economical approach in that making something good out of the bad involves a recycling process of existing materials (Warhol 1975: 93). Examining the way in which he identified and exploited opportunities, Warhol appeared to practise a type of inverse marketing technique. Using New York city as an example, he believed that living in such a large place leads people to desire objects that nobody else wants, to crave after the leftovers. So much competition with associated changing tastes means that, in order to survive, you should realise that 'changing your tastes to what other people don't want is your only hope of getting anything' (Warhol 1975: 93).

Warhol provides some interesting insight into the type of person who could work within his enterprise: ideally the individual should exhibit some degree of misunderstanding of Warhol's philosophy, not major discrepancies but certainly a small level of misinterpretation. During the communication process, the ideas expressed by the other individual sometimes interacted with his own in order to create a unique solution to the problem so that 'when working with people who misunderstand you, instead of getting transmissions, you get transmutations, and that's much more interesting in the long run' (Warhol 1975: 99). There is a message for us here in that we can either all follow the same method or all feed off each other's tangential thoughts in order to achieve transmutations and alternative visualisations of marketing theory and practice.

Securing the future through marketing artistry

Marketing, of course, has a number of set rules and regulations usually under the guise of marketing planning and strategy (McDonald 1995; Wensley 1999) that we are constantly reminded to follow in order to achieve success. Not everyone abides by these rules, adapting the formal procedures from time to time to suit individual needs or developing their own approaches. The 'Stuckist Manifesto' contains many interesting proclamations that may be of interest to adventurous marketers. Its philosophy rejects conceptualism, hedonism and egoism, while encouraging authenticity, self discovery, the promotion of a holistic perspective and mystery. The Stuckists argue that in the early days of Saatchi's BritArt, it did actually challenge The Establishment, but now due to its popularity it has become part of the very body it originally denounced, and its purpose has been lost. Translating this into the realms of marketing, it is fine to challenge those among the marketing academy as long as the people involved have something meaningful to offer in its place. Childish (1999) seems to be saying that it is all right to make mistakes and operate at a more basic level. Others try to adopt a more complicated methodology but success only comes through cleverness. Following in the footsteps of the Surrealists, the Futurists and the Stuckists, I have derived a proclamation of creativity in order to secure the future of marketing. The key elements of the proclamation stem from the working practices and philosophies of the creative individuals discussed in this work.

A proclamation of marketing artistry

- We must work towards a high level of self-belief in order to generate quality values and opinions
- We should view initiation of ideas and innovation of thought and deed as keys to success
- We should make blatant pronouncements on the value of innovatory thought
- We must work with change, rather than against it
- Creative Marketing must be promoted as prophecy, as a vision of the future
- Creative Marketing should be adopted as a weapon for change
- We should believe in the value of The Lone New Marketer attracting a following and developing a new school of thought
- We must reject the solid bourgeois family of Traditional Marketing
- We must guard the New Creative Philosophy with intense jealousy
- Creative marketers should revel in eccentricity
- We should market the mystique and aura of the future of marketing
- Creative marketers should be unrestrained in thought and deed
- Creative marketers should control, rather than be controlled
- We should believe in the value of developing kinetic and dynamic strength
- We should be prepared to make good out of the bad
- Creative marketers should promote the transmutation of ideas rather than their transmission

By attempting to embrace at least some of the ideas expressed in the Proclamation as well as continuing to search for additional creative metaphors and stories of success, this should enable us to focus on some fundamental qualities and competencies in order to work towards acquiring and generating the necessary skills for future success. Entrepreneurial marketers such as the owner/manager of the small enterprise can aim to follow such creative practice, just as much as a member of marketing academia or industry. Certainly within one of my own spheres of research on the craft microenterprise, these creative pronouncements should serve as developing improved tools of understanding managerial behaviour and motivation within domestic and export markets. Of course, not everyone can hope to possess such high degrees of self-belief, we cannot all be innovators and initiators. Some of us will work with change, while others will resist any attempt to alter the status quo. If everyone experienced similar visions, then there would be no interest since we would all behave in the same way, and believe in the same things. There would be no need for marketing prophets. What we can do is act as a forward-thinking body, set up a new *Salon des Refusés*, and turn against the bourgeois comfort of the current marketing family. Hopefully we may not need to follow such extreme measures as the Futurists and Surrealists or use Vache's bullet, but there are definite merits in adopting Wright's *Living City* ideology, Dali's power of imagination, follow Van Gogh's undying dedication for the 'cause' or believe in the power of Warhol's transmutation of thought and deed. The choice is ours to make.

References

Adams, L.E. (1996) *The Methodologies of Art. An Introduction*, New York: HarperCollins.

Adams, S. (1997) *The Barbizon School and the Origins of Impressionism*, London: Phaidon Press.

Ades, D. (1988) *Dali*, London: Thames & Hudson.

Alberge, D. (1999) 'Rebels get stuck into the Brit artists', *Times*, Thursday 26 August: 7.

Alley, R. (1981) *Catalogue of the Tate Gallery's Collection of Modern Art other than Works by British Artists*, London: Tate Gallery and Sotheby Parke-Bernet.

Amabile, T.M. (1983) *The Social Psychology of Creativity*, New York: Springer-Verlag.

Angell, C. (1994) *The Andy Warhol Museum*, USA: University of Pennsylvania.

Arndt, J. (1986) 'On making marketing science more scientific: role of orientations, paradigms, metaphors and puzzle solving', *Journal of Marketing* 49, Summer: 11–23.

Barnbrook, J. (1998) *Young British Art: The Saatchi Decade*, UK: Booth-Clibborn Editions.

Bell, J.D. (1995) 'The internationalisation of small computer software firms', *European Journal of Marketing* 29, 8: 60–75.

Brandon, R. (1999) *Surreal Lives. The Surrealists 1917–1945*, London: Macmillan.

Breton, A. (1966) *Manifestes du Surrealisme*, Paris: Gallimard.

Bridge, S., O'Neill, K. and Cromie, S. (1998) *Understanding Enterprise, Entrepreneurship and Small Business*, London: Macmillan.

Brown, N. (1998) *Tracey Emin*, UK: Art Data.

Bureau of Surrealist Research (1925) 'Declaration of 27 January 1925' (trans. by R. Howard), reprinted in M. Nadeau *The History of Surrealism*, Harmondsworth: Penguin, 262–3.

Burton, F.N. and Schlegelmilch, B.B. (1987) 'Profile analyses of non-exporters versus exporters grouped by export involvement', *Management International Review* 27, 1: 38–49.

Button, V. and Searle, A. (1997) *The Turner Prize*, London: Tate Gallery Publishing.

Carney, D.P. and Williams, R. (1997) 'The memetics of firms, entrepreneurship and the new body politic: the memetics of the marketplace', *Management Decision* 35, 5/6: 447–51.

Carson, D., Cromie, S., McGowan, P. and Hill, J. (1995) *Marketing and Entrepreneurship in SMEs. An Innovative Approach*, Hemel Hempstead: Prentice Hall.

Cavusgil, S.T., Bilkey, W.J. and Tesar, G. (1979) 'A note on the export behaviour of firms: exporter profiles', *Journal of International Business Studies* 10: 91–7.

Childish, B. (1999) *I'd Rather You Lied*, Hove: Codex.

Coviello, N.E. and Munro, H.J. (1995) 'Growing the entrepreneurial firm – networking international market development', *European Journal of Marketing* 29, 7: 49–61.

Cox, C. (1926) *Genetic Studies of Genius, Vol II. The Early Mental Traits of Three Hundred Geniuses*, California: Stanford University Press.

Dali, S. (1993) *The Secret Life of Salvador Dali* (trans. by H. M. Chevalier), London: Alkin Books.

Day, D. (1998) 'Defining the interface: a useful framework', in *Proceedings of the Academy of Marketing UIC/MEIG-AMA Symposia on the Marketing and Entrepreneurship Interface 1996–1998*, Northampton: Nene University College, Northampton.

De Long, D.G. (1998) *Frank Lloyd Wright and the Living City*, Berlin: Vitra Design Museum.

Denvir, B. (1993) *The Chronicles of Impressionism*, London: Thames & Hudson.

Desphande, R. (1983) ' "Paradigms Lost": on theory and method in research in marketing', *Journal of Marketing* 47, Fall: 101–10.

Dormer, P. (1997) *The Culture of Craft. Status and Future*, Manchester: Manchester University Press.

Edwards, S. (1999) *Art and Its Histories, A Reader*, London: Yale University Press.

Ehrenzweig, A. (1970) *The Hidden Order of Art. A Study in the Psychology of Artistic Imagination*, London: Paladin.

Ennew, C.T. and Binks, M.R. (1999) 'Marketing and entrepreneurship: some contextual issues', in *Proceedings of the Academy of Marketing UIC/MEIG-AMA Symposia on the Marketing and Entrepreneurship Interface 1996–1998*, Northampton: Nene University College, Northampton, 471–84.

Fernie, E. (1996) *Art History and its Methods. A Critical Anthology*, London: Phaidon Press.

Fillis, I. (1998) 'The craft of exporting – the creative entrepreneur in Britain and Ireland', in *Proceedings of the Academy of Marketing UIC/MEIG-AMA Symposia on the Marketing and Entrepreneurship Interface 1996–1998*, Northampton: Nene University College, Northampton, 347–54.

—— (1999) 'Exploring the marketing/entrepreneurship interface by examining the exporting of crafts to the American market', *UIC/AMA Annual Research Symposia on Marketing and Entrepreneurship*, 6–7 August, San Francisco.

Frascina, F. and Harris, J. (1997) *Art in Modern Culture. An Anthology of Critical Texts*, London: Phaidon Press.

Gabriel, C. (1990) 'The validity of qualitative market research', *Journal of the Market Research Society* 32, 4: 507–19.

Galton, F. (1870) *Hereditary Genius*, London: Macmillan.

Gibson, I. (1997) *The Shameful Life of Salvador Dali*, London: Faber & Faber.

Gill, J. and Johnson, P. (1991) *Research Methods for Managers*, London: Paul Chapman Publishing Ltd.

Glasgow Museums (1994) *Glasgow Art Gallery and Museum: The Building and the Collections*, Glasgow: HarperCollins.

Gombrich, E.H. (1996) *The Essential Gombrich. Selected Writings on Art and Culture*, London: Phaidon Press.

Goodwin, C. (1996) 'Moving the drama into the factory: the contribution of metaphors to services research', *European Journal of Marketing* 30, 9: 13–36.

Guilford, J.P. (1950) 'Creativity', *American Psychologist* 5: 444–54.

Hackley, C.E. and Mumby-Croft, R. (1998) 'Marketing entrepreneurs as creative agents in a social matrix – towards a theoretical framework for marketing entrepreneurship', in *Proceedings of the Academy of Marketing UIC/MEIG-AMA Symposia on the Marketing and Entrepreneurship Interface 1996–1998*, Northampton: Nene University College, Northampton, 505–13.

Hanson, L. and Hanson, E. (1955) *Passionate Pilgrim. The Life of Vincent Van Gogh*, New York: Random House.

Hauser, A. (1982) *The Sociology of Art* (trans. by J. Meredith), London: Clarendon Press.

Hills, G.E. (1987) 'Marketing and entrepreneurship research issues: scholarly justification?', in G.E. Hills (ed.) *Research at the Marketing/Entrpreneurship Interface*, UIC, Chicago, 3–15.

Hirschman, E.C. (1983) 'Aesthetics, ideologies, and the limits of the marketing concept', *Journal of Marketing* 47, Summer: 45–55.

Hulbert, B., Day, J. and Shaw, E. (1998) *Proceedings of the Academy of Marketing UIC/MEIG-AMA Symposia on the Marketing and Entrepreneurship Interface 1996–1998*, Northampton: Nene University College, Northampton.

Hunt, S.D. and Menon, A. (1993) 'Is it, metaphor at work, or is it, metaphors, theories and models at works?', in G. Laurent *et al.* (eds) *Research Traditions in Marketing*, Boston, MA: Kluwer, 426–32.

Johnston, W.J. and Czinkota, M.R. (1982) 'Managerial motivations as determinants of industrial export behaviour', in M.R. Czinkota and G. Tesar (eds) *Export Management: An International Context*, New York: Praeger, 3–17.

Jones, J. (2000) 'Hanging tough', *The Guardian*, Visual Arts Section, Tuesday 4 January: 14.

Kant, I. (1952) *Critique of Judgement* (trans. by J. Meredith), Part 1: 'Critique of Aesthetic Judgement', Oxford: Clarendon Press.

Kaufmann, E. (1978) 'Frank Lloyd Wright: plasticity, continuity, and ornament', *Journal of the Society of Architectural Historians* 37, March: 119–27.

Little, R. (1976) *Guillaume Appollinaire*, London: Athlone Press.

Marinetti, F.T. (1909) 'Foundation and manifesto of Futurism' (trans. by R.W. Flint and

A.A. Coppotelli), in R.W. Flint (ed.) *Marinetti. Selected Writings*, London: Secker & Warburg, 1972, 41–3.

McAuley, A. (1998) 'To grow or not to grow: that is the question: growth aspirations of Scottish craftspeople', in *Proceedings of the Academy of Marketing UIC/MEIG-AMA Symposia on the Marketing and Entrepreneurship Interface 1996–1998*, Northampton: Nene University College, Northampton, 229–38.

—— and Fillis, I. (1999) 'Creativity and the entrepreneur', *Academy of Marketing UIC/MEIG-AMA Symposium on the Marketing and Entrepreneurship Interface*, University of Strathclyde, Glasgow.

McClarence, S. (1999) 'Museum of the week', *Times*, Weekend Section, Saturday 4 September: 28.

McDonald, M.H.B. (1995) *Marketing Plans: How To Prepare Them And How To Use Them*, Oxford: Butterworth-Heinemann.

Meenaghan, J.A. (1983) 'Commercial sponsorship', *European Journal of Marketing* 17, 7: 5–73.

Morrison, H. (1998) *Louis Sullivan: Prophet of Modern Architecture*, New York: W.W. Norton & Company.

Murphy, A. (1999) *Jean-Francois Millet*, Yale: Yale University Press.

Nevett, T. and Nevett, L. (1987) 'The origins of marketing: evidence from Classical and Early Hellenistic Greece', in T. Nevett and S.C. Hollander (eds) *Marketing in Three Eras*, Proceedings of the Third Conference on Historical Research in Marketing, Michigan State University, 3–12.

Rampley, M. (1998) 'Creativity', *British Journal of Aesthetics* 38, 3: 265–78.

Rewald, J. (1973) *The History of Impressionism*, London: Secker & Warburg.

Rindfleisch, A. (1996) 'Marketing as warfare: reassessing a dominant metaphor (questioning military metaphors' centrality in marketing parlance)', *Business Horizons* 39, 5: 3–10.

Roethlisberger, F.J. and Dickson, W.J. (1939) *Management and the Worker*, Cambridge, MA: Harvard University Press.

Rose, M. (1975) *Industrial Behaviour: Theoretical Development since Taylor*, Harmondsworth: Allen Lane.

Roskill, M. (1967) *The Letters of Vincent Van Gogh*, Collins, Glasgow: Fontana Library.

Smart, D.T. and Conant, J.S. (1994) 'Entrepreneurial orientation, distinctive marketing competencies and organisational performance', *Journal of Applied Business Research* 10, 3: 28–38.

Smircich, L. (1983) 'Studying organisations as cultures', in G. Morgan (ed.) *Beyond Method*, London: Sage, 160–72.

Snow, E. (1994) *A Study of Vermeer*, Berkeley: University of California Press.

Sontag, S. (1964) 'Against interpretation', reprinted in E. Fernie (1996) *Art History and its Methods. A Critical Anthology*, London: Phaidon Press.

Stern, B. B. and Schroeder, J. E. (1994) 'Interpretative methodology from art and literary criticism: a humanistic approach to advertising imagery', *European Journal of Marketing* 28, 8/9: 114–32.

Storey, D.J. (1994) *Understanding the Small Business Sector*, London: International Thomson Business Press.

Sweetman, D. (1990) *The Love of Many Things. A Life of Vincent Van Gogh*, London: Hodder & Stoughton.

Tisdall, C. and Bozzolla, A. (1977) *Futurism*, London: Thames & Hudson.

Vache, J. (1995) *Four Dada Suicides*, Atlas Press.

Wach, K. (1996) *Salvador Dali: Masterpieces from the Collection of the Salvador Dali Museum*, New York: Abrams.

Wallach, M. and Kogan, N. (1965) *Modes of Thinking in Young Children*, New York: Holt, Rinehart & Winston.

Warhol, A. (1975) *The Philosophy of Andy Warhol. From A to B and Back Again*, San Diego: Harcourt Brace & Company.

Watson, K., Hogarth-Scott, S. and Wilson, N. (1998) 'Key issues in export market development for small and medium sized UK businesses', in *Proceedings of the Academy of Marketing UIC/MEIG-AMA Symposia on the Marketing and Entrepreneurship Interface 1996–1998*, Northampton: Nene University College, Northampton, 355–65.

Welch, E. (1997) *Art and Society in Italy 1350–1500*, Oxford: Oxford University Press.

Wensley, R. (1999) 'The basics of marketing strategy', in M.J. Baker (ed.) *The Marketing Book*, fourth edition, Oxford: Butterworth-Heinemann.

Wilson, S. (1990) *Tate Gallery: An Illustrated Companion*, London: Tate Gallery Publishing.

Wright, F.L. (1932) *The Disappearing City*, New York: William Farquhar Payson.

4 Marketers wake! a portrait of the artist as a marketing man

Anthony Patterson and Stephen Brown

Once upon a time

Once upon a time there was a storyteller *par excellence*. His name was James Joyce and he wrote compelling stories about Ireland that displayed great virtuosity and imagination. Yet in his own words, he was a 'cut and paste man', who gathered raw material from life, myth, legend and ancient tale. In his day, the popular press condemned Joyce under the vague generalisation that his work is 'something to do with drinking, a kind of verbalized vomit' (McHugh 1981: 108), and helped propagate the boundless rumours that he was, as O'Brien writes, 'a misanthrope, a cocaine addict, "*cavalier servante*" of duchesses, a Bolshevik propagandist, a spy for Austria during the war . . . (who) swam in the Seine each morning, surrounded himself with mirrors, wore black gloves in bed' (1999: 126). Nevertheless, he is still regarded as one of the finest writers there has ever been, second only to Shakespeare. Alongside Picasso in painting and Schoenberg in music he stands among the avant-garde elite of the twentieth century. In the reflective list-making frenzy that the turn of the century and the new millennium has precipitated, he has been hailed the 'Irishman of the Century' (McDonald 1999) and the Modern Library's top 100 Books of the Century has placed *Ulysses* at the top of the pile while *A Portrait of the Artist as a Young Man* comes in at number three. The date 16 June, christened Bloomsday, is celebrated by Joyceans the world over and a thriving academic industry is devoted to interpreting his literary *oeuvre*. This chapter will pay tribute to Joyce for like many of the artists mentioned in this book he had an instinctive understanding that marketing and art are kindred forms, and that the art of marketing is art and the art of art is marketing.

Our aim in this chapter is twofold. First, we will argue that Joyce was highly receptive towards marketing in his work and in his efforts to attain commercial success. Needless to say, many of the marketing activities in which he was engaged were never directly traceable to him but instead were performed on his behalf by loyal subjects such as Samuel Beckett and T.S. Eliot. Joyce, after all, lived in the modernist era, a time when true artists were expected to 'eschew publicity and feign indifference' to their commercial success or lack thereof (Dettmar 1996). Second, with the rise of contemporary commodity culture we intend to demonstrate how a central theme of Joyce's art, namely, the vernacular world of Dublin pub life has itself been busy absorbing the impact of Joyce's artistic contribution, the upshot of which has been that the cultural tradition of old has evolved into something quite new and different. Irish theme pubs, as they are known, have supplanted traditional pubs and are completely shameless in their marketing excess (see Brown and Patterson 2000). They recapitulate, as intensely as possible, what Fintan O'Toole calls, 'the virtual reality of the recreated Ireland' (1997: 161). In this chapter we describe one of these new 'theme' pubs, one that owes a special debt of gratitude to Joyce, since its theme is none other than the man himself – and why not? He has, after all, become a valuable cultural commodity. As David Norris said at the 1992 Joyce Symposium in Dublin, '"the name of Joyce" – packaged and commodified by the Joyce Industry – creates . . . "instant recognisability" and "brand identification." He goes on to thank the major sponsor of the symposium, "Baileys Irish Cream, an Irish Product like the works of James Joyce, of international recognition and excellence"' (cited in Leonard 1998: 10). In describing the James Joyce Pub in Paris we demonstrate not only how art and commodities are indistinguishable but also how, like Joyce, the best marketers – among which the theme pub entrepreneurs surely rank – stock their minds with traditional ideas and images and then set this accumulated knowledge to serve as fodder for their marketing imaginations.

'Sunny Jim': the marketing man

'Sunny Jim' as his family affectionately called James Joyce as a child, after an advertising campaign of the time,[1] was deeply ensconced in the world of marketing and advertising. Recently there has been an outpouring of articles and books by Joycean scholars on the relationship that Joyce and his work share with advertising, marketing and popular culture (see Herr 1986; Kershner 1996; Leonard 1998; Osteen 1995). It is known that Joyce had in his personal library a popular marketing book of the period, which was quite significantly entitled *The Art of Selling Goods* and, even more significantly, Osteen (1995) spotted in Joyce's 'Notes on Business and Commerce', written in Rome, that at one stage he actually considered pursuing an advertising career, a role that he later assigned to one of the main protagonists of *Ulysses*, Leopold Bloom. Osteen also notes that in many ways he did actually pursue just such a career given the enthusiastic manner in which he marketed his books, 'preparing press clippings for inclusion in review copies or presenting *Ulysses* as a real steal to recalcitrant purchasers' (1995: 111). It would be a nonsense to suggest that because Joyce made his work 'wilfully obscure' (Bishop 1986: 1) he had no interest in reaching an audience or in marketing his books because the fact is that he deliberately cultivated such wilful obscurity in order to sustain scholarly interest in his work. Joyce said that he wanted to write a book that would 'keep the professors busy for centuries arguing over what it meant', and certainly to date he has been highly successful in this respect.

Dettmar (1996) presents a detailed study of the ways in which Joyce participated in the marketing of *Ulysses*. He identified six main facets of involvement. First, the year after its Paris publication Joyce helped Sylvia Beach package copies for mailing and compile mailing lists. Second, he actively recruited sympathetic reviewers. Third, he attempted to control the very content of those reviews by setting certain phrases into circulation – essentially advertising blurbs of his own devising – that he knew would be repeated in the subsequent reviews. Fourth, he encouraged reviewers to coin slogans to describe the distinctive writing style that he pioneered. Interestingly, he actually preferred the 'mythical method' rather than the term 'stream of consciousness' that gained more popular accord. Fifth, Joyce astutely recognised the publicity value of the New York obscenity trial that was to decide whether or not the initial ban on *Ulysses* should be lifted. As it turned out, the ban was lifted, after which Joyce gleefully had an advertisement for *Ulysses* designed that incorporated Judge Woolsey's comments on the parts of the book that he thought obscene. Sixth, Joyce was the first artist to realise that not only did he have a reading public to win over but also an academic community. To this end, Joyce commissioned many critical projects, the most notable of which were Stuart Gilbert's task of setting out the Homeric parallels in *Ulysses* and the biography entrusted to Herman Gorman. Such marketing activities do not seem so very far removed from our contemporary trend towards producing an ever-escalating clatter of spin-off merchandise to accompany the launch of big budget Hollywood movies. Finally, one thing that Dettmar neglected to mention was the fact that Joyce penned such a marketing majesty in the first place. He had, after all, succeeded in writing perhaps the most salacious, most sensational, most revolutionary novel of all time, one that clearly met the needs of the market and continues to do so.

In Joyce's work too there is considerable evidence to suggest that he was deeply fascinated by the emerging commodity culture of the early twentieth century and the awakening of its foremost accomplices, marketing and advertising. A veritable academic industry is devoted to highlighting the extent to which this is so, albeit confined to the field of literary studies rather than our own. Wicke (1994) focuses on how *Ulysses* conveys the mediating power of turn-of-the-century advertising in Dublin as a means of accentuating Ireland's then pitiable status as a colonial backwater of Britain. After all, English companies selling products like Lipton's tea and Pears soap were by far the main advertisers of the day. Notably, the only exportable product that Ireland itself had at the time was Guinness stout. Perhaps, Guinness's subsequent success, both in terms of the stout it sold and in the Irish pubs that it helped to establish in foreign climes, was driven as much by a need to shake off the shackles of colonisation as they were by marketing know-how. Leonard's (1998) Lacanian exploration of Joyce's fiction holds that advertising, marketing and popular culture appearing therein often acts as a compensatory or illusory mechanism to consumers who are striving to satisfy a sense of permanent lack. According to Leonard Joyce's theory of the object, as expressed in *Stephen Hero*, based on the epiphany that could be glimpsed 'in the soul of the commonest object' closely parallels the theory of advertising that also seeks 'to make "the commonest object" appear "to leap to us" and seem "radiant"' (1998: 2). Leonard proceeds to explain how Joyce's notion of *integritas* is in keeping with how a marketer might seek to differentiate the look of his product from that of a competing product; how his notion of *consonantia* and *claritas* are similar to basic marketing theory about the importance of generating brand awareness, loyalty and equity, and finally how Joyce's notion of *quidditas* is analogous to the marketing requisite of constructing a brand with a personality or a soul. What Joyce achieves is not only to independently reckon some of the essence of marketing through the formalisation of his own aesthetic theory but also to anticipate in nascent form the premise of the present book, namely, that art and marketing are indistinguishable.

Joyce's work provides many other insights into the world of marketing; not least the inspired advertisements that Joyce had Bloom create in *Ulysses*, his awareness of 'the infinite possibilities hitherto unexploited of the modern art of advertisement' (Joyce 1992: 799). Decades before Williamson (1978), he figured that advertising was a co-productive process between advertisement and consumer, a negotiation of meaning that, whilst offering a focus for consumer desire, could never be predicted. Decades before Baudrillard (1988), he implicitly recognised that marketing and consumer discourse had the power to offer consumers a seductive type of pleasure that might be interpreted positively. Decades before fantasy was ever studied in consumer research (e.g., Rook 1988), Joyce demonstrates how an ad or physical object can initiate fantasy and act as a means towards completion of the self. Contemporary consumption-fixated 'blank' fiction – a body of literature that consumer researchers have recently studied (see Brown 1995; Patterson and Brown 1999) – was very much foreshadowed by the blizzard of brand names in which Joyce's work was immersed. Joyce revealed the hypocrisy of Yeats' Celtic Revival, which cast itself as commercially untainted when in actual fact it was big business and perhaps the main architect culpable for the rise of commodity Ireland. Joyce was among the earliest authors, his fellow Irishman Oscar Wilde being another, to collapse the distinction between 'high' and 'low' culture, happily writing about the relationship consumers shared with throwaway songs, ads, magazines, souvenirs and other items of kitsch. Little wonder that Joyce's work is sometimes described as prophetic, omniscient in scope, as encompassing all past and future knowledge (Derrida 1982). Perhaps this is why his books are among the very few that manage to survive the transition from modern to postmodern without diminishment (Kiberd 1992).

Now Joyce may have been a canny marketer, to the extent that insights into advertising and marketing issues are interwoven into his tome, but is there any evidence to suggest that his marketing ability extended beyond the literary sphere? Yes! Joyce was involved in a number of business ventures over the course of his life, some of which were more successful than others. It is a little known fact that Joyce managed to acquire successfully a concession from the Dublin Woollen Company to sell Irish Foxford Tweed to the Italians and Austrians. In an angry letter to a Dublin solicitor concerning a refusal to publish *Dubliners* he claims that this Tweed selling scheme had put 150,000 francs into the pockets 'of hungry Irish men and women since they drove me out of their hospitable bog' (Ellmann 1982: 314), though it is unclear how much he himself made from the enterprise. This success obviously whetted his appetite and ambition, for at one point he even considered importing skyrockets into Trieste. But nothing came of it.

Another decidedly more down-to-earth but equally ambitious venture was triggered by a remark made by his daughter, Lucia, when she asked of daddy why Dublin had no cinemas. For Joyce it was an opportunity too good to miss. He leapt into action contacting and establishing a syndicate, composed of four Italians, that aimed to open Dublin's first ever cinema, with a possible rollout to other Irish cities. They were so impressed with Joyce's idea that they signed a contract entitling Joyce to 10 per cent of the profits and also paid for Joyce's trip to Dublin so that he could get things off the ground prior to their arrival at a later date. Joyce went about his task with gusto, finding suitable premises for the cinema, which was to be named the Volta, getting electricity installed, acquiring benches and chairs, supervising the decoration and personally designing posters for the grand opening. Initially, the venture seemed promising, reviews were good and although attendance was low the consensus was that things would improve, and they probably would have but for the fact that Joyce returned to his family in Trieste and could no longer keep a watchful eye on the business. After only a few weeks the Italian who was left running the place cut his losses and left after selling the Volta to an English firm called the Provincial Theatre Company. They were the only party to make any money from the scheme. Nevertheless, it is clear that Joyce is not just a literary man; his persona is as much Bloom the ad-canvasser, as it is Dedalus the poet.

The pillar of the taverns

Turning from our discussion of Joyce as a marketing man, we will now consider the ways in which Joyce has become a marketable cultural commodity within the popular culture of today. As if to underline its *value* as a commodity, an Irish currency was unveiled in September 1993 and would you believe it! – the front of the ten-pound note showed a picture of Joyce, while on its reverse the opening words of *Finnegans Wake* were inscribed. The James Joyce Centre and the James Joyce Museum, which have been criticised for selling blue-and-white neckties and other such memorabilia (Beja and Benstock 1989), also profit from the commodification of Joyce. All over Ireland, an extraordinary variety of commodities are on sale that are jazzed up Joycean – tea-towels, T-shirts, biscuit tins, sepia prints, mugs and other trinkets. Bloomsday, celebrated throughout the world on 16 June, the date on which Joyce set *Ulysses* because it commemorated the first time in 1904 that he courted Nora Barnacle, also provides a huge boost to Dublin's economy. Many people, dressed in Edwardian attire, take to the streets and retrace Bloom's footsteps across the city, stopping off, of course, in Davy Byrne's pub where the gorgonzola sandwich and glass of burgundy that Bloom purchased in the novel are on sale, albeit at a considerably inflated price. Famous Irish musicians such as the Pogues, Kate Bush, Enya and Therapy, have all made allusions to Joyce in their songs.[2]

Vincent Cheug (1996) believes that alongside this 'popular conscience' of Joyce, there also exists 'a popular unconscious' that manifests itself through the occasional oblique reference to Joyce in film, book or other media. He cites numerous examples of hidden Joyceana, such as advertisements made in the style of Joyce and an episode of the television series *Thirtysomething* that is clearly modelled on 'The Dead' although no acknowledgement is ever made either in the show or the closing credits. Cheug also wonders at how both these forms of consciousness 'could be used and manipulated to sell products' (1996: 181).

One overtly conscious and highly successful utilisation of Joyce the commodity, which is inexplicably omitted from all other discussions of Joyce and marketing, is the theme pub phenomenon. As every thirsty traveller knows, there are many theme pubs dotted around the world with Joyce as their overriding theme.[3] It is against strong competition from his contemporaries – Wilde, Shaw, Yeats, Synge and O'Casey – that Joyce has managed to become the favourite literary icon of pub producers. This is partly due to his contribution towards the enshrinement of a popular Irish mythology, which has itself become a phenomenally popular pub theme (see Brown and Patterson 2000). The ideal marketability of the name – James Joyce – with its film star resonance coupled with his distinctive almost cartoon appearance – walking-cane, moustache, dickey-bow, spectacles (or eye-patch) – also contribute towards Joyce's commodity value.

Nevertheless, perhaps the most compelling reason for adopting Joyce as a pub theme lies in the fact that Joyce to a degree conforms with the stereotypical image of the Irish drunkard and also displayed a great passion for the milieu of pub life. Described by Yeats as the 'pillar of the taverns', Joyce, like his father, was often to be seen drinking in the pubs of Dublin and later too, after his voluntary exile, in the cafes and bars of Italy and Paris. Though, that he would eventually follow in his father's staggering footsteps was never a foregone conclusion. As a youth he was pious to an extreme, scornful of heavy drinkers such that his friends would often mock his own meagre intake. Gogarty, in particular, would coax and cajole Joyce to drink ever more copious quantities, in the hope that he could break his spirit, so to speak, and was delighted when Joyce eventually succumbed to its temptations. The death of Joyce's mother caused the biggest sea change in his attitude towards its consumption. Aside from its ability to quell the pain of bereavement, 'it allowed him to relax and observe the way others talked and behaved, it enabled him to discuss his anxieties and finally to sing or act the fool' (Lyons 1992: 111). Like most young men Joyce was proud of his drunken antics and would often boast about how the actresses at the Camden Hall had to step over his drink-sodden body. Total intoxication was the state of mind he sought to induce and in so striving it became a common sight, much to the chagrin of his brother Stanislaus, to see a tottering Joyce being escorted home from the pub by some kindly soul who had to bear Joyce's ceaseless singing, 'Of the good stuff let's have some more. Because I've lost the key to my door' (O'Brien 1999: 50).

The fact that Joyce was often 'plootered' did not stop him from astutely observing the pub life that he was part of and reproducing it in astonishing detail within his books, most notably in *Ulysses*, which has done more for the marketing of Dublin pubs than all the efforts of the Irish Tourist Board. Joyce said himself, in a letter to his brother Stanislaus, that 'the publicans would be glad of the advertisement' (Ellmann 1982: 332). Certainly, Joyce's opus has occasioned an outpouring of reverence for the humble Irish pub; an outpouring that expressed and continues to express itself in the publication of ever more books on the subject (see Blake and Pritchard 1985; Kearns 1996; Murphy 1994; Pepper 1994; Taylor 1994; Tohill 1990); an outpouring that has not only affirmed the pub's position as an important part of Irish culture, but which has also codified Joyce's standing therein. Nowhere is this better illustrated than in the James Joyce theme pub in Paris.

The tavern of the pillar

The James Joyce Pub, the second of eight Irish theme pubs launched to date by Brian Loughney, an Irish businessman, opened in Paris in 1995.[4] The pub boasts a prime location on the Gouvion St Cyr near the Palais des Congrès.[5] The property, originally used to sell French cheese, was retro-fitted in the style of a traditional Irish pub according to Loughney's exacting specifications. His aim was to provide punters with both a slice of Joycean culture and an 'authentic' experience of Irish pubs comparable to that on offer in Dublin.

With the exception of an enormous plastic pint of Guinness, that totally overshadows the recess of a first floor window, the exterior of the James (as it is known to the locals) could have been swiped from a souvenir Irish picture book of the type so beloved of tourists. Every detail of tradition has been lovingly reproduced. Small columns and stained glass windows ascend to hold the entablature that bears the name James Joyce Pub. This sparks the questions (at least to the uninitiated) – Is this Joyce's pub? – Did he ever come here? – Is he actually in there? – an avuncular publican behind the bar, pulling pints and making jolly with the customers, like the dead Bygmister Finnegan in *Finnegans Wake* who somehow wakes and transmutes into Humphrey Chimpden Earwicker, a Dublin publican.

The pub rests on a street corner, facilitating customer access via either a front or a side entrance, but its doors are much more far-reaching. They function as a direct portal to visitors travelling from and going to Joyce's Dublin. Nor are we speaking metaphorically for Loughney has secured a wonderful marketing coup, an agreement with Ryan Air, an Irish airline, whereby all visitors flying from Ireland with Ryan Air are deposited outside the pub via an express coach and returned via the same route. How appropriate that the pub should become a point of origin and departure, of beginning and ending, just like the circuitous structure of Joyce's *Finnegans Wake*. The fascia is predictably painted a dark emerald green and is completed by a gold trim surround; the name too is emblazoned in gold and is cast in a classical calligraphy. While the whole façade reeks of Oirishness with a capital 'O', there is no sign of Joyce save an unobtrusive little drawing printed on a double-sided wooden advertising placard. No explanation whatsoever is made of Joyce's identity or achievements. It seems to be implicitly assumed that punters will be drawn into the pub either through simple curiosity, the Ryan Air marketing stratagem or purely by the magic words, *James Joyce Pub*.

Inside, the first Joycean symbol encountered is an unusual abstract sketch of Joyce near the main entrance, his face little more than a coarse caricature, painted meagrely in the colours of Ireland's flag – green, white and a splatter of gold. Objects have been incorporated into the painting, twisted metal, wire, rope and an askew frame all serve to contort the image. All of which contributes to this celebration of Joyce's weirdness. The portrait is striking not only in composition but also in that it is a Joycean artefact that is not simply one of the hackneyed pictures that are readily available for visual consumption in the pages of Ellmann's prodigious biography and suchlike. Needless to say, there are plenty of the usual Joycean pictures scattered around the place, framed photocopies from Ellmann's book and so on, but their sheer multitude and careful arrangement endows them with a certain mystery and power.

Featured prominently in the pub are narrow stained glass windows, specifically commissioned by Loughney to showcase the Joycean theme. Patterned after those in the Book of Kells and cast in shimmering jewel tones, each has a unique centrepiece, such as a building historically associated with Joyce – The Martello Tower, Clongowes Wood College, The National Library of Ireland and The Berlitz School. Again these buildings will be familiar to many, but the point of this pub is not the unearthing of hidden character or fresh insight but rather the celebration of familiarity and of personal intimacy with an Irish cultural icon.

The pub does not exclusively display Joycean items, however. There are also many other Irish references, both contemporary and historical, scattered willy-nilly about the place. Olde mirror ads for Guinness and Powers Whiskey, an 1899 ad selling Dublin as a holiday destination, archaic implements and products like Oxo cubes, Gold Bond Mixture, Caster oil, Three Nun's Tobacco and so on. In another corner there is a group picture signed by all the actors from *The Commitments*, a hugely popular Irish film of 1991. The film penned by one of Ireland's most reputable contemporary authors, Roddy Doyle, who like Joyce writes realistic visions of Irish life, awash with alcohol and profanity, and believes that the ordinary is the proper domain of the artist. In addition, there are many pictures of contemporary Irish Rugby – a signed picture of a recent Irish squad and numerous action shots of aggressive men, dressed in green shirts and white shorts, sprinting to a certain try or frozen in mid-dive stretching for the line. The rugby ethos in the pub is particularly strong: certainly, rugby fans rather than the literati constitute the biggest proportion of customers. Apparently, the pub is a favourite haunt of the Irish rugby players themselves who enjoy a pint of stout or two after a tussle with the French homeboys. This privileging of rugby need not take away from the literary dimension of the place. They can co-exist, as one rugby fan proved to Joyce back in the 1930s. The fellow had came to Paris to watch an Ireland–France rugby match and Joyce was genuinely touched when he recited some of his favourite Joyce passages by heart (Fallon 1999).

That said, the focal point of the pub is undoubtedly the television rather than the very impressive assortment, on loan from a special library collection, of first edition copies and landmark critical studies, all encased in a glass display cabinet. Bemoaned as the curse of every pub, the introduction of the television along with piped music[6] has been blamed for bringing about an end to the art of conversation and storytelling that supposedly characterised pubs of yesteryear. It is ironic that Joyce was the first man to bring the cinema to Dublin. That he had a good understanding of cinema's narrative techniques is not in doubt, as is evident from his use of flashback in *A Portrait of the Artist* and the dissolving of one scene into another in *Finnegans Wake*. He even discussed with Russian director Sergei Eisentein the possibility of filming *Ulysses* and also had planned to shoot the Anna Livia Plurabella episode of *Finnegans Wake* (Ellmann 1982). Clearly he understood the power contained in those onscreen images and had an inkling of their potential to supplant written text as the medium of the future. People in the pub can be observed staring at the TV, the sound turned off, seemingly spellbound, staring at nothing in particular, totally transfixed. In truth, none of the Joycean artefacts could ever hope to effect a similar response. If proof were ever needed of the existence of Lyotard's (1984) 'zero consciousness' then this is it.

On the wall immediately beside the television screen there is a huge mural of Joyce. Close examination reveals that interspersed throughout the sepia-toned artwork there resides what is perhaps the most comprehensive collection of visual references to Joyce ever gathered in one place: Bernard Kiernan's pub; The Abbey

Theatre; Nora young and old; his children, Lucia and Charles; every photo, portrait and sculpture of Joyce in existence – his death mask, the Dublin statue, a youthful casual confident Joyce, Joyce in middle age; then, pictures of the Parisian cafes he frequented, snippets of his hand-writing; his parents, his brothers and sisters; the other buildings that he made famous, either in fiction or reality. Interestingly, there are pictures of the James pub itself, and even pictures of pictures that are in the James Joyce pub, such as the abstract painting described earlier, which all serve to historicise the pub itself and make it part and parcel of the contemporary making of Joyce. From a distance all the elements of the collage, this concentrated distillation of what we know of the visual Joyce, unite to form an image of Joyce presiding over the spectacle before him, smartly dressed in shirt and tie, spectacles, overcoat and hat. He has a knowing, self-assured look about him, that seems to say, 'The artist like the God of the creation, remains within or behind or beyond or above his handiwork, invisible, refined out of existence, indifferent, paring his fingernails' (Joyce 1993: 483).

In its entirety, the contents of the suitably dark interior, the photographs, paintings, drawings, letters, first editions and other memorabilia conspire to create a shrine to Joyce and the brand of Irishness that he was so helpful in propagating. A visitor might be inspired to think, as Joyce once did, on arriving at a Dublin hotel, after an absence of some time, 'The place is very Irish. I have lived so long abroad and in so many countries that I can feel at once the voice of Ireland in anything' (Ellmann 1982: 306).

The morning after

For thinking drinkers and drinking thinkers alike, the James Joyce pub epitomises the postmodern condition. It is an amalgam of hyperreality, glocalization, commodification, retrospection and de-differentiation. It is a place where high and low culture meet up and down a few while pontificating on art's imitation of life and vice versa. Purists, admittedly, might complain that it expropriates, and execrates the image of James Joyce, Ireland's greatest ever artist (Lodge 1997). But, as this chapter has sought to suggest, Sunny Jim himself would hardly have complained, since he was a consummate marketing man. We suspect, indeed, that Joyce would have been wholly sympathetic to the theme pub concept and cognisant of the reasons for their ubiquity.

The success of the James Joyce pub – and let us not forget that it is successful, being one of the busiest pubs in Paris – stems from the fact that consumers today are disappointed with reality. To cater for these consumers, dreary reality has been transfigured by the creative imagination of people like Loughney whose version of experience is one with which consumers can enjoy. Of course, it is not necessarily an accurate portrait of the artist, as Joyce said himself, 'The truth probably is that I am a quite commonplace person undeserving of so much imaginative painting' (Ellmann 1982: 509), but the point is that through creativity a process of 're-enchanting the disenchanted' (Ritzer 1999), is enacted.

Indeed, it can legitimately be argued that the eponymous pub is a perfect, if unwitting, metaphor for the life of Joyce, insofar as his lifelong aim of re-writing Ireland is analogous to what theme pub imagineers, like Loughney, do with the text of their built environments. In the course of his career, Joyce encountered incredible opposition, narrow-minded critics, obstinate publishers and puritan printers, all of whom sought to repress and resist the vision of Joyce's imagination. Loughney, likewise, has had to endure opprobrious attacks of a similar ferocity, from critics resistant to the idea of the Irish theme pub. For instance, Glancy (1997: 6); considers them to be 'hideous constructions, banal beyond all redemption' Hayes (1997: 17); contends that they are 'kitsch bastardized versions of the real thing' and Lezard (1998: 9) pulls no punches when he states, 'theme pubs are rubbish. Let me explain in brutally simple terms. I do not go into theme pubs because I am not a moron. Does that sound snobbish? I do not give a damn if it does'.

Degraded they may be, but Irish theme pubs – akin to James Joyce, marketing man extraordinaire – are larger than life; they are hyperreal to the nth degree, they are Ireland in essence, in exclesis, in absentia. Above all, theme pubs provide a sense of home, a fulfilment of the nostalgic impulse, a chance to recapture the memory of paradise lost. There is an old Irish interrogative 'have you no homes to go to?' that the publican is heard to cry at closing time in an attempt to usher out the barflies. This statement takes on new meaning for Irish emigrants like Joyce who do not actually have any homes to go to, well at least homes on Ireland's own swampy soil. His voluntary exile, which could be interpreted as a pretext for losing his identity, in the end actually accentuates it. Joyce wrote in the last page of *A Portrait of the Artist* that his goal in life was 'to forge in the smithy of my soul the uncreated conscience of my race'. In so doing he rewrote Ireland according to the marketing principles that he laid down in his own aesthetic theory of art. He found the epiphany in the commonest entity that is Ireland and sold it to us all. It is time, that we, as marketers, followed Joyce' lead, otherwise we may well be guests at our own funeral. Marketers wake!

Notes

1 The character Sunny Jim was the hero of numerous jingles that advertised a breakfast cereal called FORCE.
2 The front sleeve of a Pogues' album actually features Joyce as one of the band members.
3 Aside from the James Joyce in Paris, there are many other Joycean pubs scattered around the world, in San Francisco, Prague, Durham, London and New York, as well as a nineteen-strong chain of Finnegan's (sic) Wakes owned by the brewer, Whitbread,

in the UK. There is also a James Joyce pub in Zurich, which boasts the original interior of the Jury's Hotel of Dame Street that features in *Ulysses* complete with its unique décor and nineteenth-century furniture. The Union Bank of Switzerland bought the pub interior at an auction in the early 1970s just before the original pub was demolished and subsequently had it dismantled, transported and reassembled in Zurich where it re-opened in 1976.

4 Paris is famed for its avant-garde past, cradling movements such as Cubism and Surrealism and spawning artists such as Picasso, Cézanne, Braque, Man Ray and Duchamp. It is also a city of which Joyce was especially fond. In 1920, while on his way to London, Joyce decided to spend a few days there and ended up staying for twenty years. He especially relished the frequent drinking sessions where he fraternised in the cafes with the local literati and prostitutes. In *Dubliners* too he wrote, 'Everything in Paris is gay . . . They believe in enjoying life . . . they've a great feeling for the Irish there. When they heard I was from Ireland they were ready to eat me, man' (Joyce 1993: 87).

5 Loughney also has Irish pubs in Brussels, Madrid (2), Boston, Dublin and Galway and another in Paris. Aside from the James Joyce Pub of this study they are all named 'Kitty O'Shea's', who was the lover of a famous Irish parliamentarian, Charles Stewart Parnell. Parnell was the only Irish figure Joyce had any sympathy for, to the extent that he compared the course of their lives in 'Gas from a Burner' (Ellmann 1982).

6 This pub played all kinds of contemporary pop music from Abba to U2 and steers clear of any kind of fiddle dee dee.

References

Baudrillard, J. (1988) in M. Poster (ed.) *Selected Writings*, Stanford: Stanford University Press.

Beja, M. and Benstock, S. (1989) *Coping with Joyce: Essays from the Copenhagen Symposium*, Columbus: Ohio State University Press.

Bishop, J. (1986) *Joyce's Book of the Dark: 'Finnegans Wake'*, Madison: University of Wisconsin.

Blake, L. and Pritchard, D. (1985) *Irish Pubs*, Bray: Real Ireland Press.

Brown, S. (1995) 'Psycho shopper: a comparative literary analysis of the dark side', in F. Hansen (ed.) *European Advances in Consumer Research 2*, Provo, UT: Association for Consumer Research, 96–103.

Brown, S. and Patterson, A. (2000) 'Knick-knack paddy-whack, give a pub a theme', *Journal of Marketing Management* 16,6: 647–62.

Cheug, V.J. (1996) 'The Joycian unconscious, or getting respect in the real world', in R.B. Kershner (ed.) *Joyce and Popular Culture* (The Florida James Joyce Series), Gainesville: University Press of Florida, 181–91.

Derrida, J. (1992) *Acts of Literature*, New York: Routledge.

Dettmar, J.H. (1996) 'Selling *Ulysses*', *The James Joyce Quarterly* 31, 4: 795–812.

—— (1982) *James Joyce*, London: Oxford University Press.

Fallon, B. (1999) *An Age of Innocence: Irish Culture 1930–1960*, Dublin: Gill and Macmillan.

Glancy, J. (1997) 'A renaissance down the boozer', *The Independent*, 7 March, 6–7.

Hayes, T. (1997) *Gift of the Gab!: The Irish Conversation Guide*, Dublin: O'Brien.

Herr, C. (1986) *Joyce's Anatomy of Culture*, Chicago: University of Illinois Press.

Joyce, J. (1992) *A Portrait of the Artist as a Young Man*, London: Wordsworth Editions.

—— (1993) *James Joyce: A James Joyce Reader*, London: Penguin.

Kearns, K.C. (1996) *Dublin Pub Life and Lore: An Oral History*, Dublin: Gill and Macmillan.

Kershner, R.B. (1996) *Joyce and Popular Culture* (The Florida James Joyce Series), Gainesville: University Press of Florida.

Kiberd, D. (1992) 'Introduction', in J. Joyce *Ulysses*, London: Penguin.

Leonard, G. (1998) *Advertising and Commodity Culture in Joyce* (The Florida James Joyce Series), Gainesville: University Press of Florida.

Lezard, N. (1998) 'Two pints of lager and a silly hat, please', *The Independent*, 17 July, 9.

Lodge, D. (1997) *The Practice of Writing*, London: Penguin.

Lyons, J.B. (1992) 'The drinking days of Joyce and Lowry', *The Malcolm Lowry Review* 31/32: 112–21.

Lyotard, J. (1984) *The Postmodern Condition*, Manchester: Manchester University Press.

McDonald, H. (1999) 'My Irishman of the century', *The Observer*, Sunday 26 December, 20.

McHugh, R. (1981) *The Finnegans Wake Experience*, Dublin: Irish Academic Press.

Murphy (1994) *Irish Shopfronts and Pubs*, San Francisco: Chronicle Books.

O'Brien, E. (1999) *James Joyce*, London: Penguin.

O'Toole, F. (1997) *The Lie of the Land: Irish Identities*, London: Verso.

Osteen, M. (1995) *The Economy of Ulysses: Making Both Ends Meet*, New York: Syracuse.

Patterson, A. and Brown, S. (1999) 'The confessionalist manifesto: consumer behaviour and self-construction in *High Fidelity* and *Bridget Jones's Diary*', in McAuley, A. (ed.) *Proceedings of the Academy of Marketing Annual Conference*, Stirling: University of Stirling, CD-Rom.

Pepper, B. (1998) *Irish Pubs*, Orpington: Eric Dobby Publishing.

Ritzer, G. (1999) *Enchanting a Disenchanted World*, Thousand Oaks: Pine Forge.

Rook, D.W. (1988) 'Researching consumer fantasy', in E.C. Hirshman and J.N. Sheath (eds) *Research in Consumer Behaviour*, 3, Greenwich, CT: JAI Press, 247–70.

Taylor, S. (1994) *The Bushmills Irish Pub Guide*, Belfast: Appletrees Press.

Tohill, I.J. (1990) *Pubs of the North*, Portaferry: Tohill.

Wicke, J. (1994) '"Who's she when she's at home?' Molly Bloom and the work of consumption', in R. Pearce (ed.) *Molly Blooms: A Polylogue on 'Penelope'*, London: University of Wisconsin Press, 174–95.

Williamson, J. (1978) *Decoding Advertisements*, London: Marion Boyers Publishing Ltd.

5 Dealing with death: art, mortality and the marketplace

Stephanie O'Donohoe and Darach Turley

Introduction

As an antidote to the potentially dehumanising effect of the scientific focus in medical education, final year students at Aberdeen University may take a course in literature on topics such as death and bereavement. According to Dr Blair Smith, who developed the course,

> Literature in all its forms has always been a major influence on society and omission of its study must therefore leave one exposed. Furthermore, its study provides insights into many aspects of historical and contemporary life, experiences and emotions . . . A doctor who can only face death or birth with a cold equanimity cannot pretend to practise humanely.
>
> (Smith, in Cochrane 1998: 8)

Dr Smith's argument resonates with concerns expressed in the social science and marketing literature about the dominance of the scientific, positivistic paradigm (see, for example, Belk 1986; Holbrook 1995). As postmodern perspectives gain a foothold, however tentative, in the mountains of marketing theory, they bring with them a greater belief in art as an important means of organising human experience; indeed, works of art may 'enable us to commune momentarily with something eternal, something majestic, something ineffable, something over and above ourselves . . . offering evanescent intimations of immortality' (Brown 1998: 75–6).

Taking the research path less travelled, several scholars have demonstrated the insights to be gained into marketing and consumption practices from cultural artefacts including novels, films, magazine articles, comic books, television programmes and advertising (Belk and Pollay 1985; Brown 1995, 1998; Hirschman 1987, 1988; Holbrook 1995; Holbrook and Grayson 1986). The world of literature often has much to say about the marketplace, and as Brown (1998) demonstrates, in some cases it is novelists rather than consumer researchers who first identify emergent market-related attitudes and behaviour.

If works of art can inspire marketers and consumer researchers to practise humanely, nowhere is this needed more than in the area where marketing meets mortality (Turley 1997). In the next section, we discuss two recent novels that address the relationship between marketing and mortality, serving as mirror images of each other. Our reading of these novels suggests that the distinction between the sacred, the profane (Belk *et al.* 1989) and the secular (Hirschman 1990; O'Guinn and Belk 1989) is a useful one for exploring marketing's dealings with mortality. One of the characteristics of the sacred discussed by Belk *et al.* (1989) is *kratophany*, the powerful competing tendencies it elicits to approach and to avoid. We outline these two analytical frames and use them to explore treatments of death in advertising discourse. Finally, since meaning is co-produced by a text's readers (Scott 1994; Stern 1989), we home in on consumer complaints about portrayals of death and dying in print advertising; we ask what these reactions tell us about our understanding of death, dying and bereavement, and where the boundaries might be between the sacred and the sacrilegious in advertising's treatment of death.

Mortality and morality in the marketplace: a tale of two novels

Two recent novels allow us a glimpse of contemporary interactions between the sacred and sacrilegious, the profound and the profane that occur when death is firmly located in the marketplace. There are several striking parallels between *Jesus and the Adman* (Brook 1998) and *Way to Go* (Spence 1998). Published in the same year, each book documents the life of a young man after the death of his father. Remote and apparently unloving in life, each father in death is a catalyst, making mortality his son's personal and professional business.

Johnny Yells, the profane protagonist of *Jesus and the Adman*, is a junior copywriter with a leading advertising agency. He is excited by the opportunity to pitch for the business of LifeGen, a life insurance company described by his creative director as:

> the new boys in life assurance. They're regarded as being a little brash in what is a highly conservative industry . . . They want people to sit up and take notice. Traditionally life assurance is hard to sell: it's dull and prosaic and people are superstitious – they don't like anything that makes them think about death. You've got to overcome these fears, reassure them, tell them they can trust LifeGen.
>
> (Brook 1998: 37)

During this meeting, Johnny is called out to be told of his father's death. Even as he speaks to his stepmother, her words feed his ideas for a campaign for LifeGen and he is more anxious to get back to the briefing than console his stepmother or think about his father. Still thinking about life assurance at the funeral, he notices in the church an unusual painting of Christ smiling, inscribed 'He who believes in me shall have eternal life'. Inspired to start 'cashing in' on God's claim, Johnny develops a phenomenally successful campaign for LifeGen featuring the 'Smiling Jesus' image and the headline 'For Life after Death, talk to LifeGen'. Although his creative partner refuses to work on the campaign, Johnny's conscience is clear:

> The fact that the idea had come to him in the middle of his father's funeral merely underlined the truth of Wollard's maxims: there is no telling where an idea might appear; everything is raw material for the adman; the only sacred thing in advertising is a good idea.
>
> (Brook 1998: 54)

Johnny abandons and betrays his former partner as he wins plaudits and promotion and extends the LifeGen campaign to television. These ads take Belk's (1985) notion of 'terminal materialism' quite literally; one shows a man at the point of death confronted by a great light and a booming voice asking what he has not done in life. The man immediately thinks of overcharged clients, neglected family and charitable giving, but the Voice has something else in mind: 'For heaven's sake man. LifeGen. Did you talk to LifeGen?' (Brook 1998: 153–5).

Although the campaign brings Johnny the success he desires, it also brings him to the brink of madness. He looks at his 'Smiling Jesus' posters and becomes convinced that Jesus is no longer smiling at him. Obsessed by the question of what happens after death, he is stalked by fear and dread of nothingness. Unable to talk to friends about death, he becomes isolated. Breaking into the church where he first saw the 'Smiling Jesus' painting, he searches for the minister to ask what happens when we die. Having injured himself badly during the break-in, however, he almost dies himself. Again, this experience is raw material for his work: his ideas for the television ad are dictated from his hospital bed. The novel ends with Johnny surrounded by fame, fortune and fashionable clothing, but with intimations that fear of death, as well as death itself, will consume him in the end.

The destiny of Neil McGraw, narrator and central character in *Way to Go*, is shaped by death from the outset. Born to a mother who died in childbirth and a father who was the local undertaker, his childhood home was truly funereal. Although Neil resists his father's attempts to draw him into the family business, he acquires a taste for gallows humour and the question of what happens when we die. Leaving his Scottish home as soon as he can, he heads for London and becomes part of a household of hippies. This phase in his life ends when the household's father figure dies suddenly, but the friends find comfort in the unorthodox funeral ceremony that they improvise for him. Neil then travels around the world for fifteen years, gathering jokes and stories about death and witnessing funeral ceremonies wherever he goes. He falls sick in India, still asking his big question, and is saved from dehydration and death by Lila, the woman who becomes his wife. Planning to live in London, they are called back to Scotland on the death of Neil's father. Neil takes care of the funeral and his father's body:

> I put up his shirt collar, fastened the plain black tie in a simple knot, folded the collar down again and smoothed it flat. Then the polished black shoes, size nines with the hard toecaps. Right first, then left, double knot the laces. Better. What he'd have wanted, to be properly dressed. I nodded, smiled. Good.
>
> (Spence 1998: 157)

Although Neil had planned to sell the family business and return to London, a neighbour looks to him when her husband dies. As Lila predicts, he cannot refuse 'the poor soul that's turning to you for help' (Spence 1998: 173), and the family business is reincarnated: friends from his past join him in the new venture, and the name changes from 'McGraw and Sons' to 'Way to Go'. The company's brochure emphasises the commitment to keeping prices down and to offering choice from the simplest to the most elaborate of funerals. Furthermore,

> When someone close to you dies, it's a time to grieve, for there's nothing as deep as that pain of loss. But it's also a time to celebrate the person's life, give thanks for having known them, give them a good send-off. We're here to help with that, whatever way you want. We're an old family business and can still do things the traditional way, if that's what you'd prefer . . . But if you want a ceremony that's a little out of the ordinary, we'll work on it with you. We can make customised hand-painted coffins . . . We can help with your choice of music and readings, make the whole event a performance – funeral as theatre. If you decide on cremation, we can help with suggestions as to what can be done with the ashes, in some cases taking inspiration from the ancient traditions of other cultures . . .
>
> (Spence 1998: 188–9)

The business becomes successful, famous and controversial. Despite the weird and wonderful caskets and ceremonies, Way to Go focuses on helping people devise meaningful ceremonies and ways of memorialising the dead. Its ethos is contrasted with that of large corporations, exemplified by Lila's outrage on discovering that another firm had taken the body of a young AIDS victim from the family home against the mother's wishes and had deposited it on the floor of a garage outside the company premises, with 'AIDS' daubed in red on the body bag.

And at the service in the crematorium, the boy's mother made a speech and thanked us, especially Lila, for not treating her boy like a leper, for giving him dignity, for helping her give him a decent send-off.

(Spence 1998: 241)

Neil receives several offers from larger undertaking businesses to merge with them or sell out to them, but he refuses to be 'swallowed up by some monstrous conglomerate' (p. 249). A large multinational company, Universal Rest Incorporated, brings its Funeral Roadshow to Scotland. At a trade presentation describing how revenue can grow in tandem with 'increased consumer choice' and 'enhanced customer satisfaction', Neil cannot stay silent. He launches a diatribe that could have come directly from Jessica Mitford (1998), hound of Casketville, herself:

'The whole pitch today is about maximising profits'.
'And what's wrong with that?'
'It shouldn't be above all else . . . And whatever way you tart it up, maximising profits means squeezing your customers, persuading them to spend more. And I just think it's sick to do that to people when they're vulnerable'.

(Spence 1998: 249)

Way to Go remains independent and continues with its alternative vision of undertaking. The last client we read of is Neil himself, facing an untimely death from cancer. His personal and professional lives fusing for the last time, he and Lila plan his funeral. The book ends with the funeral and the dispersal of his ashes in fireworks that light up the sky: as Neil is still narrating the story, the reader is left with a sense that he has finally found the answer to his question.

Mortality and the marketplace

Jesus and the Adman could be read as a modern retelling of the Faustian myth, crossed with elements of Dorian Gray, while Way to Go draws on exposés of the funeral industry in fact and fiction (Mitford 1963, 1998; Waugh 1948), recent Western interest in the handcrafted coffins of Ghana (Secretan 1995) and concerns about high-pressure sales tactics being imported into the British funeral industry from America (see, for example, Ahmed 1998). For our purposes, however, these two books illustrate the powerful tensions between the sacred, the secular and the sacrilegious, and the related tension between fear and fascination, which are also evident in advertising discourse surrounding death.

The sacred and the profane

There is 'a fundamental distinction structuring social life . . . between what is set apart and regarded as sacred and what is regarded as profane or ordinary' (Belk *et al.* 1989: 2). The boundaries between the sacred and the profane appear to be shifting in contemporary society, however, illustrating 'the selectively permeable nature of these domains of experience' (p. 13). Belk and his colleagues examine the secularisation of institutionalised religion and the sacralisation of secular (non-religious) realms of experience, showing how people enact the sacred/profane distinction in the context of consumption:

> We take the sacred in the realm of consumption to refer to that which is regarded as more significant, powerful and extraordinary than the self. Sacred occurrences may be ecstatic: they are self-transcending . . . The profane, by contrast, is ordinary and lacks the ability to induce ecstatic, self-transcending, extraordinary experiences.
>
> (Belk *et al.* 1989: 13)

Within the secular sphere of consumption, Belk *et al.* found sacredness perpetuated by temporal or spatial separation from the profane, whereas 'desacralisation' involved desingularising objects or experiences and turning them into saleable commodities. 'Irreverent' attitudes or behaviours with respect to sacred places, people, places, times, events or experiences were similarly seen as sacrilegious.

Although treating sacred objects as saleable commodities is a form of sacrilege, sacred and monetary value may also coexist, as O'Guinn and Belk (1989) discovered in their analysis of Heritage Village, USA. Indeed, '[t]he admixture of the religious and the commercial in this religious theme park defies any axiomatic belief that the sacred and the secular represent distinct and non-overlapping spheres' (p. 227).

Johnny Yells and Neil McGraw clearly inhabit opposite ends of the sacred–profane spectrum. Indeed, Hirschman (1988: 348) could have had Johnny in mind when she described how secular consumers sought products as ends in themselves, obtaining these by acts of treachery, deceit and betrayal. In pursuit of fame and fortune, Johnny betrays his partner and plunders his father's death and his own near-death experience. Furthermore, he appropriates a sacred image for a campaign that trades in people's greatest fears. As Belk *et al.* observe:

> Because mixing the sacred with the profane threatens to destroy the sacred, advertising is often seen as threat, having the potential to trivialize the sacred by its copresence . . . With religion, as with art, advertising threatens to banish the ecstasy achieved in formerly sacred contexts. The other threat is

that commodities seek to appropriate the sacredness of royalty, art or religion through contamination. This appears to be the concern of critics . . . who find it offensive that advertising should feature art masterpieces or religious figures.

(Belk *et al.* 1989: 25)

However, as Hirschman notes, there is a spiritual price to pay for such actions: secular consumers 'were typically lonely, unloved, envied, and distrusted by others . . . unable to form or to maintain family relationships and friendships' (1988: 348). Johnny may have a girlfriend, but the relationship does not appear strong; he is a protegé, a competitor, or an acquaintance rather than a friend to others. As he is tormented by the spectre of nothingness, no one he knows is prepared to discuss questions of life and death with him, and he becomes increasingly withdrawn and alienated. Although the novel ends with Johnny still surrounded by the trappings of success, there is also a sense that he is destined for a further breakdown.

Neil McGraw, on the other hand, embodies the virtues of the sacred consumer described by Hirschman:

Sacred consumers displayed little interest in acquiring technologically produced material goods. They were not fashion conscious; they did not seek or use products in a competitive manner. Typically, they were engaged in some form of productive activity that connected them to the earth or to some other natural resource. When faced with a choice, they consistently declined the pursuit of monetary gain in favour of family nurturance, friendship, loyalty, or honesty. As a result, they were trusted by others, they had a supportive network of friends and/or family members.

(Hirschman 1988: 348)

Thus, Neil eschews the production-line of large funeral corporations for handcrafted coffins and customised funeral ceremonies. Disregarding competition and profits, Neil and his team seek to provide support for dying and bereaved members of their community. We see his nurturing nature in the tender care he shows in preparing his own father's body for burial, and this spirit is reflected in Lila's actions as she takes over the funeral of the young man who died of AIDS. In contrast to Johnny, Neil is surrounded and nurtured by friends; he is not isolated in searching for answers to the question of what happens when we die, and when the time comes for him to die, it is seen not as a tragedy or a release, but as part of the mysterious but natural cycle of life itself.

Death accepted or death denied?

The concept of *kratophany* outlined by Belk *et al*. (1989) resonates with the debate in the thanatological literature concerning how we stand *vis-à-vis* our future demise. Although answers span the emotional spectrum – neglect, disdain, defiance, ignorance, longing, avoidance, dread, stoic acceptance – two camps may be identified, each proposing different characteristic responses to human mortality in contemporary life.

The first, and numerically the more prevalent, is broadly negative in character where death is either denied, dismissed, disbelieved in, avoided or ignored. Articulating the fundamental link between death, mortality, culture and consumption, Bauman notes that:

> There would probably be no culture were humans unaware of their mortality
> . . . Culture would be useless if not for the devouring need of forgetting;
> there would be no transcending were there nothing to be transcended . . .
> Thus, the constant risk of death – the risk always knowable even if flushed
> down to the murky depths of the subconscious – is arguably, the very founda-
> tion of culture.
>
> (Bauman 1992: 31)

For Aries (1974, 1981) we live in an epoch of death denied. Following the Victorian crusade against dust, odours and bodily excreta we have inherited a loathing for death and dying and a distaste for their physical concomitants. Modesty forbids death being spoken of, particularly to those who are dying. The stark trauma of death has been expunged from the vocabulary of mourning; euphemism reigns supreme. Dying has been deported, handed over to medical bureaucracy. Death too has been sequestered and privatised; funerals rarely disrupt the ebb and flow of economic and social life.

A common theme among authors subscribing to the view that death has been sequestered and concealed is the 'pornography of death'. First coined by Gorer (1965), it is the logical outcome of a process whereby death itself has been expunged from social discourse, dying has been institutionalised and the moribund moved to a marginal social orbit. This social exclusion of the topic confers a taboo status and thereby renders it suitable material for the joker and the prurient. This pornographic dividend of death can be either furtively savoured through horror films or self-righteously condemned via protestations at the levels of explicit violence on television programmes (Gorer 1965). On a related point, Moller (1996) notes how a certain genre of Hollywood blockbuster either deliberately or inadvertently abets the denial of death agenda by pushing popular cultural images that make death and dying unreal.

The second group of thanatologists mentioned above *is* characterised by the view that the denial–avoidance trait in contemporary Western society is at best overstated. Certainly, there are several alternative explanations for the apparent sequestration of death. At one level demographic trends may not have been fully appreciated. The increase in life expectancy means that more people die older having enjoyed a full demographic life, siblings and peers may have pre-deceased them; they are likely to have left mainstream economic and social life behind. As a result, their passing on is likely to be more sequestered (Badham and Ballard 1996; Walter 1991). The advent of AIDS, coupled with the fame of some celebrities living with the HIV virus, has done much to resurrect and rehabilitate death as an acceptable subject for social discourse (Davies 1996; Zagor 1992). It could also be the case that what was formerly seen as denial of death was in fact an aversion and distaste for concomitants of contemporary death – loneliness, meaninglessness, disability and dependency (Moller 1996). There may also be a crucial difference between devaluing death and denying it. 'Like the skid row bum, who exists physically but whose human worth is devalued and disregarded, the phenomenon of dying is not obliterated. Instead, the social status of dying persons is diminished' (1996: 22).

In a more upbeat tone, Seale (1998) challenges the thesis that modern societies are death denying, since social organisation for death in late modernity is remarkably active, realistic and death accepting. Modernist medicine, through the activities of certifying doctors, pathologists, coroners, social statisticians and health educators, ensures that an awareness of the risks of death permeates modern consciousness and governmentality (Seale 1998: 99). He also distinguishes between the psychological denial of death and the sociological sequestration of death by public and caring professions. The thesis that death is denied is a more tenable explanation at the psychological level, however, for Seale it can be argued that such denial is an essential precondition for our own survival. 'If we were to be constantly preoccupied with thoughts of our own death, participation in society and culture would lose all meaning' (1998: 70).

Johnny Yells appears to be consumed by kratophany. Using others' fear of death for his own commercial purposes and steeped in a materialistic existence, he becomes obsessed by the question of what happens after death and terrified by the void he anticipates. Neil McGraw seeks to mitigate rather than capitalise on people's fear and pain of death. His thanatological taste for bad jokes and worse puns is not pornographic in Gorer's sense, but reflects his curiosity and acceptance of death as a sad but inevitable part of life. Like Johnny, Neil is constantly asking what happens when we die, but unlike Johnny, he has the spiritual capital to engage with and embrace death.

Advertising and the double dialectic of death

Advertising, the 'literature of consumption' (Scott 1994), communicates much more than the benefits of products or services (Leiss *et al.* 1990; Williamson 1978). As Twitchell observes:

> Although advertising cannot create desire, it can channel it. And what is drawn down that channel, what travels with the commercial, is our culture . . . what is carried in and with advertising is what we know, what we share, what we believe in. It is who we are. It is us.
>
> (Twitchell 1996: 4)

As McCracken (1987) and reader-response theory (Scott 1994) remind us, however, consumers are the 'final authors' of advertising; we actively negotiate the meaning of ads in the context of our own life themes, life projects and our historical, social and cultural contexts (Mick and Buhl 1992). This brings us into the realm which Holbrook terms 'consumer aesthetics', the study of:

> consumers' appreciative responses to artworks, to entertainment, to advertising, to the media, or to other products that provide aesthetic experiences ranging in intensity from the simplest hedonic pleasure to the most profound ecstatic rapture . . . As some of the most compelling human experiences, they deserve the most dedicated investigation from a variety of methodological perspectives.
>
> (Holbrook 1995: 11)

This suggests that advertising is implicated in the ways that our culture speaks to itself about death and dying. Consistent with this view, Hirschman and Holbrook wonder whether 'the use of death in films and ads may help purge anxieties regarding death and dying or alternatively, desensitise consumers of their fear of death' (1982: 96). We may then ask how (or whether) advertising comports itself in this area, and how consumers respond. Does advertising heighten, assuage or ignore our fear of death? And in its dealings with death, where are the boundaries between the sacred, the profane and the sacrilegious?

Zagor suggests that the advertising world has recently 'lifted the veil from the last taboo of the late 20th century and started exploring the use of death, or at least mortality, as a messenger' (1992: 17). Certainly, dead celebrities have haunted commercial breaks for more than a decade. Zagor notes that this trend may have begun in 1986 with Yul Brynner's endorsement of the American Cancer Society. Recorded for use after his death from cancer, his message was 'Now that I'm gone, I tell you, don't smoke – whatever you do, just don't smoke'. Within the advertising industry, it has been suggested that there is a trend away from 'fluff and peripheral imagery and towards more substance and reality', which may lead to greater acceptability of death-related themes (Zagor 1992). An alternative and less worthy explanation is offered by Falk (1997). He argues that the pursuit of more powerful imagery and effects in advertising may be linked to the need to rise above the clutter from competing brands and the broader mediascape of films, television programmes and so on.

Recent uses of death imagery in advertising

It is hardly surprising that campaigns related to drink-driving, cancer or life insurance have alluded to or depicted death. However, themes relating to death and dying have also been used in ads for charities, cigarettes, clothes and telephone services. An Advertising Standards Authority (ASA) report identified 'three no-go areas for advertisers: death, religion and bad language' (ASA 1996: 1). It may be, however, that death in itself is not taboo, but that the focus and intention of ads dealing with mortality will be subject to careful public scrutiny. Indeed, The Independent Television Commission (ITC) has warned advertisers that:

> while viewers often accept emotionally disturbing material if it is in advertising for charities or for public health and safety issues, they are generally not as tolerant of its use in advertising which has commercial objectives, where it is more likely to be regarded as gratuitous.
>
> (ITC 1997: 9)

How, then, do advertisers represent death, dying and bereavement? Some have depicted skeletons alongside products to 'demonstrate' the longevity or indestructible nature of the latter; the award-winning Kadu shorts ad is a case in point (Falk 1997). A recent campaign for a NatWest account used the strap line 'After all, YOU ONLY LIVE ONCE', and various ads depicted memorials to people who had died without fulfilling their dreams. One, for example, featured a park bench bearing a plaque declaring it to be 'In loving memory of Gary Tapp, who passed into the next world really cheesed off he hadn't seen more of this one'. This ad can hardly be accused of denying death. Neither does it particularly encourage fear of death, marrying *memento mori* with *carpe diem*. Its treatment of death inhabits the profane end of the spectrum, both in its use of colloquialisms (the dead are not usually described as 'really cheesed off' about anything) and in the implication that the dreams not fulfilled could have been bought with money.

Other advertisers proclaim more serious and lofty intentions in their depictions of death. One BT ad, for example, shows a solemn little boy in dark clothes, perhaps his school uniform. He is standing in the open air; the background is blurred but suggests a cemetery. A black-clad adult's hand on his head and the arm of another adult, similarly attired, are also in the picture. 'A death in the family is always hard', the telecommunications company advises, but 'it's even harder when you don't understand what death is'. The link between this scenario and BT lies in the company's support for projects 'where better communication can help solve people's problems', such as Winston's Wish, a charity that seeks to help bereaved children. This is not an ad about defiance or denial of death but rather seeks to communicate BT's appreciation of the sacred nature of death and the company's nurturing nature, helping children to accept and cope with the death of people they loved.

The most famous examples of death tamed in the service of branding come from Benetton, a company not known for treading lightly on the sacred. Oliverio Toscani, art director for Benetton's advertising campaigns and editorial director for *Colors*, a Benetton magazine, recently devoted an entire issue of the magazine to death. His rationale for this was that 'death is something that everyone has to do but nobody ever mentions it . . . Death is probably the last pornographic issue left' (O'Reilly 1998: 10). Notorious for ads that have attached the brand's logo to news pictures of devastation, Benetton has included in its campaigns images of war graves, a dead soldier's bloody clothes, an electric chair and a murder victim. It has also shown a picture of AIDS victim David Kirby on his deathbed. Although 'catastrophe aesthetics' existed in the news media before being transferred to advertising, Falk (1997) suggests that the 'Benetton–Toscani effect' has led to a broader range of advertising representations, incorporating new ways of using the negative register in advertising discourse, and a secondary circulation of ads in the media, as their appropriateness is debated.

The David Kirby ad offers an excellent example of commodities seeking 'to appropriate the sacredness of royalty, art or religion through contamination' (Belk *et al.* 1989: 25); indeed Toscani (1998) even refers to it as his 'Pieta'. The ad shows David Kirby close to the point of death, surrounded by distraught family or friends, including a woman trying to comfort a distressed child. When Benetton used the ad in Britain, the Advertising Standards Authority received two complaints. Judging it to be in breach of the British Codes of Advertising and Sales Promotion, the ASA 'deplored the advertisers' apparent willingness to provoke distress with their advertising approach' (1992: 9). In April 1994, 133 complaints against Benetton were received for its ad showing the army fatigues and blood-stained T-shirt with a bullet hole belonging to Marinko Gagro, a soldier killed during the conflict in the former Yugoslavia. Complainants saw the ad as exploitative, cynical and offensive, and the ASA 'considered that the advertisements had caused grave and widespread offence and deprecated the advertisers' failure to recognise people's objections to such depictions' (1994: 7).

Undeterred by such responses, Benetton has recently launched another campaign confronting consumers with stark representations of death. The ads feature photographs of Death Row inmates with 'SENTENCED TO DIE' stamped over the images. The photographs, taken by Toscani over a period of two years, also form the centrepiece of the company's recent catalogue. Benetton claims that the ads are '*about* capital punishment' and 'aim at giving back a human face to the prisoners on death row' (Benetton 2000: 1). The company sees itself as tearing down walls of indifference, raising awareness of universal problems and paving the way for innovative modes of corporate communication. Many do not share Benetton's rosy view of itself, believing that Benetton desacralises and desingularises images of death and devastation by employing them to sell knitwear (Kerrigan 2000). For some, however, the current campaign has given Benetton's critics pause for thought. Garfield for one characterised previous Benetton campaigns as 'an assault on the sensibilities of unsuspecting readers, who have no expectation to be confronted with human tragedy by the ready-to-wear industry', but finds the current ads 'too powerful and provocative to be summarily dismissed' (Garfield 2000: 1).

Death themes in advertising: a study of ASA complaints

Our concern with representations of death, dying and bereavement in advertising, and the tensions between approach and avoidance, sacred and profane, led us to examine Monthly Reports from the Advertising Standards Authority. The ASA administers the British Codes of Advertising and Sales Promotion, investigating press, poster and cinema ads, direct marketing and sales promotion material that appear to be in breach of the codes. Although the ITC also compiles monthly reports on advertising complaints, this involves a much smaller number of ads. This, together with space constraints, led us to focus on ASA reports here.

We read each ASA Monthly Report since January 1995, examining every case that referred to death, dying or bereavement in any way. This material is a rich source of information on problematic advertising content and public response to this, but there are several limitations to the data that should be borne in mind. The reports do not include complaints that were not deemed worthy of investigation, so there could have been other complaints involving the use of death-related themes other than those reported by the ASA. There may also be some under-representation of the number of complaints made about particular ads, since those received after the adjudication has been published are not detailed. Finally, if they have appeared at the same time, different ads within a campaign are combined within the one case report, and the number of complaints is not broken down by the ads involved. None the less, this examination yielded a sample of 113 cases where a complaint had been made about an ad on a death-related theme.

Analysis of complaints

Since January 1995, a total of 858 complaints have been recorded against 113 death-related ads or campaigns. Looking through the reports, six main categories of advertiser seemed to be associated with death-related themes. *Animal groups* included organisations such as the League Against Cruel Sports, the International Fund for Animal Welfare, various anti-vivisection groups and The Vegetarian Society. These organisations typically made claims regarding numbers of animals killed for commercial, sporting or research purposes. They often described in graphic detail how animals were killed, and pictures frequently accompanied the text. *Other groups* refers to non-profit groups whose concerns are unrelated to animals, such as the British Diabetic Association; it also includes Government departments, such as the Department of Health. The *Financial services* category is self-explanatory, as is *Funeral etc.* except that this grouping includes will-making and monument services. One board-game is included in the *Games* category, but the remainder relate to computer or playstation games. Included in *Media and cultural* are ads for magazines, films, television programmes, music and cultural or tourist attractions such as Madame Tussaud's. The *Other* category covers various commercial products and services, ranging from recruitment services to jeans and pagers. The breakdown of ads and complaints by category of advertiser is presented in Table 5.1.

The first point to note here is that complaints about death-related themes and images represents a minuscule proportion of complaints to the ASA each year; in 1998, for example, the ASA received 12,217 complaints (ASA 1999). This suggests that advertisers rarely venture into this sacred territory, and/or that they touch upon it with great sensitivity. This does not mean that such complaints deserve to be dismissed; on the contrary, they allow us to observe how the powerful tensions discussed above are played out in the marketplace. Several patterns of interest emerge from our analysis. Looking at the totals column for each year, we see that the number of death-related ads complained about has been quite stable over the period examined, with a relatively sharp increase in 1999. It will be interesting to see whether this indicates rising concerns about such

Table 5.1 Number of death-related ads (and complaints) * 1995–9 by category of advertiser

	Animal groups	Other groups	Financial services	Funeral etc.	Games	Media, cultural	Other	Total
1995	5 (381)	3 (5)	2 (4)	5 (5)	–	4 (18)	4 (6)	23 (419)
1996	5 (11)	5 (7)	–	1 (1)	4 (52)	2 (2)	3 (13)	20 (86)
1997	1 (4)	5 (149)	–	4 (5)	4 (7)	1 (1)	5 (6)	20 (172)
1998	6 (28)	3 (5)	1 (1)	7 (8)	1 (13)	1 (1)	2 (4)	21 (60)
1999	6 (28)	6 (34)	1 (2)	3 (3)	3 (15)	2 (7)	8 (32)	29 (121)
Total	23 (452)	22 (200)	4 (7)	20 (22)	12 (87)	10 (29)	22 (61)	113 (858)

* Figures in parentheses refer to number of complaints rather than number of ads complained about.

portrayals and references, or whether 1999 was exceptional. The number of complaints has fluctuated dramatically over the five years, indicating the impact that a few particularly controversial ads – or an energised lobbying group – can have. Looking at the categories of advertiser, ads from animal groups account for the greatest number of ads and complaints. Animal groups' ads attracted over half of all complaints, and were the largest category of ads complained about. Although there does not appear to be a great difference in the number of ads between animal groups and several other categories, it should be pointed out that it is in the animal groups category that the number of ads is understated; two cases here consisted of multiple death-related ads combined into the one case report.

At first glance, the high number of complaints recorded concerning ads showing the death of animals appears to fit the stereotype of animal-loving Britons. The nature of the complaints received in this category does not support this interpretation, however. Some distress and offence were registered at representations of animal suffering, but the overwhelming majority of complaints disputed advertising claims concerning the nature and number of animal deaths, and may have come from individuals associated with particular interest groups. For example, an advertising campaign from the RSPCA calling for support for the Wild Mammals Protection Bill met with 98 complaints, and ads on a similar theme from the International Fund for Animal Welfare attracted 271 complaints.

Other groups appeared to be responsible for the next most problematic category of ads. Again, the figures are slightly distorted by the 1997 Gun Control Network campaign. This campaign features on two separate occasions in the ASA reports, and one of those cases combines two different ads. A total of 93 complaints were registered against the two press ads in June 1997, and another 56 against a cinema ad in July. In the wake of the Dunblane massacre, the Gun Control Network was seeking a ban on all handguns, a position – and advertising campaign – contested vigorously by those who enjoyed target shooting as a sport. Other cases in this category include ads from Amnesty International and Baby Milk Action; here complaints tended not to reflect distress at accounts of death related to commercial or political matters, but often challenged particular claims, such as those concerning the numbers of deaths. Several charity ads, however, focused on specific causes and risks of mortality. Action Research, for example, mailed new and expectant mothers with a leaflet highlighting the incidence of cot death and meningitis. An ad from the Cancer Research Campaign asked people to 'Help save a life. There's a one in five chance it'll be yours.' Complaints about ads like these were a mixture of disputed claims and concerns about unwarranted fear appeals used to raise funds. Complaints against one ad, however, seemed to fit with the denial of death thesis. A 1999 ad for Help the Aged was headed 'Thousands of elderly people will stop feeling the cold this winter'. The ad showed six pairs of feet, wearing death tags indicating causes like pneumonia, hypothermia and bronchitis. There were seven complaints registered against the ad, and these reported that the references to death were 'offensive' and 'frightening'. The ASA upheld complaints about two ads in the *Other groups* category, and partly upheld seven more.

At first sight, complaints in the *Funeral etc.* category might indicate that denial of death is alive and well, or that the sacred nature of death gives grieving relatives a very narrow latitude of acceptance of how undertakers promote their services. These explanations are not supported by the data, however: of the 22 complaints received, 19 were from funeral directors challenging their competitors' claims regarding costs, endorsement or ownership. Only one complaint referred to distress, which was hardly surprising since it concerned the use in a promotional brochure of a particular headstone, without the family's knowledge or permission – an act of desecration worthy of Johnny Yells himself. The ASA upheld complaints against 15 of the 20 ads in this category, and partly upheld one more. The impression from these cases, then, is not of a perturbed or death-denying public, but of an industry keeping a watchful eye on its own activities.

The relatively high number of complaints attracted by ads for computer and playstation games is not surprising given the high body count and gore factor in the games themselves. An ad for a game called *Gender Wars*, for example, was headlined 'How many women have you shot up today?' It featured a drawing of a man wearing a helmet and visor, and holding a smoking gun, in front of a pile of women's bodies. Ads for *Blade Runner* showed a photograph of a woman slumped across the base of a pillar, apparently in a cemetery, with the headline 'I stared death in the face. Yup, she was dead.' Many of the games had been advertised in computing and games magazines, but a few (like the *Blade Runner* ad) had used the much less targeted poster medium. Given the murder and mayhem depicted in the ads, it should not be surprising that all complaints about these ads were upheld.

The murder and mayhem theme was also dominant in the *Media and cultural* category, but the ads here tended not to be restricted to specialist media. An example in this category was a poster for Madame Tussaud's that showed wax-works of four bleeding, decapitated heads on poles. The accompanying text read 'Heads of state, heads of Parliament, and . . . er . . . heads'. All except one ad (for the television series *The Bill*) had the complaints against them upheld. Turning to the very small number of *Financial services* ads, these tended to talk most directly about the causes and risks of mortality. As was the case with some charity ads, complaints here tended to be based on disputed claims, and/or concern about unwarranted fear appeals. For example, a 1999 ad for a Norwich Union Healthcare income protection policy claimed that nearly one in three premature deaths amongst women in Britain are due to coronary heart disease. Two ads in this category (including this one) had complaints against them partly upheld.

Turning finally to miscellaneous advertisers – the *Other* category – we have noted already that this covers a range of goods and services. Some of these made quite tangential references to death, and one even hinged on the interpretation of the Latin phrase *usque ad mortem bibendum*. A complainant interpreted this as a reference to being permanently dead drunk, but the advertiser, Allied Domecq, reassured the ASA that it simply meant 'enjoy drinking until you die'. Other ads in this category were far more problematic, defiling sacred space and appropriating or perhaps parodying the pornography of death. A 1998 ad for Diesel Jeans showed a man sawing the hand off an arm. All around him were bodies and dismembered body parts, some of which were burning in a furnace; others were wrapped in black plastic and one was hanging from the ceiling. The ad claimed that Diesel jeans were suitable for 'labourers, clubbers, murderers, or anyone else who needs lots of odd shaped pockets'. Although the two complainants realised that the ad featured mannequins, they argued that parodying violent murders and the dismemberment of women was deeply offensive. In other cases, advertisers exploited specific cases of human distress for commercial ends. For example, a catalogue featured an ad for Black Flys sunglasses, in the form of a cartoon strip. The strip was headed 'People are dying to get their hands on Black Flys! A TRUE STORY'. The ad then went on to tell the story of a young man who stole a pair of the sunglasses and fell to his death while being pursued. Eleven complaints were received, including some from the dead man's family. A number of advertisers saw suicide as a scenario conducive to their commercial purposes. One case where a complaint was upheld was a magazine ad for Patrick Cox shoes, showing the legs and feet of a man apparently hanged from a tree. In another case, a psychiatrist's complaint that an ad offensively trivialised suicide was not upheld. That cinema ad for Shellys Shoes begins with black and white scenes of shoes in the act of suicide: shoes are shown stepping over the edge of a railway platform, over the top of a high building, or covered with pills. A voice-over informs the audience that 'it doesn't have to be like that', as the ad turns to colour. Coloured shoes are seen crowding around a graveside as a coffin is lowered into the ground, bearing the inscription 'RIP grey slip-ons size 9'.

The end

This overview of death's incarnations in one particular genre of marketing-related artefacts throws light on a number of issues. It lends support to the research focus that seeks to uncover symbolic meanings presented in cultural texts (Hirschman and Thompson 1997). The proliferation of accounts of 'the final things' in popular art forms attests to lively development and exchange of meanings relating to death-denied, death-defied, dying and the dead. It can also be said that the material discussed in this chapter offers further evidence of what Belk *et al.* (1989) term the 'sacralisation of the secular and the secularisation of the sacred', and the nexus of relationships between religion, culture and consumption

(O'Guinn and Belk 1989). These were central concerns in the two novels cited at the outset, *Way to Go* and *Jesus and the Adman*.

It was noted earlier that a key hallmark of the sacred identified by Belk *et al.* (1989) is *kratophany*, an approach–avoidance dialectic, 'an ambivalent reaction combining fascination and devotion with repulsion and fear'. Much of the material examined in this chapter illustrates this ambivalence in the context of the market-place. Whilst death is not yet a taboo-free topic, it does seem to be firmly established among advertising practitioners' thematic repertoires, sometimes deliberately employed in campaigns that are at best indirectly linked to mortality. At the same time, usage of specific death-related imagery is tentative and sporadic.

Holbrook calls for 'the most dedicated investigation from a variety of method-ological perspectives' (1995: 11) into consumers' responses to art, entertain-ment, advertising and other products providing aesthetic experiences. In keeping with Holbrook's injunction, the second half of this chapter began to explore consumers' responses to death-related themes and imagery in advertisements. Here, at the level of the consumer, ambivalence was once again in evidence. On one hand, a surprising finding was that many readers' reservations were unlikely to be based on distaste or disapproval of death itself; many of them seemed oblivious to explicit death-related elements in their determination to pursue political, cause-related or financial agendas. On the other hand, a significant num-ber of the responses examined above were, in Holbrook's terms, of the 'pro-found' variety. Clearly a sense of death's extraordinary and sacred character endures. Vestiges of its taboo status remain. The sensibilities of those recently touched by death require special attention. Children should be shielded from explicit portrayals; as with Dracula himself, the lid should come off only after dark. It is really an adult matter and needs to be rationed, as instanced by those who felt that decorum and death's otherworldly aura might be better preserved if its usage in advertising could be confined to the service of causes rather than commerce.

Clearly, representations of death, dying and bereavement in marketing dis-course merit further attention. This analysis focuses on contemporary British print advertising; the balance between sacred, sacrilegious and profane, and between denial, defiance and acceptance may vary according to the media, prod-uct categories, cultures and periods studied. The tensions discussed in this chapter may manifest themselves in other forms of marketing discourse. Given the sacredness and sensitivity of this area, consumers' readings of death-related ads deserve to be explored in more depth and detail than allowed by the ASA reports, which after all summarise complaints received from a self-selecting group. Debates within advertising agencies (and between agencies and clients) surround-ing the use of such imagery may also offer insights into the construction and consumption of death in the marketplace.

References

Advertising Standards Authority (1992) 'Benetton spa', *ASA Monthly Report* 11, April: 9.
—— (1994) 'Benetton spa', *ASA Monthly Report* 35, April: 7.
—— (1996) 'Drawing the line', *ASA Monthly Report* 63, August: 1.
—— (1999) 'Overview of 1998 and statistics', http://www.asa.org.uk
Ahmed, K. (1998) 'Funeral firm tries to ban TV expose', *The Guardian*, 12 May: 7.
Aries, P. (1974) *Western Attitudes Towards Death: From the Middle Ages to the Present*, Baltimore, MD: Johns Hopkins University Press.
—— (1981) *The Hour of Our Death* (trans. H. Weaver), London: Allen Lane.
Badham, P. and Ballard, P. (1996) 'Facing death: an introduction', in P. Badham and P. Ballard (eds) *Facing Death: An Interdisciplinary Approach*, Cardiff: University of Wales Press, 1–4.
Bauman, Z. (1992) *Mortality, Immortality and Other Life Strategies*, Oxford: Polity.
Belk, R. (1985) 'Materialism: trait aspects of living in the material world', *Journal of Consumer Research* 12, December: 265–80.
—— (1986) 'Art versus science as ways of generating knowledge about materialism', in D. Brindberg and R.J. Lutz (eds) *Perspectives on Methodology in Consumer Research*, New York: Springer-Verlag, 3–36.
—— and Pollay, R. (1985) 'Images of ourselves: the good life in twentieth century advertising', *Journal of Consumer Research* 11, March: 88–97.
——, Wallendorf, M. and Sherry, J. (1989) 'The sacred and the profane in consumer behavior: theodicy on the Odyssey', *Journal of Consumer Research* 16, June: 1–38.
Benetton (2000) 'Looking at death in the face', Press release, http://www.benetton.com, 1–2
Brook, R. (1998) *Jesus and the Adman*, London: Flamingo.
Brown, S. (1995) 'Sex 'n' shopping: a "novel" approach to consumer research', *Journal of Marketing Management* 11, 7: 681–706.
—— (1998) *Postmodern Marketing 2: Telling Tales*, London: International Thompson Business Press.
Cochrane, L. (1998) 'Doctors to study death and illness in literature', *The Scotsman*, 3 June: 8.
Davies, D. (1996) 'The social facts of death', in G. Howarth and P.C. Jupp (eds) *Contemporary Issues in the Sociology of Death, Dying and Disposal*, London: Macmillan, 17–29.
Falk, P. (1997), 'The Benetton–Toscani effect: testing the limits of conventional advertising', in M. Nava, A. Blake, I. MacRury and B. Richards (eds) *Buy this Book: Studies in Advertising and Consumption*, London: Routledge, 64–83.
Garfield, B. (2000) 'The colors of exploitation: Benetton on Death Row', *Advertising Age*, http://www.adage.com/news_and_features, 1–2.
Gorer, G. (1965) *Death, Grief, Mourning in Contemporary Britain*, London: Cresset.
Hirschman, E. (1987) 'Movies as myths: an interpretation of motion picture mythology', in J. Umiker-Sebeok (ed.) *Marketing and Semiotics: New Directions in the Study of Signs for Sale*, Berlin: Mouton de Gruyter.
—— (1988) 'The ideology of consumption: a structural-syntactical analysis of *Dallas* and *Dynasty*', *Journal of Consumer Research* 15, December: 344–59.

—— (1990) 'Secular immortality and the American ideology of affluence', *Journal of Consumer Research* 17, June: 31–42.

—— and Holbrook, M.B. (1982) 'Hedonic consumption: emerging concepts, methods and propositions', *Journal of Marketing* 46, Summer: 92–101.

—— and Thompson C.J. (1997) 'Why media matter: toward a richer understanding of consumers' relationships with advertising and mass media', *Journal of Advertising* 26, 1: 43–60.

Holbrook, M. (1995) *Consumer Research: Introspective Essays on the Study of Consumption*, Thousand Oaks: Sage

Holbrook, M. and Grayson, M. (1986) 'The semiology of cinematic consumption: symbolic consumer behavior in *Out of Africa*', *Journal of Consumer Research* 13, December: 374–81.

Independent Television Commission (1997) 'Volkswagen Polo', *Television Advertising Complaints Report*, June: 9.

Kerrigan, M. (2000) 'Death Row adverts could put Benetton in the frame', *The Scotsman*, 28 January: 2.

Leiss, W., Kline, S. and Jhally, S. (1990) *Social Communication in Advertising*, London: Routledge.

McCracken, G. (1987) 'Advertising: meaning or information?', in M. Wallendorf and P. Anderson (eds) *Advances in Consumer Research*, 14, Provo, UT: Association for Consumer Research, 121–4.

Mick, D. and Buhl, C. (1992) 'A meaning-based model of advertising experiences', *Journal of Consumer Research* 19, December: 317–38.

Mitford, J. (1963) *The American Way of Death*, London: Hutchinson.

—— (1998) *The American Way of Death Revisited*, London: Virago Press.

Moller, D.W. (1996) *Confronting Death: Values, Institutions and Human Mortality*, New York: Oxford University Press.

O'Guinn, T. and Belk, R. (1989) 'Heaven on earth: consumption at Heritage Village, USA', *Journal of Consumer Research* 16, December: 227–38.

O'Reilly, J. (1998) 'Death is probably the last pornographic issue left', *Media Guardian*, 2 February: 10–11.

Scott, L. (1994) 'The bridge from text to mind: adapting reader-response theory to consumer research', *Journal of Consumer Research* 21, December: 461–80.

Seale, C. (1998) *Constructing Death: The Sociology of Dying and Bereavement*, Cambridge: Cambridge University Press.

Secretan, T.(1995) *Going Into Darkness: Fantastic Coffins from Africa*, London: Thames & Hudson.

Spence, A. (1998) *Way to Go*, London: Phoenix.

Stern, B. (1989) 'Literary criticism and consumer research: overview and illustrative analysis', *Journal of Consumer Research* 16, December: 322–34.

Toscani, O. (1998) 'Toscani on advertising', http://www.benetton.com

Turley, D. (1997), 'A postcard from the very edge: mortality and marketing', in S. Brown and D. Turley (eds) *Consumer Research: Postcards From the Edge*, London: Routledge, 350–77.

Twitchell, J. (1996) *Adcult USA*, New York: Columbia University Press.

Walter, T. (1991) 'Modern death – taboo or not taboo?', *Sociology* 25, 2: 293–310.
Waugh, E. (1948) *The Loved One*, London: Chapman Hall.
Williamson, J. (1978) *Decoding Advertisements*, London: Marion Boyar.
Zagor, K. (1992) 'Death as a salesman', *Financial Times*, 30 April: 17.

6 'Trust no one': science fiction and marketing's future/present

Warren Smith and Matthew Higgins

Introduction

Science fiction seems to stir up some extreme reactions. On the one hand dismissed as cultural trash produced for purely commercial gain and consumed by dreadful obsessives terminally disengaged from 'serious' concerns. On the other, a genre that usefully offers scientific extrapolation and social criticism. Hence we find a self-satisfied distancing from the vulgarity of mass consumption contrasted with an over-earnest maintenance of a 'methodology' that produces prediction and/or critique.

In this chapter, we argue that marketing is not mere 'subject matter' for science fiction, something that science fiction has periodically addressed, usually by attacking its wanton and socially destructive materialism. Marketing and science fiction, we argue, has an implicate relationship. Most obviously the demands and opportunities of commerce were, and continue to be, significant in the development of the genre. Indeed the relationship between reality and its literary representation is not uni-directional. There are some well-known examples of this complicity that illustrate how science fiction has impacted upon actual technological change. We are all familiar with Arthur C. Clarke's conceptualisation of the geo-stationary satellite, an idea that he regrets not having patented. It has also been argued that mobile phones were inspired by *Star Trek's* communicators. Ronald Reagan's short-lived outer-space laser defence system was dubbed *Star Wars* and the associated imagery, drawn from a film where a clean-cut Western hero triumphed against the forces of an evil empire, was helpful in mobilising support (Davies 1990: 1). In the late 1970s, Sperry Univac, a large IT company, sponsored a series of seminars exploring the potential social consequences of contemporary science fiction. It fell to John Pascoe of Sperry UK to write a foreword to the published proceedings. He explains that Sperry's interest in the project was prompted by business considerations:

A clue is found in the description of our activity. We live and work in a technology that changes at a very rapid rate, a rate unique in the history of all technologies, and one that may to the outsider sometimes seem frightening. Between twenty and forty per cent a year improvement in performance for the same price – the industry refers to this as the price/performance ratio – is the historic norm since the industry began in the early fifties and no end is in sight. Our own computers today are probably half the size and cost of their predecessors of as short a time as three years ago. Had this rate of technological advance, of improvement in the price performance ratio been matched in the aircraft industry over the last thirty years, you would by now be able to cross the Atlantic in seconds for less than the price of a packet of cigarettes. At this point our interest in science fiction and its relation to reality might become a little clearer, for some aspects of the science fiction future are for us no more than our tomorrow.

(Malik 1980: vi–vii)

John Pascoe was the *marketing* director of Sperry UK at the time. Here we have science fiction as a tool for new product development.

We want to suggest that science fiction is not simply a literary genre that comments upon the future/present. Although we open the chapter with a review of what might be called *reflectionist* engagements by science fiction with marketing, this provides a point of opposition. Our motivation in writing about marketing and science fiction is not simply to draw attention to a useful 'resource' that we can then interrogate for meaningful messages. We seek not merely to draw attention to these parallels, but to begin to unsettle the positions that produce them. In this attempt we allow ourselves to draw one comparison; that the extreme characterisations with which we opened this chapter, a self-satisfied distancing from the vulgarity of mass consumption opposed by an over-earnest maintenance of a 'methodology' that produces prediction and/or critique, can also be seen within contemporary debates in marketing. We argue that much contemporary science fiction has a disturbing effect, that it increasingly threatens (without entirely dissolving) the boundaries that made its *reflectionist* commentaries possible. We value science fiction's engagement with marketing not because it offers support for a particular position, but because it disturbs *in toto*. However, we do not see ourselves entirely moorless in this environment. With reference to a process of 'alien-ation' found in science fiction, we suggest that we are drawn to contemplate the boundaries produced by its disturbances. A purely detached, coolly critical position is impossible. But this does not mean that we are passively beguiled.

Let us begin, however, by considering some conventional accounts of marketing in science fiction.

Science fiction on marketing

For Isaac Asimov (1971: 285) science fiction offers a mode of thought to question and imagine change, 'We've got to think about the future now. For the first time in history, the future cannot be left to take care of itself; it must be thought about.' His work was therefore a form of 'social science fiction', a means to speculate, extrapolate and moralise over the effects of technological, political and sociological change. Indeed for those who had not appreciated its serious intent, critical texts have been produced that direct us to its pedagogic value. Both Greenberg *et al.* (1975) and Ofshe (1977) are collections of science fiction stories for sociology students to be used to sharpen social awareness via comprehension and discussion exercises.

Such 'purposeful' science fiction is therefore a forum where alternative realities are presented that reflect the social trends and preoccupations of the time. The assumption is that science fiction produces evidence that can be read as critiques of contemporary society and its possible future directions. These readings are, according to Kuhn (1990), both sociological and psychological in nature. By revealing these preoccupations science fiction, in *reflectionist* mode, captures the cultural moment. The classic example is the association of 1950s science fiction cinema with the Communist threat. Thus both *Invasion of the Body Snatchers* (1956) and *The Thing from Another World* (1951) were seen to mirror the perceived dangers of the Red Menace. Where such lessons cannot be directly 'read off' the film's symbolism, Kuhn (1990) sees science fiction as reflecting the largely repressed mental states shared across societies. Consequently the *Godzilla* cycle of films in Japan are interpreted as expressions of subconscious fears of the consequences of the nuclear bomb. Similarly Tarrat (1977) argues that aliens and extraterrestrial forces are actually externalisations of civilisation's conflict with the drives and sexual desires of the primitive unconscious. Therefore under a reflectionist interpretation, whether concerned with sociological critiques or repressed psychological desires, science fiction is a representation of reality. Its value lies in the messages that it produces.

There are many examples of science fiction having something (usually critical) to say about marketing. Perhaps the most famous example is Pohl and Kornbluth's (1953) *The Space Merchants*. Here advertising agencies have taken over many of the roles of government, and advertising executives are the elite of society. However, the hero, Mitchell Courtney, an estranged ad-man, begins to understand the error of his former ways. Realising the disastrous ecological consequences of materialistic values, he joins an underground conservation movement, which attempts to expose the manipulations of the agencies. Finally driven out, the rebels establish an anti-advertising society on Venus.

The Space Merchants was strongly influenced by styles of advertising of the time. Designed to ensure product recall, commodities were represented via jingles based on a logic of memorisation and recall. These slogans were repeated over and over again (Goldman and Papson 1994). The fear of subliminal messages and the role of marketing in creating false needs was a key theme. This critique was developed in Frederick Pohl's (Kornbluth had long since died) somewhat belated sequel. In case readers missed its critical intent *The Merchants' War* (1984) was puffed via its social message, 'A new look at the advertising culture . . . *The Merchants' War* may not silence the snake oil merchants in our society, but it may reduce the number of people willing to swallow their potions' (excerpt from Newsday review, St Martin's Press edition, 1984). And indeed, whilst *The Merchants' War* returns to many of the preoccupations of *The Space Merchants* it also reflects some contemporary developments in marketing technique. In the sequel an un-materialistic Venus is contrasted with an Earth increasingly segmented according to consumer/economic category. Those few areas as yet uncolonised by the agencies are subjected to a technology of persuasion that uses light, sound and smell to create a seductive spectacle that encourages consumption.

The plot centres on Tarb and Mitzi, two Earth diplomats seconded from their advertising agencies to maintain relations with Venus but actually charged with surreptitiously undermining the Veenie cause. However, the Veenies become aware of their underground activities, kidnap Mitzi and replace her with a body double. Returning to Earth and their advertising posts, Tarb quickly becomes a victim of a competing advertising agency's 'unethical' new product – *Mokie Koke*. A thinly veiled reference to *Coca-Cola*, *Mokie Koke* is instantly addictive. Tarb's addiction leads to a rapid fall from grace in the corporate world. In contrast, Mitzi's double becomes a stockholder in the agency. Conspiring with a fellow Veenie sympathiser, the advertising agency's share price is inflated allowing Mitzi to sell out and establish a new advertising agency. This enables the Veenies to use the same technologies of persuasion to generate sympathy for their cause.

The Space Merchants and its sequel are excellent examples of individual novels that criticise marketing and its methods. However, it was with the rise of the 'New Wave' that the estrangement between science fiction, marketing and the wider corporate world became a defining theme. The 'New Wave' consisted of a body of largely European writers who were profoundly cynical of the potential of science and technology to provide a better society. Accordingly science fiction became less preoccupied with technologically assisted prophecies. Instead it turned inwards; technology was no longer something directed towards the stars.

Initially 'New Wave' writers worked to protect reason from the perversions of materialism, to preserve the prospect of humanistic emancipation. Soon, however, they lost faith in this possibility and resigned themselves to plotting the course of its fateful assimilation. Reason, science and technology were found to be irrevocably subservient to the interests of monopoly capitalism (Jordin 1984). 'New Wave' science fiction therefore became a liberal critique of the experience of individuals within capitalist society. J.G. Ballard, a leading light of the 'New

Wave', produced a number of stories portraying the consumerism of a decadent future/present. Ballard's (1973) short story *The Subliminal Man* is perhaps his most notable attack on the consequences of unfettered marketing. Anticipating the sprawling megalopolis that a decade later became synonymous with Ridley Scott's *Blade Runner*, *The Subliminal Man* is set in a society of huge motorways linking massive commercial centres. At each intersection hotels, shopping malls and huge car parks dominate the skyline.

The story revolves around Franklin, a local doctor who is harassed by one of his psychotic patients, Hathaway. Hathaway is certain that new gigantic signs being erected on the freeway are a medium for subliminal messages. However, Hathaway's predilection for conspiracy theories makes Franklin sceptical. Franklin enjoyed all the trappings of consumerism but was beginning to reflect upon their meaning. He was forced to work during his weekends on private consultancy to help pay for the house that was heavily re-mortgaged. Credit bills for holidays and consumer gadgets were a constant drain on his income. The only time Franklin had to himself was the drive to and from work. Even here he did not escape the clutches of materialism. Obsolescence was built into the structure of society. The motorways were covered with a mesh of small rubber studs. These studs allowed smooth driving at precise speeds of 40 mph, 50 mph, 60 mph and 70 mph. When they wore out they were replaced with new studs that had been designed only to be effective with the latest tyre designs. Driving at intermediate speeds caused the chassis to shake leading to mechanical damage. Franklin had replaced his car only three months after buying it; since it was cheaper to trade in than begin to pay the maintenance costs.

One day, driving along the motorway and encountering the huge signs, Franklin remembered Hathaway's warnings. The signs were indeed enormous, though they contained no message. Their purpose was unclear – it was generally believed that they were a technology to assist the airport. Returning home, Franklin finds his wife sprawled in front of the television. Although there were four television channels, the programmes were the same, only the advertisements differed. All telephone conversations were free, however the calls were interrupted by a commercial break. The ratio of free speech to advertising was dependent on the distance of the call. Franklin's wife was watching *Spot Bargains* a programme that listed the offers in local shops. The supermarkets never closed and shoppers, like anxious stockbrokers, darted from one supermarket to another to take advantage of the ever-changing prices. Supermarkets further reinforced consumption by listing the highest spenders in the local area. They were socially rewarded because their spending increased the rate of discount for everyone. In contrast, the lowest spenders became social outcasts.

Franklin finally decides to investigate one of the huge concrete signs. He notices a powerful humming emanating from the structure. Through a reflection in a shop window, he sees that the sign carries two messages: one '*Keep away*', the second

'*Buy cigarettes*'. His curiosity aroused, Franklin returns to the sign the next day during rush hour. There he finds Hathaway, who, having scaled the construction, is surrounded by armed police. Hathaway had succeeded in blowing the sign's fuse enabling the text to be 'seen' by the spectators below:

BUY NOW BUY NOW BUY NOW BUY NOW BUY
NEW CAR NOW NEW CAR NOW NEW CAR NOW
YES YES YES YES YES YES YES YES YES YES YES

(Ballard 1973: 74)

Although Franklin is unable to prevent the police opening fire on the triumphant Hathaway, he remains strangely unperturbed. Accepting the situation he goes out and buys a new car.

The critique of marketing and its methods contained in these stories is fairly clear.[1] There are also some remarkably prescient predictions. It is interesting to note how nearly all the commentaries contained in these stories on product obsolescence, selling methods, privacy, materialism and environmental impacts have found their way into Kotler *et al.* (1999) as contemporary ethical issues. Ballard's *The Subliminal Man* and the seductive technology in *The Merchants' War* are literary equivalents of Packard's *Hidden Persuaders* (1961) and its successors. Indeed the fear that the assumed rationality of the individual is being subverted via surreptitious methods is still played out today. A recent article in *The Guardian* (Cleverly 1999) warns of a new form of marketing, 'stealth advertising', which conjures up images of cloaked media preying on unenlightened consumers. It is soon apparent that our obsession with subliminal advertising goes beyond the famed James Vicary experiment to seduce consumers to buy popcorn and *Coca-Cola* in 1950s American cinema houses. Ambient promotions, the use of non-visual or aural advertising, can be experienced in almost every supermarket and remains a popular focal point for Internet discussion on conspiracy theories.[2] It is also notable that at the end of *The Merchants' War* the consumption brainwashing technology is used to support the Veenie cause. An anticipation of social marketing? Contemporary social causes are no longer squeamish about using the hard-nosed methods of the corporate world (Bruce 1994; Kotler and Levy 1969).

These stories are less than flattering in their representation of the marketer. Usually they are given egotistical motivational drives but minimally developed moral scruples. It is only when Courtenay in *The Space Merchants* and Tarb in the *The Merchants' War* are released from their top-ranking positions as marketing executives that they realise the consequences of their former trade. The portrayal of humanity is equally bleak. The tales outline how economic forces have produced a world infatuated with consumption. Consumers are represented as blindly duped, addicted either to the 'product' or browbeaten by constant advertising.[3] Those individuals who withdraw from consumption are often portrayed as deranged victims or societal outsiders. Implicit in all the stories is that marketing's role in the maintenance of the economic system has created a lack of regard for humanity and the environment. Thus in *The Space Merchants* and *The Merchants' War* the majority of the world's population is dependent upon genetically modified, synthetic food. In *The Subliminal Man* the desire to constantly expand GNP means that products are rapidly abandoned. The land alongside the motorway becomes a dumping ground for goods in perfect working order.

Marketing science fiction

But there is something dreadfully deadening about these *reflectionist* readings. Their pessimistic asceticism tends entirely to ignore our entirely self-conscious engagement with the consumption opportunities presented by marketing. We will return to this point in due course. More immediately, however, we have to recognise how the *production* of the science fiction genre is, in particular, tied up with marketing activities.

In most accounts science fiction appears either as a beguiled propagator of jet-propelled futures, a mental laboratory for earnest social speculations or, as in our previous discussion, a moralistic commentator upon late capitalism. But if science fiction's engagement with marketing has frequently fallen into the latter category, its wringing hands are not entirely unsoiled. It is revealing how many 'serious' histories of science fiction stress the importance of commerce. This is not merely a recognition of its trashy origins, a disreputable heritage subsequently left behind. Instead the viability of the genre is seen to move hand in hand with the development of commercial opportunity. Such histories (e.g. Aldiss 1973; Amis 1960; Asimov 1971) usually begin with a whistle-stop tour of proto-science fictions. Plato's Atlantis story from the dialogue *Critias*, More's *Utopia*, Rabelais's *Gargantua* and Swift's *Gulliver's Travels* are oft cited. Appropriate respect is paid to Mary Shelley's *Frankenstein*. But it is the founding of the magazine *Amazing Stories* by Hugo Gernsback in 1926 that marks science fiction's emergence from its primitive era. This is because authors now had a consistent commercial outlet for their work, as Isaac Asimov acknowledges, 'although the concept of science fiction had been born, the economic basis for the support of science fiction did not exist' (1971: 270). This was the era of pulp fiction, inexpensive mass-produced literature aimed at an increasingly literate citizenship. The target audience was the archetypal teenage male who was provided with an endless stream of formulaic tales of mad scientists, their recalcitrant creatures, heroes and heroines.

The edging of science fiction towards respectability, the beginning of its so-called 'Golden Age', is similarly associated with the development of commercial outlets. At the same time, the atomic bomb played an important role in rescuing SF from far-fetched futures in that its extravagant predictions were being seen to be realised. A wider audience began to take notice; John W. Campbell's editorship of *Astounding Futures* directed science fiction away from tales of adventure towards issues of politics and morality. These 'serious' concerns attracted 'respectable' publishing houses: Doubleday and Simon and Schuster became particularly identified with the genre. Hence the importance of corporate support is heavily stressed. The Golden Age is associated with a transformation from pulp hobbyists to professional authors, 'suddenly writers found they were in the writing *business*' (del Ray 1980: 222).

And what about those austere, non-materialistic members of the 'New Wave'? Surely they finally disentangled science fiction from vulgar commerciality? Of course the fact that business was now its biggest target meant that it remained a central preoccupation. However Klein's (1977) account of an antagonistic middle class authorship offers a less charitable reading. Whilst we may prefer to see them as principled defenders of lost values, their background is that of frustrated ambition. Once expecting to become the secular priesthood of modernity, their hopes became frustrated. The middle classes no longer felt themselves to be in control; instead they too had been assimilated by the forces of capital. The privileges that had been anticipated, indeed that had been promised, failed to arrive. Big business and big science were not a simple point of opposition but an estranged and deceitful partner. Under this interpretation the 'New Wave' appear as spurned collaborators, lashing out at those who had used them. Their real regret was not that the corporate world is destructive and exploitative, but that it had failed to deliver upon its promises. The instrumental benefits expected by the dominant class had somehow slipped elsewhere.

The revival of a more optimistic form of science fiction in the mid-to-late 1970s was also stimulated by commercial success. Many of these examples were mainstream Hollywood feature films that, by nature, are strongly market driven. For many the success of *Star Wars* (1977) and *Close Encounters of the Third Kind* (1977) reinvigorated the whole genre. Of course both were resolutely old-fashioned films. One is a tale of princesses, Evil Empires and valiant knights;[4] the other shows how 'humanity' is also extraterrestrial. But more than anything, the restored viability of this somewhat reactionary science fiction was measured by the films' sheer profitability. For these so-called blockbusters, massive investment is protected by similarly massive marketing budgets. And whilst science fiction is not the only form of mass entertainment that is heavily marketed, the relationship, particularly on film, is increasingly intertwined. The *Star Wars* phenomenon is of course the clearest example. The initial three *Star Wars* films netted over £2.4 billion in merchandising alone (Wilde 1999). The announcement two years ago of the production of the prequel trilogy started another round of licensing and sponsorship deals. PepsiCo reportedly paid £600 million for merchandising rights, whilst Lego committed £200 million to market toy figures.

Increasingly these deals are not merely product tie-ins. Marketing has become complicit in the production of films through the sale to corporations of product placements. Whilst this is conventionally achieved through the clear branding of the film's artefacts, this has recently gone a step further with the virtual reality thriller *The Matrix* (1999). Although the film itself might be read as a critique of capitalist society, humanity's (literal) labour power is exploited whilst it is pacified via a (literal) false consciousness, the script's reliance on mobile phones presented an opportunity for joint advertising. Thus newspaper and television campaigns simultaneously sell the film and phones, Nokia communications becomes '*The link between reality and the dream*'. It has been suggested that this relationship is often inverted. Instead of marketers taking advantage of the opportunities offered in the script, the script is shaped to offer marketing opportunities. George Lucas, the creator of the *Star Wars* films, has been heavily criticised for the insertion of characters that can be turned easily into cute toys. Hence the Ewoks in the *Return of the Jedi* (1983) are effectively walking, squeaking teddy bears. The computer-generated Jar Jar Binks in *The Phantom Menace* transforms easily into a space age version of Disney's bendy Goofy.

Marketing and the science fiction film has therefore moved from the merchandising of secondary products, to the insertion of brands into filming, to finally driving the creative process. Here we are close to science fiction's trashy origins, a genre driven solely by commercial gain. Films like *Independence Day* (1996) and *Godzilla* (1998) mine the choicest science fiction motifs and rebrand them for a new generation. Marketing for such films occurs simultaneously with production. Teaser trailers are produced long before the film has been completed. Usually these trailers feature extravagant special effects. *Independence Day's* nefarious alien invaders gleefully detonate the White House, whilst *Godzilla's* huge foot crushes terrified commuters. Size, we were told, *is* important. Indeed these films' heavy use of special effects is frequently used to dismiss them as abstract light shows, a grotesque spectacular devoid of serious comment. Thus this science fiction fetishises technology, in the same way that advertising fetishises commodities. The name of George Lucas's massively profitable special effects company, Industrial Light and Magic, is highly revealing – a clearer statement of technological disenchantment is hard to imagine. In fact many science fiction films are 'sold' on the basis of their special effects by either publicising the number of effects shots, for instance *Lost in Space* (1998), or by stressing the size of the budget. *Total Recall's* (1990) actual budget was substantially less than was used in publicity material. *Terminator 2: Judgment Day* (1991) was reviewed in the business section of the *New York Times* a week before it opened on general release (Hoberman 1991: 23).

Trust no one

Nevertheless this analysis fails to capture the power of much contemporary science fiction. This has a more comprehensive ability to disturb. In this way it also serves to undercut the strategies that have produced the preceding critiques. Thus whether reading a science fiction text as a piece of social criticism, or alternatively subjecting its production to similar critique, we inevitably demarcate various actors, most obviously the author(s), the textual reading, contemporary marketing reality, the mainstream audience, the audience as consumer and so on. Indeed all social criticism depends on these strategies of division. As Kellner (1998) shows, this process of boundary drawing is central to critical theory. It first notes how capitalism is a form of reification, a process of abstraction by which the privileges of certain categories are justified. The response of the critical theorist is to draw their own boundaries and make use of abstractions to illuminate social processes. Hence they criticise positivistic approaches that simply mirror existing social realities. Instead they call for social theory to abstract itself from current society in order to produce critical perspectives and alternatives, 'this abstractness, this radical withdrawal from the given, at least clears a path along which the individual in bourgeois society can seek the truth and adhere to what is known' (Marcuse 1968: 150–1). These abstractions are the means by which we can uncover the 'actual' social processes that take place behind the back of the individual. For instance, Ritzer's (1997) McDonaldisation thesis, in showing how the processes of production and consumption have slipped into the ordering of the non-commercial, separate the normal from the abnormal. The assumption is that there is something 'authentic' that has been distorted. We will have a few more words to say about McDonaldisation in due course.

In fact, much contemporary science fiction is powerful because it threatens the assumption that things *can* be known. This science fiction serves to transgress, twist and unsettle the sites from which critique can be launched. McHale (1991) in a wider review of postmodernist fiction sees science fiction as the archetypal postmodern genre. Its 'dominant' or focusing component is ontological, invoking such questions as 'Which world is this?' 'What kinds of world are there and how are they constituted?' 'Which of my selves is to engage in this world?' David Cronenburg's *Videodrome* (1982) is a good example of such science fiction. On the surface it has many of the elements expected in a critique of the pervasive powers of the mass media. A pirate TV station transmits programmes of sexual depravity that are found to induce brain tumours. This tumour, 'a new organ . . . a new outgrowth of the human brain' makes the brain hallucinate. Once detached from reality the body becomes a literal (the body acquires slots to receive tapes) receptacle for re-programming. But hallucination is laid upon hallucination. Through this endlessly replicating hallucinatory virus, *Videodrome* does not simply criticise the effects of representation but moves everything into representation (Bukatman 1993). Its transmission does not create a pseudo-reality but destroys any sense of something that is separate from representation, any sense of authenticity. 'Professor' Brian O'Blivion, the film's media guru caricature of Marshall McLuhan, informs us that 'Television is reality, and reality is less than television.' Our subjectivity is entirely constituted through the act of viewing.

Traditional science fiction and attempts to be critical about science fiction have a similar problem in that both seem to require commitment to the existence of something separate, unaffected and untainted. *Videodrome's* ultimate revelation is of a global conspiracy headed by a company called 'Spectacular Optical' (mission statement – 'We make inexpensive glasses for the Third World and missile guidance systems for NATO'). However, the nefarious activities of Spectacular Optical may or may not be just another hallucination. But it is ultimately irrelevant – in *Videodrome* the death of the subject and the death of representation is mutual, complicit and final. In this environment, no longer is it possible to conceptualise images as representations of reality and judge them for their veracity and reliability. No longer can we identify distortions and dissimulations. Instead the simulations and the real are so intertwined that we cannot distinguish one from another.

Marketing and alien-ation

Although this PoMo hyper-reality has a certain vertiginous attraction, we remain somewhat uncomfortable with the message that it sends about our relationship with marketing. We want to explore the complex nature of this process of engagement by returning to and reinterpreting the notion of the 'alien'. Of course the alien plays a central role within science fiction. However, this role is played out in different ways. Here we identify three versions: the alien as destructive 'other'; the alien as symbolic of lost or threatened values; and finally, the alien as representative of a pervasive process of 'otherness' (Sobchack 1987).

In its first version, whether deriving from unknown origins, artificially constructed or a perverted version of what is held to be natural, the alien is obviously demarcated as monstrous. It is something that is clearly 'Other' and something that must be stopped before it threatens what is held to be valuable. This is the archetypal 'monster from outer space' found in such works as *The War of the Worlds* (1953), *The Thing* (1951, 1982) and the *Alien* (1979, 1986, 1991, 1997) films. An alternative formulation sees the alien itself as representative of conservative values. In this science fiction the alien is held apart from the human, but only in order to display a nostalgic message about lost humanity. For instance, in films like *The Day the Earth Stood Still* (1951), *Close Encounters of the Third Kind* (1977), *ET* (1982), *Starman* (1984), and of course in the various *Star Trek* incarnations, aliens often demarcate the border with the human by being better than us, more human than human. Instead of destroying, they embody and protect humanist values that are felt to be increasingly under threat.

Finally, in what might be called postmodern science fiction, it is questioned whether there is any original model of humanness from which the alien can be distanced (or alternatively seen to represent). In a world where traditional signifiers have been lost, we are all aliens whether human or extraterrestrial (Sobchack 1987). Distinctions drawn from such binaries as alien/human are increasingly troubled. Hence this science fiction breaks down divisions such as male/female, real/imaginary, human/other, literal/metaphorical, factual/fictional, plausible/incredible. The meaning of alienation is eroded if, as in certain science fiction, colonisation is no longer the result of invasion by an identifiable Other. Science fictions 'no longer symbolically figure the alien-ation generated by a whole new economic world system, but rather our *incorporation* of that new system and our *absorption* by it' (Sobchack 1987: 252 – emphasis in original). *Invasion of the Body Snatchers* (1956), *Solaris* (1961), *Blade Runner* (1982) and the previously discussed *Videodrome* (1982) all produce this ontological confusion.

When we allow these characterisations to resonate with approaches to marketing, we find different, but somewhat familiar messages produced. The postmodern view, as discussed earlier with reference to *Videodrome*, presents the division between the marketing and the non-marketing world as no longer sustainable. Marketing is seen to have conducted its own programme of colonisation. Through this process the language, practice and ordering processes of marketing have become irretrievably taken for granted in the creation of our-selves. Like 'postmodern' science fiction, marketing is preoccupied with the ontological. It fragments, builds and re-builds worlds. Some elements of marketing likes to think that it can build better worlds. But we cannot step outside. There is no outside world separate from marketing. The movement of marketing techniques into the 'normal environment' is now complete (Cleverly 1999).

If this is a broadly Baudrillardean perspective, then the other versions use the alien to implicitly draw upon critical theory. Hence they follow a similar rationale but switch their symbolism. Thus the alien either threatens 'authentic' values or represents and protects them. It is a similar type of engagement that we have seen applied *by* science fiction to marketing, but also *to* science fiction because of its strong commercial instincts. Both positions are constructed from a position of certain superiority, a position that allows condemnation and revulsion. Thus much science fiction[5] dismisses marketing as a force that stimulates unfettered consumption whilst numbing us to the destructive effects of its materialism. In turn the contemporary SF blockbuster is subjected to the same critiques that science fiction has directed at the world of marketing. Thus Hartwell (1984) argues that science fiction was a televisual narcotic directed at the adolescent population of the United States. These cultural dopes are the archetypal science fiction 'anoraks', 'pimple faced nerds in rubber Vulcan ears or wrapped in multi-faceted scarves, overweight women clutching collectibles and dolls' (Tulloch and Jenkins, 1995: vii). Personified in this pitiful spectacle is all that critical theorists despise – blind consumerism, an obsession with trivia, a fixation with gadgetry, a loss of dignity and respect and either a retreat from the pressing issues of the real world or, worse, a total inability to decipher fact from fiction (see Alvesson 1994).

But those who offer these criticisms cannot preserve their detachment. For instance Adorno's (1991) treatment of the capitalist culture industry distinguishes it from art because of its commercial vulgarity. Yet of course this analysis proceeds on the basis of deep knowledge. The products of the culture industry have been thoroughly sampled before they are rejected. For Umberto Eco this exposes an ill-concealed desire:

> the barely disguised manifestation of a frustrated passion, a love betrayed, or rather, the neurotic display of a repressed sensuality, similar to that of the moralist who, in the very act of denouncing the obscenity of an image, pauses at such length and with such voluptuousness to contemplate the loathsome object of his contempt that his true nature – that of carnal, lustful animal – is betrayed.
>
> (Eco 1994: 25–6)

The critic has to face the implications of involvement with the object of her criticism.

In her essay *The Imagination of Disaster*, Susan Sontag (1971) discusses the nature of our engagement with alien inhabitants of science fiction. This engagement is, she argues, the:

> Undeniable pleasure we derive from looking at freaks, beings excluded from the category of the human. The sense of superiority over the freak conjoined in varying proportions with the titillation of fear and aversion makes it possible for moral scruples to be lifted for cruelty to be enjoyed. The same thing happens in science fiction films. In the figure of the monster from outer space, the freakish, the ugly, the predatory, all converge – and provide a fantasy target or righteous bellicosity to discharge itself, and for the aesthetic enjoyment of suffering and disaster.
>
> (Sontag 1971: 316)

Yet this account gives no attention to the implicate nature of the alien gaze. Sontag speaks of the monstrous 'Other', something that is so obviously apart that it receives only our scorn. But the aliens in science fiction are often neither obviously apart nor completely absorbed. One of the most successful examples of contemporary science fiction is the *X-Files*, a television series notable for its menagerie of alien types, alien/human hybrids and freaks of nature.[6] Indeed the episode 'Humbug' (1995) takes place in a community of freaks in which a series of murders have taken place. Mulder and Scully are sent to investigate. Rapidly the hierarchical distinction between the 'normal' FBI investigators and the freak is brought into question. In a key scene, one morning Scully is awoken by Lenny, a freak with an incipient conjoined twin. Scully still dazed from sleep is unable to resist searching for signs of Lenny's physical abnormality, the attachment of his brother to his waist. At the same time Lenny is drawn to Scully's partially exposed breasts. Realising what they have been doing, both restore normality by covering themselves. Soon it is the physical normality of the FBI agents that sets them apart. Mulder's bland dress sense and his catalogue model good looks begin to cause revulsion.[7] The story soon becomes a battle with the assumptions of (ab)normality. The rational Scully is faced with a troubling paradox. She has to convince the local Sheriff, formerly 'Jim, the Dog Faced Boy', that just because he regards his community as 'normal folk' does not mean that they cannot be killers. Most serial killers, she explains, are regarded as mundane by those who know them. No longer, then, can we be certain of the limits of normality.

These limits are never entirely lost. But, neither are they secure. We are continually troubled by the trace of their presence. The alien as freak then cuts a liminal figure, but one that causes us to reflect upon ourselves. We, to paraphrase Eco, contemplate the loathsome object but are forced to consider our own nature, and pause to wonder whether it is, in fact, natural.

Conclusions

Science fiction is more than a reflexive resource through which to gaze upon marketing. Reading it as just another site of criticism misses first the complicity of its relationship with commerce but, more importantly, that science fiction ultimately ends up problematising the stability of these sites. The drawing of boundaries between ourselves and the Other, alien and human, the subject and critic is often uncertain. This is not to say that they entirely disappear, but the boundaries themselves become matters of debate.

This tensile movement is wonderfully illuminated by a tale of Sunday afternoon lunch. It is an encounter with the golden arches of McDonald's that Morris Holbrook (1999) relates in the *Journal of Macromarketing*. The story revolves around Morris and his wife's Sunday afternoon drives. On route to nowhere in particular, they stop at McDonald's. McDonald's offers an Arch Deluxe for $2.99 and an Arch Deluxe with Bacon for $3.29. Morris' wife orders an Arch Deluxe without bacon and also without cheese. This request causes great consternation for the waitress who, trained in the art of standardised meal order inputs, is unable to find an appropriate key on her till for the order. She ultimately resorts to inputting an Arch Deluxe with Bacon, whilst shouting to the kitchen to void the cheese and the bacon. Despite such efforts the burger naturally comes in its pre-ordained form, with cheese and bacon. Whilst this story is unusual only in its mundanity, most of us having probably enjoyed a similar experience, what is of interest is the way in which Holbrook takes great pleasure and pride in recounting this tale; the knowing relish of being able to see the opponent's hand, the (smug) satisfaction of being at the receiving end of Ritzer's (1997) 'irrationality of rationality'. Indeed George Ritzer himself, in a presentation at a recent conference,[8] showed the slipperyness of our corporate encounters when he spoke of (another)

McDonald's purchase. Wishing to make an argument about the 'invisibility' of the visible kitchen areas, he began to sense that the audience were beginning to wonder why he continues to frequent such awful places. Rizter explained that he was 'really thirsty' and that there was really nowhere else to go in the busy international airport terminal. Catching himself, he then wondered out loud why he always felt obliged to indulge in such shaky self-justifications.

Despite our desire to perceive Ronald McDonald as the new threat from outer space,[9] many of us remain customers, viewers, followers and critics. And what is more delicious than being able to perform all these roles? Would McDonald's be half the fun without the half-hearted, manufactured smiles, the product placements, the bucket seats and garish décor, the slow fast-food and being able to complain about standardised milk shakes 'tasting different'. And those burgers are so damn tasty. A new type of total customer experience – dissatisfaction and satisfaction rolled into one ecstatic bundle; an opportunity to bemoan the failings of service delivery whilst enjoying the pleasures of flesh.

This form of alien-ation forces us to question a somewhat superior, motivated no doubt by some notional sense of authenticity, critical distancing from marketing's vulgar horrors. But this does not mean that we must fall victim to the vertiginous pull of the corporate abyss. The passive, programmable, bewilderment of the *Videodrome* is similarly simplistic. Both positions have something in common. They rest ultimately in static states. Either the security of knowing something to be true. Or the security of knowing everything is false. But both these stabilisations give us little purchase on our engagement with marketing. Clearly we are neither entirely critical nor entirely beguiled. We participate, withdraw, display wonder, show disgust, believe, are sceptical, test, play, enthuse, and detach. Science fiction exposes the fluidity of these positions. Asseverations are diluted. Like tears in rain.

Notes

1 C.C. MacApp's (1968) short story 'And all the world a grave' is another excellent critique of marketing's construction of desire. An accountancy error provides a coffin manufacturer with a massive advertising budget. Soon death becomes the latest status symbol.

2 See for example http://www.parascope.com/articles/0397/sublim.htm 'Subliminal threat : The Subliminal Scares'.

3 It is no coincidence that in Ray Bradbury's (1953) *Fahrenheit 451* drugs and television are similarly addictive.

4 Some would be tempted to be debate whether *Star Wars*, given its reliance on fantasy archetypes, is science fiction. We find such questions remarkably tedious and prefer to admire Darth Maul's light sabre.

5 Of course we must be suspicious of distinctions between 'good' and 'bad' science fiction given that many 'classics' were originally dismissed as trash.

6 Recently the series has increasingly parodied itself – in a recent episode a weary Fox

Mulder investigating the tale of an alien (extraterrestrial) baseball player asks, 'So I assume that you're speaking metaphorically?' His subject, the brother of the originator of the X-Files replies 'Speaking metaphorically is for young men like you agent McGuyver, I don't have time for that. I only have time for speaking the truth.' Mulder comes to the point, 'Is X a man who is metaphorically an alien, or an alien who is metaphorically a man, or a something in between who is literally an alien-human hybrid?'

7 Dr Blockhead sneers at society's entirely abnormal desire for conformity, 'I've seen the future, and the future looks just like him.'

8 'Critical Interventions: Obscene Powers: Corruptions, Coercion and Violence', 11–12 December, 1999, University of Southampton.

9 See http://absurdgallery.com/arch.shtml

References

Adorno, T.W. (1991) *The Culture Industry: Selected Essays on Mass Culture*, London: Routledge.

Aldiss, B. (1973) *Billion Year Spree: The History of Science Fiction*, London: Weidenfeld & Nicolson.

Alvesson, M. (1994) 'Critical theory and consumer marketing', *Scandinavian Journal of Management* 10, 3: 291–313.

Amis, K. (1960) *New Maps of Hell*, London: Harcourt Brace.

Asimov, I. (1971) 'Social science fiction', in D. Allen (ed.) *Science Fiction: The Future*, New York: Harcourt Brace Jovanovich, 263–91.

Ballard, J.G. (1973) 'Subliminal man', in J.G. Ballard (ed.) *The Disaster Area*, London: Panther.

Bradbury, R. (1953) *Fahrenheit 451*, New York: Ballantine.

Bruce, I. (1994) *Meeting Need: Successful Charity Marketing*, Hemel Hempstead: ICSA Publishing.

Bukatman, S. (1993) *Terminal Identity: The Virtual Subject in Postmodern Science Fiction*, Durham: Duke University Press.

Cleverly, C. (1999) 'Life's a pitch – and then you buy', *The Guardian Media Section*, Monday 14 June: 8–10.

Davies, P.J. (1990) 'Science fiction and conflict', in P.J. Davies (ed.) *Science Fiction, Social Conflict and War*, Manchester: Manchester University Press.

del Rey, L. (1980) *The World of Science Fiction, 1926–1976: The History of a Subculture*, New York: Garland Publishing.

Eco, U. (1994) 'Apocalyptic and integrated intellectuals: mass communication and theories of mass culture', in R. Lumley (ed.) *Apocalypse Postponed*, London: British Film Institute.

Goldman, R. and Papson, S. (1994) 'Advertising in the age of hypersignification', *Theory, Culture and Society* 11: 23–54.

Greenberg, M.H., Mislead, J.W., Oleander, J.D. and Warwick, P. (1975) *Social Problems Through Science Fiction*, London: St Martin's Press.

Hartwell, D.G. (1984) *Age of Wonders: Exploring the World of Science Fiction*, New York: McGraw-Hill.

Hoberman, J. (1991) 'Nietzsche's boy', *Sight and Sound*, September, 22–4.

Holbrook. M. (1999) 'Higher than the bottom line: reflections on some recent macro-marketing literature', *Journal of Macromarketing* 19, 1: 48–75.

Jordin, M. (1984) 'Contemporary futures: the analysis of science fiction', in C. Pawling (ed.) *Popular Fiction and Social Change*, London: Macmillan, 50–75.

Kellner, D. (1998) *Boundaries and Borderlines: Reflections on Jean Baudrillard and Critical Theory*, Online Available, http://www.uta.edu/huma/illuminations/kell2.htm

Klein, G. (1977) 'Discontent in American science fiction', *Science Fiction Studies* 4, 1: 3–13.

Kotler, P., Armstrong, G., Saunders, J. and Wong, V. (1999) *Principles of Marketing*, 2nd European edn, New Jersey: Prentice-Hall.

—— and Levy, S.J. (1969) 'Broadening the concept of marketing', *Journal of Marketing* January: 10–15.

Kuhn, A. (ed.) (1990) *Alien Zone: Cultural Theory and Contemporary Science Fiction*, London: Verso.

MacApp, C.C. (1968) 'And all the world a grave', in F. Pohl (ed.) *The Eighth Galaxy Reader*, London: Pan Books.

Malik, R. (1980) *Future Imperfect: Science Fact and Science Fiction*, London: Francis Pinter.

Marcuse, H. (1968) *One Dimensional Man*, London: Sphere Books.

McHale, B. (1991) *Postmodernist Fiction*, London: Routledge.

Ofshe, R. (1977) 'Introduction', in R.Ofshe (ed.) *The Sociology of the Possible*, 2nd edn, New Jersey: Prentice-Hall.

Packard, V. (1961) *The Hidden Persuaders*, London: Penguin.

Pohl, F. (1984) *The Merchants' War*, New York: St Martin's.

—— and Kornbluth, C.M. (1953) *The Space Merchants*, London: Heinemann.

Ritzer, G. (1997) *The McDonaldization Thesis: Explorations and Extensions*, London: Sage.

Sobchack, V. (1987) *Screening Space*, 2nd edn, New York: Ungar.

Sontag, S. (1971) 'The imagination of disaster', in D.Allen (ed.) *Science Fiction: The Future*, New York: Harcourt Brace Jovanovich, 312–25.

Tarrat, M. (1977) 'Monsters from the ID', in B.K. Grant, (ed.) *Film Genre*, New Jersey: Scarecrow Press, 161–81.

Tulloch, J. and Jenkins, H. (1995) *Science Fiction Audiences: Watching* Doctor Who *and* Star Trek, London: Routledge.

Wilde, J. (1999) 'Buyer beware', *The Guardian, The Guide* 24–30 April: 8–10.

7 The good, the bad and the jolly: taste, image and the symbolic resistance to the coca-colonisation of Denmark

Søren Askegaard and Fabian F. Csaba

Telling fairy tales

> And accordingly Jack the Dullard was made a king, and received a crown and a wife, and sat upon a throne. And this report we have wet from the press of the head clerk and the corporation of printers – but they are not to be depended upon in the least.
>
> (Hans Christian Andersen 1855/1995)

'Once upon a time there were three brothers,' the narrator begins while we are shown a parchment map of Denmark. 'The two oldest considered themselves rather attractive . . .', two brothers appear, one cruising in a convertible another on a motorcycle, both wearing heavy make-up and Baroque garments, '. . . but of course they had been to America and now they wanted to marry . . .', we see a princess on a screen, '. . . the lovely Princess Tina'. The camera zooms out and we discover that the screen is mounted on a traditional Danish mobile hot-dog stand ('pølsevogn') where a ragged dork is completely dazed by her beauty. The stiff squeezes a half-litre bottle of cola of the 'Jolly' brand down in his right front pocket and sets off. While we see him driving his moped set against the parchment map, the narrator explains, 'The youngest brother was called Prince Jolly . . . but no one really counted on him. Nevertheless he also headed for the castle where Princess Tina was inspecting all her suitors.' A camera suspended from the ceiling moves over the line-up of hopefuls including the fancy older brothers of Prince Jolly. The wooers appearing on her monitor clearly do not excite her. 'In the middle of the ceremony,' the narrator goes on, 'Prince Jolly walks in and shouts "Hey, aren't you the one with the ripe fruits?" The princess looked down at him and she looked closer.' The camera moves down the body of the Prince and stops at the bulge in his trousers. The princess is clearly intrigued and steps down from her throne and approaches him. Prince Jolly, now in courtly attire, is seen holding the hand of his bride in front of a castle, both smiling blissfully. This image of the happy couple then appears on a photo. Another picture next to it shows three children. Between the family portraits is a half-full bottle of Jolly Cola. The story ends: 'And then they lived happily ever after. And if you think that it was his big Jolly Cola she fell for, think again. But it was good for the thirst . . . afterwards . . .'

This pastiche of Hans Christian Andersen's fairy tale *Klods Hans* (in English *Jack the Dullard*[1]) is one example in a series of advertising efforts to reinvigorate the image of the Danish soft-drink Jolly Cola and reclaim the strong market position it had enjoyed throughout the 1960s and 1970s. Something of an anomaly in Europe, Jolly had managed to defend its home turf against the American cola-giants and remained the dominant cola until it began to loosen its grip on the market in the early 1980s, plunging to a mere 6 per cent market share in the late 1990s. The advertising fairy tale is a thinly veiled allegory. In Hans Christian Andersen's story, Jack the Dullard succeeds through limited means, making good use of whatever he comes across (a billygoat for transportation, a dead crow, a wooden shoe and a pocketful of wet clay). The prepared speeches and rehearsed wit of the older two brothers let them down in the strange scenario that the fussy and demanding princess has staged. Jack's improvised, bold and crazy repartee, however, paves the way for an absurd interplay that wins her over. The commercial appears to be a projection of management's dream of outwitting the forceful, fancied and fanciful American contenders and winning the Danish consumer . . . and, of course, living happily ever after. The allegory, in fashioning the brand personality after Jack the Dullard, would suggest that Jolly was in a bad shape image-wise. And besides, as H.C. Andersen concludes his tale, it 'is not to be depended upon in the least'.

This chapter examines the efforts of Denmark's once favoured national cola, Jolly Cola, to resist the advancement of Coca-Cola and, to a lesser degree, Pepsi. In moving our looking glass to the struggles of this obscure Danish product, we seek to move the debate on globalisation, consumption and culture home to our own 'back yard'. From here, we offer a refreshing story, drawn from our local narrative tradition and woven together with advertising imagery, about the 'symbolic' resistance to the Coca-colonisation of Denmark. The story is partially inspired by Baudrillard's (1976) observation that each term in a disjunction excludes its other, its opposition, whereby the opposition becomes the imaginary of the former term. Hence, the American 'other' becomes the central imaginary against which references to Danishness are constructed. One of our key arguments is that marketing forms a central part of this particular imaginary whereby 'Americanness' becomes a particular element in the Danish approach to imagining marketing. This imagination takes it outset both in the very real representations of Coca-Cola's and Pepsi's marketing efforts and in the supra-sensual imaginations (Wunenburger 1991), formulae of intuitive and creative genius that are believed to be the secret behind the success of the American marketing magic. We will look further into the seemingly futile marketing efforts to end and reverse the decline of Jolly Cola, a product which of course also represents a piece of Danish popular culture and commercial history. The purpose is not to perform a premature autopsy of Jolly, but to explore further the symbolic meanings of cola in relation to globalisation and consumption through the story and advertising imagery of an ailing local cola.

Initially, we will elaborate on the point and scope of the inquiry into cola symbolism, by offering a counterpoint to the study of Jolly Cola in Denmark, namely a recent ethnographic study of Coca-Cola in Trinidad by Daniel Miller (1998). This will be followed by an argument for the role of Coca-Cola in relation to the twentieth-century *Zeitgeist* and against what we see as Miller's attempt to 'banalise' Coca-Cola as a consumer object. We then turn to a discussion of the story of Jolly Cola faced with the intruding global competitors: the complexities of the symbolic battles between Americanness and Danishness in the initial advertisement responses by Jolly and the subsequent references to a specific US-based marketing imaginary countered by Danish 'anti-marketing' imaginations. We conclude by discussing the story of Jolly in the light of various conceptualisations of globalisation, using the case of colas in Denmark as one particular example of the global–local nexus of marketing and consumption processes.

The symbolism of coke

Coca-Cola is frequently invoked in debates on globalisation, culture and consumption. The ubiquity and uniformity of the product appears to support what has been called the 'global homogenisation paradigm'. According to this view, cultural differences are increasingly being eroded through the world-wide replacement of local products with mass-produced and internationally marketed goods (Howes 1996: 3). The influx of (Western) consumer products, it is argued, tends to serve as a catalyst for cultural and political change. Social and cultural critics see this as a new type of commercial and cultural imperialism that is sometimes conveyed in the catchy figure of Coca-colonisation (Hannerz 1992). In a polemic against this outlook, Daniel Miller has recently argued that Coca-Cola seems to have acquired the status of a meta-symbol,[2] which means that it may 'be filled with almost anything those who wish to either embody or critique a form of symbolic domination might ascribe to it' (Miller 1998: 170). Because of this flexibility and the powerful expressive and emotive foundations on which they operate, it is very difficult to subject meta-symbols to analysis and refute what they are claimed to stand for (ibid.). The figure of Coca-Cola thus contributes to perpetuate clichés and dubious claims in discourse on global homogenisation, Americanisation, commodity power and imperialism. Miller sets out to refute the meta-symbolic status of Coca-Cola. He first comments on the existing literature on the company, arguing that 'irrespective of whether it is enthusiastically in favour or constructed as a diatribe against the drink, acts to affirm the assumption that the significance of the drink is best approached through knowledge of company strategy' (ibid.: 171). Miller suggests that this is an error in that it presupposes that the company controls its own effects and ignores the local contextualisation of global forms by consumers and local producers. The title of the article, 'Coca-Cola: A Black Sweet Drink from Trinidad' alludes to the distinction made in Trinidad between sweet red and sweet black drinks, and the local production and export of Coca-Cola and its syrup. The title and the ethnography itself illustrates poignantly how local categories that are imposed on global products alter their original meanings in a process of domestication and recontextualisation. This approach represents what David Howes defines as 'the creolization paradigm' (1996: 5) in cultural anthropology. Drawing on linguistic sources, the concept of 'creole' suggests cultures that are intrinsically of mixed origin, the confluence of different historical currents, which interact in a centre/periphery relationship (Hannerz 1992: 264).

There is an ironic twist to the idea of cultural creolisation, when applied to the relationship between Europe and the United States. Over the past century, the centre seems to have moved across the Atlantic and the main direction of cultural flow the other way. Now it is the European cultures that are being creolised as they appropriate American cultural forms (Kroes 1996).[1] The 'paradigm of creolisation' and its application to a European context (rather than the more 'exotic' realms it is conventionally applied to) obviously have implications for the way we conceive of Americanisation and Coca-colonisation. As Kroes (1996) suggests, even 'in the case of a clear and undeniable impact of American culture [. . .], the word Americanisation is unduly alarmist'. It reduces the complex processes of cultural influence, borrowing, imitation and reception, to a zero-sum game where any degree of Americanisation would imply an equal degree of de-Europeanisation (ibid.: xi). So it is clear that it is necessary to be on guard against certain symbolic meanings attributed to Coca-Cola. But in his analysis, Miller in his attack on the premises of 'global homogenization paradigm' comes close to reducing Coke to just 'a particular soft drink' (Miller 1998: 170). He does not question Coke's 'ability to objectify globality' but in order to 'plunge us down from a level where Coke is a dangerous icon' (ibid.), Miller seems to play down the rich complex, contradictory symbolic meanings with which Coca-Cola is imbued. Rather than aiming to dissociate Coke from certain concepts that have polarised its meaning, we might explore them as a part of the varied mythology Coke supports. Rather than engaging in a kind of iconoclasm against cola as a 'meta-symbol', we would like to approach it as what Barthes called a 'totem-drink' in his essay on the symbolic meaning of wine in France: 'Like all resilient totems, wine supports a varied mythology which does not trouble about contradictions' (Barthes 1993: 58). The fact that John Pemberton before inventing Coca-Cola produced a forerunner called French Wine Coca perhaps justifies the analogy

(Pendergrast 1993: 24). Just like Jolly, French Wine Coca was a direct imitation product (ibid.) (or is it appropriation?). We will first examine the special symbolic properties that has enabled Coke to transcend cultural boundaries and become a 'sign of the times', an icon of modern life. Then we will proceed with our appropriation of Miller's idea of going local with cola in the pursuit of insights into globalisation, culture and consumption, where the scope includes the cultural history of Coke as an icon identified with America in anti-American discourse.

Cola and the spirit of the age

It has been suggested that one of the dominant indications of contemporary (post)modern consumer culture is the aestheticisation of everyday life (Feather-stone 1991: 65–82), referring to at least three different cultural processes: the rapid flow of signs and images in contemporary life worlds, the effacing of bound-aries between high art and popular culture, and the project of turning life itself into a work of art – a stylised performance of whatever would constitute 'the good life' for the individual. Featherstone sees these processes as inherent in a society of mass consumption; a point already made by Morin (1962) in his clair-voyant treatise on the characteristics of the new cultural form of mass culture. Metaphorically speaking, few products symbolise these new times better than the industrially produced, often artificially flavoured, bubbly, happy and nutritionally utterly superfluous product of 'soda pop'.

As Witzel and Young-Witzel (1998) demonstrate, the soft drink or soda pop as a category underwent a transformation from a product claiming medical benefits to one of the product-emblems of twentieth-century pop culture. This is particu-larly evident in the story of the particular type of soda called 'cola' (Pendergrast 1993). The advertising and merchandising of soft drinks in general and cola in particular reveals the mythology of youth, of leisure, of happiness and of func-tionalism (in terms of refreshment), which are central to modern consumer culture. Hence, Cola epitomises what Morin (1962) saw as *l'esprit du temps* where the individual in contemporary mass culture is qualified as a consumer consuming her or his personal existence. This kind of personal existence – of which the colas are general exponents – is spun up in a modern mythology built on two prin-ciples. The first is one of generalised sympathy: of love, happiness and happy endings, and – what are usually seen as – feminine values. The other principle is that of leisure: of youthful adventure and excitement, of sexuality, and pop stars are those who realise this mythological life to the fullest. They are in Morin's eyes 'the new Olympians' (ibid.: 143). Coca-Cola and Pepsi at present seem to repre-sent those two aspects of modern consumer mythology, albeit with different emphases. Coca-Cola is 'democracy in a bottle'. It is the self-designated carrier of the hope of universalisation of the mass cultural mythology, as expressed in the now-classical Coca-Cola song containing the line 'I'd like to buy the world a coke and keep it company' – in short, it is *the* symbol of global friendship and community (Witzel and Young-Witzel 1998: 105). Pepsi, on the other hand, takes on the role as the challenger, the youthful innovator of values and styles based mainly on (teeny) pop stars representing the style of the future: 'Generation neXt'. As such, Coca-Cola and Pepsi become a sort of global set of communicating vessels, the term Morin (1962) uses for the dedifferentiation processes in modern mass culture. The universes of colas, the mythological elements used in the marketing communications, become part of the 'new, cosmopolitan folklore' of global mass culture. According to Morin, the cosmopolitanism of this mass culture is of a double nature. It is on the one hand anthropological: an appeal to some of the emotional preconditions in a 'universal fantasy person', not too different from the child or the archaic human being but nevertheless always present in the modern *Homo Faber* (Morin 1962: 224–5). But, on the other hand, it is also the result of the promotion of a new type of human being created and socialised through the mediation of mass culture itself. The mutual support of these universalisms, anthropological and modern, is the prime carrier of the spreading of the modern consumer culture, 'coca-colonisation'. Coca-Cola's marketing efforts in particular are exponents of this aspect of mass culture: the hope for progress and salvation for the world's population in what Morin called a terrestrial religion of salvation (ibid.: 234). Its strong mythological and magical universe linked to profane, mundane and easily accessible products reflects exactly the inner contradiction of modern mass or consumer culture – a contradiction that according to Morin is both a weakness and a strength. He writes, '[Mass culture] maintains and develops religious processes about the most profane and mythological processes about the most empirical. On the other hand, it establishes empirical and profane processes around the basic idea of modern religion: individual salvation' (ibid.: 235). The cola-products are world-wide missionaries for the *leitmotifs* of harmony and change that are dynamic forces in the modern consumer environment. But their country of origin is the United States of America.

Ambiguities of Americanisation: the coca-colonisation of Denmark

After a series of angry protests against Coca-Cola in France just after World War 2, the company's local representative suggested that 'the best barometer of the relationship of the US with any country is the way Coca-Cola is treated' (Pendergrast 1993: 243). The identification of Coca-Cola with the interests and cultural values of America is essential to the product and has played a crucial role in its global expansion. The special bond between America and Coca-Cola was firmly established during WW2, where the soft-drink company and the US Army joined together in an openly co-operative arrangement to supply the soldiers with the drink wherever in the world they were fighting. The Coca-Cola Company's patriotism and opportunism not only forged enduring emotional ties to war-weary soldiers with the sweet taste of home, but also opened the door to the world for the drink. By the end of the war, Coke had been introduced to millions of people around the world, and the company had gained valuable experience in supplying it. At the end of the war, America found itself in the position as the pre-eminent military, economic and political world power. American administration and rebuilding efforts after the war paved the way for a massive cultural and commercial influence that eventually provoked the rise of anti-American senti-ments and accusations of American imperialism. The terms 'Americanisation' and 'Coca-colonisation' surfaced in the ideological debates in cold-war Europe and have floated in social and cultural discourse ever since (ibid.: 242). But what does Americanisation actually mean? In a broad sense, of course, it refers to the impact of American culture abroad. But considering the complexity of American culture we are clearly dealing with a very diffuse concept. The impact and assessment of American culture abroad is of course highly situated. Obviously, a distinction needs to be made between the West and the rest, given Europe's role in the formation of modern American civilisation. But even European countries have their unique experiences of Americanisation and concepts of what constitutes the American, depending on factors such as religion, language, political traditions and institutions, social stratification, extent and time of emigration to America. The history of Jolly reflects the changing and ambiguous reception of American cul-ture in Denmark as well as the country's economic and political relationship with the United States.

Coca-Cola came to Denmark in 1938 but only for a brief spell because of the shortages and rationing of sugar during the war. A high special tax on cola was imposed to protect the Danish market and this meant that Coke did not return until 1959. By the time the cola-tax was removed, sixteen Danish breweries and soft-drink bottlers had joined forces to produce a Danish version of the American soft drink and prevent an American invasion. The name 'Jolly', with its rhyme on by-then popular names such as Tommy or Johnny, seems to have been chosen as a reference to the still vivid images of the merry Anglo-Saxon 'Tommies' – liber-ators of Denmark after the German occupation during WW2. Furthermore, its meaning was a direct reference to the leisurely values of the rising consumer society, inspired by the above-mentioned missionaries of new consumer values, but in the hope that a local carrier would be able to hold the intruding strangers at bay. With an efficient and strong distribution system already in place, Jolly Cola quickly established itself and was advertised heavily in cinemas and popular weekly magazines. In the early 1970s, Jolly Cola was still the dominant brand. Its advertis-ing campaigns featured groups of male and female teenagers relaxing and having fun together in the Danish summer, rowing canoes, splashing together in the sea on an inflatable mattress or strolling down a country road. The image of Coca-Cola and Pepsi (that entered the market in 1971) seemed to suffer from the

Marxist current in Danish youth culture in the 1970s. Danish playwright Nils Schou's piece *Marx and Coca-Cola* (1982) looks at this period in retrospective and suggests just how ideologically loaded the soft-drink was at the time. Both the title and the role of the product in the plot – the protagonist, a hypocritical young revolutionary, betrayed by his preference for the brown fluid, turns out to be a bourgeois in disguise – show how antithetical the product was to 'politically correct values'. America and its mass commodities were identified with imperialist capitalism. Anti-American feelings were also fuelled by the Vietnam War and years later Danish marketers would joke that it would take another Vietnam War or something of that order to help Jolly Cola rebound. From the late 1970s the cultural mood seems to have changed. New generations had less use for unambiguous, security-giving relations to the nation, the people, the Danish language or 'psyche', that sustained, and was sustained by, the patrolling of the nation's economic and cultural borders. As the restraining factors weakened, the American colas quickly gained ground. Media development became an important factor in the 1980s. The monopoly of the Danish state television was broken in 1988 and a new national network, TV2, began airing TV commercials for the first time in Denmark. Satellite and cable channels followed quickly. Coca-Cola made the most of the new advertising opportunities and at one point bought a whole commercial break and showed a range of its international Christmas ads. Confronted with such an overwhelming marketing attack, the dwindling local brand had to mount some kind of 'symbolic' defence of its remaining market share. The ad campaigns we describe were produced in the face of this bleak marketing reality. One of the commercials dealt very explicitly with the identification of Cola with America.

A young, blond woman approaches US customs and is stopped by a gruff US customs officer. The dialogue is in English but with Danish subtitles. The officer says in a brusque tone, 'Hey you!' Somewhat confused, the woman points to herself, 'Me?' 'That's right lady. Where do you come from?' In a clear, crisp voice with a Danish accent, the woman replies, 'Den-mark'. 'Let's see your luggage. Open it up!' He examines her bag and discovers a Jolly Light and exclaims, 'What the fuck is this: Jolly Light! What the hell is wrong with you, trying to bring a Danish light cola into the United States? Don't you realize that United States of America, ma'am, is the home of cola?' Unintimidated, the woman suggests, 'Why don't you taste it.' He opens the bottle, gulps a big mouthful and hesitates a moment. 'Hmmm. Not bad! We'll have to keep the rest for further investigation.' Cut. We see a huge storage room with confiscated items. On one shelf we see three empty bottles of Jolly Cola appear.

Product–country images are especially powerful narratives about the meanings and values transferred by products from their origin to their destination (Askegaard and Ger 1998; Bell and Valentine 1997). Contrary to the widespread belief that country images lose significance in a market increasingly driven by strong brands, uniform technology and production standards, imagery linking products and places are as strong as ever, not least because of the tendency of consumer culture to become culture consumed (Firat 1995).

Confronting the product–country image with respect to cola, the advertisement projects quite different images of America than Coke and Pepsi commercials do. Bosscher *et al.* (1996: 1) explain that the Americanisation of Western Europe 'throve in part on the appeal of cultural forms which were experienced as clearly sensually expressive, shrill, unvarnished, enthralling and overwhelming'. We find such expressions in campaigns like Coke's 'Can't Beat the Feeling' and recognise the skill with which a range of powerful human emotions and sentiments are engaged. Representatives of European high culture would label such American cultural forms 'vulgar' and 'superficial', but this hardly discourages young consumers, on the contrary. Jolly could try to replicate the feeling in the Coke ads but could hardly match the American resources and talent in this respect. Besides, playing at being American and keeping a straight face might not have been easy or credible anyway. Instead, Jolly engages in a sort of negative advertising that plays with aspects of the European repertoire of images of America. The choice of representative of American culture in the ad is rather conspicuous. The coarseness of the customs officer represents a different kind of vulgarity. He looks more like the archetypical bad cop, reminding us that beneath America's ideals of freedom, justice and equality is a reality of corruption, bigotry and brutality. The face of America in the ad, the officer, also contradicts the stereotypical values attributed to America in the standard commercial vernacular namely individualism, anti-authoritarianism and youth. In fact the visual imagery, mood and symbolism of the ad is reminiscent of Apple Computers classical '1984' commercial, which dramatises old fears of the totalitarian and authoritarian consequences of technological and social modernisation, which is part of what Americanisation has represented to Europeans. As Duhamel wrote in his 1931 book with the emblematic title *America the Menace: Scenes from the Life in the Future*, 'no nation has thrown itself into the excesses of industrial civilization more deliberately than America' (Duhamel, quoted in Bødker 1999: 92). The question is, however, whether Danish youth care about Americanisation while they sink their burgers with a Coke at one of the many new McDonald's or Burger King franchises that have mushroomed in Denmark in the past decade. They have a taste for American mass culture and in appropriating it they are increasingly asking for (or perhaps just being served) the real thing. It has become difficult to see America and its popular cultural forms as alien *per se*. Younger Danes seem to have a 'double cultural citizenship' or at least find it increasingly irrelevant to draw a clear line of distinction between Danish and American culture. It is typical of nations to affirm their own identity through a focus on the differences in relation to others (Morin 1984). Arguably, Danish national identity formation has shifted during the last decades. The EU and various immigrant groups have taken on the role as 'the Other' against which a national 'Self-hood' is defined. The paradoxical nature of the popular fear of the so-called 'Islamisation' of Danish society is so much more obvious as there is hardly a single minaret or real mosque in Denmark, but lots of temples for American consumer culture. A look at the names of even local companies or shops in the inevitable pedestrian shopping area of even the smallest provincial towns will provide ample evidence of the extension of the *lingua franca* of modern commercial culture.

The contrasting and contesting images of Danishness and Americanness in both this and the Jack the Dullard commercial illustrate the complex relationship between the local and the global analysed by Robertson (1995) and Pieterse (1995) among others. Images referring to the national folklore (blond women, 'pølsevogn', the Danishness of Andersen's fairytale, etc.) as well as 'global folk-lore' (the fairytale narrative, the reference to the USA as the land of know-how, performance and excellence, the myth of the meek that will inherit the world) join to constitute a new commercial folklore, making explicit the fact that adver-tising is the new format of the fairytale with the product in the role of the helper in classical narratological analysis (Heilbrunn 1998). This commercial folklore is addressing the same kind of cosmopolitan *anthropos* that we saw Morin (1962) refer to in his analysis of mass cultural phenomena.

'Coca-Kotlerization': cracking the cola-code

Coca-Cola has become the sacred canopy of the marketing imaginary. Its position as one of the exemplar products of mass consumer culture, hedonism and happi-ness does not only make Coca-Cola a multi-dimensional consumer icon visible and accessible in most parts of the world. It also seems to have obtained a status as a standard example of marketing excellence and a most beloved case as such in various marketing and consumer textbooks. Not a single textbook with aspir-ations of being taken seriously can avoid at least a few references to the marketing practices of this global product-icon. Consequently, Coca-Cola itself can be understood in terms of Brown's (1998) notion of 'Coca-Kotlerization'. Brown (1998: 63) wrote: 'After all, the most pernicious and pervasive form of colonial-ism in marketing [. . .] inheres in the whole Coca-Kotlerization process, the absolute and seemingly unbreakable dominance of American marketing scholar-ship in general and the Kotlerite model of analysis, planning, implementation and control in particular'. Marketing is God and Kotler is his prophet – for academics and teachers all over the world. However, for many practitioners, the global success story of Coca-Cola has won it a similar position as world exponents for 'good' marketing practices, in both senses of the word. In terms of practice, the prophet is Coca-Cola! (Perhaps a couple of others count too.) The universe of Coca-Cola is absolutely good, from its sponsoring efforts in connection with world celebrations of sports events like the soccer World Cup or the Olympics, to its (re)invention of the modern Santa Claus, the cuddly ice bears, nice family gatherings in the garden, happy spontaneous outbreaks of musical energy, or a world united under the colours of Coca-Cola. The unification of the world in itself symbolises the success and the marketing excellence of the Coca-Kotlerite approach, and underlines one more time the point of Usunier (1996), that the first cross-cultural thing to note about (modern) marketing is that (modern) marketing is inherently an American phenomenon.

Reverting to the Jack the Dullard theme, this slick professionalism and over-whelming 'know-how' − a term that also rings an American bell in Danish, since in its original English form it is a part of colloquial speech − occupies a certain position in the Danish context. At the same time admired and frowned upon, it represents the efficiency and profitability of 'business American-style' as well as the intrusion and the aggression of this foreign element in the calm and consensus-driven little garden-kingdom called Denmark. Confronted with such powers, few Danish advertisers would obtain any credibility in seeking to play the same game or even to beat the intruding giants in a marketing cacophony. Leaving the loud marketing screams to Pepsi's pop music kings and queens, Jolly instead provided yet another answer that revealed the company's acceptance of the Coca-Cola mastery of marketing magic and simultaneously gave it an ironic twist. Jolly took to the possibly most fundamental icon of the icon: the unique, curvaceous bottle, the shape of which had become so synonymous with the product that the Coca-Cola Company in the 1990s decided to put a picture of the bottle on the Coca-Cola cans! A campaign was run, featuring a test lab, where a voice-over presents the spectator with the fundamental marketing problem: that Jolly Cola does well in blind tastes and compares also in price but that the fundamental problem must be that the product comes in an ordinary Danish soda bottle. Hence a series of mock tests is shown with consumers commenting on a prototype for a new Jolly bottle: 'Problem: It quenches thirst magnificently, but is perceived as unoriginal. Cause: It sounds and tastes like the foreign colas and the bottle is a non-sexy Danish soft-drink bottle.' A bottle of Jolly Cola is opened in front of a microphone and poured over a glass full of ice cubes. Then the picture suddenly changes. Through a test observation camera picture with an on-screen green frame, digits and status messages we look into a laboratory setting where two scientists in white coats are preparing a test experiment. 'But we are now testing an alternative.' A very phallic bottle (awkward-looking, long necked, and curved; not unlike those heat-twisted Coca-Cola bottles found in souvenir stores) is pre-sented to various test subjects. 'It looks like . . . uhmm . . . ' a young man wearing sunglasses says. Another tilts backwards on his chair in sheer astonishment. A reappearing character, a long-haired guy wearing a big hat, howls and makes odd gestures, and finally starts dancing, using the bottle as a maraca singing 'la cucara-cha'. Two young women are delighted, and one of them turns to a researcher and asks him if he (his) had been the model. An older woman is disgusted and calls the researcher a pig. The narrator continues, 'Conclusion: the bottle provokes excit-ing responses. However, the idea has been dropped in favour of a new light bottle that simply contains twice as much.' 'Neither original nor sexy. But good against thirst.' The final slogan (Neither original . . .) appears on the screen.

In this parody on marketing research, Jolly Cola simultaneously acknowledged the indisputable fact that there is something 'magic' about the marketing icons such as the Coke's hobbleskirt bottle and logo. But on the other hand, it invited (Danish) consumers to turn their back on the marketing magicians and go for the (stereo)typically Danish, down-to-earth, no-nonsense (functional) approach to what constitutes a suitable product. The fetishism attached to the Coca-Cola bottle further underlines the extremely strong symbolic values attached to the product – maybe best underlined by what Pendergrast (1993) has termed the largest business blunder ever in history; the disastrous launching of the New Coke at the height of the cola wars in 1986. Now it stands as a classical example of poor application of marketing research and a company's lack of comprehension of the character of its own product and consumers' 'co-ownership' of a brand.[4] This evidence of the primacy of image over taste (or an extended product definition over a narrow one) was corroborated in the Danish context. Jolly Cola at one point in time decided to alter the taste slightly in order to bring it closer to the taste of the big colas. In spite of the fact that tests demonstrated consumers' appreciation of the new taste, it did not help much. And what is perhaps more depressing, no public outrage followed as in the case of the new Coke. A more recent campaign made direct references to the American cola wars and, more explicitly, to the Pepsi Challenge campaign. When Pepsi in the early 1990s ran a Danish version of the Pepsi (taste) Challenge, inviting loyal Coca-Cola drinkers to pick their favourite cola in a series of blind taste sessions led by MTV-hostess Maiken Wexø, Pepsi at the time concluded that, '52.6 per cent preferred Pepsi', a number that was insignificant to all but the totally innumerate in the audience. Would pseudo-scientific evidence in a format that looked like a revival of a patent medicine hoax really be taken seriously? Not by Jolly, who offered the following spoof on the blind-test in a recent ad: a blindfolded man is trying to find his seat at a table in front of the picture. We are in a large storage area with Jolly Cola boxes stacked to the roof. In the background three blindfolded women from the national Danish handball team are sampling the drink. The man is introduced on the screen as 'Tage Stilling, Jolly's head of advertising' (in Danish the name is a pun meaning 'decide', 'to decide' or 'take a stand'). 'Ooops. Well now it is not that we want to be invisible, but we are actually conducting a blind test of the new Jolly with professional assistance from the Jolly-girls,' he says making a gesture backwards towards the handball players. The Danish female national handball team have been the whole nation's favourites by winning the gold medal at the (Coca-Cola) Olympics in Atlanta, 1996. They were known as the 'Metal-girls' then. Jolly had only recently taken over the sponsorship from the Danish (overwhelmingly male) steelworkers' union. Blindfolded, Tage Stilling turns the glass the wrong way around and spills Jolly Cola out on the table as he tries to pour from the bottle. He discovers the mistake and manages to fill his glass. After having tasted the drink he exclaims, 'mmm . . . Yes . . . it's now proven that Jolly tastes good. Even in the dark. Isn't it girls?' He turns around, disoriented and unable to locate the women.

Structuring the common differences

We are now better able to understand the powers the modern Danish cola-version of Jack the Dullard is up against. The hegemony of Coca-Cola (and Pepsi) on the world market lie not only in their overpowering marketing machines and their relative control over distribution systems around the world, but also as much, if not more, in the sheer fact that symbolically they have set and are setting the scene for the so-called battle over the consumers' minds (Ries and Trout 1981).

Since the big colas stepped up their efforts in Denmark around 1980, the constant representations of a global youth culture by the major colas and the growing influx of 'global food' (represented first and foremost by multinational fast food chains) has fundamentally changed the situation for what already appeared like an oxymoronic phenomenon: the 'national' (Jolly) cola. This is not to argue that Coca-Cola and Pepsi are entering the Danish market as true global products. As pointed out by Pieterse (1995) and Robertson (1995), among others, the global always transforms to a hybrid or glocalised phenomenon by the local context. And both Friedman (1990) and, as discussed earlier, Miller (1998) demonstrate how Coca-Cola takes on locally contextualised meanings. As one Coca-Cola slogan goes, 'We are multi-national, we are multi-local' (quoted in Bell and Valentine 1997: 190). This has also been the case in Denmark. The presence and, indeed, once dominant position of Jolly Cola surely has shaped the particular market context and the significations of all present cola brands. On the other hand, to claim that Coca-Cola is 'a remarkably unsuitable candidate for [the] role as the key globalized corporation' (Miller 1998: 171) is probably to underestimate the significations Coca-Cola carries beyond the specificities of one or the other market context.

In many ways, we believe that 'cola', and in our particular case the constellation of the two giant American Colas together with Jolly Cola, constitutes a phenomenon that could be characterised much like Wilk (1995) characterises the global institution of the beauty pageant. Cola, like the beauty pageant:

> presents the basic paradox of globalisation in an especially clear form; in each place the [cola] is made into a local institution, embedded in specific social relationships, invested with meaning by unique groups in a particular histor-ical context. But at the same time, in some ways, the [cola] also creates larger

relations of uniformity, casting local differences in ways that, on a global scale, are predictable and surprisingly uniform.

(Wilk 1995: 110)

The situation of the very local Jolly Cola is caught up in those 'global structures of common difference', a term proposed by Wilk (1995), defined by the global strategies and imagery of Coca-Cola and Pepsi respectively. It is difficult, if not impossible, for Jolly to 'change the script' (as Pepsi's slogan would have it).

Ritzer is 'hard pressed to see McHuevos [Uruguay] or McLaks [Norway] or elegant dates at fast food restaurants as significant local variations on the homogenizing process of McDonaldization' (1998: 86). Similarly, the situation of Jolly reminds us of the unequal distribution of power between the global and local players in the market. As Ritzer points out, neither the continued distinctiveness of local markets, nor the deterritorialisation of global products and consumption patterns (Appadurai 1990) annihilates the continued relevance of the territory from which the global product emanates, largely the United States. In accordance with Ritzer then, and without denying the complexities of the globalisation process, the story of Jolly demonstrates that the West in general and the United States in particular today holds the upper hand in the global exchanges of consumer imagery and products.

The structures of common difference, then, rest on the powerful imagery attached to the 'territory of origin' and of the global marketing of the cola companies but these efforts would be in vain if it was not for the willingness of the local audience to engage in and perpetuate the myths of the 'always the real thing', a.k.a. the 'all-American drink' or the 'choice of a new (global) generation'. The advertising efforts of 'Jolly Cola' showed us the field of significations in which the positioning battle of the colas in Denmark that are played out against each other are set by the local 'Americanness' of the two giants, their references to world culture, their wars against each other, and the whole mythology created and maintained in the interplay between (especially) Coca-Cola, the product, and Coca-Cola, the icon of consumer culture. This way, paradoxically, the local character of Jolly Cola has only one point of gravity: the globality of the competitors. The 'tragedy' for the local company is that all these efforts have not led to a stronger national identification. Hence, Jolly's resistance has, for the last decade, been symbolic in the double sense of the word: it has been played out in a register of symbolic images copying and countering the marketing imagery of the global competitors. This, however, has been largely in vain, generating some sympathy in terms of the communication efforts, but constantly trailing the competitors in terms of number of exposures and having had no positive impact in raising the market share of the brand.

The mere existence of a 'national cola' is in itself a result of the global structures of common difference, as is witnessed by the introduction of the product in

1959 as a response to the opening of the Danish market for Coca-Cola. As phrased by Wilk, 'while different cultures continue to be quite distinct and varied, they are becoming different in very uniform ways' (1995: 118). Jolly Cola may be Danish, but it is still a cola (and its name is suggestive of the foreignness of this product). Furthermore, Jolly Cola has altered (adapted) its taste with reference to the taste of American colas, it has altered its bottle types according to its American competitors, and it has consistently throughout the last fifteen years positioned itself against the symbolic universes of Coca-Cola and Pepsi. Thus, the uniform ways in which cultures differ in this case seem to be totally designated by the global forces rather than the local ones, which is exactly the kind of hegemony that arises also from Wilk's analysis.

The ugly . . .

The story of the good (global harmony, family values, etc.), the bad (challenging youth culture, Michael Jackson, etc.) and the jolly (numskull, village fool) cola in Denmark elucidates one of the problems of a local producer trying to 'outlocal' global producers (Ger 1999). Jolly Cola whether playing with or against the 'Coca-Cola commercial vernacular' can never become much more than the equivalent of a spaghetti-Western: a diverting imitation but never really 'it' and never, never 'the real thing' that defines the category. Recently, the rights to Jolly Cola were bought by the regional brewery and bottler Albani and thus became even more local. The company believes that the previous ownership, dominated by Carlsberg, who in the meanwhile had started a Nordic collaboration with Coca-Cola, had neglected the brand. A current ad begins with Tage Stilling confiding in the audience, 'I might as well say it as is, we need to sell some more Jolly C . . . C . . . C . . .', he cannot pronounce cola, smiles apologetically and goes on to explain, 'that not many know it but Jolly has got a new taste'. It also seems to have lost the 'cola' tag, which does not appear on its new label. The advertisement borrows ideas from some of the most successful national ads of the past year, for instance Tuborg's ad for its strong domestic 'Squash' brand of orange soda. In this ad the protagonist has tried to ask for a 'Tuborg Sq . . . Sq . . . Squa . . . Squaaaa . . .' in a drugstore for a decade without being able to pronounce the English word 'squash'. Whether it helps to lose the cola, as if to avoid comparisons to the credible colas, is questionable. Some might say it is the 'jolly' that ought to be lost instead. When was that word part of the popular idiom anywhere? But of course then what would be left? Albani is situated in Odense, the Alma Mater of Hans Christian Andersen, where they – we – keep retelling his world famous tales, especially the one about the ugly duckling who, in spite of the trials and tribulations, grew up to become a beautiful swan.

Notes

1 In English, the fairy tale is known under the titles: Clod Hans, Clod-poll, Clumsy Hans, Numskull Jack, and Simple Simon.

2 A term introduced in Malcolm Quinn's (1994, quoted in Miller 1998: 186) analysis of the history of the swastika. The word 'swastika' derives from the sanskrit 'svastika', which means 'conductive to well-being', the essence of Coke's core brand identity.

3 The picture is of course more complex, since the USA is not the only source of new cultural forms affecting Europe. The global cultural flows are immensely complex, and creolisation perhaps a general cultural condition.

4 Of course, ultimately Coca-Cola rebounded impressively after the blunder, re-establishing much of their reputation and regaining their market share and more. Miller fails to note this in his first argument against seeing the Coca-Cola Company role as a key example of a globalised corporation. His second point, that Coke is based on a franchise system and therefore not representative, is equally dubious (consider McDonald's, Avis, etc.).

References

Andersen, H.C. (1855/1995) *Samlede eventyr og historier*, Copenhagen: Hans Reitzels Forlag.

Appadurai, A. (1990) 'Disjunction and difference in the global cultural economy', in M. Featherstone (ed.) *Global Culture*, London: Sage, 295–310.

Askegaard, S. and Ger, G. (1998) 'Product-country images: towards a contextualized approach', in B. Englis and A. Olofsson (eds) *European Advances in Consumer Research*, 3, Provo, UT: Association for Consumer Research, 50–8.

Barthes, R. (1993) *Mythologies*, London: Vintage Books.

Baudrillard, J. (1976) *L'éxchange symbolique et la mort*, Paris: Gallimard.

Bell, D. and Valentine, G. (1997) *Consuming Geographies. We Are Where We Eat*, London: Routledge.

Bosscher, D. *et al.* (eds) (1996) *American Culture in the Netherlands*, Amsterdam: VU University Press.

Brown, S. (1998) *Postmodern Marketing 2: Telling Tales*, London: ITBP.

Bødker, H. (1999) *Distance and Immersion: 'America' Across the Atlantic – Three Twentieth Century Practices*, unpublished doctoral dissertation, SDU Odense University.

Featherstone, M. (1991) *Consumer Culture and Postmodernism*, London: Sage.

Firat, A. F. (1995) 'Consumer culture or culture consumed', in J.A. Costa and G.J. Bamossy (eds) *Marketing in a Multicultural World*, Thousand Oaks, CA: Sage, 115–35.

Friedman, J. (1990) 'Being in the world: globalization and localization', in M. Featherstone (ed.) *Global Culture*, London: Sage, 311–28.

Ger, G. (1999) 'Localizing in the global village: local firms competing in global markets', *California Management Review* 41, 4: 64–83.

Hannerz, U. (1992) *Cultural Complexity. Studies in the Social Organization of Meaning*, New York: Columbia University Press.

Heilbrunn, B. (1998) 'My brand the hero? a semiotic analysis of the consumer-brand relationships', in M. Lambkin *et al.* (eds) *European Perspectives on Consumer Behaviour*, London: Prentice Hall Europe, 370–401.

Howes, D. (ed.) (1996) *Cross-Cultural Consumption. Global Markets, Local Realities*, London: Routledge.

Kroes, R. (1996) *If You've Seen One, You've Seen the Mall: Europeans and American Mass Culture*, Urbana: University of Illinois Press.

Miller, D. (1998) 'Coca-Cola: a black sweet drink from Trinidad', in D. Miller (ed.) *Material Cultures: Why Some Things Matter*, Chicago: University of Chicago Press, 169–87.

Morin, E. (1962) *L'Esprit du temps*, Paris: Editions Grasset.

—— (1984) 'Pour une théorie de la nation', in *Sociologie*, Paris: Fayard, 129–38.

Pendergrast, M. (1993) *For God , Country and Coca-Cola*, New York: Collier Books.

Pieterse, J.N. (1995) 'Globalization as hybridization', in M. Featherstone, S. Lash and R. Robertson (eds) *Global Modernities*, London: Sage, 45–68.

Ries, A. and Trout, J. (1981) *Positioning: The Battle for Your Mind*, New York: McGraw-Hill.

Ritzer, G. (1998) *The McDonaldization Thesis*, London: Sage.

Robertson, R. (1995) 'Glocalization: time-space and homogeneity-heterogeneity', in M. Featherstone *et al.* (eds) *Global Modernities*, London: Sage, 25–44.

Schou, N. (1982) *Marx og Coca-Cola*, Gråsten: Drama.

Usunier, J.-C. (1996) *Marketing Across Cultures*, London: Prentice-Hall Europe.

Wilk, R. (1995) 'Learning to be local in Belize: global structures of common difference', in D. Miller (ed.) *Worlds Apart. Modernity Through the Prisms of the Local*, London: Routledge, 110–33.

Witzel, M.K. and Young-Witzel, G. (1998) *Soda Pop! From Miracle Medicine to Pop Culture*, Vancouver: Raincoast Books.

Wunenburger, J.-J. (1991) *L'imagination*, Paris: Presses Universitaires de France, coll. Que sais-je.

Section II
Aesthetics

New Shoes

I'm on a mission to buy black shoes
Of which I have a lack
I only own three dozen pairs
Eight pairs of which are black

I really need these new black shoes
The latest style you see
To go with my brand new black suit
A Diderot unity

I really must have them, and soon
It's a genuine need
An absolute necessity
A calling I must heed

My conscience hurts me a little
When I see all my shoes
The thought of all those starving kids
That I see on the news

Instead I focus on the suit
And how great it will feel
To have a complete ensemble
From neck right down to heel

Evaluation of Alternatives:

For weeks I have been vigilant
Scanning others' footwear
Watching all the advertisements
To see what is out there

Shoes are important for image
Right there for all to see
One is judged by foot attire
So I choose carefully

It is a complex task to choose
The shoes just right for me
They must reflect my place in life
And do it blatantly

My job, my marital status,
My age, my sex, my roles
Each must be accommodated
By these leather and soles

Should they be modern or classic?
Should they have heel or none?
Pointed toe or square? I am quite
Confused before begun

This choice is very important
I care what others think
My time, my energy, my hopes,
And my money I sink

144

The Purchase:

Off I go all ready to buy
Keen to find the right pair
At last I have a style in mind
Now to find them out there

As I set off I see myself
So well accessorised
With those new shoes I have in mind
That I've seen advertised

How hard can it be, so much choice
So many shoes and stores
My pair must be out there somewhere
My spirits start to soar

But soon I remember the past
Those aborted attempts
To find a pair that fit with style
I become pale and tense

Sneakers are what I want deep
    down
Comfortable and secure
But they don't meet the image need
For this I need much more

Why can't I have style and comfort
In just one pair of shoes?
Can't both be accommodated?
Why does one have to lose?

Why is it that the comfy ones
Are not acceptable?
Instead I have to have the ones
That pinch, pressure, and pull

Plodding through endless stores and
    malls
They start to look the same
Have we already done this one?
I'm now sick of this game

I want to spend my hard-earned cash
I have it in my hand
But the more I try to spend it
The less I find I can

The pressure mounts, my husband
    groans
Our toddler's bored to tears
How long can I keep on going?
The surrender time nears

Attendant after attendant
Their eyes glazing over
Try to assist me with my cause
But soon run for cover

I feel bad for bothering them
Guilt tempered with desire
I need their unending patience
Even though they tire

My wits are dulled, my spirits low
I make a selection
I go for a compromise pair
A grudging decision

Cognitive Dissonance:

Now I have a pair of shoes
That don't meet my criteria
They're quite stiff and uncomfortable
The style is inferior

Now every time I wear my shoes
I sink a bit inside
I should have bought those other ones
I feel quite self-maligned

But one point of comfort remains
Soon they'll be outdated
Then I can buy another pair
To be satiated!

Simone Pettigrew

8 Presenting the past: on marketing's re-production orientation

Stephen Brown, Elizabeth C. Hirschman and Pauline Maclaran

The postmodern . . . is an attempt to think the present historically in an age that has forgotten how to think historically in the first place.

(Jameson 1991: xi)

Introduction

In January 1998, the 'new' Volkswagen Beetle was launched in the United States to resounding critical acclaim and unalloyed customer approval. Designed by leading automotive imagineer, J. Mays, and manufactured at a state-of-the-art plant in Puebla, Mexico, the new Beetle combined the distinctive bubble shape of the old VW Bug with the latest automotive technology to produce a futuristic car with anachronistic styling (*The Economist* 1998).

Although the new Beetle is not the first retro-vehicle – the Mazda Miata started the trend in 1989 – its rapid acceptance and mass-market appeal have stimulated a significant about turn in the automobile industry (Pearman 1999a). Most major manufacturers have announced variations on the 'yestertech' theme. Examples include the Chrysler PT Cruiser, a pastiche of the upright sedans of the 1940s; the BMW Z07, which evokes the two-seater Ferraris of the 1950s; and the 'new' Ford T-Bird, an affectionate homage to the style, if not the under-braked, over-powered performance, of the 1954 original (Hutton 1999).

The neo-VW and its automotive imitations may exemplify the 're-production orientation' of the motor industry (re-production, insofar as it involves producing the old anew, not reproducing the old as was), but they are not alone. Retro-styling is *de rigueur* in numerous product categories including motor cycles, coffee makers, cameras, radios, refrigerators, telephones, watches, toasters and perfumes, to name but a few (Brown 1999). Retro, moreover, is apparent across the various components of the marketing mix, from faux-antique packaging and repro retail stores to on-line auctions, which represent a hi-tech throwback to pre-modern pricing practices (Alexander 1999). In addition to the cyber-souk, the recent, rapid rise of heritage parks suggests that retroscapes are taking their place in the marketing pantheon alongside brandscapes, servicescapes, marketscapes, mindscapes and several other 'scapes' besides (Appadurai 1986; Bitner 1992; Sherry 1998a, 1999; Venkatesh 1998).

Naturally, these presentations of the past have not gone unnoticed by marketing academicians. Some commentators consider this retroactivity to be part and parcel of the much-heralded postmodern condition (Brown 1993,1995; Firat and Venkatesh 1993, 1995), whereas others have examined the advent of nostalgic themes in advertising and the significance of consumer nostalgia generally (e.g. Belk 1991; Holak and Havlena 1992; Holbrook 1993; Holbrook and Schindler 1996; McCracken 1988; Stern 1992). Path-breaking though such publications have proved, there remains ample scope for additional research. The postmodern approach, for example, is predicated on theoretical speculation rather than empirical investigation and analyses of consumer nostalgia have tended to concentrate on a single component of the marketing mix – advertising and promotion. There is scope, therefore, for postmodernist empirical analyses of non-promotional phenomena such as retro-products, retro-services and, as the present chapter will show, retro-scapes.

This chapter, then, aims to examine marketing's re-production orientation by means of a detailed empirical study of three heritage parks. After outlining the emergence, growth and proliferation of the heritage park concept, it contends that the work of a prominent postmodern literary theorist, Fredric Jameson, provides an appropriate means of reading the heritage retroscape. The chapter continues with a summary of the empirical research programme; interprets the heritage text in terms of five key Jamesonian themes; and concludes with a succinct discussion of the future of retro-marketing. In keeping with the interpretive research tradition, which aspires to idiographic insightfulness rather than the theory-building nomothetism of neo-positivistic scholarship, this chapter does not attempt to construct a general model of re-production orientation. Instead, it seeks to draw attention to an important marketing phenomenon – presenting the past – and thereby contribute to the growing stream of postmodern marketing scholarship.

The heritage age

In recent years, it has often been suggested that the 'modern' era, which dates from the Enlightenment of the seventeenth century, has given way to a new historical epoch, tentatively termed postmodernity (Bauman 1997; Best and Kellner 1991, 1997; Connor 1997; Sim 1998). Not everyone concurs with this contention, as the virulent pro- and anti- debate readily testifies. Nevertheless, it is widely accepted that museums epitomise the hypothesised shift from a modernist to a postmodernist sensibility (Featherstone 1991; Rojek 1993, 1995; Urry 1990) and few would deny that museological issues have exercised the imaginations of the postmodern intelligentsia (e.g. Baudrillard 1994; Bourdieu 1984; Clifford 1988; Derrida 1987; Eco 1986; Haraway 1984–5; Harvey 1989; Huyssen 1995).

Traditionally regarded as an august repository of aesthetic accomplishment, artistic genius and, not least, national pride, today's museums have increasingly abandoned their elitist associations, serried ranks of tedious display cases and reverential aura of silent contemplation (Belk 1995; Brown 1995). Participation, excitement, performance, multimedia effects and spectacular 'blockbuster' shows, with their attendant memorabilia, tie-in products and promotional activities, are the order of the day (Berger 1998; Moore 1997). Dullness has been discarded, information overload eschewed and customer delight has become the measure of success. Museums are moving, in effect, from a product to a marketing orientation and marketers, in turn, are becoming increasingly interested in museological issues. Customer surveys (Fife and Ross 1996; Hooper-Greenhill 1988; Merriman 1989), user typologies (Bagnall 1996; Macdonald 1996; Umiker-Sebeok 1992), object relations (Fitchett and Saren 1998; Kelly 1993; McCracken 1990), the poetics and politics of display (Dubin 1999; Duhaime *et al.* 1995; Gable 1995), plus all manner of planning, strategy and implementation issues (Butler 2000; Kotler and Kotler 1998; McLean 1997) are occupying the fertile minds of marketing academicians and museum administrators alike.

Heritage parks, or open-air museums, are symptomatic of the growing interpenetration of museology and marketing, with all the associated tensions concerning commercialisation and commodification (Walsh 1992). An often uneasy amalgam of traditional museum and theme park, they typically comprise an array of replica, reconstructed or reproduction buildings on an historical site and, as often as not, are peopled with attendants in period costume who perform suitably antiquarian tasks (shoeing horses, baking bread, spinning thread, etc.). There is, admittedly, considerable variation on the heritage theme theme (Leon and Piatt 1989). At one extreme lies Disney's aborted Heritageland USA, with its money-spinning rides, restaurants and residential facilities (Lowenthal 1998). At the other extreme are 'authentic' archaeological sites like Newgrange, Ireland, which comprises little more than a car park, low-rise visitors' centre and the tastefully refurbished megalithic tombs themselves (O'Kelly 1996). In between lie all sorts of heritage marketing hybrids: megabrand museums (Belk 1995; Pine and Gilmore 1999), museum stores (Brown 1999; Costa and Bamossy 1995), corporate collections (Joy 1993; Samuel 1994), Nike Town-style flagships (Harrigan 1998; Sherry 1998a) and festival shopping malls, many of which occupy historic buildings, as in the celebrated cases of South Street Seaport, New York, and Powerscourt House, Dublin (Boyer 1992; Maclaran and Stevens 1998). Be that as it may, all such historically themed recreations are as one in their attempts to present the past for profit, or a semblance of profit.

Although heritage parks are widely considered to be characteristically post-modern, they are not prototypically postmodern. To the contrary, the heritage park concept dates from 1891, when the Museum of Scandinavian Folklore opened on a 75-acre site just outside Stockholm. Testimony to the *fin de siècle*'s preoccupation with the past and the contemporaneous invention of national traditions (Hobsbawm and Ranger 1983; Lears 1983), Artur Hazelius' Skansen park was swiftly followed by several Scandinavian facsimiles, most notably the Danish National Museum of 1901, which comprised a collection of reconstructed rural buildings set in a 90-acre park (Walsh 1992). Disseminated, furthermore, by the world's fairs of the late nineteenth century – many of which incorporated egregious national tableaux – the folk-life format took hold overseas, especially in the United States (Ettema 1987; Wallace 1986). The first of many American heritage parks opened in 1929 at Greenfield Village, Dearborn, Michigan. Funded in its entirety by Henry Ford, the museum consisted of:

> A traditional New England green with church, town hall, courthouse, post office and general store; the Scottish Settlement schoolhouse Ford attended as a boy; the Plymouth, Michigan, carding mill to which Ford's father took wool; Noah Webster's house; William Holmes McGuffy's Pennsylvania log-cabin birthplace; a 500-ton stone Cotswold Cottage; and the Sir John Bennett jewelry shop from Cheapside, London, with its clock graced by statues of Gog and Magog.
>
> (Walsh 1992: 96)

History, for Ford, may have been bunk but heritage parks clearly had their place. And, where Ford led, others inevitably followed. John D. Rockefeller Jr. underwrote Colonial Williamsburg, Virginia, to the tune of $79 million. The Wells Brothers of the American Optical Company sponsored Old Sturbridge Village, Massachuetts, and, suitably impressed by the success of these first-generation facilities, Walt Disney took things to their logical conclusion in 1955. Main Street USA, which was fashioned on Disney's rose-tinted recollections of his turn-of-the-century childhood in Marceline, Missouri, is the epitome of ersatz history and frequently denounced as such. Yet it is generally acknowledged within the heritage industry that Disneyland set the standard against which contemporary developments continue to be measured and, indeed, its enormous popularity did much to fuel the post-war heritage boom (Bryman 1995; Fjellman 1992; King 1991; Sorensen 1989). More than half the 15, 000 museums in the United States are less than forty years old and heritage facilities comprise approximately 55 per cent of the total (Kotler and Kotler 1998). Analogous attractions, furthermore, have been opened in almost every corner of the globe (The Polynesian Cultural

Center, Hawaii; Kyongju World Tradition Folk Village, Seoul; Tjapukai Cultural Theme Park, Cairns, Western Australia; Museum of Welsh Life, Cardiff, etc.).

Needless to say, the proliferation of heritage parks, sites and centres has spawned a prodigious scholarly literature on the merits and demerits of such phenomena (see Lowenthal 1985, 1989a, 1989b, 1998). As a rule, these assessments are unremittingly hostile, focusing on the meretriciousness rather than the meritoriousness of the museums' mutant offspring. Their popularity with the paying public is of course acknowledged, as are their beneficial economic effects, especially in areas of high unemployment and social deprivation. But heritage facilities, generally speaking, are treated with ill-disguised disdain (Boniface and Fowler 1993; Chase and Shaw 1989; Hewison 1987; Pearman 1999b). They misrepresent the past; they entertain rather than educate; they destroy what they purport to preserve; they eviscerate visitors' sense of place; they display decontextualised artefacts without proper explanations or labelling; they employ the apparatus of scholarship to legitimise anti-scholarly practices; they are all the same, despite minor surface variations; they tell sanitised, depoliticised, hopelessly distorted stories about the homogenised heritage in question; they are in thrall to the machinations of multi-national capital and mendacious marketers, with their bogus logos, banal branding exercises, prosaic strategic plans, cheapjack souvenir stalls and embarrassing promotional stunts. In short, they trivialise, they titillate, they twist the truth to the point of travesty and, worst of all, they pander to the lowest common denominator in pursuit of filthy lucre, customer throughput and profit maximisation.

Marketing, then, is held largely responsible for the flagrant philistinism of the heritage industry. It is widely regarded as a necessary evil at best and grand larceny at worst (Belk 1995; Cosgrove 1993; Fowler 1992; Samuel 1994; West 1988; Wright 1985). Indeed, the cultural studies literature is replete with condemnations of customer-led gimmickry and the dangers of 'Disneyfication' (Moore 1997). Such criticisms, however, not only misconstrue the nature of marketing but they misrepresent the purpose of heritage. According to Lowenthal's (1998) recent manifesto, it is important to distinguish between heritage and history. The former is not simply a crass, commodified, over-commercialised version of the latter, it serves a different purpose entirely. Unlike history, heritage does not engage with the past in order to better understand 'what actually happened'. It is, rather, a celebration of the past, an attempt to exploit the past for essentially non-scholarly but equally legitimate purposes – entertainment, edification and ethnic glorification, in the main. Heritage and history interpenetrate, to be sure, but to denounce heritage as biased or 'bad' history is to miss the point. The critics, what is more, presuppose that history comprises a body of objective, scientifically established facts that are demonstrably 'true', or as true as can be given the inadequacies of the historical record. The truth, however, is that history is not true, as such, nor is it free from subjectivity.

On the contrary, history is constantly being revised, revoked, remade, remoulded, reworked, rewritten. As the latter-day postmodern turn in historiography has made clear, the past is inaccessible by definition and all avenues to the past are paved with textual material – archives, secondary sources and, not least, the story-telling endeavours of professional historians. The modernist search for historical truth has been superseded by the postmodernist emphasis on historical text (Iggers 1997; Jenkins 1997; Munslow 1997; McCullagh 1998).

Postmodern textuality and the Jameson effect

History, of course, is only one among many academic disciplines – marketing included – to be affected by postmodern textuality (Doherty *et al.* 1992; Hollinger 1994; Rosenau 1992). Not every commentator, admittedly, considers the textual trope to be the 'essence' of postmodernism, not least because essentialism is an anathema to postmodernists. Yet few would deny that contemporary scholarly discourse is heavily inflected by a textual dialect (Thompson 1998a). As numerous researchers have shown, meaningful insights into marketing phenomena can be obtained when they are treated as texts and the apparatus of literary theory is brought to bear on advertisements, shopping centres, service encounters or whatever (e.g. Belk 1986; Hirschman and Holbrook 1992; McQuarrie and Mick 1992, 1996; Scott 1994; Stern 1989). Somewhat surprisingly, however, the work of America's leading postmodern literary theorist, Fredric Jameson, has not figured prominently in these deliberations. It has, of course, often been alluded to (Belk and Bryce 1993; Firat and Venkatesh 1993, 1995; Peñaloza 1994; Scott 1992; Thompson 1999) but, in light of the direct relevance of his ideas to retro-marketing, much more remains to be divulged and, indeed, demonstrated.

In certain respects, Fredric Jameson is the forgotten figure of postmodern thought. Although he has been described as 'the foremost contemporary literary critic' (Kellner 1994: 424) and 'the most important cultural critic writing in English today' (McCabe 1992: ix), he has not been accorded the megastar status of, say, Michel Foucault, Jacques Derrida, Jean Baudrillard or Roland Barthes. Whereas the latter theorists come equipped with an enormous secondary literature of 'readers', 'anthologies', 'commentaries' and, made simple, summaries, bite-sized introductions to Fredric Jameson are conspicuous by their absence. The few that there are, furthermore, are almost as abstruse as the original and most definitely not 'for dummies' (Dowling 1984; Homer 1998; Kellner 1989).

The comparative neglect of Fredric Jameson is hard to comprehend, given the fecundity of his thought, but it is largely due to a notoriously difficult writing style. His sentences are well-nigh Proustian in their interminability. They are embedded, what is more, in prodigiously long paragraphs, which stretch without missing a beat to the distant horizon of his seemingly unending essays. In this regard, of course, Jameson is not alone. Postmodern writing *per se* is deliberately, often wilfully inaccessible, but it is fair to say that Jameson's style lacks the redeeming features of, say, Derrida's ready wit, Baudrillard's aphoristic bent, Foucault's empirical leanings or Barthes's brilliant *bon mots*. Although he is widely cited, not least by marketing scholars, it is striking that the bulk of these citations refer to a single – and uncharacteristically lucid – paper on postmodernism and consumer society (Jameson 1985).

Despite the difficulties of Jameson's less than limpid literary style, his work is particularly pertinent to the heritage park phenomenon and retro-marketing generally. Granted, he only actually mentions heritage sites on one occasion (Jameson 1991), albeit even then the reference is to a 1950s retroscape contained in a 1960s science fiction novel set in the then distant 'future anterior' of 1997! Yet, a Jamesonian approach may help shed some light on what he terms (after Lyotard, 1984) 'nostalgia for the present'. Like so many postmodern thinkers, what is more, style and content are inseparable; that is to say, the *way* Jameson makes his case is *part* of the case. For the purposes of the present discussion, nevertheless, five themes pertinent to heritage parks can be identified: *absence, narration, hyperspace, retrotopia* and *connectivity*.

Absence

Without doubt, the most striking aspect of Fredric Jameson's writing style is that it is absolutely replete with absences, evasions and deferrals; insofar as his publications are full of remarks like 'as will become apparent', 'which shall be examined presently' and 'to be considered below'. Although this tendency may seem like little more than a literary affectation, it is integral to Jameson's overall project, which is predicated on the Hegelian–Marxian procedure of dialectical reasoning. Dialectics, in essence, assumes that every object or concept contains within it that which it is not and that both are necessary for things to make sense (Adorno and Horkheimer 1973; Anderson 1983; Bhaskar 1993). Hence, day is only comprehensible in terms of night, male in terms of female, rural in terms of urban, good in terms of evil, life in terms of death, etc. It is the task of the theorist to investigate such absent presences and combine ostensibly contradictory positions in order to attain higher levels of understanding. In this respect, the style of Jameson's writing, characterised as it is by enormous dialectical sentences hingeing on a semi-colon, seeks to explicate and exemplify at one and the same time. His literary form literally informs.

Narrative

To be sure, Jameson's life-long commitment to dialectical reasoning is typical of his overall approach (Kellner 1994; Williams 1995; Young 1990). Unlike many postmodern thinkers, such as Baudrillard, Foucault and Barthes, whose research has been characterised by marked changes of direction and periodical epistemological breaks, Fredric Jameson has told a fairly consistent story. And the story he tells is about storytelling. From his earliest work on Sartre (Jameson 1961) to his recent reflections on Brecht (Jameson 1998a), narrative and narrativity are central to the Jamesonian corpus. As he trenchantly observed in his breakthrough text, *The Political Unconscious*, 'the all-informing process of *narrative* is the central function or *instance* of the human mind' (Jameson 1981: 13). What is more, whereas rival postmodern pundits have famously announced the demise of 'grand narratives' – scientific progress, human emancipation, economic growth and so on – Jameson resolutely refuses to alter his stance on narration. Not only does he consider narrative all pervasive, evident in everything from casual conversation to philosophical system-building, but also history itself consists of nothing but narratives (since the actual events of 'real' history are inaccessible to present-day investigators).

Hyperspace

Ironically, however, Jameson's preoccupation with narrative is belied by his own texts, which tend to be organised spatially (like patchwork quilts) rather than the traditional temporal alignment – from once upon a time to happily ever after – that is the linear, narrative norm in the Western literary tradition (Eagleton 1986). His works, in fact, have been described as 'pretend' books, as 'simulacra', as 'hyperreal' and this assessment is again very much in keeping with Jameson's preoccupation with postmodern architecture in general and decentred hyperspace in particular (Homer 1998). Space is a fundamental organising principle of postmodernism and it is fair to say that Jameson is best known for his representations of spatial representations (Los Angeles' Bonaventure Hotel, in particular). Like Jean Baudrillard (1983) and Umberto Eco (1986), two other noted authorities on the realer-than-real that is hyper-reality (Perry 1998), Jameson brilliantly evokes the total confusion (disorientation), unfocused arrangement (de-centredness) and blurred boundaries (de-differentiation) of postmodern architecture.

In this respect, Jameson (1984, 1985, 1994, 1998b) repeatedly opines on the difficulties of representing such utterly bewildering, increasingly ubiquitous, placelessly anonymous spaces (see Augé 1995; Relph 1987; Sherry 1998b) and, to this end, posits 'cognitive mapping' as a meaningful methodological possibility. Although it is based on the familiar map-drawing procedure posited by urban planner Kevin Lynch (1960), the technique is transformed in Jameson's dexterous hands to include poems, plays, paintings and various alternative forms of non-cartographic representation. Unlike Derrida's deconstruction, indeed, it is more than a mere anti-method methodology, a procedure for representing the unrepresentable. Cognitive mapping provides a means of linking the individual with society, the local with the global, the past with the present (Jameson 1992, 1998c).

Retrotopia

Just as the swirling confusion of the typical Jamesonian sentence encapsulates the discombobulating experience of postmodern hyperspace (McCabe 1992), so too a retrotopian orientation pervades his prodigious academic output. On the one hand, his writings are curiously old-fashioned, notwithstanding the contemporary subject matter, since his Marxist lexicon of 'hegemony', 'reification' and 'false consciousness' is somehow redolent of 1970s radicalism (Jameson 1991). This imbues his publications with a not unpleasant but slightly anachronistic tone, the textual equivalent of a retro product or television series. On the other hand, his style is 'truly utopian', a monumental accumulation of magisterial sentences, each one grammatically correct, laboriously constructed and flawlessly executed, with every sub-clause cemented firmly in place (Eagleton 1986). Like utopianism itself, they are unbearably, stupefyingly, excruciatingly perfect.

In this regard, however, Jameson (1971, 1985, 1998b) consistently defends humankind's utopian inclination, the unending search for something better, arguing that it is inscribed in even the most banal cultural artefacts from airport art and the *Reader's Digest* to romantic fiction and Las Vegas kitsch. But whereas modernists maintain that utopia resides in the infinite future, postmodernists look to the illimitable past. One of the central precepts of postmodernism is that stylistic innovation is to impossible, since everything has already been done, and all that remains is to recombine or evoke existing styles and methods in an ironic, playful, reflexive manner. According to Jameson (1984), the postmodern is characterised by *pastiche*, the imitation or amalgamation of different forms, categories and modalities, and *schizophrenia*, a disconcerting loss of historical depth – the very sense of history – since all possible pasts are perpetually present in the here and now. The apotheosis of these traits is the nostalgia or retro film (e.g. *American Graffiti*, *Blue Velvet* or, more recently, *Pleasantville*), which recreate the feel, shape and tone of older films whilst remaining incontestably up to date. Nostalgia in postmodernity, then, has nothing to do with emotional trauma, a deeply felt longing for past times (Davis 1979; Lowenthal 1985; Robertson 1990; Tannock 1995; Turner 1989), but the depersonalised, pseudo-historical appeal of a bygone aesthetic. History is no longer reached through the archive, but by means of stylistic recuperation and temporal stereotyping, which convey various forms of past-ness, be it 1930s-ness, 1950s-ness or an eternal 1970s beyond historical time.

Connectivity

The past is not only inexhaustible and infinitely recyclable (there have been several 1970s revivals since the 1970s), but it is readily rearranged. As postmodern architecture, with its mélange of (say) neoclassical, rococo and modernist motifs readily testifies, it is perfectly possible to have several contrasting 'pasts' occupying the same space at the same time. For many, in fact, it is this hybridisation, this juxtaposition of opposites, this tendency to connect the unconnected, that is the hallmark of postmodernism (Firat and Venkatesh 1993, 1995). It is, furthermore, one of the signature stratagems of Fredric Jameson, albeit such composite compositions cannot be divorced from his dialectical approach, which is predicated on openness, fluidity, catholicism and interweaving diverse conceptual positions. Dialectics takes everything in, leaves nothing out, notes analogies between what are normally regarded as separate domains in order to make unexpected connections and ultimately induce a 'dialectical shock' of recognition in the reader (Jameson 1991). Regardless of his rationale, the essential point is that connections and correspondences are everywhere in Fredric Jameson from political stance to literary style. As Eagleton (1986: 77) rightly observes, Jameson's work is characterised by 'coruscating connections and brilliant analogies'; his texts are an 'immense combinatoire' of other people's ideas, albeit with a novel twist; and, if his project had to be encapsulated in a couple of (suitably intertextual) words, they would be, 'only connect'.

Research sites and methods

Heritage sites, as Leon and Piatt (1989) note, are not only many in number but also exceedingly diverse in form, fame and freedom of curatorial expression. They range from internationally renowned individual buildings (Monticello, Mount Vernon), through eerily empty battlefields (Manassas, Culloden) to populist purveyors of pseudo-history, both good and bad (Balinesia, Busch Gardens). With the best will in the world, it is very difficult to draw a 'representative' sample from such an assemblage and, in keeping with analogous interpretive research (e.g. O'Guinn and Belk 1989; Sherry 1990, 1998a; Stern 1996; Thompson 1998b; Wallendorf et al. 1998), the present study comprises analyses of three contrasting yet closely related exemplars: the Museum of Appalachia, The Ulster–American Folk Park and The Ulster Folk and Transport Museum.

The Museum of Appalachia

Situated adjacent to the I-75, sixteen miles north of Knoxville, Tennessee, the Museum of Appalachia is dedicated to preserving the way of life of the people from the region. It consists of sixteen substantial buildings, plus outhouses and ancillary facilities, scattered in a loose semi-circle around an open, tree-fringed meadow. Exceptionally picturesque, especially in springtime, the 65-acre park is the life's work of John Rice Irwin, a former school teacher turned folklorist and author. The museum, consisting of a single log cabin, opened in 1969 and, thanks to the founder's boundless enthusiasm, local celebrity and collector's eye for a bargain, it has steadily expanded, with further developments in train (Irwin 1987).

In addition to the punctiliously reconstructed, fully refurnished and carefully maintained wooden buildings, which range from Mark Twain's family cabin to an implement festooned blacksmith shop, the museum includes a commodious Display Barn and three-storey Hall of Fame. The former contains the largest collection of pioneer artefacts in the United States – barbed wire, bear traps, band saws, beehives and many more besides – whereas the latter is a shrine to the region's renowned sons and daughters, though it also contains displays of toys, quilts, baskets, barrels, bayonets, unusual musical instruments, Native American relics and multitudinous Appalachian ephemera. A small restaurant, selling traditional, home-cooked vittles from the working farm, and a craft-cum-antiques shop, stocking locally manufactured gift items and excess objects from the founder's collection, are an integral part of the heritage park, as is a small, 100-seat auditorium, where musical performances (*A Night in Old Appalachia*) are staged for groups of visitors.

Although none of the three-strong management team has formal marketing qualifications, nor indeed undertakes systematic market research – visitor comment cards excepted – the Museum boasts an impressive year-round promotional programme. Most events, admittedly, are modest. As a rule, these involve one or two musicians on the veranda of the Smoke House, playing requests and chatting to visitors, or are tied to the inviolate requirements of the agricultural calendar: planting, ploughing, hoeing, harvesting, repairing outbuildings and Yuletide relaxation. However, the Annual Fall Homecoming, a four-day festival devoted to music-making, craft-working, storytelling and celebrating indigenous Appalachian culture, is the highlight of the year, attracting 50,000 people to the Museum. The surrounding publicity, coupled with a professional press pack and occasional articles in *The Smithsonian*, *Readers' Digest* and *Home and Garden*, ensures that the park remains firmly in the public eye. Several television series have been filmed on site and it features in a video, shown countless times per season to millions of tourists, at Walt Disney World. All told, the Museum attracts 100,000 visitors annually, making it the third largest attraction, after Dollywood and Opryland, in the state of Tennessee.

Ulster–American Folk Park

Ireland has long had close links with the United States. No less than twelve American presidents, from Jackson to Clinton, are of Irish descent, as are figures as diverse as Andrew Carnegie, Ulysses S. Grant, John Wayne and, strange though it sounds, Alex Haley (Kennedy 1996, 1997, 1998; Lazenblatt 1999). While most Americans are familiar with the massive Irish influx of the mid-nineteenth century, which largely consisted of Roman Catholics from the south and west of the island, an earlier, no less enormous wave of immigration took place in the seventeenth and eighteenth centuries (Akenson 1996). In the main, this consisted of Protestant dissenters from the north and east of Ireland, the forebears of whom had previously emigrated from Scotland. Industrious, obdurate and belligerent by turns, the Scots-Irish settled in the Carolina Piedmont and quickly spread throughout the Appalachians, Alleghenies and Tennessee Valley, as far west as east Texas. Numerous icons of pioneer legend – Jim Bowie, Davy Crockett, Kit Carson, etc. – are of Scots-Irish stock and, in keeping with Hirschman's (1985) thesis on primitive aspects of consumption, many present-day behaviours and activities are traceable to Scots-Irish antecedents (e.g. country music, clog dancing, place and family names). Indeed, it is often asserted that the settlers were attracted to the area on account of its topographical similarity to northern Ireland and that striking parallels in speech patterns and even the physical appearance of the two peoples are still apparent (Bracefield 1999; Wright 1999).

Opened in July 1976, to coincide with the US Bicentennial, the Ulster–American Folk Park celebrates the historic link between the two countries by focusing on the emigration experience (Montgomery 1991, 1997). Situated in the rural hinterland of Belfast, Northern Ireland, the park consists of two 'halves': one devoted to the Irish and the other to the American ends of the trans-Atlantic journey. These are linked by a full-scale, part-replica of an early nineteenth-century sailing vessel, *The Brig Union*, which is abutted on either side by recreated Irish and American streetscapes. The emigrant experience is further evoked by the guiding thread of the Mellon family, who left Ulster in the early nineteenth century, settled in Pennsylvania, founded the famous banking dynasty and, to this day, remains part of the east-coast establishment. Thus, the Old World half of the park is centred on the original, if substantially rebuilt, Mellon farmhouse, and the New World half consists of full-scale reconstructions of their first farmsteads in the United States. The park, in fact, is part-funded by the family, who also sponsored an impressive exhibition hall and indoor museum.

Although the Ulster–American Folk Park is primarily devoted to the Scots-Irish emigration of the seventeenth century, the nineteenth-century Irish-Catholic exodus is also encapsulated, both in stone and by means of an extensive genealogical database, which is available to visitors in search of their roots. In total, the park consists of eighteen buildings, from weavers' cottage and working forge to spirit grocers and subterranean corn-crib, plus a museum shop, restaurant and Center for Emigration Studies. Plans are afoot, furthermore, to extend substantially the American half of the park and, coupled with its imaginative promotional programme of fake wakes, re-enacted weddings, costumed recreations of rural events and an annual Bluegrass Festival, the Folk Park is likely to add to its current annual total of 130,000 visitors (Wilson 1995).

Ulster Folk and Transport Museum

By far the largest of the three heritage parks under consideration, the Ulster Folk and Transport Museum occupies a 227-acre site in the rolling hills on the eastern outskirts of Belfast, Northern Ireland. It opened (as the Ulster Folk Museum) in 1964 and nestles in the thickly wooded but carefully manicured grounds of Cultra Manor, a nineteenth-century stately home that now houses the museum's education, conference and catering offices. Somewhat akin to its Appalachian counterpart, the museum is the brainchild of a single individual, E. Estyn Evans, a prominent local academician who spent his career cataloguing the lifestyle of northern Irish country-folk. Inspired by its indefatigable founder, the folk park was originally devoted to recreating the Ulster countryside as it was at the start of the twentieth century. Buildings, roads, hedgerows, fields, farm animals, waterways, agricultural activities and even the landscape itself were relocated, reconstructed and reconfigured to reflect the rural milieu around the individual reassembled buildings (Gailey 1986).

By the time of its 1972 merger with the Ulster Transport Museum, however, the focus of the park had shifted from rural to urban, thanks to the construction of a small Ulster town, complete with church, chapel, courthouse, school, grocery store, newspaper offices and several terraces of housing. What is more, the lower part of the site has seen the construction of airy Transportation Galleries, which are given over to the museum's internationally renowned collection of steam engines, buses, automobiles, motorbikes and, naturally, macabre memorabilia of Belfast's best known product, *The Titanic*. The museum also contains an indoor exhibition hall, devoted to static displays of agricultural implements; a small residential centre in a cluster of renovated nineteenth-century buildings; several separate car parks scattered across the capacious if uncoordinated site; and an administration block, which houses the archives, library and material relating to less tangible aspects of local heritage (music, dance, folklore, etc.).

As befits a two-time winner of the prestigious Museum of the Year award (Britain in 1972, Ireland in 1986), the Ulster Folk and Transport Museum employs a full-time, professionally qualified marketing director. Although market research is not gathered on a systematic basis, and although formal marketing plans are not prepared, a comprehensive programme of promotional events helps attract 180,000 visitors per year. During the busy summer season, moreover, several of the buildings are staffed with attendants who demonstrate rural crafts and respond to queries from customers. Unlike some of the better-known living history museums, such as Plimoth Plantation (Snow 1993), the attendants are uncostumed, their responses are unscripted and questions are dealt with in the third rather than the first person (that is, they do not act the part of nineteenth-century country bumpkins, feigning disbelief when confronted with cameras, cars and the accoutrements of contemporary life). This practice may change, however, as part of a recent reorganisation of museums' administration in Northern Ireland, which incorporates the Ulster Folk and Transport Museum and the Ulster–American Folk Park into a larger umbrella organisation, The National Museums and Galleries of Northern Ireland (Wilson 1995).

Research methods

The three parks, then, are not 'representative' in any statistical sense but they are reasonably typical of heritage attractions, with interesting individual points of comparison and contrast. Despite the academic attention lavished on large, high-profile facilities like Greenfield Village and Old Sturbridge (Kirschenblatt-Gimblett 1998), most heritage sites are fairly small, often only a single building (Kotler and Kotler 1998). All three institutions in the present study are medium sized, though the Ulster Folk and Transport Museum is more than three times the acreage and attracts twice as many visitors as the Museum of Appalachia, with the Ulster–American Folk Park somewhere in-between. All three parks, furthermore, fall in the middle of Mills' (1990) authentic-synthetic spectrum, insofar as the buildings are neither original *in situ* (Colonial Williamsburg), nor ersatz renditions (Disneyland), but careful re-builds or exact replicas (albeit the Ulster–American Folk Park is based on the original Mellon homestead and boasts a Disneyesque brig, to boot). All three locations, likewise, provide living history tableaux, such as crafts demonstrations and customer–attendant interactions, though there is considerable variation in the degree of commitment to such practices. All three facilities, finally, are somewhat lacking in professional marketing expertise – again typical of the industry and again with individual variations – despite impressive publicity and promotional programmes. Most meaningfully perhaps, all three parks are interlinked thematically, insofar as the Museum of Appalachia celebrates a culture that was transplanted by people from the north of Ireland (Ulster Folk and Transport Museum), who emigrated to the United States in the eighteenth century (Ulster–American Folk Park). As such, they are worthy of careful consideration and, while theoretical generalisations are neither expected nor necessary in the interpretive research tradition, the findings may help contribute to a better understanding of marketing's re-production orientation.

In keeping with the interpretive paradigm, the research programme comprised a combination of qualitative approaches. After several familiarisation visits, each heritage park was studied for five consecutive days in summer 1998. A total of 200 interviews were conducted, on exit or in res. media, with individual visitors and groups of visitors. These ranged from 25 minutes to 4.5 hours. The longest of the interviews involved a sub-sample of fifteen patrons, who were accompanied by a researcher as they explored the parks. Their encounters with and reactions to the exhibits were noted and discussed as the visit progressed. Other day-trippers were observed unobtrusively as they went about the business of enjoying themselves. Lengthy unstructured interviews were also undertaken with curators, administrators and various employees of the parks (attendants, handymen, guides, musicians, shop clerks). What is more, a number of promotional events were attended and video- or audio-recorded (Annual Bluegrass Festival, *A Night in Old Appalachia*); more than 150 photographs of the exhibits and displays were taken; and the voluminous published material pertaining to the development of the parks and the individual buildings therein – maps, slides, videos, pamphlets – was systematically collected, collated and culled. Key informants in the heritage sector were interviewed at one of the industry's annual conferences; visits were paid to analogous heritage sites, both in Europe and in the United States; and each of the researchers kept a diary or wrote an introspective account of their individual experiences. All told, the textual database consists of approximately 500 pages of interview transcripts and an equivalent amount of non-interview evidence. Although this body of qualitative data cannot be considered comprehensive, it is considerable enough to facilitate comprehension of the heritage park experience.

Before the findings are presented, it is necessary to stress that research predicated on literary theory is slightly different from 'mainstream' qualitative inquiry (Arnould and Wallendorf 1994; Spiggle 1994; Thompson 1997). The latter typically assumes that salient themes and constructs *emerge* naturally from engagement with the raw data (albeit in practice interpretive analyses are rarely if ever entirely innocent or devoid of theoretical presuppositions). A process of extended immersion in the textual material eventually triggers creative insights that bubble to the surface, or alternatively burst through in a dramatic Eureka-esque fashion. Research premised on literary criticism, by contrast, openly acknowledges its theoretical position and ordinarily reads with *intent* (Scott 1994; Stern 1989). That is to say, the relevant texts are interpreted from a stated theoretical standpoint, be it Marxist, Psychoanalytical, New Critical or whatever. Thus feminist literary critics seek to expose androcentrism in the texts they study; post-colonialists do likewise with Western cultural imperialism; and deconstructionists show how texts inevitably contradict themselves and thereby undermine the very arguments they are seeking to advance. Of course, this does not mean that literary critics' preferred stance is rigid or doctrinaire, or involves imposing a pre-ordained conceptual framework on the chosen texts (though the New Critics' process of close reading was often accused of this, as was Deconstruction in the hands of the so-called Yale School). On the contrary, literary criticism involves an iterative, to-ing and fro-ing dialogue between the texts under investigation and the preferred theoretical stance, with flexibility the overriding principle, as is the case in all competent qualitative research.

Results: reading retroscapes

The flexible, intuitive and open-ended character of literary inquiry is amply illustrated in the present heritage parks study. The researchers' initial experience of the Museum of Appalachia with its admixture of buildings from different historical periods, seemingly anachronistic artifacts (such as a 1930s radio in a 1830s farmstead) and apparent lack of a central focus immediately suggested Jameson's well-known notions of pastiche and decentred hyperspace. As heritage parks are frequently cited as exemplars of postmodernism's preoccupation with spatial concerns and paradoxical juxtapositions, this connection is hardly original. However, the linkage was serendipitously reinforced by a period of residence in Knoxville's Regency Hyatt, designed by John Portman, who was also responsible for the legendary Bonaventure Hotel in Los Angeles. This intuitive sense of appropriateness was further strengthened as the study progressed, the researchers' grasp of the intricacies of Jamesonian thought developed, and additional themes emerged from the interviews, observations and archival analysis. The theoretical and empirical exercises thus ran in tandem, each affecting, informing and enriching the other. Although all three parks exhibit the principal Jamesonian themes, the essential point is that the concepts were not intentionally imposed upon the data, nor did they miraculously emerge in the course of the interpretive process. They emerged with intent.

Absence

Absence is present everywhere in the heritage parks, paradoxical though this may appear. The *raison d'être* of the parks is to preserve – or, rather, reproduce – a way of life that has disappeared, or is in danger of disappearing. They celebrate, in effect, what no longer exists, be it in the form of log cabins, farm implements, household furnishings, breeds of animal and, in the case of the Ulster Folk and Transport Museum, the very physical landscape of the late nineteenth century. All-but abandoned handicrafts, industrial processes, culinary arts and various traditional skills – which by their very nature are absent from view – are also made immanent, at least momentarily, as are intangible aspects of folk culture such as song, music, dance, language and re-enacted rural festivities like the fake wake (itself a tribute to the dear departed). Indeed, the Ulster–American Folk Park epitomises this all-pervasive sense of absence, insofar as it is entirely devoted to disappearance – emigrants' high-risk departures from one place for an uncertain short-term (the crossing) and long-term future (the New World). It is little wonder that 'living' wakes were held for those about to undertake the journey. In a similar vein, the Museum of Appalachia was born out of the founder's deep conviction that the remarkable people of the region had been overlooked, belittled and forgotten by the

American majority, despite their astonishing achievements in decidedly unpropitious circumstances.

Another absence conspicuous by its presence is the park-keepers' preoccupation with what is not there. Plans for future facilities, exhibits and developments are constantly referred to, both in conversation and in writing. The Ulster–American Folk Park intends to extend the American half of the attraction with reconstructions pertaining to pioneer life in Western Pennsylvania, the Shenandoah Valley and the Appalachian Frontier. The Museum of Appalachia has ambitious plans to develop a 1930s-style TVA tableau, though the upper storey of the Hall of Fame and an exhibition devoted to *Charlie*, a made-for-TV movie filmed in the park, represent more immediate priorities. Similarly, the Ulster Folk and Transport Museum is sorely in need of a visitors' centre and another two indoor exhibition halls, in order to orient properly its disorientated customers (see below).

Customer information, moreover, is disconcertingly absent in all three parks due to the lack of formal market research into visitor motivation, behaviour and satisfaction. The curators hope, of course, that customers will 'take something with them', the exhibits naturally excepted. Ideally, this comprises an enhanced understanding of past times or, failing that, a craft-shop souvenir or two. But there is some uncertainty whether customers actually depart with the museum's intended message. Indeed, it is arguable that visitors actually leave with an overwhelming sense of absence, a vaguely anti-climactic feeling that they have visited the park at the wrong time. Intra-park discourse is dominated by discussions of non-presence, unavailability and anticipated occurrences. ('The rural wedding re-enactment is next week'; 'the band starts playing at 7.30 tonight'; 'the person you should talk to is not here right now'.) The Museum of Appalachia, in particular, is characterised by the constantly recurring refrain of The Fall Homecoming. The park, in effect, is only fully present for four days per year. The rest of the time it indulges in absenteeism and functions as a promotional trailer for the main event.

R1: At the Homecoming they have 300 musicians here on this space.

I: It must be a huge thing.

R1: Yeah. The Homecoming has three stages. This is the main stage and they have a stage in the overhang barn and a stage at the other end.

I: That's fantastic. They have crafts people here too?

R1: Oh yeah, they weave, spin, make apple butter, hominy grits. They split rails and make molasses.

I: I like molasses. I remember that.

R1: Well they make it right here. All down to the fence they'll be people selling their stuff. They got painters and books and the authors who write the books.

R1: He tries to keep the craft people being Appalachian type craft.

R2: We don't want nothing made in Japan.

I: That wouldn't work would it?

R1:   It's all wooden toys, corn-chip dolls and a woman comes down from Kentucky and spins and weaves dog hair.

I: How does he find these people?

R1:   I guess they find him.

R2:   In the old days he had to go find them.

R1:   He had to find them. Now it's people waiting 'til somebody dies so they can move in. He's got enough crafts and no room for any more.

I: That's wonderful.

R1:   They do it all. You just wouldn't believe it. Anywhere from 50–80,000 people usually show up.

R2:   Second week in October.

(interview with musicians, male, 70s, MoA)

Absence, to be sure, makes the heart grow fonder and it is this sense of something missing, of hidden depths, of secrecy, that appeals to many patrons. Such is the wealth of artefacts on display – one tableau in the Museum of Appalachia consists of 225 identical mule-bits – that it is simply impossible to take it all in on a single visit. In fact, many visitors absent themselves from large parts of the parks, such as the New World side of the Ulster–American Folk Park, and focus instead on a small area in order to absorb fully what is on offer. Yet even here absence is perpetually present, since they inevitably encounter all manner of incomprehensible implements, artefacts and displays, rusting signifiers of vitally important but long-forgotten agricultural chores.

This unfathomability, however, is by no means unpleasant. In certain respects, it is entirely appropriate as it resonates with visitors' own states of mind and general attitude. Interviewees frequently refer to the fact that they were completely unaware of the existence of the park or, alternatively, had repeatedly deferred their visit – sometimes for years – until such times as it was unavoidable. In addition to requiring an excuse to visit, it seems that heritage is always the responsibility of someone else, usually a member of the family – a sister, a cousin, a great aunt – who has taken it upon themselves to tend the family tree. In fact, even the most avid consumers of heritage, those searching for information about their forebears, are missing something. The genealogical information they have is unfailingly incomplete, full of holes or, as often as not, riddled with inconsistencies and anachronisms. Genealogy, in truth, is ultimately about absence, because there is always an empty space at the end of the search, when whatever information there is finally runs out.

I: How far have you been able to trace your family back here?

R: So far I've gotten one great, great grandparent born in 1797 or 1798. We're trying to get back beyond that. Our dad has reached the same

point I have, him going in one direction and me going in the other, but I
would like to go beyond that. I think probably we would not be able to
go back beyond the 1600s. I don't think so, from what I understand.

I: The records?

R: Right.

(American tourist, female, UAFP)

Not every visitor, of course, is enamoured by absence and, in truth, it is the
gaps in their representational records that are responsible for much of the oppro-
brium heaped on heritage parks *per se*. As previously noted, historians repeatedly
denounce the peddlers of past times for presenting a distorted, not to say sanitised, picture of the past, one that ignores disease, oppression, conflict, political
activism and the struggles of minority groups. A number of informants, certainly,
felt that the parks failed to present a fully rounded portrayal of past times. The
Museum of Appalachia was described as 'very masculine' on occasion, due to the
profusion of picks, shovels, chain saws, sledge hammers and manifold macho
farming implements. The Ulster Folk and Transport Museum, by contrast, was
deemed overwhelmingly middle class, though this has less to do with the artefacts
themselves than its situation in an affluent suburb, colloquially known as 'the Gold
Coast'. The Ulster–American Folk Park, meanwhile, was considered by some to
be slightly one-sided in its treatment of emigration, on account of its emphasis on
the Protestant, Scots-Irish experiences of the eighteenth century to the neglect of
the mass Catholic migrations of the nineteenth.

There is something else the park's not saying. There is a bias towards the
Scots migration as opposed to Catholic, Irish Catholic migration. So there's a
bias on that. It's heavily biased towards the emigration of the Ulster-Scots.
There is one chapel and there's one priest's house and there's some stuff on
the Archbishop of New York but essentially it's an early Ulster-Scots migration which means it's not the same as the later, heavily Catholic migration.
They're very different migrations. They went to different places. They did
different things. They became different types of people. For a lot of Irish
Americans coming back this would not be their migration. This is not their
migration. This is the migration of the people that became the Presidents of
the United States, not the people who went to Boston, Chicago, New York or
wherever. It's not their migration.

(American tourist, male, UAFP)

Given the Ulster–American Folk Park's location in the north of Ireland and its
original remit with regard to the Mellon family, this focus is only to be expected.
In fairness, furthermore, the curators are acutely aware of the gaps in their
representations and the accompanying literature goes to great lengths to present a

fuller, more nuanced picture. However, there seems to be a resigned acceptance that, in today's polyvocal postmodern times, it is impossible to control what opinionated customers bring to and get from museums. Prejudices tend to be reinforced regardless of the representations, and pre-existing stories are there to be confirmed rather than challenged.

Narrative

Be that as it may, stories are the coinage of the heritage realm. Although many of these narratives suffer from runaway inflation or are debased in a literary twist on Gresham's Law – bad stories, self-evidently, drive out good – there is no question that 'getting the story straight' is the common currency of history in general and heritage in particular. The circulation of narrative capital, moreover, occurs at several different levels. There is the story of the heritage industry *per se* and its attempts to turn the use value of historical events into the exchange value of tourist attractions. Then there are the seemingly unique but in fact highly stylized chronicles of the heritage parks themselves, from fairy tale beginnings, though the various Rostowesque stages of narrative growth, to (presumably) self-sustaining storytelling.

And then again there are the copious stories told in and by the heritage parks, many of which are simulacra of Adam Smith's dictum that collective benefits flow from individual pursuit of fame and fortune. Indeed, it can be contended that the comparative under-performance of the Ulster Folk and Transport Museum (which is more than three times the size and much richer in resources than the other two) is due to the fact that it is somewhat lacking in the specie of stories. Whereas the Ulster–American Folk Park uses the Mellon epic as an exemplar of Scots-Irish emigration and the Museum of Appalachia is replete with Horatio Algeresque accounts of great achievement, from Mark Twain and Roy Acuff to John Rice Irwin himself, the Ulster Folk and Transport Museum is decidedly lacking in the capital of chronicle. However, this shortfall in its storytelling portfolio should be settled when and if the narrative manufacturing facility that is the proposed visitors' center is eventually brought into commission.

Above and beyond the political economy of storytelling, the narratives produced by and in the parks are not dissimilar to the 'patchwork quilts' of Fredric Jameson. They are many, varied, overlapping and highly decorative, whilst possessing a semblance of an overall pattern. Each of the parks, for example, provides a spatial trail of tales, a suggested sequence of exhibit visits. These are indicated by arrows on the visitors' maps, which are automatically issued on entry and, if followed to the letter, give the customer a synoptic sense of how the narrative quilt unfolds. Interwoven into the basic story-line of emigration (Ulster–American Folk Park), material progress (Museum of Appalachia), or geographical difference (Ulster Folk and Transport Museum), are the tales pertaining to the individual buildings and the people associated with them. In some cases, these are immortalised on display boards, plaques or panels and attached to the buildings themselves – though the Ulster Folk and Transport Museum is particularly parsimonious in this regard – but in all cases they are available in the accompanying textual material (guidebooks, maps, pamphlets, etc.). The employees in attendance also have their tales to tell, not simply about the building or its former inhabitants, but also about the activities they are demonstrating (weaving, cooking, metalwork), the folkways of times past and, not least, the manifold objects, implements and furnishings on display.

In addition to attendant-inflected narratives about families, food and farming, the fullest stories are found in the exhibition halls, visitors' centres and indoor galleries, where the various tableaux are described in great, possibly excessive detail. These range from the familiar tale of *The Titanic* in the Ulster Folk and Transport Museum to the almost-forgotten story of Sergeant York, a distinguished World War One hero, whose fifteen minutes of immortality (including a 1944 biopic. starring Gary Cooper) are remembered in the Museum of Appalachia's Hall of Fame. They are typified, however, by the remarkable achievements of the commercially minded Campbell brothers retailed in the Ulster–American Folk Park:

> Robert Campbell, who went on to become a fur-trapper and builder of Fort Laramie, was born in this house in 1804. Robert emigrated to America in the early 1820s to join his older brother Hugh, who had emigrated in 1818. Robert moved west for health reasons and soon became involved in the fur trade. By 1936 Robert left his active life in the mountains and settled in St. Louis, where he continued to supply expeditions of trappers and pioneer settlers as they set out on the Oregon Trail . . .
>
> Hugh Campbell emigrated to New York in 1818 aboard the Phoenix. He kept a journal of his voyage which sheds much light not only on his character but also on the nature and organization of the early nineteenth-century emigrant trade. Hugh became one of Philadelphia's most prominent merchants before eventually going to St. Louis where he entered into partnership with his brother Robert.
>
> (plaque on Campbell Cabin, UAFP)

Commendable though the chronicles of buildings and their past occupants undoubtedly are, the really striking stories stem from contemporary consumers' engagement with the parks. Unanticipated encounters with resonant objects, be it a tin bath, a room setting or a complete exhibit, call forth all sorts of meaningful visitor narratives, which are verbally recounted to the accompanying family group, to unrelated bystanders or to the staff in attendance. Often all three. Indeed, the instantaneous response to what are ostensibly trivial artefacts – a three-legged pot, a china doll, a haystack – is invariably highly animated, verging on rapturous. In keeping, what is more, with this essentially aesthetic reaction, the memories evoked by the objects are routinely described in appropriately poetic language ('I like those rolled-up haystacks because when they get snow on them they look like raisin bread.')

Equally poetic are the stories that consumers have to tell about themselves, though this may have more to do with the frequency of their retelling than any inherent poesy. Every single interviewee had a tale or two up their sleeves, which they were ready, willing and able to recount. As might be expected, most of these chronicles concerned the individual informant, their background and biographical details, albeit accounts of holiday experiences, the reasons behind their visit and the current day's events in particular, also figured prominently. Nevertheless, by far the most compelling stories – or, rather, the best rehearsed – were historical in character, insofar as they referred to the convoluted genealogy of the informant's family.

Interestingly, the content of these ancestral sagas is compatible with Northrop Frye's four-category classification of narrative archetypes: comedy, tragedy, irony and romance (Stern 1995). Thus, there are richly comic tales of dastardly forebears (horse thieves, mistaken identities); profoundly tragic tales of those who failed to make it or narrowly escaped death (turned back at Ellis Island, lost in the San Francisco earthquake); inadvertently ironic tales like the wealthy couple committed to healthy living, whose family fortune was made from tobacco; and, more often than not, deeply romantic tales of star-crossed lovers, tearful reunions and all's well that ends well. In practice, as Stern rightly observes, these categories overlap considerably and it is not unusual for a family saga to contain elements of two or more narrative archetypes, as in this typical 'just so' story.

> *R1:* I know on my mom's side there were people who came over because of the famine. I'm not sure if that was the case on my dad's side. But I know with her it was. And then of course, my great grandmother, she came over for other reasons. She was in love with a Frenchman and the family didn't want her to marry him. So they sent her to America 'cause she was young and they figured she could work her passage back or whatever. She came through Ellis Island, and they used to go down to the island and hire whoever came off the ship. And they hired her to work in a quarry as a cook and a waitress and she could never get back to her Frenchman. However, one day about a year later there he was sitting at the end of the table. He had come to America and was then hired by the same company.
>
> *I:* Incredible!
>
> *R2:* She was carrying a tray of fish and dropped them on the floor!
>
> *R1:* She dropped her tray of fish and they got married. They both made the journey and it was meant to be, I guess.
>
> (American tourists, male and female, UAFP)

'Everyone', according to several heritage park informants, 'has a story to tell' and this is indubitably the case. Yet it is equally true to say that many personal and family chronicles are incomplete, fragmented or hopelessly muddled. Again and again the retold tales simply failed to make sense. Part of this difficulty, admittedly, may be due to the interview situation. Not everyone is a natural raconteur, after all. Nevertheless, it is not unreasonable to suggest that it is this very lack of coherence that prompts people to undertake genealogical research in the first place. Part of the pleasure of such historical investigations comes from fitting the family puzzle together to create a coherent narrative. Of course, the problem with being a detective in one's own detective story is that the trail goes cold. The clues eventually run out or become irritatingly ambiguous. And it is at this point of chronological break-down that heritage parks come into their own. By telling an exemplary or stereotypical tale, they enable genealogically-minded visitors to acquire the story wholesale or appropriate pertinent details. Whatever they need, in fact, to make their own narrative cohere. Postmodern patrons of heritage parks adopt a pick 'n' mix attitude to the narratives on offer, taking only the bits and pieces they require.

I: In particular, why were you interested in Mellon?

R: I think because of what they had done for America and where they had come from and their ambition and sometimes coming from nothing and what they were able to do with their lives. We talked about the native intelligence they had to start with, because they had nothing and my own father came from a farm here and had to leave at the age of seven. This is an old story but he was one of the many who came over and he eventually became a policeman in America but he had the native intelligence, although only a sixth grade education . . . His roots were similar to some of the stories I saw in the park. He didn't become a huge success but he was very successful coming from the background that he did, so that's sort of brought memories into it.

(American tourist, male, UAFP)

The museum-keepers, meanwhile, are preoccupied with 'getting their story across', whether it be within the confines of the park itself or in terms of communicating the message to outside audiences by means of PR material concerning the annual cycle of events. However, this obsession with telling a cogent story that customers can take away, or developing new promotional angles on old stories, or their lack of control over 'moments of fiction', the stories told by museum attendants at the point of sale, stands in very sharp contrast to consumers, who are less interested in getting *the* story straight than *their* story straight. The meta-narratives of modernity have been superseded by the petit-narratives of postmodernity.

Hyperspace

Postmodernity, to be sure, involves much more than individual micro-stories, important though narrative and autobiography undoubtedly are. For many commentators, space and its representations are especially salient features of the postmodern moment. Temporal issues, admittedly, are by no means ignored, but spatial matters loom large in postmodern debates, whether it be in global–local terms or in relation to the alleged inauthenticity of theme parks and analogous hyperreal environments.

Fredric Jameson, as noted earlier, is one of the prime movers of this spatial paradigm shift and his evocative descriptions of postmodern hyperspace have proved particularly influential. Although he does not deal with them directly, except in response to questions posed in a published interview (Stephanson 1987), heritage parks are exemplars of Jamesonian hyperspace. Unsurprisingly, then, all three sites under investigation are appropriately *decentred*, *disorientating* and *de-differentiated*, albeit to different degrees and with slight but significant variations from park to park.

When it comes to decentredness, for example, the studied spaces differ in the extent to which they lack a focal point. The Museum of Appalachia is semi-circular in arrangement, with an empty meadow in the middle and it is thus the most decentred. The Hall of Fame, considered the focus of the facility by its owners, occupies a somewhat eccentric spatial situation, very much in the wings of this natural amphitheater. Indeed, if there is a focal point at all it is entirely intangible; namely, the bluegrass music that wafts over the meadow thanks to the players on the porch. More intangible still are the fanciful tales of the legendary Fall Homecoming, which succeeds in filling the empty, central space with 50,000 people for four magical days per year.

The Ulster–American Folk Park, by contrast, possesses a very clear focal point. The sailing ship and dockside area not only acts as a hinge between the Irish and American halves of the heritage park, but is also the highlight of most people's visit to this popular tourist attraction. At the same time, the dockside is the single most 'inauthentic' exhibit, a complete mock-up of part of a prototypical wind-jammer. As such, it flies in the face of the park's previous spatial and intellectual focus, the original, the 'actual', the 'authentic' Mellon farmstead. Fakery has thus displaced the real, in accordance with the precepts of postmodernity.

The Ulster Folk and Transport Museum, on the other hand, falls somewhere in between. Overall, the three geographically dispersed parts of the park – transport galleries, rural area and township – combine to convey a strong sense of spatial decentredness. However, the individual components are decentred to different degrees. The transport galleries are very compact; the rural area is deliberately diffuse; and, bizarrely, the township is a bit of both. Its buildings are clustered, horseshoe-like around an empty, as yet undeveloped central space. Indeed, for aficionados of Irish townscapes, which typically comprise a single main street with closely packed buildings on either side (Buchanan 1987), this decentred arrangement is particularly disorientating, verging on the surreal.

Disorientation, however, is everywhere apparent in the studied heritage parks. Despite the museum-keepers' diligent attempts to orientate their patrons, through signposts, arrow-strewn maps and the best verbal efforts of on-site employees, visitors frequently fail to follow the suggested spatial sequence. It is not unusual to find confused customers turning cartographic cartwheels trying to work out where, exactly, they are and what building stands before them. Once again, this is true in all three cases, though it is especially strongly marked in the Ulster Folk and Transport Museum, largely on account of its sheer geographical extent and the fact that the story it tells is spatial rather than temporal. That is to say, the park depicts different parts of Northern Ireland, both urban and rural, at a single point in time. Unfortunately, the guidebook fails to stress this basic point and, as the individual buildings often predate this chronological anchor (even though their fixtures, fittings and furnishings relate to the designated date), customer disorientation is the inevitable outcome. The lack of adequate signposting, coupled with a marked reluctance to indicate which buildings are which and, not least, a visitors' map containing misdirected arrows pointing out misnumbered buildings, only adds to the confusion!

In fairness, there is method in the museum's madness. As the stated intention is to re-present the north of Ireland exactly as it was in or around 1900, the case against obtrusive signposts and nameplates is incontestable, from a curatorial if not a customer standpoint. However, even if the signage were adequate, as it is in the Ulster–American Folk Park and the Museum of Appalachia, and even if the visitors were forced to follow the suggested sequence of exhibits (which of course they are not), a degree of disorientation would still obtain. As previously noted, the objects, artefacts and displays are inherently discombobulating. By their very nature they are no longer in use; they pertain to a bygone era and a predominantly rural lifestyle, which has long since disappeared. Just as communist asylum-seekers of the 1960s were purportedly rendered speechless by the sheer abundance of consumer goods in American supermarkets (Johnson 1996), so too the suburbanised children of today's consumer society are completely thrown by the accoutrements of agricultural production, by the handles, cogs and gear wheels of the pre-push-button epoch.

This disorientation, it must be emphasised, should not be taken to mean dissatisfaction or discontent. The opposite, in fact, is the case. Disorder, distraction, disconcertion and detective work – wondering where they are, what things were and where to next – are an important part of the heritage park experience and enjoyed up to a point. Some consumers, admittedly, adopt an essentially instrumentalist approach to the attractions, focusing on prices, accessibility, signage, catering facilities and so on. The entire 'day out' agenda, in other words. For others, however, the whole heritage experience has a slightly phantasmagoric, pleasantly blurred, agreeably confusing quality. De-differentiation, the judicious melding of past and present, here and there, education and entertainment, is their *raison d'être*.

De-differentiation, indeed, is especially evident in spatial, inter-personal and representational senses. Spatially, the boundaries of the parks are not clear-cut on account of their open-air qualities. What is and what is not part of the heritage park, be it a propinquitous farmhouse or barn or meadow, is not readily apparent to visitors. Similarly, on-site activities, such as building work or agricultural tasks, are liable to be interpreted as part of the 'performance' rather than the necessary workaday activities that they actually are (albeit the museum-keepers are aware of this and seek to capitalise on any such 'living history' connotations). The same is true of inter-personal interactions among visitors, since the interactee may or may not be an employee of the museum and, even when they are not, may still provide useful historical information or answer a burning question. Consumers, in fact, are especially tickled when they are mistaken for a member of staff or taken to be part of a tableau.

> R: I was sitting down changing film in the camera and one of the Austral-
>   ians came around and he looked over at me.
> I: He thought you were one of them?
> R: He reckoned I looked like one of the exhibits because there was only
>   one chair and I was sitting on it changing film!
>
> (Australian tourist, male, UFTM)

Most importantly perhaps, the parks brilliantly succeed in blurring the boundaries between fake and real. Although the buildings are reconstructions or replicas and, in most cases, stocked with artefacts that were not originally *in situ*, they are none the less regarded as 'really, really real'. They are presentations of the past not representations of the past, both for the consumers and producers of such historical tableaux. Even when the artificiality of the exhibit is foregrounded, as in the case of the Mark Twain cabin in the Museum of Appalachia (which contains a photomontage of the original dilapidated building), this does not detract from the perceived authenticity of the experience. Consumers not only accept that a certain amount of poetic licence is necessary but also that the most poetically licensed parts of the park are the most authentic. The producers, likewise, are absolutely adamant that their representations are real and take great exception to any suggestion otherwise. At the same time they are fully aware of the essential artificiality of the heritage exercise and their complicity therein.

In these paradoxical circumstances, questions are inevitably raised about cognitive mapping processes. How are people making sense of the heritage park experience, which is patently fictional yet taken to be fact? According to

MacCannell (1989), tourists are engaged in a search for authenticity and this is obligingly staged by purveyors of package tours. Ritzer (1998), by contrast, contends that today's post-tourists are looking for inauthenticity, the ersatz familiarity of Disney, McDonald's, Pizza Hut and Holiday Inn. This may be so, but the present study suggests that the authentic–inauthentic dichotomy has itself been de-differentiated and people are looking for authentic inauthenticity. Authenticity no longer resides in unvarnished historical facts but in real people performing real tasks with real implements in real buildings. True, the people are actors, the skills have been learnt for the purposes of display, the implements are as genuine as the legendary hammer that has had five replacement shafts and three new heads, and the buildings have been constructed, at least in part, with new materials by today's rude mechanicals. However, it is these demonstrations of the art of work in an age of reproduction mechanicals that makes the heritage park experience real. Indeed, one of the most frequent complaints about the sites under study is that there are insufficient people performing suitably pseudo-tasks or spinning fake yarns, both literal and metaphorical. Historical truth, so it seems, cannot be separated from the living truth. History is rendered true by its staging, by the manufacture of truth effects, by the authentic-ness rather than the authenticity of the experience.

Retrotopia

The importance of authentic-ness is nowhere better illustrated than in the dockside exhibit at the Ulster–American Folk Park. Almost without exception, the interviewees felt that this facsimile of part of a sailing vessel gave a real sense of the emigration experience. True, their experience takes all of six minutes compared to six weeks; the 'sea' is flatter than flat calm; the 'sky' is a concrete ceiling fifteen feet above the deck (albeit painted black to simulate night-time); the cramped below decks area, containing the human cargo, is uncrowded, uncluttered and completely odour-free; and there is not a single original artefact anywhere on display.

Yet, in keeping with Jameson's conceptualisation of historical consciousness in postmodernity – as a bygone aesthetic, a stylistic evocation, a sense of a sense of the past – this dockside sensorium seems real to the people passing through. It may well be a pastiche, a piece of historical theatre, but the very act of 'embarking' and 'disembarking', as well as handling the bolted-down barrels, bunks and analogous 'artefacts', gives people a much better idea of what it must have been like to leave home, and undertake a perilous trans-Atlantic trip, than any number of written accounts or static, look-don't-touch tableaux.

> I: Tell me what you think of it.
> R1: The buildings are marvellous, aren't they?
> R2: They've done a great job.

R1:   It's spectacular here. It really is spectacular, especially when you get to the boat. I mean, we had ancestors who came over on boats, though not quite as bad as that. But think of the people.

I: It's amazing.

RI: Yes, really. To put that many people on a little boat like that. It just, it's terrifying. You can feel your stomach churning over.

(American tourists, male and female, UFTP)

Just as heritage parks, with their congeries of reproduction buildings from markedly different times (and places) are a pastiche, an egregious 'perpetual present', so too consumers respond to them in a decidedly schizophrenic fashion. As noted previously, encounters with resonant objects can and do induce paroxysms of rapture amongst consumers. Everything from wooden outhouses and broken butter churns to ribbed-glass wash boards call forth poetic personal narratives. When confronted, moreover, with particularly mysterious objects, consumers are inclined to concoct little stories to account for them, at least to their own satisfaction.

Rapture, however, is the exception rather than the rule, because the bulk of objects are regarded with bemusement, amusement, shoulder-shrugging or, on occasion, curiosity concerning the curatorial mind-set (why on earth would anyone want to collect 200 identical bridle-bits, or padlocks, or augers, or nails?). In the heritage park context, it thus seems that some objects are freighted with considerable personal significance, whereas others are treated with sublime indifference. Interestingly, the word 'interesting', with its aptly ambivalent connotations of intrigue and insipidity, is a very frequently used expression. When asked, furthermore, many post-trip interviewees found it quite difficult to specify what part of the parks proved particularly memorable. The whole thing is a bit of a blur.

Heritage parks, then, produce a schizophrenic reaction from consumers, a strange combination of animation and apathy. They are regarded as absolutely authentic, the real thing, a presentation of the past exactly as it was. No more, no less. At the same time, heritage parks are two-a-penny these days. They are all pretty much the same offering minor variations on the weaver's cottage, working smithy, ye-olde attendants and souvenir key-rings. Heritage sites, in many ways, are the historical equivalent of the Big Mac, tasty at the time but quickly forgotten. In these circumstances, it is not surprising that consumers don't take things too seriously. People visit heritage parks for many reasons – to wallow in nostalgia, to find out about family history, to repay people for their hospitality, to 'do something' with house guests or vacationing school-kids, because it's on the itinerary of the tour bus etc. – but prominent among them is diversion, escapism, fun. A day out. Hence, they tend to adopt a wry, ironic, droll, facetious and, not least, playful attitude. They frequently joke about the implements, artefacts, exhibits and times past, particularly their forebears' patent lack of height. The museum attendants, furthermore, often enter into this bantering, jesting, post-tourist spirit of mockery, repartee and persiflage. Many visitors, in short, play at being visitors and are ever ready to reflect irreverently on their experiences and adventures, interview included.

R: How long are you doing this interviewing, son. What's it all about?

I: We're doing a research project on the Scots-Irish, the ethnic group. I come from the north of Ireland and this part of America was settled by the Irish.

R: So, you're catching up on the culture?

I: Yeah, because it's very similar. The surnames for example and the way people talk, the music, all sorts of things, such as the dancing you do. It's very similar to Irish dancing.

R: So you ought to have on one of them little skirts?

I: I don't have the legs for it . . .

(Adult male, 70s, MoA)

More importantly, perhaps, they also reflect on their reactions to the past and, once again, an air of ambivalence prevails. On the one hand, glimpses of times past generate enormous admiration for their forebears. These were people who had little in the way of material resources or labour-saving devices; who faced enormous privation and ever-present threats of physical violence; who eked a living from difficult and unyielding environments; who were ravaged by disease and died before their time; and, who lived lives that were nasty, brutish and short. Nevertheless, they won through in the end. They raised their children, who raised their children in turn. They not only managed to manage, but also built a great country by the sweat of their brows and unshakeable belief in the Lord. They did not have much but, as they were unaware that they did not have much, they were perfectly content.

I: What's your reaction when you see places like this?

R: I love it. I think the quality of life in some ways was much better back then.

I: Why do you say that, in what sense?

R: Because I don't think temptation was as prevalent for most people, 'cause they didn't have TV and all that stuff to taunt them. They just had what was around them and they made do with what they had. But in other ways you could die from a broken arm and in other ways there were other hardships. I think people were probably more content. They had more of a purpose. They had to work. Not like these days.

I: So, do you feel then that we've lost something?

R: We've definitely lost something and it will never come back. When I see places like this I'm disappointed that we lost so much, maybe.

(Adult female, 40s, MoA)

On the other hand, not a single interviewee would choose to live in times past, given the opportunity to do so. Some older informants, admittedly, were prepared to consider changing places, but only because the buildings brought back roseate memories of long-departed childhood. Even here, however, realism usually won out insofar as the parks were often criticised for being too perfect and underplaying the problems that had to be endured. Admirable though their ancestors' achievements undoubtedly are; closer though families and communities may well have been back then; simpler, slower-moving and less-stressful though past times sometimes appear, they were also exceedingly hard times; they were filthy and demanding times; they were hellish as well as heavenly times. The material benefits of modern society – television, refrigeration, supersonic transportation, medical miracles – are not to be relinquished lightly, even though they are accompanied by degeneracy, drug addiction and environmental despoliation. It seems that material progress and moral decline go hand in hand. The past, in short, is a foreign country and diverting though occasional package tours are, one would not want to live there.

> *I:*   So what do you think people get from their visit? What do they take away from here?
>
> *R:*   I think they take away a greater appreciation of the hardships that people had. I get sort of tired hearing about the good old days because they were good in a lot of ways but man they were hard, they were so hard and I think people come away with that feeling. I'm so thankful for what we have, I'm thankful from where I came from and I'm thankful that I don't have to live in those times. But I think it also makes them feel better about themselves. So many times you go to places . . . I don't want to criticise it, Dollywood is fine, it serves a purpose . . . but many times you go to places like that and all you come away with is a feeling you spent your money. You don't, I don't know, maybe . . .
>
> (Marketing manageress, 30s, MoA)

Consumers' overall attitude towards the good old bad old days is unambiguously ambiguous. Postmodern nostalgia is not an unreflexive wallow in days gone by. Nor does it regard the past from a presentist position of self-satisfied superiority. Nor, for that matter, is it a straightforward combination of pleasure and pain – pleasure in the past and pain that it has passed. It is rather a combination of pleasure and pain for *both* the past and the present, what Jameson (1991: 251) terms *eudemonization*. The present is characterised by material progress and moral decline, the past by moral probity and material deficiency. Utopia, therefore, does not lie in the future, because material advance will come at a moral cost. Nor does it lie in the past, since a material price has to be paid for moral worth. It resides, rather, in the interaction of the two – retrotopia – where the best of the past meets the best of the future, where handicraft embraces hi-technology, where form and content combine.

Connectivity

Making connections, indeed, is the essence of the heritage park experience. Just as Jameson's work is encapsulated in the words 'only connect', so too heritage is all about connectivity. It connects, what is more, on several different levels. For example, the principal purpose of heritage parks *per se* is connecting the present with the past by means of artefacts, displays and demonstrations of what life was like 'back then'. More specifically, the Ulster–American Folk Park is predicated on ancestral connections between Ireland and the United States, as epitomised by the Mellon dynasty. The Ulster Folk and Transport Museum connects town and country, as well as cataloguing the history of the vehicles that connected them. The Museum of Appalachia, moreover, is ultimately about making connections between image and reality. The prevailing image of the Appalachian people, as backward, in-bred hill-billies, is challenged, contradicted and counteracted with the realities of industriousness, generosity and achievement despite seemingly insurmountable odds.

Visitors to the parks are also engaged in making connections. Some are happy to commune with their ancestors by the medium of genealogical inquiry or simply by encountering objects akin to those in their predecessors' possession (bibles, quilts, ornaments, jewellery, rocking chairs, etc.). Others are content to be connected with connectedness; that is, to the kin, the community, the culture, the country from whence they came and, by vicarious association, to its celebrities, its struggles, its triumphs, its accomplishments. And yet others are bent on a personal quest for days of yore, for their former selves, for happy memories of childhood and the protective parental cocoon.

In most cases, however, this connectivity involves both past and present inasmuch as multi-generational family groups are the single largest category of visitors. Presentations of the past thus act as a catalyst for inter-personal and inter-generation communication – parents with children, grandchildren with grandparents, globe-trotting relatives with settled stay-at-homes – thereby providing an opportunity to reinforce the familial bonds that are neglected in the hurly-burly of day-to-day existence. Children, especially, are expected to benefit from their encounters with heritage, albeit in a punitive, take-your-medicine-it's-good-for-you sense. By seeing at first hand the drudgery, deprivation and sheer destitution of life in the past, today's youth may be persuaded to appreciate their good fortune and treat their elders and betters with due respect thereafter. In theory at least.

I: What have you been learning while you're here?
R1:   About the past and all.

I: Do you think you'd rather be a kid today, or a kid back then?

R1:   Today.

R2:   No hesitation.

I: Yeah, why is that?

R2:   Cobwebs in the houses and all.

I: Cobwebs in the houses?

R2:   Better sweets now.

I: Better sweets now, yeah.

R1:   What about the school?

R2:   Very strict and all. It's not that strict now.

I: The school looked pretty strict to you? And it's easier. The teachers are nicer now, you think?

R2:   Um hum.

(Irish children, male, 10 yrs, UFTM)

The marketing of the parks, furthermore, is predicated on connectivity. Apart from heavy reliance on repeat business, word-of-mouth recommendations and establishing long-term relationships with valued customers through databases, newsletters and the like (all of which rest on the notion of connection), heritage park marketers go to great lengths to forge links with local schools, universities and special interest groups, such as historical societies. Promotional activities, likewise, are driven by a connectivity imperative. This ranges from combining eclectic events into a coherent package, as in the Ulster Folk and Transport Museum's 'Championship Day', to major ventures like the Museum of Appalachia's Fall Homecoming, which expressly utilises connectivity – getting in touch with one's roots – as its root metaphor and, appropriately enough, allocates the first of its four days to children and family-oriented activities.

Marketing, to be sure, is inherently connective, since it has traditionally sought to bridge the gap between producer and consumer. Yet the parallel is completely lost upon historical purists and analogous academic commentators on heritage, who continue to regard marketing as a necessary evil at best or a capitalist conspiracy at worst. Marketing, after all, is the bane of historical integrity. Using the past to move merchandise is considered iniquitous bordering on blasphemous. Selling contaminates, it profanes the sacred, sacralises the profane and deprives precious memories of their sanctity, notwithstanding ample historical evidence of God and Mammon's co-mingling (McDannell 1995; Moore 1994).

Set against this, the evidence clearly indicates that some of the most nostalgic-ally freighted exhibits in the parks are associated with commercial life. The candy store in the Ulster Folk and Transport Museum, the pharmacy in the Ulster–American Folk Park, the post office, barber's shop and, especially, general store in the Museum of Appalachia all triggered exceptionally happy memories. Bygone brands, passé packages and long-forgotten foodstuffs are especially salient, generating all sorts of pleasurable recollections about the comparative merits of the products concerned. Even cure-all-ills patent medicines, containing 40 per cent alcohol and liberal doses of opium, are bathed in the numinous light of anamnesis, as are the promotional vehicles – namely, itinerant medicine shows – that accompanied them.

I: Does this store remind you of your childhood?

R1: Yeah, it does. It does.

R2: I see some products that were still around when I was growing up.

I: Such as?

R2: The Rinso soap powder. Robin Starch was around. Maxwell House coffee.

R1: That chewing tobacco, there.

R2: That powder was popular with people, at one time.

I: What was it?

R2: A kind of tonic that people drank.

R1: That came after World War Two, didn't it?

R2: I don't remember the timing exactly. All over the country they were drinking that, thinking it was the greatest tonic in the world. But it was 35 per cent alcohol and they didn't even know it!

R1: It would cure everything!

R2: Two or three summers in a row, when I was a kid, they'd come by selling that sort of stuff.

I: What, like the way they do it in the movies, with the guy selling the, you know, snake-oil?

R2: Yeah, they had a show with comedians and then they'd take a break every so often and go up and down the aisles trying to sell.

R1: Like commercials.

R2: They sold some candy and they sold some sort of tonic. I well remember that.

(Adult male and female, 70s, MoA)

Clearly, some of this affability may be attributable to confirmatory bias, on account of the presence of self-confessed marketing researchers, but it was equally apparent when the interactions of consumer and consumption were observed unobtrusively. Whereas display cases of broken drill-bits or disused padlocks are contemplated with mild curiosity and not a little bewilderment, the sight of a glass Coke bottle, an empty packet of Lucky Strikes, or an old-fashioned, candy-striped barber's pole, is greeted like a long-lost friend. Products pertaining to unmentionable bodily functions are especially popular and, in keeping with the carnivalesque, liminoid, away-day ethos of tourism, invariably give rise to all manner of ribald and jocular remarks. Indeed, it is striking that the biggest single complaint about the parks under consideration concerns their marketing shortcomings, their failure to promote themselves properly, their lack of consideration for paying customers and tendency to hide their lights under a bushel of museological integrity.

Marketing, then, is an integral part of the heritage package. Its place, admittedly, continues to be challenged by the curatorial cabal, those who remain committed to pursuing the chimera of historical truth and absolute realism with regard to its representation. The ultimate irony, however, is that the most marketing-inflected aspects of heritage parks – the enactments, the costumes, the gimmicks – are the very things that render them realistic for consumers. In this regard it is worth recalling that the 'authenticity' of the parks is not judged against fidelity to the historical 'facts' but in terms of its presentation of the facts relative to other heritage centres and competing attractions with an historical ethos (Williamsburg, Dollywood, etc.). In postmodernity, historical truth inheres in the true-ness of the representations not in representations of the truth, the whole truth and nothing but the truth.

Postmodern consumers, in short, are inclined to authenticate heritage time in terms of heritage space. Like Jameson, moreover, they are prone to make meaningful metaphorical – or, rather, analogical – connections while partaking of the heritage repast. The layout of the Museum of Appalachia, with its geographically eccentric Hall of Fame is considered symptomatic of Appalachians' perceived marginalisation within American society as a whole. The disorientation felt in the Ulster Folk and Transport Museum, in particular, is equivalent to peoples' relationship with unfathomable times past. For American visitors to the Ulster–American Folk Park, the dangers of the emigrants' sea voyage are analogous to their own high-risk decision to visit riot-torn, bomb-blasted Northern Ireland. For Irish visitors, by contrast, the richer furnishings, larger buildings, elevated situation and, interestingly, higher prices in the replica retail stores on the New World side of the park are symbolic of what the land of opportunity had to offer prospective emigrants, in both days gone by and, to some extent, the present.

According to one museum official, indeed, heritage parks are homologues for tourist marketing as a whole. The more visitors marketing succeeds in attracting to the parks, the less pleasurable the experience for those who are there. More people, moreover, means greater wear and tear on the collection, the surrounding environment and the academic integrity of the museum. Granted, a judiciously implemented segmentation strategy would obviate this perceived problem, but as Belk (1995) artfully observes, such activities are contrary to museums' all-comers-welcome tradition (even though visitor profile studies (see Merriman 1989) suggest otherwise). In practice, however, populism is widely regarded as a signifier of philistinism, customer delight an indicator of erroneous curatorial decision taking and marketing a metaphor for mendacity, money-grubbing and museological myopia (Moore 1997). Except, of course, when government grants are cut.

Discussion

Marketing may be an anathema in certain superannuated museological circles, but as both institutions are considered symptomatic of the postmodern condition, it seems eminently sensible to consider postmodern museums from a postmodern marketing standpoint. The present chapter has examined three heritage parks, using the work of Fredric Jameson as a theoretical template. While the findings are of some relevance to the managers of the museums concerned, they also have broader implications, though these are indicative rather than exact.

Prior attempts to account for the staggering popularity of heritage parks have focused on three key factors: migration, demographics and technophobia. The rise of urbanism in the nineteenth century and its acceleration in the twentieth has transformed much of the Western world from a settled agrarian society into an itinerant urban one, with the consequent loss of rural rootedness, community spirit and a sense of place. Open-air museums and heritage parks thus offer a welcome, if fleeting, glimpse of *Gemeinschaft* for alienated city slickers. Similarly, the greying of the baby-boom generation has prompted a psychic return to the comforts, certainties and conflict-free times of childhood when people were polite, picket fences pearly white and mom's apple pie perpetually cooling on the stoop. Granted, like the golden age of the ancients, this rose-tinted retroscape never actually existed, outside of Hollywood studios, but the concept certainly does and it is expropriated, exaggerated and artfully exploited by the hucksters of heritage. This culturally mandated yearning for past times is also often attributed to the pace of contemporary technological change, with its attendant stresses and strains for those required to keep up, keep moving, keep ahead of the game. In these circumstances, it is perhaps unsurprising that individuals react to this new round of time–space compression by pining for the simpler times, slower times, sentimental times portrayed in friendly neighbourhood heritage parks.

Although few would deny the importance of such factors in explaining the rise of retroscapes – and, perhaps, retromarketing *per se* – the above study suggests that other factors are also at work. The parks succeed because of their inherent mystery, the fact that the objects are inscrutable yet strangely compelling, as is the past itself. The parks succeed because they are a narrative-mart, one of the few remaining places where inter-generational stories are bought, sold, swapped, exchanged and put together from the museum's bespoke collection. The parks succeed because they tangibilise the intangible and make unreality real – realer than real – even though they rely on artificial arte*facts* to produce authentic 'arti*fictions*' as it were. The parks succeed because they use the past to make the present bearable. The world may be going to the dogs but most people are not required to live in kennels, attractively primitive though such retro-residences are. The parks succeed, furthermore, because they connect, they resonate, they contain something meaningful for everyone, something that fills the emptiness, spawns a story or two and provides transportation to a different time and place, a retrotopia that is nice to visit but not to buy a condominium. In an increasingly depthless world of resident aliens, the heritage park time-share provides the perfect postmodern solution.

Despite its popularity at present, the future of the past is uncertain, at least in its heritage park manifestation. The heritage product is predicated on connectivity, a congeries of objects that ignite the narrative spark and radiate the warm glow of nostalgia. As the market ages, however, fewer and fewer customers are capable of relating to, or have any direct experience of, the artefacts on display. Today's older generation may possess fond memories of being bathed by the fire in an aluminium tub or turning a hand-cranked butter-churn for hours on end, but the number of customers so blessed is steadily diminishing. Naturally, this demographic imperative does not mean that heritage parks are obsolescent, since there will always be some interest in the way things were. Nevertheless, as time goes by, the nostalgia evoked *in* the heritage park will gradually be superseded by nostalgia *for* the heritage park itself, for the visitor's childhood experience of being taken to the heritage park by a nostalgic grandparent. This neo-nostalgia, or 'nostalgia squared', as Jameson (1991) terms it, has obvious managerial implications. Up and running for thirty-something years, heritage parks have a heritage of their own, which they have thus far failed fully to exploit. The future of the past, then, may increasingly involve presentations of past presentations of the past (as in, for instance, the 'original' Disneyland).

Set against heritage parks' potentially negative prospects, dialectical reasoning suggests a positive side to the heritage encounter. In many ways, the most intriguing outcome of the foregoing empirical study is consumers' happy memories of pre-modern marketing phenomena, a finding replicated in several similar studies (Fife and Ross 1995; Merriman 1989; Moore 1997). Even the most questionable marketing practices, such as the snake-oil selling medicine show and its dubious cure-all-ills catholicons, are drenched in the clement cascade of memory. Clearly, this finding can be interpreted in several, completely different ways. It can be taken as tentative evidence that marketing is no longer deemed diabolical, notwithstanding the continuing deprecations of die-hard museologists and left-wing academicians. It may be an indicator that marketing has lost some of its rambunctious, roll-up-roll-up spirit as it has become formalised, analytical and increasingly scientific in orientation. Then again, it could simply mean that retromarketing succeeds by utilising the positive connotations of nostalgia to offset the negative connotations of marketing. Retromarketing, in short, seems to be a way of softening the hard sell, something that may be especially important when the product is intimidatingly hi-tech or associated with high-pressure salesmanship.

Automobiles, for example, are not only the cockpit of marketing chicanery but their silicon-chip powered engines are beyond the mechanical acumen of most amateurs, enthusiasts and tinkerers. Hence, they are beginning to look sufficiently old-fashioned to counteract any latent feelings of impotence in the face of hi-tech engineering.

It remains to be seen, of course, whether this finding is the same outside the heritage park context or, for that matter, applies at the 'authentic' end of the historical spectrum. This is true of all five Jamesonian themes, which may or may not be sufficiently robust to survive the journey from one domain to another. However, there is no shortage of retro products, service-scapes and marketing milieux that they can be tested on. Consider *Star Wars*. The sixteen-year *absence* of additional episodes in George Lucas's inter-galactic epic generated the most unprecedented demand in modern movie history. *Narrative*, further-more, is an integral part of the *Star Wars* saga, since *The Phantom Menace* is the first episode in the second third of three trilogies, so to speak. Indeed the entire *Star Wars* cycle is often described as a postmodern myth, a retro-fairy tale for and of our time. *Hyperspace*, likewise, is self-evidently pertinent to Lucas's inter-galactic chronicle (consider the various geographical locations, all of which look considerably realer than real), albeit movies *per se* are frequently described as exemplars of postmodern hyperspace, simulacra for which no original exists. As for *retrotopia*, it is not difficult to regard this celluloid cosmos as a bigger, better, well-nigh utopian world where old-fashioned heroes, villains and Jedi knights disport themselves. It is a technologically advanced world that is set in the past ('A long time ago, in a galaxy far, far away'). The film, in fact, is ultimately about *connectivity*. Aside from the convoluted narrative connections between the com-ponent parts of Lucas's cinematic saga, there are important elements of connect-ivity in the viewing experience. Those who were taken to the 1977 original as children now have their own children to take and, just as the original pushed back the frontiers of special effects, so too *The Phantom Menace* is required to do the same. Anything less represents a failure to recapture the nostalgic magic of the cutting-edge original. Bearing in mind that *Star Wars* was a retro-movie to start with, as Fredric Jameson (1985) astutely observed, *The Phantom Menace* is actually a neo-retro movie that nostalgically trades on nostalgia for Lucas's nostalgic classic.

Fredric Jameson, to be sure, is more than a brilliantly insightful critic of postmodern cultural texts, be they movies or multinational corporations. His corpus contains copious concepts that are pertinent to marketing and consumer research. To cite but two contrasting examples: until his latter-day spatial turn, Jameson (1979,1981) devoted much time and effort to *historicism*, the nature of the relationship between past and present. In this regard, he distinguishes four kinds of historicism: *antiquarianism*, which valorises the past and prefers it to the present; *existentialism*, which attempts to understand the past in its own terms;

structuralism, which seeks to uncover the deeper meanings of past events; and, *anti-historicism*, which lionises the present and elevates it over the past. It does not take much of an imaginative leap to recognise these particular mindsets in the above heritage parks study. Some visitors wish to return to the halcyon days of youth; others seek a sense of what life was like back then; yet others, curators in the main, try to grasp the bigger historical picture; and then there are those who look to the past in order to affirm contemporary accomplishments. However, testing the validity of such a typology is perhaps better tackled by quantitative research methods, which are ideally suited to investigating insights, issues and ideas identified by qualitative inquiry (Hooper-Greenhill 1994; Moore 1997; Umiker-Sebeok 1992).

While this is fine in theory, the second issue arising from Jameson's work involves the intractable question of how best to study postmodern marketing phenomena. Since postmodernism challenges the methodology, epistemology and ontology of conventional marketing research – truth, validity, reliability, objectivity, predictability, generalisation, etc. – the use of modern methods to make sense of postmodern marketing phenomena seems singularly inappropriate, not to say impossible. To be sure, this does not mean that established tools and techniques *cannot* be applied to postmodern products and services. On the contrary, there are any number of compelling modernist portrayals of postmodern marketing conditions. Just because a product is postmodern does not mean that postmodern research methods are necessary to make sense of it. Yet the appropriateness of such approaches remains moot. The difficult decision facing marketing scholars, as it has faced other fields grappling with postmodernist incursions, is whether the discipline is engaged in postmodern marketing research or researching postmodern marketing.

Conclusion

Approximately twenty years ago, an architectural festival was held in Italy, as part of the Venice Biennial. Entitled 'Presenting the Past', it was the first exhibition devoted specifically to postmodernism (Anderson 1998). It boasted buildings by the leading lights of the postmodern movement – Paulo Portoghesi, Robert Venturi, Charles Jencks amongst others – and, more meaningfully perhaps than the individual participants, it intimated to all and sundry that the modernism of Le Corbusier and Mies van der Rohe had run its course. Not only did the festival announce and, in certain respects, legitimise the new architectural order, but it also served to identify postmodernism's distinguishing features, as the title suggests. Not everyone, admittedly, would accept that postmodern architecture is characterised by imaginative combinations of past (styles, motifs, detailing) and present (materials, technologies, fittings, etc.). But, few would deny that the retro look is becoming increasingly ubiquitous. As amply demonstrated by the profusion of retro products, service-scapes and promotional paraphernalia – from sports cars to *Star Wars* – the past has never been so present.

Retro-marketing, to be sure, has not been ignored by academic authorities and management commentators. However, most investigators hitherto have explained it in terms of the nostalgic inclinations of aging baby-boomers or the rise of postmodernism, an aesthetic movement that espouses the appropriation and amalgamation of past styles. The present chapter has sought to extend this line of thinking by applying the principles of a prominent theorist of postmodern nostalgia, Fredric Jameson, to three closely related retroscapes. Working on the standard postmodern premise that academic marketing artefacts are 'texts' – both literally (secondary sources, interview transcripts, etc.) and metaphorically (advertisements, shopping centres) – and thus amenable to literary analysis, the retroscapes were read in terms of five salient Jamesonian themes. These revealed that heritage parks are authentically artificial places where consumer stories are constructed, completed and communicated, the essence of past times is encapsulated, intergenerational and genealogical connections are made and, last but not least, consumers combine meaningful reflections on their roots with a good day out.

Further research is necessary in order to establish the relevance of such readings to a wider range of retro-marketing phenomena. Nevertheless, the Jamesonian approach adopted herein has considerable research potential. His spatial theories are directly relevant to marketing's growing interest in the long-neglected 'P' of place (Sherry 1998b). His approach to the utopia-ideology dialectic may creatively combine two marketing issues that have been treated separately hitherto (Hirschman 1993; Maclaran and Stevens 1998). And, his strikingly original treatment of reification could help resolve a debate that has bitterly divided several prominent marketing philosophers (Hunt 1989; Monieson 1989). Most suggestively perhaps, Jameson's fondness for analogical reasoning – identifying correspondences between ostensibly different domains – can be fruitfully applied to marketing thought itself. Is relationship marketing a form of retro-theorising, an hi-tech reversion to pre-modern commercial practices? Are marketing principles textbooks the intellectual equivalent of heritage parks, populist reconstructions of bygone ideas in an aesthetically pleasing but hopelessly superficial format? Has marketing, having failed in its grand, modernist, customer-orientated ambitions, opted for a modest, postmodern, re-production orientation?

References

Adorno, T. and Horkheimer, M. (1973 [1944]) *Dialectic of Enlightenment* (trans. J. Cumming), London: Verso.

Akenson, D.H. (1996) *The Irish Diaspora: A Primer*, Toronto: P.D. Meany.

Alexander, G. (1999) 'Online shops bring back haggling', *The Sunday Times*, Business, 11 April: 10.

Anderson, P. (1983) *In the Tracks of Historical Materialism*, New York: Verso.

—— (1998) *The Origins of Postmoderity*, New York: Verso.

Appadurai, A. (1986) 'Introduction: commodities and the politics of value', in A. Appadurai (ed.) *The Social Life of Things: Commodities in Cultural Perspective*, Cambridge: Cambridge University Press, 3–63.

Arnould, E. and Wallendorf, M. (1994) 'Market-orientated ethnography: interpretation building and marketing strategy formulation', *Journal of Marketing Research* 31, 4: 484–504.

Augé, M. (1995 [1992]) *Non-places: Introduction to an Anthropology of Supermodernity* (trans. J. Howe), New York: Verso.

Bagnall, G. (1996) 'Consuming the past', in S. Edgell, K. Hetherington and A. Warde (eds) *Consumption Matters*, Cambridge, MA: Blackwell, 227–47.

Baudrillard, J. (1983 [1981]) *Simulations*, New York: Semiotext(e).

—— (1994 [1981]) *Simulacra and Simulation* (trans. S.F. Glaser), Ann Arbor: University of Michigan Press.

Bauman, Z. (1997) *Postmodernity and its Discontents*, Oxford: Polity.

Belk, R.W. (1986) 'Art versus science as ways of generating knowledge about materialism', in D. Brinberg and R. Lutz (eds) *Perspectives on Methodology in Consumer Research*, New York: Springer-Verlag, 3–36.

—— (1991) 'Possessions and the sense of past', in R.W. Belk (ed.) *Highways and Buyways: Naturalistic Research From the Consumer Behavior Odyssey*, Provo, UT: Association for Consumer Research, 114–30.

—— (1995) *Collecting in a Consumer Society*, London: Routledge.

—— and Bryce, W. (1993) 'Christmas shopping scenes: from modern miracle to postmodern mall', *International Journal of Research in Marketing* 10, 3: 277–96.

Berger, A.A. (1998) 'Postmodern/postmuseum? Popular culture and museums in contemporary society', in A.A. Berger (ed.) *The Postmodern Presence: Readings on Postmodernism in American Culture and Society*, Walnut Creek: Altamira, 88–102.

Best, S. and Kellner, D. (1991) *Postmodern Theory: Critical Interrogations*, New York: Guilford.

—— (1997) *The Postmodern Turn*, New York: Guilford.

Bhaskar, R. (1993) *Dialectic: The Pulse of Freedom*, New York: Verso.

Bitner, M.J. (1992), 'Servicescapes: the impact of physical surroundings on customers and employees', *Journal of Marketing* 56, 2: 57–71.

Boniface, P. and Fowler, P.J. (1993) *Heritage and Tourism in 'The Global Village'*, New York: Routledge.

Bourdieu, P. (1984 [1979]) *Distinction: A Social Critique of the Judgement of Taste* (trans. R. Nice), London: Routledge.

Boyer, M.C. (1992) 'Cities for sale: merchandising history at South Street Seaport', in M. Sorkin (ed.) *Variations on a Theme Park: The New American City and the End of Public Space*, New York: Hill & Wang, 181–204.

Bracefield, H. (1999) 'Let Erin remember: the Irish-American influence on traditional music in Ulster', in B. Lazenblatt (ed.) *America and Ulster: A Cultural Correspondence*, Jordanstown: University of Ulster, 29–43.

Brown, S. (1993) 'Postmodern marketing?', *European Journal of Marketing* 27, 4: 19–34.

—— (1995) *Postmodern Marketing*, London: Routledge.

—— (1999), 'Retro-marketing: yesterday's tomorrows, today!', *Marketing Intelligence and Planning* 17, 7: 363–76.

Bryman, A. (1995) *Disney and his Worlds*, London: Routledge.

Buchanan, R. (1987) *Province, City and People: Belfast and its Region*, Antrim: Greystone.

Butler, P. (2000) 'By popular demand: marketing the arts', *Journal of Marketing Management* 15 (in press).

Chase, M. and Shaw, C. (1989) 'The dimensions of nostalgia', in M. Chase and C. Shaw (eds) *The Imagined Past: History and Nostalgia*, New York: Manchester University Press, 1–17.

Clifford, J. (1988) 'On collecting art and culture', in *The Predicament of Culture: Twentieth Century Ethnography, Literature, and Art*, Cambridge: Harvard, 215–51.

Connor, S. (1997) *Postmodernist Culture: An Introduction to Theories of the Contemporary*, Oxford: Blackwell.

Cosgrove, S. (1993) *Flogging a Dead Horse*, Manchester: Cornerhouse.

Costa, J.A. and Bamossy, G.J. (1995) 'Culture and the marketing of culture: the museum retail context', in J.A. Costa and G.J. Bamossy (eds) *Marketing in a Multicultural World: Ethnicity, Nationalism, and Cultural Identity*, Thousand Oaks, CA: Sage, 299–328.

Davis, F. (1979) *Yearning for Yesterday: A Sociology of Nostalgia*, New York: Free Press.

Derrida, J. (1987 [1980]) 'Envois', in *The Post Card: From Socrates to Freud and Beyond* (trans. A. Bass), Chicago: University of Chicago Press, 1–256.

Doherty, J., Graham, E. and Malek, M. (eds) (1992) *Postmodernism and the Social Sciences*, Basingstoke: Macmillan.

Dowling, W.C. (1984) *Jameson, Althusser, Marx: An Introduction to 'The Political Unconscious'*, London: Methuen.

Dubin, S.C. (1999) *Displays of Power: Memory and Amnesia in the American Museum*, New York: New York University Press.

Duhaime, C., Joy, A. and Ross, C. (1995) 'Learning to "see": a folk phenomenology of the consumption of contemporary Canadian art', in J.F. Sherry, Jr. (ed.) *Contemporary Marketing and Consumer Behavior*, Thousand Oaks: Sage, 351–98.

Eagleton, T. (1986) 'Fredric Jameson: the politics of style', in *Against the Grain: Selected Essays 1975–1985*, London: Verso, 65–78.

Eco, U. (1986) *Travels in Hyperreality* (trans. W. Weaver), New York: Harcourt Brace.

Ettema, M.J. (1987) 'History museums and the culture of materialism', in J. Blatti (ed.) *Past Meets Present: Essays About Historic Interpretation and Public Audiences*, Washington, DC: Smithsonian Institution Press, 62–87.

Featherstone, M. (1991) *Consumer Culture and Postmodernism*, London: Sage.

Fife, G. and Ross, M. (1996) 'Decoding the visitor's gaze: rethinking museum visiting', in S. Macdonald and G. Fyfe (eds) *Theorizing Museums*, Cambridge, MA: Blackwell, 127–50.

Firat, A. F. and Venkatesh, A. (1993) 'Postmodernity: the age of marketing', *International Journal of Research in Marketing* 10, 3: 227–49.

—— (1995) 'Liberatory postmodernism and the reenchantment of consumption', *Journal of Consumer Research* 22, December: 239–67.

Fitchett, J. and Saren, M. (1998) 'Baudrillard in the museum: the value of Dasein', *Consumption, Markets and Culture* 2, 3: 311–35.

Fjellman, S.M. (1992) *Vinyl Leaves: Walt Disney World and America*, Boulder: Westview.

Fowler, P.J. (1992) *The Past in Contemporary Society: Then, Now*, London: Routledge.

Gable, E. (1995) 'Maintaining boundaries or "mainstreaming" black history in a white museum', in S. Macdonald and G. Fyfe (eds) *Theorizing Museums*, Cambridge, MA: Blackwell, 177–202.

Gailey, A. (1986) 'Creating Ulster's folk museum', *Ulster Folklife* 32: 54–77.

Haraway, D. (1984–5) 'Teddy bear patriarchy: taxidermy in the Garden of Eden, New York City, 1908–1936', *Social Text* 11: 19–64.

Harrigan, K. (1998) *Fantasy City: Pleasure and Profit in the Postmodern Metropolis*, New York: Routledge.

Harvey, D. (1989) *The Condition of Postmodernity*, Oxford: Blackwell.

Hewison, R. (1987) *The Heritage Industry: Britain in a Climate of Decline*, London: Methuen.

Hirschman, E.C. (1985) 'Primitive aspects of consumption in modern American society', *Journal of Consumer Research* 12, September: 142–54.

—— (1993) 'Ideology in consumer research, 1980 and 1990: a Marxist and Feminist critique', *Journal of Consumer Research* 19, March: 537–55.

—— and Holbrook, M.B. (1992) *Postmodern Consumer Research: The Study of Consumption as Text*, Newbury Park: Sage.

Hobsbawm, E. and Ranger, T. (1983) *The Invention of Tradition*, Cambridge: Cambridge University Press.

Holak, S.L. and Havlina, W.J. (1992) 'Nostalgia: an exploratory study of themes and emotions in the nostalgic experience', in J.F. Sherry, Jr. and B. Sternthal (eds) *Advances in Consumer Research*, 19, Provo, UT: Association for Consumer Research, 380–7.

Holbrook, M.B. (1993) 'Nostalgia and consumption preferences: some emerging patterns of consumer tastes', *Journal of Consumer Research* 20, September: 245–56.

—— and Schindler, R.M. (1996) 'Market segmentation based on age and attitude toward the past: concepts, methods and findings concerning nostalgic influences on customer tastes', *Journal of Business Research* 37, 1: 27–39.

Hollinger, R. (1994) *Postmodernism and the Social Sciences: A Thematic Approach*, Thousand Oaks: Sage.

Homer, S. (1998) *Fredric Jameson: Marxism, Hermeneutics, Postmodernism*, New York: Routledge.

Hooper-Greenhill, E. (1988) 'Counting visitors or visitors who count?', in R. Lumley (ed.) *The Museum Time Machine*, London: Comedia, 213–32.

—— (1994) *Museums and their Visitors*, London: Routledge.

Hunt, S.D. (1989) 'Reification and realism in marketing: in defense of reason', *Journal of Macromarketing* 9, Fall: 4–10.

Hutton, R. (1999) 'Time machines', *The Sunday Times*, Sport, 7 March: 23.

Huyssen, A. (1995) 'Escape from amnesia: the museum as mass medium', in *Twilight Memories: Marking Time in a Culture of Amnesia*, New York: Routledge, 13–35.

Irwin, J.R. (1987) *The Museum of Appalachia Story*, Atglen, PA: Schiffer.

Jameson, F. (1961) *Sartre: The Origins of a Style*, New York: Columbia University Press.

—— (1971) *Marxism and Form: Twentieth-Century Dialectical Theories of Literature*, Princeton: Princeton University Press.

—— (1979) 'Marxism and historicism', *New Literary History* 11: 41–73.

—— (1981) *The Political Unconscious: Narrative as a Socially Symbolic Act*, London: Methuen.

—— (1984) 'Postmodernism, or, the cultural logic of late capitalism', *New Left Review* 146: 53–92.

—— (1985) 'Postmodernism and consumer culture', in H. Foster (ed.) *Postmodern Culture*, London: Pluto Press, 111–25.

—— (1991) *Postmodernism or, The Cultural Logic of Late Capitalism*, London: Verso.

—— (1992) *The Geopolitical Aesthetic: Cinema and Space in the World System*, Bloomington: Indiana University Press.

—— (1994) 'The antinomies of postmodernity', in *The Seeds of Time*, New York: Columbia University Press, 1–71.

—— (1998a) *Brecht and Method*, New York: Verso.

—— (1998b) 'Theories of the postmodern', in *The Cultural Turn: Selected Writings on the Postmodern 1983–1998*, New York: Verso, 21–32.

—— (1998c) 'Notes on globalisation as a philosophical issue', in F. Jameson and M. Miyoshi (eds) *The Cultures of Globalization*, Durham, NC: Duke University Press, 54–77.

Jenkins, K. (1997) *The Postmodern History Reader*, London: Routledge.

Johnson, P. (1996) 'It's always Christmas in the supermarket', in *To Hell With Picasso and Other Essays*, London: Weidenfeld & Nicolson, 8–11.

Joy, A. (1993) 'The modern Medicis: corporations as consumers of art', in J.A. Costa and R.W. Belk (eds) *Research in Consumer Behavior*, 6, Greenwich, CT: JAI Press, 29–54.

Kellner, D. (1989) *Postmodernism/Jameson/Critique*, Washington, DC: Maisonneuve.

—— (1994) 'Jameson, Fredric', in M. Groden and M. Kreisworth (eds) *The Johns Hopkins Guide to Literary Theory and Criticism*, Baltimore: Johns Hopkins University Press, 424–6.

Kelly, R.F. (1993) 'Vesting objects and experiences with symbolic meaning: summary of a special session (with discussant's remarks)', in L. McAllister and M.L. Rothschild (eds) *Advances in Consumer Research*, 20, Provo, UT: Association for Consumer Research, 232–4.

Kennedy, B. (1996) *The Scots-Irish in the Shenandoah Valley*, Belfast: Ambassador.

—— (1997) *The Scots-Irish in the Carolinas*, Belfast: Ambassador.

—— (1998) *The Scots-Irish in Pennsylvania and Kentucky*, Belfast: Ambassador.

Kotler, N. and Kotler, P. (1998) *Museum Strategy and Marketing: Designing Missions, Building Audiences, Generating Revenue and Resources*, San Francisco: Jossey-Bass.

King, M.J. (1991) 'Theme park experience: what museums can learn from Mickey Mouse', *The Futurist* 25, November–December: 24–32.

Kirschenblatt-Gimblett, B. (1998) *Destination Culture: Tourism, Museums and Heritage*, New York: Routledge.

Lazenblatt, B. (1999) *America and Ulster: A Cultural Correspondence*, Jordanstown: University of Ulster.

Lears, T.J.J. (1983) *No Place of Grace: Antimodernism and the Transformation of American Culture 1880–1920*, Chicago: University of Chicago Press.

Leon, W. and Piatt, M. (1989) 'Living-history museums', in W. Leon and R. Rosenzweig (eds) *History Museums in the United States: A Critical Assessment*, Urbana, IL: University of Illinois Press, 64–97.

Lowenthal, D. (1985) *The Past is a Foreign Country*, Cambridge: Cambridge University Press.

—— (1989a) 'Nostalgia tells it like it wasn't', in C. Shaw and M. Chase (eds) *The Imagined Past: History and Nostalgia*, New York: Manchester University Press, 18–32.

—— (1989b) 'Pioneer museums', in W. Leon and R. Rosenzweig (eds) *History Museums in the United States: A Critical Assessment*, Urbana: University of Illinois Press, 115–27.

—— (1998) *The Heritage Crusade and the Spoils of History*, New York: Cambridge University Press.

Lynch, K. (1960) *The Image of the City*, Boston: MIT Press.

Lyotard, J.-F. (1984 [1979]) *The Postmodern Condition: A Report on Knowledge* (trans. G. Bennington and B. Massumi), Manchester: Manchester University Press.

MacCannell, D. (1989) *The Tourist: A New Theory of the Leisure Class*, 2nd edn, Basingstoke: Macmillan.

Macdonald, S. (1996) 'Theorizing museums: an introduction', in S. Macdonald and G. Fyfe (eds) *Theorizing Museums*, Cambridge, MA: Blackwell, 1–18.

Maclaran, P. and Stevens, L. (1998) 'Romancing the utopian marketplace: dallying with Bakhtin in the Powerscourt Townhouse Centre', in S. Brown, A.M. Doherty and W. Clarke (eds) *Romancing the Market*, London: Routledge, 172–86.

McCabe, C. (1992), 'Preface', in F. Jameson *The Geopolitical Aesthetic: Cinema and Space in the World System*, Bloomington: Indiana University Press, ix–xvi.

McCracken, G. (1988) *Culture and Consumption: New Approaches to the Symbolic Character of Goods and Activities*, Bloomington: Indiana University Press.

—— (1990) 'Matching material cultures: person–object relations inside and outside the ethnographic museum', in R.W. Belk (ed.) *Advances in Nonprofit Marketing*, 3, Greenwich, CT: JAI Press, 27–47.

McCullagh, C.B. (1998) *The Truth of History*, London: Routledge.

McDannell, C. (1995) *Material Christianity: Religion and Popular Culture in America*, New Haven, CT: Yale University Press.

McLean, F. (1997) *Marketing the Museum*, London: Routledge.

McQuarrie, E.F. and Mick, D.G. (1992) 'On resonance: a critical pluralist inquiry', *Journal of Consumer Research* 19, September: 180–97.

—— (1996) 'Figures of advertising rhetoric', *Journal of Consumer Research* 22, March: 424–38.

Merriman, N. (1989) *Beyond the Glass Cage: The Past, the Heritage and the Public in Britain*, Leicester: Leicester University Press.

Mills, S.F. (1990) 'Disney and the promotions of synthetic worlds', *American Studies International* 28, 2: 66–79.

Monieson, D.D. (1989) 'Intellectualization in macromarketing revisited: a reply to Hunt', *Journal of Macromarketing* 9, Fall: 11–16.

Montgomery, E. (1991) *The Ulster-American Folk Park: How it all Began*, Omagh: Scots-Irish Trust of Ulster.

—— (1997) *Ulster-American Folk Park*, Omagh: Ulster-American Folk Park.

Moore, K. (1997) *Museums and Popular Culture*, Leicester: Leicester University Press.

Moore, R.L. (1994) *Selling God: American Religion in the Marketplace of Culture*, New York: Oxford University Press.

Munslow, A. (1997) *Deconstructing History*, London: Routledge.

O'Guinn, T.C. and Belk, R.W. (1989) 'Heaven on earth: consumption at Heritage Village, USA', *Journal of Consumer Research* 15, September: 227–38.

O'Kelly, C. (1996) *Concise Guide to Newgrange*, Cork: Houston.

Pearman, H. (1999a) 'Curiouser and curiouser', *The Sunday Times*, Culture, 16 May: 14–15.

—— (1999b) 'This is the pits', *The Sunday Times*, Culture, 12 June: 12.

Peñaloza, L. (1994) 'Crossing boundaries/drawing lines: a look at the nature of gender boundaries and their impact on marketing research', *International Journal of Research in Marketing* 11, 4: 359–80.

Perry, N. (1998) *Hyperreality and Global Culture*, London: Routledge.

Pine, B.J., II and Gilmore, J.H. (1999) *The Experience Economy: Work is Theatre and Every Business a Stage*, Boston, MA: Harvard Business School Press.

Relph, E. (1987) *The Modern Urban Landscape*, London: Croom Helm.

Ritzer, G. (1998) *The McDonaldization Thesis: Explorations and Extensions*, London: Sage.

Robertson, R. (1990) 'After nostalgia? Wilful nostalgia and the phases of globalization', in B.S. Turner (ed.) *Theories of Modernity and Postmodernity*, London: Sage, 45–61.

Rojek, C. (1993) *Ways of Escape: Modern Transformations in Leisure and Travel*, Basingstoke: Macmillan.

—— (1995) *Decentring Leisure: Rethinking Leisure Theory*, London: Sage.

Rosenau, P.M. (1992) *Post-modernism and the Social Sciences: Insights, Inroads and Intrusions*, Princeton: Princeton University Press.

Samuel, R. (1994) *Theatres of Memory. Volume 1: Past and Present in Contemporary Culture*, London: Verso.

Scott, L.M. (1992) 'Playing with pictures: postmodernism, poststructuralism and advertising visuals', in J.F. Sherry, Jr. and B. Sternthal (eds) *Advances in Consumer Research*, 19, Provo, UT: Association for Consumer Research, 596–612.

—— (1994) 'The bridge from text to mind: adapting reader-response theory to consumer research', *Journal of Consumer Research* 21, December: 461–80.

Sherry, J.F., Jr. (1990) 'A sociocultural analysis of a midwestern flea market', *Journal of Consumer Research* 17, June: 13–30.

—— (1998a) 'The soul of the company store: Nike Town Chicago and the emplaced brandscape', in J.F. Sherry, Jr. (ed) *Servicescapes: The Concept of Place in Contemporary Markets*, Chicago: NTC Books, 109–46.

—— (1998b) 'Understanding markets as places: an introduction to servicescapes', in J.F. Sherry, Jr. (ed.) *Servicescapes: The Concept of Place in Contemporary Markets*, Chicago: NTC Books, 1–24.

—— (1999) 'Distraction, destruction, deliverance: the presence of mindscape in marketing's new millennium', in S. Brown and A. Patterson (eds) *Proceedings of the Marketing Paradiso Conclave*, Belfast: University of Ulster, 14–25.

Sim, S. (1998) *The Icon Critical Dictionary of Postmodern Thought*, Cambridge: Icon.

Snow, S.E. (1993) *Performing the Pilgrims: A Study in Ethnohistorical Role Playing*, Jackson: University Press of Mississippi.

Sorensen, C. (1989) 'Theme parks and time machines', in P. Vergo (ed.) *The New Museology*, London: Reaktion, 60–73.

Spiggle, S. (1994) 'Analysis and interpretation of qualitative data in consumer research', *Journal of Consumer Research* 21, 3: 491–503.

Stephanson, A. (1987) 'Regarding postmodernism – a conversation with Fredric Jameson', *Social Text* 17: 29–54.

Stern, B.B. (1989) 'Literary criticism and consumer research: overview and illustrative analysis', *Journal of Consumer Research* 16, December: 322–34.

—— (1992) 'Historical and personal nostalgia in advertising text: the *fin de siècle* effect', *Journal of Advertising* 21, 4: 11–22.

—— (1995) 'Consumer myths: Frye's taxonomy and the structural analysis of consumption text', *Journal of Consumer Research* 22, 2: 165–85.

—— (1996) 'Deconstructive strategy and consumer research: concepts and illustrative exemplar', *Journal of Consumer Research* 23, September: 136–47.

Tannock, S. (1995) 'Nostalgia critique', *Cultural Studies* 9, 3: 453–64.

The Economist (1998) 'Return of the Beetle', *The Economist*, 10 January: 80.

Thompson, C.J. (1997) 'Interpreting consumers: a hermeneutical framework for deriving marketing insights from the texts of consumers' consumption stories', *Journal of Marketing Research* 34, 4: 438–55.

—— (1998a) 'Living the texts of everyday life: a hermeneutic perspective on the relationships between consumer stories and life-world structures', in B.B. Stern (ed.) *Representing Consumers: Voices, Views and Visions*, London: Routledge, 127–55.

—— (1998b) 'Show me the deep masculinity: Jerry Maguire's postmodernised identity crisis and the romantic revitalisation of patriarchy (or the mythopoetic subtext of relationship marketing)', in S. Brown, A.M. Doherty and W. Clarke (eds) *Romancing the Market*, London: Routledge, 56–73.

—— (1999) 'Postmodernism and postmodern consumer goals made easy!!!', unpublished manuscript.

Turner, B.S. (1989) 'A note on nostalgia', *Theory, Culture and Society* 4, 1: 147–56.

Umiker-Sebeok, J. (1992) 'Meaning construction in a cultural gallery: a sociosemiotic study of consumption experiences in a museum', in J.F. Sherry, Jr. and B. Sternthal (eds) *Advances in Consumer Research*, 19, Provo, UT: Association for Consumer Research, 46–55.

Urry, J. (1990) *The Tourist Gaze*, London: Sage.

Venkatesh, A. (1998) 'Cyberculture: consumers and cybermarketscapes', in J.F. Sherry, Jr. (ed.) *Servicescapes: The Concept of Place in Contemporary Markets*, Chicago: NTC Books, 343–75.

Wallace, M. (1986) 'Visiting the past: history museums in the United States', in S.P. Benson, S. Brier and R. Rosenzweig (eds) *Presenting the Past: Essays on History and the Public*, Philadelphia: Temple University Press, 137–61.

Wallendorf, M., Lindsey-Mullikin, J. and Pimentel, R. (1998) 'Gorilla marketing: customer animation and regional embeddedness of a toy store servicescape', in J.F. Sherry, Jr. (ed.) *Servicescapes: The Concept of Place in Contemporary Markets*, Chicago: NTC, 151–98.

Walsh, K. (1992) *The Representation of the Past: Museums and Heritage in the Post-modern World*, London: Routledge.

West, B. (1988) 'The making of the English working past: a critical view of the Ironbridge

Gorge Museum', in R. Lumley (ed.) *The Museum Time Machine: Putting Cultures on Display*, London: Comedia, 36–62.

Williams, P. (1995) 'Fredric Jameson (1934–)', in S. Sim (ed.) *The A–Z Guide to Modern Literary and Cultural Theorists*, London: Harvester-Wheatsheaf, 229–33.

Wilson, A. (1995) *A Review of Major Museums in Northern Ireland*, Bangor: Department of Education for Northern Ireland.

Wright, L. (1999) 'Ulster and America: a visual correspondence', in B. Lazenblatt (ed.) *America and Ulster: A Cultural Correspondence*, Jordanstown: University of Ulster, 103–15.

Wright, P. (1985) *On Living in an Old Country: The National Past in Contemporary Britain*, London: Verso.

Young, R. (1990) 'The Jameson raid', in *White Mythologies: Writing History and the West*, London: Routledge, 91–118.

Section III
The avant-garde

THE SPIRAL

Left alone in the spiral, forced to fight for myself
I reached out for something, something to help me feel,
    A mark, a sound, a space, a symbol
For I am not what I was, the spiral helped define me
    A symbol solidifies me in time and space
    It defines me, who I am
    It brings me into the light

I grow, I accept, I realize, I learn
Creation is not just for God, not just for heaven and earth,
    But creation is for us.
I create myself, out of the spiral, out of the loss, out of the moment.
My creation is life; my symbol is peace, hope, and love.
All that I am, all that I can be radiates from that point
I learn, I live, I become
I redefine myself
I emerge out of the darkness and look into the light
    the light I have created, the light I symbolize, the light that radiates
    from that which I burn into myself.

To define, to love, to display
It creates itself each day
We create ourselves each day.
Embodied somewhere in the paint, the mark places me in time
    allowing me to transcend time.
Scar me, paint me, change me
Let me grow, the spiral is life; I join and reach for the light.

Does it scream to others or does it just scream to me.
God created heaven and earth; and I create and recreate myself.

Joel Watson

9 Tupperware, Tommy Moore, Teddy Bear and Tipper Gore – Pete, Jamie, Stew, Oyster and Morrie's High School Reunion: titillation and titivation in entelechic entitulation

Morris B. Holbrook

Introduction: wake up and smell the kafka

Back in the 1950s and 1960s, marketing scholars argued incessantly about whether their discipline was a science or an art – partly, on the fallacious assumption that if it's not one, it must be the other. Subsequently, after most of us had given up the ghost on the former possibility, many concluded that if not a science, marketing must be an art. Some cynics might suspect that marketing would not qualify as an art any more than it can pass for a science, but rather that it has all the earmarks of a rather clumsily practised craft. But meanwhile, those who argue for the artistic stature of marketing would contend that what we write about our discipline constitutes a body of literature.

If – for purposes of argument – we grant this rather grandiose premise, a question immediately arises concerning how we ought to evaluate the literary fruits of our scholarly labours. In this connection, I wish to make the simple claim that you can and should judge a book by its cover. Indeed – in this age of amazon.com, when we often do not even get to see the cover before we buy – you can and should judge a book by its title. The title says it all. And there is no point in moving beyond that level of information unless you want more pedestrian and pedantic details than most of us will ever care about.

I call this general epistemological phenomenon the *Principle of Entelechic Entitulation* and regard it as the key to both *titillation* and *titivation* – that is, being entertained or excited plus getting 'smarter', where 'smarter' implies *both* more intelligent *and* more beautiful (thereby connecting directly with what literary critics used to refer to as 'instruction' and 'delight'). In other words, choose a catchy title – pick a snappy headline, design a fetching cover – and, hey, you've got it made.

This Principle of Entelechic Entitulation hinges, of course, on the role of *entelechy* – that is, the inherent force or immanent agency that regulates realising or manifesting the essence of something or someone. In other words, entelechy is what leads someone or something to *become* what he, she, or it potentially *is* – which, to paraphrase President Billy Jeff Clinton, 'depends on what the definition of "is" is'. Now some authorities – for example, the ones who compiled *Webster's Ninth New Collegiate Dictionary* – will try to convince you that entelechy is 'hypothetical' and 'not demonstrable by scientific methods'. But according to that logic, so is the Product Life Cycle, the Wheel of Retailing, the Elaboration-Likelihood Model, the Theory of Reasoned Action, the Method of Honest Catology, the Influence of Anxiety, and any number of other paradigms without which we marketers could not go about our daily job of saving the world. Tell me the title and – via the magic powers of entelechy – I will extrapolate the whole meaning of the text. In fact, I will write the whole book in my own mind a lot faster than I could manage if I actually had to take the time to read it. If you humour me, I will do it without even removing the shrink wrap. To some, this approach might seem ass-backwards. But I say, instead of letting the tail wag the dog, it is having Morris the Cat wag the tale. And what could be better than that?

I view this Principle of Entelechic Entitulation as the path to truth – as the royal road to sweetness and light. In this connection, some fool once argued that inspiration is 1 per cent of our labours and that the rest is perspiration. No way! Sprucing up the title – making it 'smart' for titivation to the max – is 99 per cent of the task, and the rest is just a sweaty drop in the bucket. Erich Auerbach said it all in *Mimesis* when he emphasised the Point of Departure or 'Ansatzpunkt' – the idea that the whole meaning of a work can be unfolded from a brief chunk of the text, just as the whole organism is encoded in one DNA molecule or the entire hologram in a tiny fragment. Of course it can. You could select virtually any short passage or obscure phrase at random. But why bother searching around when the title just sits there – big as life, up front, in your face – and begs to be picked as the obvious Ansatzpunkt of choice? Once you have seen the title, surfacing the rest of the meaning requires just a moment's worth of elaboration.

Writing, of course, is just the flip-side of reading. Or as the reader–response theorists would have it, the two activities are basically the same thing. Consequently, as an author who knows that he knows what he knows about the role of entelechic entitulation, I spend the vast majority of my energy dreaming up titles, confident in the conviction that the entelechy of each will realise itself and manifest its essence upon the printed page. I slave away to invent a bold headline and then leave the remainder of the job to my word processor. Once you have given Microsoft Word or Corel WordPerfect a titillating and titivating entitulation to work with, either of these marvellous literary engines knows how to do the rest, more or less in the manner of Robert Frost's horse. Point the critter in the right direction, and it will take you home.

So – faced with the challenge of contributing to a book about *Imagining Marketing* – I obviously need a humdinger of a title. Which means alliterative. And cinematic. And obscure beyond belief. Hmm, let's see. How about . . . 'Tupperware, Tommy Moore, Teddy Bear, and Tipper Gore – Pete, Jamie, Stew, Oyster, and Morrie's High School Reunion: titillation and titivation in entelechic entitulation'?

Morrie – the movie: honing and homing the Principle of Entelechic Entitulation

Just as successful marketing strategy follows the precept of concentrating all efforts in the marketing mix (honing) on a suitable target segment of customers (homing), so the Principle of Entelechic Entitulation needs to be sharpened and pointed at the appropriate victim – namely, *you*, Dear Reader. Towards that end, I have shaped the theme of this chapter to fit its title. Meanwhile, I have chosen the title because the first and third parts alliterate, while the second part alludes to a recent movie in which Lisa Kudrow and Mira Sorvino – playing two eponymous young women who attend *Romy and Michele's High School Reunion* (1997) – give one of the funniest performances ever seen on the silver screen.

I believe that almost any alliterative sequence of words is worth appreciating merely because it is assonant, consonant, or otherwise sonorous. And speaking of Romy, Michele, and their reunion adventures, I also believe that the world should take note of the remarkable circumstance – indistinguishable from a felicitous concatenation of marketing triumphs – by which at least four of my cohorts from a graduating high school class of only twenty-five students at the Milwaukee Country Day School (MCDS) have reached national and indeed international prominence (surely an astonishingly high hit rate for a bunch of kids from a small and dwindling beer town in America's Midwest to attain). With affection and respect, the friend they used to call 'Morrie' dedicates this chapter to Pete, Jamie, Stew and Oyster.

Tupperware: the prepotency of post-packaging

What could be more postmodern – more differentiating, eclectic, hyperreal, self-contradictory – than packaging a product *after* you have bought and consumed it? If, as Montaigne insisted, a handkerchief affords a truly loathsome way to wrap up some human excrement and carry it around with you in your pocket, then surely we should not be surprised to find that, during the 400 years of progress since his snot-related diatribe first appeared, we have evolved the inherently disgusting habit of boxing our garbage and keeping it in the refrigerator.

During the burgeoning boom in consumerism of the 1970s, suburban house-wives who had nothing better to do with their spare time and who did not shrink from the danger of recapitulating the horror satirised in Ira 'Rosemary's Baby' Levin's *Stepford Wives* (1975) – in which Connecticut women whose bodies have been taken over by maliciously programmed consumption-oriented automatons come to care deeply about their kitchens – played their roles as prototypical members of the Culture of Consumption by serving as hostesses at orgies of domesticity known as 'Tupperware Parties'. In essence, such an event consisted of inviting a group of your friends to come over for coffee or sherry and then punishing their affiliative loyalty by shamelessly trying to sell them some small plasticised containers for the safe storage and prolonged preservation of left-over food. My wife Sally attended such a gathering once and inevitably acquired a pile of rubberised boxes that, I assure the sceptical reader, worked just fine for keeping Friday night's goulash – or, as Ira Levin would have it, ghoulash – indelibly if not so delectably edible until (say) lunch on the following Thursday. Our refrigerator quickly became a marvel of organised compartmentalisation. Every moribund morsel in its plastic pigeonhole; every detrital delicacy in its proper place; every ration of rotting ratatouille in its wrapper on the rack.

Retrospectively, this episode conjures up a horrific vision of wholesome con-sumption gone somehow awry or even rancid. In a sense, consumers of the 1970s – which, at the time, invariably meant housewives – had found a way to convert their own kitchens into food-processing plants for the home production of some-thing resembling the infamous Swanson TV Dinners of the 1950s – the recollec-tion of which still makes me shudder with fright – that is, precooked food ready to be unwrapped, reheated (not to mention rehated), and eaten with a minimum of fuss and bother or, if you prefer the marketing-based terminology, a maximum of convenience. The only difference between TV Dinners and Tupperwared Left-Overs lies in the dubious distinction between prepackaging and postpackaging. Both manifestations of convenience entail an essentially puke-ish culinary experience.

The few remaining doubters and churls are essentially the same lost souls who resonated to T.S. Eliot's admonitions against measuring out one's life with coffee spoons. When I first read *Prufrock* as a high school senior, I could not fathom what this phrase meant – any more than I could understand the part about wearing your trousers rolled or daring to eat a peach (though I did OK with the singing of the mermaids, whose plaintive siren's song I often found deafening). But on contem-plating the regimenting force of those Tupperware containers all neatly stacked and lined up in a compulsively ordered array of ineluctably preprogrammed future menus, I readily come to appreciate the tyrannical terrors of the T-Ware Syn-drome, the menacing threat that we could glimpse our future gustatory life passing before our eyes by simply glancing at the parade of postpackaged left-overs perched on the shelves of our fridge.

Fortunately for me, one of my high school buddies at MCDS *did* understand what Eliot meant by his coffee-spoon analogy – namely, Pete, our class poet laureate and nonpareil jazz *aficionado*. When Pete joined our freshman class, I was an aspiring pianist still listening to my father's collection of old Benny Goodman records and still clueless with respect to the beauties of (say) Charlie Parker or Dizzy Gillespie. By the time we graduated from high school, Pete had hipped me to an avid appreciation for Be-Bop (Bird, Diz, Thelonious . . .), the West Coast Masters (Chet Baker, Art Pepper, Gerry Mulligan . . .), and the East Coast Hard Boppers (Miles Davis, Horace Silver, Sonny Rollins . . .). By the time we finished college four years later (he in Wisconsin, I in Massachusetts), Pete had launched his trajectory as an aspiring writer. And by the time I had completed my doctoral programme a decade after that, Pete had made so much money on his internationally best-selling novel *Ghost Story* that he needed to move back to the USA from England to avoid the British income taxes.

How did Pete do all this so quickly and prosperously? The answer is simple: HORROR. Like Stephen King – another highly successful purveyor of this grisly genre – Pete's long list of blockbuster triumphs comprises a trail of terrifying tales full of murders, madness, brutality, blood, guts, gore and generally gruesome ghastliness. O, yes, and innumerable names of our favourite jazz musicians.

In this, Pete tacitly declares his allegiance to the essence of jazz as the basic engine that drives his literary creations – that is, improvisation as the art of breaking rules, violating norms, departing from structures, disrupting regularities, or confounding expectations – with horror as the paragon of the improvisatory impulse in literature. Think of the most surprising notes you can play and somehow manage to make them fit the context of the tune – that's jazz. Think of the most shocking abominations you can imagine and somehow manage to weave them into the fabric of your story – that's horror. Fundamentally, both impulses embody an irresistible impetus to escape from the coffee-spoon problem. They are the exact opposite of pre- or post-packaged regimentation – the Aghast Antithesis of TV Dinners, the Anathema of Tupperware, the Nemesis of Normality. In this, they both also provide models for how consumers can lead more fulfilling lives.

Tommy Moore: playing on passion

Another name for the Anti-Tupperware Aesthetic is . . . *passion*. T-Ware is inherently logical, rational, orderly, classical, reasonable, Enlightenment-friendly. Passion breaks away from all that and lurks in the dark corners of the dingy dives where jazz musicians congregate or dwells in the anguished screams of the defenceless maiden in a horror novel just before the evil monster slits her open and rips her guts out. Somewhat more subdued but none the less admirable passion also appears, obviously, in other more temperate walks of life – in sports, of course; in the classroom, on occasion; or, speaking of horror stories, in our courts of law. In the latter, especially when portrayed on television, we experience the perennial tension between jurisprudence and juicy prurience.

Face it: our legal system imposes a decidedly decent decorum that belies, disguises and otherwise sanitises the profound pain, agitation, or suffering often experienced below the surface by those participating in its judicial processes. Only rarely do the true underlying emotions break through and expose themselves publicly. Only occasionally do the real feelings get expressed. But when they do . . . Wow! It's fireworks time.

I am thinking here of a climactic moment featuring Al Pacino at the end of . . . *And Justice For All* (1979). Pacino has discovered that his own client is as guilty as sin. Abrogating his prescribed duty as a defence attorney, Pacino points the damning finger of accusation himself, knowing that the penalties for violating protocol in this manner will likely involve disbarment. In other words, his jurisprudential behaviour – his contempt of court – stems less from prudence (good judgement) than from juice (passion).

In the real world, something similar happens in the courtroom appearances of Tommy Moore – a legendary Irish-American trial lawyer in New York City, whose specialty involves righteous law suits brought by damaged patients against malevolent or mendacious medics in general and against derelict doctors or harmful hospitals in particular. My wife Sally once served on a jury that heard a case brought by Tommy Moore against some negligent physicians who, Moore made it seem, had practically assassinated one of his clients. At the time, she regaled me with tales of Moore's charisma – his unique style of viciously cross-examining hostile witnesses, of turning his silver-tongued charm in the direction of the jury, and of breaking into an increasingly insistent Irish brogue as the passion of his arguments intensified. But nothing prepared me for the force of Tommy Moore's expressive moral suasion when, years later, I finally found a chance to observe him in action on Court TV.

The case in question concerned the demise of a young woman, Libby Zion, who checked into a NYC hospital one evening with some flu-like symptoms and who, inexplicably, was dead by the next morning. Libby's father – Sid Zion, a respected journalist – decided to sue the doctors and hospital involved for their alleged malpractice and chose the rhetorical powers of Tommy Moore as the main vehicle for presenting his side of the story. This Tommy Moore did, with a vigour and vehemence seldom encountered in the courtroom.

The Libby Zion Trial happened to coincide with the O.J. Simpson extravaganza in Los Angeles. So, for months, we sat spellbound in front of these bicoastal litigatory blockbusters. Of the two, the adventures of Tommy Moore against the NYC medical establishment were by far the more engaging. By the end of the Zion trial, we found Moore railing against the incompetence, insensitivity and ineptitude of New York doctors and hospitals in a closing statement that bore more resemblance to the conclusion of *Oedipus* or *King Lear* than to the normal yawn-inducing fare typically found on courtroom television:

> It could not have happened. But for the system, it could not have happened. It would be impossible . . . Isn't that the truth? Isn't that the truth . . .? You don't have to look far to see the lie exposed . . . They knew it back in May of 1984, and they have fought and fought and fought it since. And they cannot stop fighting until you give them the verdict. Then let all tongues be silent . . . what sum of money do you award for [the] pain and suffering of Libby Zion . . .? What do you say would be just and fair compensation . . .? Would the sum of two million dollars be just and fair compensation for the last hours of Libby Zion's life in terms of what she endured . . .? Is that too much? Is that too little? Only you can tell . . . She touched many in life. But, ladies and gentlemen, my last topic is that she should touch the world in death – that her death should not be in vain. There was gross negligence in this case . . . This is what this case stands for. The only life she had is gone, but her message can live forever if you, ladies and gentlemen of the jury, examine this evidence . . . You must make a statement on this. Society begs you to. This is your unique opportunity . . . Ladies and gentlemen of the jury, I said to you on opening statement that, despite all that has been written and talked about, the Libby Zion Story had not been told. Well, now, it's been told – almost. But you are the authors of the final chapter. Ladies and gentlemen, the final words in that final chapter would fittingly be . . . NEVER AGAIN!

Where resides such civic-minded passion among my former classmates from the Milwaukee Country Day School? The answer appears in the adventures of my one politically inclined MCDS chum – Jamie – who was a member of my immediate cohort for fourteen years, all the way from four-year kindergarten through the twelfth grade. For a decade and a half, Jamie was our only civically awake classmate. He was the President of our Young Republican Club and, indeed, its only member – not so much because we had many Democrats in our midst as because none of us really gave a hoot about the remote contests between (say) Eisenhower and Stevenson or Nixon and Kennedy. But Jamie cared – cared very deeply – and this pattern of passionate involvement would propel him towards his later career in Washington, DC.

When my mother recently sold her house in Milwaukee and moved full time to Florida, we helped her empty out her attic and carried much of this old stuff back to our cramped apartment in New York – including my childhood photo album, whose pictures had been badly damaged by being stored for over forty years in a part of the house subjected to the vicissitudes of Wisconsin's wildly fluctuating temperature extremes. Because there was Scotch tape involved – do not *ever* use it to mount photographs! – many of the priceless pictures from my youth had been irretrievably stuck together in a gooey mess. After returning to NYC, I embarked on the painstaking project of trying to salvage what I could of these ruined photographs and began the delicate task of going through the album, image by image, and trying gently to pry the pictures apart while watching the evening's television offerings for the sake of some distracting amusement. Occupied thus, I eventually came upon two aging blow-ups of Jamie and Morrie – one from about fourth grade showing me with my arm wrapped around his shoulder and the other from grade six showing us both presiding over the voting booth at some long-forgotten school election. Simultaneously and altogether astonishingly, I was amazed to find Jamie himself – now fifty-five-plus years of age – addressing me from the TV tube. In his current role as the senior Republican on the House Judiciary Committee, Jamie appeared as the first in line to speak from the floor of the Senate on behalf of Democratic President Bill Clinton's impeachment. Jamie made the most of his fifteen minutes of fame:

> We are here today because President William Jefferson Clinton decided to put himself above the law not once, not twice, but repeatedly . . . The United States House of Representatives has determined that the President's false and misleading testimony to the grand jury and his obstruction of justice in the Jones Lawsuit are high crimes and misdemeanors within the meaning of the Constitution . . . And for these actions, he must be held accountable through the only constitutional means the country has available, the painful and difficult process of impeachment . . . The President engaged in a conspiracy of crimes to prevent justice from being served. These are impeachable offenses for which the President should be convicted. Over the course of the days and weeks to come, we, the House managers, will endeavor to make this case. May these proceedings be fair and thorough. May they embody our highest capacity for truth and mutual respect.

Though I did not personally agree with most or even much of what Congressman Jamie said on that particular occasion, any more than I had agreed with most or even much of what he said when he served as the self-appointed leader of the Young Republicans at Milwaukee Country Day, I was deeply moved by the degree of his passion – a passion for politics that has sustained him throughout what has emerged as a distinguished political career.

But where can we find such passion at the more mundane level of ordinary everyday consumption?

Teddy Bear: D.W. Winnicott meets Winnie the Pooh

One paradigm for such passionate involvement in consumption experiences – that is, cathexis in the everyday realm of fantasies, feelings and fun – appears in the concept of the *transitional object* as developed by D. W. Winnicott. Much as a four-year-old cannot happily exist without his security blanket (like Linus in the Peanuts cartoons), many consumers develop an extraordinary attachment to one or more special objects with which they are deeply involved – a Teddy Bear, a stamp or coin collection, a 1955 MG, a photo album from their childhood in Belfast, a bookshelf full of 1950s West Coast jazz recordings. Where such passionate involvement occurs, we naturally find a tremendous opportunity for . . . well . . . profit.

Recently, a heightened level of this phenomenon has appeared in the form of electronically animated toys such as the 'pet' *tamagotchi*. Originally an obsession of Japanese school children before emigrating to America, this tiny keychain-sized gadget behaves much like a real animal companion. It has needs that must be met – sounding an alarm when it wants to be fed, cleaned, or otherwise cared for. Children love it and sometimes learn an enhanced sense of responsibility from it. But if they neglect their tamagotchi, it dies. Gotcha! The emotional repercussions can be devastating.

We have heard it all before. Once upon a time, Christopher Robin-like little boys cherished their Winnie-the-Pooh-like Teddy Bears. Tiny girls played with their doll collections – eventually graduating to the big-breasted, slim-wasted Barbie, who has become a global icon. Cabbage-Patch Kids and Beanie Babies pushed the merchandising hysteria up a notch or two. And all tamagotchi did was to add an element of behavioural involvement based on its digitised demands for tender loving care while subtracting an element of realism associated with physical appearance and tactile sensations.

Who better to push this progression to its logical extreme – housing microchip intelligence in a cuddly exterior – than another one of my old high school classmates: Stew. Joining our class in the freshman year, Stew lived directly across the street from Country Day. So several of us hung out at his house a lot and got to know his whole family. Later – following a stint in the Marines – Stew earned a college degree from Columbia University and, ultimately, received his MBA from the Harvard Business School. After successfully pursuing his business interests in the corporate marketing jungle for a few years, Stew went to work for his wife's family, who happened to own a major toy company, Ideal Toys. There, during the 1970s, Stew developed and introduced the creation of a remarkable Eastern European inventor – the fabulously successful Rubik's Cube.

Needless to say, no matter how hard I tried, I was far too limited in both intellect and manual dexterity to solve Rubik's Cube. Obviously, I was also far too lazy and clumsy to run a 27-mile foot race. Stew, of course, could do both. With aplomb. No problem. One night – suffering from a severe head cold – he slept over at our apartment, rising the next morning at the crack of dawn to compete heroically in the New York City Marathon. We met Stew at the finish line and brought him back to soak in a hot tub, expecting a long evening of nursing him back to health. But to our surprise, when Stew emerged from the bathroom, he plopped down on the couch, picked up our son's Rubik's Cube, and – in a flurry of furiously rapid wrist twisting – solved it on the spot in about two and a half minutes.

Clearly, someone with Stew's stamina and brains was destined for marketing greatness. Twenty-five years later – now working for Tiger Toys – Stew returned to form with a monumental business bonanza. It's Furby! Arguably the greatest commercial hit of the 1998 Christmas Season – so popular that it was out of stock at all regular retailers and was selling for fourfold multiples of its list price at various dot.com Websites – Furby combines the opportunity for passionate commitment to a simulated animal companion with another feature crucial to the logic of the present essay. Specifically, Furby possesses language. Furby's got the gift of the gab.

Furby begins by speaking his own language – Furbish. But, over time, he learns the vocabulary of his owner. In other words, Furby can talk to you, and you love him for it.

So can Tipper Gore.

Tipper Gore: Al's gal wraps rap

My first awareness of Tipper Gore – not unrelated to our earlier observations on pre- and post-packaging – sprang from her concern with language in general and from her campaign during the late-1980s against what she and her fellow pressure-group members considered the morally offensive lyrics to songs by certain rock and rap groups. Specifically, Mrs Al Gore wanted voluntary warning labels attached to the packages of rock recordings featuring words construed as obscene or sociopathic. She wanted packages that would protect children against violent, profane and sexually explicit lyrics in the music they were listening to. Hey, she wanted to change the way they wrap rap.

When I first heard about this, mistakenly thinking that Mrs Gore favoured censorship, I considered her campaign an affront to free speech as supposedly protected by the First Amendment to the US Constitution. I pictured her as a cold, calculating, cynical, castrating Iron Maiden – the tip(per) of a Comstockian iceberg with a foundation of frozen frigidity hidden below her water line. But then I began listening to some of the music impugned by Mrs Gore and realised that the measures she had suggested were, if anything, far too restrained. So I came to view Tipper's campaign for voluntary warning labels as just another sort of free speech that also deserved to be protected. While she was at it, she should have asked for warnings not only about the nasty content of the words but also about the bad quality of the 'music' itself.

I put 'music' in scare quotes because I believe that much of what we find on contemporary recordings is not really music at all. It's like . . .: there is no melody, no harmonic scheme, no chord progression, no consistent metric structure, no careful rhyming. There is just a sing-song and simplistically syncopated sort of versification that somebody who wanted to be way polite would call doggerel. (The names of artists like Snoop Doggy Dog just *cannot* be a mere coincidence.) I acknowledge that sometimes contemporary rock or rap deals with themes of societal significance – sex, violence, misogyny, unemployment, hatred for the police or other authority figures, and so forth. Such effusions might well have meanings of interest politically. They might qualify as bad urban street poetry. But, musically, most rock is schlock and most rap is crap.

So I was wrong about Tipper Gore. She is a mensch. Moreover, I was also wrong about Tipper Gore on another dimension – my biased and incorrect attributions concerning her personality, which turns out to be quite warm and altogether charming. After she became 'second lady' or 'vice lady' – that is, wife of the Vice President – Tipper began appearing on talk shows and revealed an engaging manner boosted by an aptitude for her true avocation . . . photography.

Harking back to Mrs Gore's earlier career as a photojournalist for the *Tennessean* in Nashville, these skills appear in her book *Picture This: A Visual Diary* (1996). This book espouses one version of an emerging contemporary ethos – namely, the belief that virtually any life (even that of Tipper's notoriously wooden husband Al) deserves documenting in depth by means of all the available audio-visual technology at our disposal.

The American predilection for video verité reached its early heights of absurdity in a PBS series on the Loud Family – whose willingness to have the movie cameras occupy their home to record their private lives led inexorably to the destruction thereof, as portrayed in the heard-about-but-never-seen-by-me documentary *An American Family* (1973). This famous scenario has been satirised frequently in motion pictures about the disastrous results of having one's most private moments chronicled by an invasive TV or movie crew – *Real Life* (1979), *Meet the Webbers* (1993), *The Truman Show* (1998), or *EdTV* (1999). And we recently witnessed a return engagement of video verité in the ten-hour PBS special on an inter-racial couple depicted by *An American Love Story* (1999). Truly, I do not believe that prime-time TV has ever managed to surpass the glacier-like sense of boredom that pervades this latest piece of documentary self-indulgence. But that is not the point. The point is that the *pas de deux* between the reciprocal impulses towards exhibitionism and voyeurism pervades our society and apparently knows no bounds. Everybody wants his or her fifteen minutes of fame. Everybody respects celebrities who are, in Daniel Boorstin's oft-cited definition, well-known for being well-known. Even the most ordinary people want to be watched. And viewers in vast droves want to watch them.

Using her trusty single-lens reflex, Tipper Gore conducts a sort of self-inflicted version of the same torture test but, unlike the Louds or the heroes and heroines of the other stories just listed, manages to emerge from this self-analytic clinic more or less unscathed and with her lifestyle, her marriage and even her dignity pretty much intact. As far as I can see, her salvation in this direction stems from the purposeful reflexivity of her project – the facts that she is consciously studying herself with controlled integrity and that she is actually a talented photographer with a trained eye for composing her work to produce a set of artistically interesting pictures.

In high school, our class photographer with the fine eye for interestingly artistic images was Bob or, as everybody called him for long-forgotten reasons (perhaps because we thought he had a pearl inside), Oyster. Oyster was an OK student and, like me, a non-starter on the football team. But, unlike Morrie, Oyster had sense enough not to sit on the bench and subject himself to the ignominy of serving as a human tackling dummy. Rather than enduring such abuse – not unlike the hero of *Pecker* (1999) – Oyster became the unofficial MCDS photojournalist and roamed everywhere with his 35-mm SLR. Ultimately, he took probably 95 per cent of the photographs that eventually composed our graduation yearbook, *The Arrow, 1961*.

The next time I saw him – at an impromptu mini-high-school-reunion gathering attended by Pete, Stew, and Morrie (but not Jamie) in New York City – Oyster had moved to NYC and had joined a business run by his brother-in-law in partnership with a well-known rock producer, Albert Grossman. This partnership managed such renowned rock groups and other musical mega-stars as Bob Dylan; The Band; Janis Joplin; Tom Rush; Blood, Sweat, and Tears; Seatrain; Procol Harum; and so forth. Thanks to free tickets that Oyster generously offered, we hung out with him during many rock concerts at the old Fillmore East. The night Sally went into labour with our son Chris in March 1969, we had just attended a concert by Procol Harum. To this day, we believe that the resoundingly loud bass notes on 'A Whiter Shade of Pale' literally shook Chris loose from the womb. At any rate, Oyster had arrived. He was practically in charge of the rock-'n'-roll business single-handedly, or so we thought. And the music he was helping to manage was some of the most celebrated in the history of pop culture.

Note the irony implicit in the reversal whereby Tipper Gore has progressed from attacking the lyrics of contemporary rock and rap to producing photographic essays on her family and friends, whereas Oyster evolved in exactly the opposite and countervailing direction from an ardent interest in photography to a lofty position in the business of commercialising rock stars. By the time he got to New York, Oyster had laid down his camera. Later, he abandoned the music business as well. Hearsay suggests that he found the people in this industry a little too crazy for comfort. After staging some sort of rumoured *cri de coeur* allegedly involving a parked vehicle and a tyre iron, Oyster apparently realised that the pressures of the rock-related lifestyle were to blame for his malaise and moved to sunny California to pursue various personal business ventures including real estate, trendy restaurants and the personal management of at least one highly successful writer of horror novels.

In the marketing-related comparison between Tipper and Oyster, method-
ologically speaking, I find myself leaning strongly in the direction of Tipper as the
desirable model to follow. Tipper has found an approach that – in studying herself
as a consumer – bears a strong resemblance to the method that my colleague
Takeo Kuwahara and I have been calling the *collective stereographic photo essay*.
Specifically, recalling her background as a photojournalist, she uses *photographs* (in
her case, conventional two-dimensional pictures rather than the stereo 3D images
that we have advocated) to document insights represented in her private (rather
than collective) application of what I would call the 'subjective personal introspective' or SPI *essay*. The resulting *photo essay* or *visual diary* holds much interest
for us – in part, because it portrays the life of an important political figure (her
V-P Husband Al) but even more, in my view, because it reports her own life as
a consumer (her everyday uxorial consumption experiences). A consumer
researcher wishing to construct a photographic essay on the consumption experience (stereographic and collective or otherwise) could do worse than to emulate
Tipper Gore.

Is Tipper Gore a great photographer on the order of (say) Alfred Stiglitz or
Edward Steichen? Probably not. She has a slightly careless tendency to let the odd
arm, head, or car door protrude into her pictures. She often shows a stubborn
insistence on putting the object of interest at the exact centre of an image instead
of at some off-centre position where it would be better balanced against other
large shapes. She frequently composes her shots with the people gazing out of
instead of into the frame. She sometimes pushes the shutter release after rather
than before the relevant focus of attention has started to leave the scene. She
appears to have a horror of cropping, even where a photo would be
vastly improved by chopping out some extraneous material. Things like that,
collectively, convert *Picture This* from an art book into a personal memoir.

But, that said, Mrs Gore does manage to capture some truly remarkable images
along the way. For example: a child's face surrounded by the folds of an American
flag (p. 19); her daughter Sarah perched precariously on a lofty banister as seen
from the bottom of a spiral staircase (p. 32); a vivid juxtaposition of Hillary
Clinton (suited and coifed as if she had just stepped out of a feature in *Vogue*)
talking to Winnie Mandela (wearing a bright green dress to match an amazing hat
that must be seen to be believed) with Jesse Jackson reaching between the two
ladies to extend a welcoming hand (p. 58); a panoramic shot of the desert in Egypt
with a camel at the far left and a pyramid at the far right (p. 73); a simple but
powerful portrait of a Rwandan refugee mother nursing her child in Kibumba,
Zaire (p. 85); the fastidiously tidy encampment of a 'homeless' person near
Washington, DC (p. 90); two cute little girls on the porch of their gorgeously
colourful tin house – painted yellow and orange with blue and green trim – in La
Boca, Buenos Aires (p. 131); the head and horns of a bull framed against the bright
purple of a toreador's cape (p. 135); the engaging reflexivity of 'dueling cameras'

in shots of the press corps taking pictures of Tipper taking pictures of themselves (pp. 142–3).

More important to our present focus, Tipper Gore's premise for her visual diary buys into the concept that guides our own use of the photo essay – namely, the desire to capture consumption experiences as they unfold in the emotionally self-reflective moments of everyday life:

> When I'm feeling something intensely, or I know that I'm witnessing a significant moment, I often reach for my camera . . . This book is a visual diary . . . and, like any diary, it is highly idiosyncratic . . . how I see events says as much about me as it does about the subjects I've photographed . . . I was trained to use a camera as a tool for communication . . . But over the years, I have come to appreciate photography even more as an art form and a means of self-expression.
>
> (pp. 1–2)

This Tipperian worldview turns out to be closely allied with what Beth Hirschman and I have called the 'fantasies, feelings, and fun' of consumption experiences:

> I also want to be remembered as someone who enjoyed life. This may sound frivolous, but just about everybody needs to take more time to have fun. People work too hard, and they take themselves too seriously . . . As the kids say: Get a life! . . . there is so much joy in life . . . When I take pictures, I try to find the joy.
>
> (p. 18)

Via this preoccupation and its resonance in the world of ordinary diurnal consumption activities, Mrs Gore manages – almost subliminally – to depict innumerable facets in the lives of VP-family members as everyday consumers.

As an example, Tipper's account of moving from the home they loved in Arlington to the Vice-Presidential Residence in Washington does not mention verbally what the photographs reveal quite clearly at the visual level (pp. 28–9) – namely, the fairly modest socioeconomic status of the old neighbourhood and the more or less humble furnishings of her child Albert's room (cheap bureau and desk, tubular metal bunk bed, etc.). Clearly, the Gores would have felt right at home in a decor as declassé as that inhabited by (say) the Holbrooks. No wonder that, when they moved into the comparative opulence of the Vice-Presidential Mansion (which had been partly furnished by the apotheotically wealthy Nelson Rockefellers), they 'felt more comfortable having some of [their] old familiar pieces around' (p. 32). This comment is tellingly juxtaposed with the photo of a secret service dog sniffing for hidden bombs in the Gore Family's new living room

(p. 33). Potential terrorist invasions of the parlour strike the viewer as chillingly incompatible with the presumed safety and security of a homey atmosphere.

Moreover, the visual diary appears to reveal some aspects of the Gore lifestyle that may not even have been intentionally encoded until the photos were later assembled and categorised. One example concerns the inordinate amount of time that Husband Al apparently spends on the telephone – a propensity that has, indeed, proven somewhat problematic politically with respect to his alleged habit of seeking campaign contributions via calls made from the White House. I personally do not really care whether Mr Gore makes donation-soliciting calls from his private chambers or dutifully trudges across the street to drop a dime in the pay phone. At any rate, public interest in the Vice President's teleconferences appears to have subsided in the wake of Monica Lewinsky's revelations concerning what President Clinton himself does while talking on the phone. Meanwhile, in a rapid-fire series of images captured by his wife, we find Al Gore on the telephone in the limo; holding two receivers up to both ears simultaneously; and making a call from the isolation booth installed in his hotel room during a trip to Moscow (pp. 44–5). Later, we see that Al likes to dress up as Frankenstein while taking phone calls (p. 112) – the excuse being a Halloween party for the press corps. Apparently, this telephonic obsession is contagious or even genetic; the main activity needed to prepare daughter Kristin to leave for college involves *not* packing the piles of laundry strewn around her room but *rather* . . . you guessed it . . . talking on the phone (p. 108).

As I write this, Vice President Al Gore wages a battle against former US Senator Bill Bradley for the Democratic presidential nomination. Bradley's chief claim to fame is his exemplary role as a fast-gunning forward for the championship New York Knickerbockers in the early 1970s on the great Knicks team that included (among others) Willis Reed, Walt Frazier and Earl Monroe. Gore's chief claim to fame is his knack for positioning himself sympathetically on ecological, welfare and other worthy issues. So how do I choose between a Knick and a knack? Though Bradley is a personal hero of mine, I believe that Mrs Gore tip(per)s the balance in Al's favour. Four-to-eight years of Tipper's camera in the White House would be too fascinating to resist.

Conclusion: bringing home the Kevin Bacon

A popular millennial parlour game – recently played globally via much-visited sites on the World Wide Web (www.fas.harvard.edu/~salm/student/sdokb/) – is called 'Six Degrees of Kevin Bacon'. Named after John Guare's play and the subsequent motion picture entitled *Six Degrees of Separation* (presumably, because 'Bacon' rhymes with 'Separation' and because this actor has made over thirty films in the last twenty years), the game stems from the premise that – via $N \leq 6$ stages – any movie star that one happens to choose can be linked via intermediate stars in intermediate films to a motion picture starring Kevin Bacon (www.cs.virginia.edu/oracle/). Or, for that matter, any star can be linked to any other star of interest (www.cs.virginia.edu/oracle/star_links.html). For example, take two actors who have portrayed very different versions of male heroism: Gene Autry and Sylvester Stallone Fig. 9.1.

Comparable logic supports the validity of my claim that any title we happen to like – through readily available chains of associations – can take us exactly where we want to go . . . in my case, to Audrey Hepburn rather than to Kevin Bacon, but that's another story. Put differently, the proposed Principle of Entelechic Entitulation says that the meaning of a title – *any* title – can be anything we want it to be.

Clearly, then, the main point of the preceding comments lies not so much in any light that they might shed on the infelicities of pre- or post-packaged consumption; the role of passion in the lives of consumers; the cathexis-inducing aspects of pet-like, animated, or linguistically gifted electronic toys; or the powers of the (collective stereographic) photo essay to reveal important aspects of such market-related phenomena. And not so much in any interest that the reader might find in the lives and livelihoods of Morrie's singularly talented high school classmates – Pete, Jamie, Stew and Oyster. But rather in the not-so-hidden assumption that has served as the crucial foundation for my approach in this chapter – namely, the conviction that a theme deserves exploration merely or even especially because it

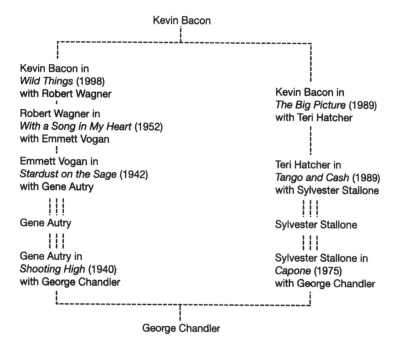

Figure 9.1 Bringing home the Kevin Bacon

rests on nothing more than a fetching play on words or a resonantly catchy titular alliteration.

I have often been castigated for an excessive reliance on the stylistic habits of consonance, assonance, recurring sounds, rhymes and the like. The thrust of the present project is that some set of themes may well deserve exploration solely because their combination produces a harmonious ring – for example, Tupperware, Tommy Moore, Teddy Bear and Tipper Gore. Anyone with half a heart – which clearly, Dear Reader, means *you* – will surely acknowledge that I have managed to tell a story about consumer behaviour and marketing with nothing more than some alliterations and some reflections on my remarkable high school classmates as a starting point.

Some churls might wonder why we need the self-conscious rhymes. To this, I can only respond that – without the pattern wherein TWare:Pete || TMoore: Jamie || TBear:Stew || TGore:Oyster – I would not have bothered with this exercise in titillating and titivating entelechic entitulation. And you, Dear Reader, would be sitting there with a £60 book containing about twenty-five fewer pages, thereby shrinking the value of your literary investment by some substantial proportion that you, if you are anything like me, can ill afford.

Even less charitable curmudgeons might loudly demand a more learned justification of the proposed approach. For this, we need look no farther than the work of Stephen Brown, who has recently applied an interpretive perspective suggested by the literary critic Harold Bloom. Specifically, Brown adopts Bloom's dictum that *any* reading is a *mis*reading. From this interpretive stance, it follows that a given reading tells us more about the interpret*er* than it does about the interpret*ee* or the interpret*ed*. The critique reveals more about the one conducting it than about the material on which it is conducted. In that sense, every interpretation is an act of self-revelation. Every critical analysis is an essay in subjective personal introspection. All reading, which is to say all knowledge, reduces to the approach that I have advocated all along – namely, self-reflection, self-discovery, self-exfoliation. This perspective is as congenial to an avowed postmodernist like Brown as to an inveterate subjective personal introspectionist like Holbrook.

We conclude that it really does not matter *what* we interpret – only *that* we do in fact find *something* worthy of our inevitably self-saturated interpretive endeavours. The entelechic force resides less in the book than in its title; less in that title than in its readers; and less in those readers than in their capacity – *your* capacity – to channel the potential meanings of the underlying metaphors. In short, MeTaPhors Be With You.

All this means – to invert the logic of Ted Levitt – that even if we *do* know where we are going, any route will *still* get us there. As in the Kevin Bacon game, any approach and, yes, any title will take us where we want to go. Unlike the old story about the farmer and the travelling salesman, you *can* get there from here. Unlike the claim by Thomas Wolfe, you *can* go home again. Unlike the poem by

Robert Frost, the path taken or not taken does *not* make all the difference. Rather, hyperreality only clothes the surface of an underlying structure based on hypertext. Our window on the world resembles a Website running on html. You *can* get to anywhere from anywhere else.

In the end, as students of marketing and consumer research, we can choose. We might choose to interpret verbal protocols supplied by a small group of customers and retailers encountered at a swap meet in New Mexico. We might choose to interpret British movies or Danish novels with some potential relevance to the nature and meaning of consumption experiences. We might choose to interpret our own autobiographical essay on the agonies of our weekly Saturday morning trip to the Crazy Prices grocery store. We might choose to interpret the answers of 1,692 respondents to a survey conducted on a representative sample of Japanese men and women over eighteen years of age. Or we might choose to interpret the meanings of a title chosen because the first and third parts alliterate, while the second part alludes to a movie in which Lisa Kudrow and Mira Sorvino give one of the funniest performances ever seen on the silver screen.

10 Going out in a blaze of glory: southern white trash retrospections on my personal relationship with Jesus, Hank Williams, Elvis Presley and a Pentecostal-Elvis-impersonating-professional-wrestling-snake-handling-minister-who-sang-Hank-Williams'-songs

Craig J. Thompson

A chapter that begins with two song lyrics[1] cannot help but invoke the spectre of Stephen Brown (1995, 1998), who has argued for years that the arts offer the most revealing insights into marketing and consumer culture. Building a chapter around this Brownian insight (which can only be described as Belkian) makes me feel strangely impelled to act upon some deep, deep impulse (which can only be described as Dichterian) to reclaim, rework and refashion it into a form that is far more original, far more audacious, far more revelatory and uniquely, unequivocally mine and only mine while masking the dread awareness that it will forever remain derivative, treading along a well-worn, already blazed path. Yes, that is a damn long sentence. But sometimes a sentence is not just a sentence. Sometimes, it is a raging war machine fuelled by deep-seated *anxieties of influence* (Brown 1999, *damn not again*!!!!) whose rhetorical weapons are ostentatious displays of loquaciousness (a tactic that can only be described as Sherryesque though it sorely lacks Holbrookian eloquence) launched against Patriarchy's Symbolic Order in vain hope of winning a desperate struggle to vanquish the dominating discourses of all those who have spoken before through an endless assault of portentous erudition that fills the existential voids, penetrates the depths of all masculine insecurities, and imposes an all-encompassing discursive hegemony (an undertaking that can only be described as Thompsonian though I'll never admit that deeply repressed fact).

I know what you are thinking: 'What the Fuck?' That is the right question too in an oblique sort of way. In this chapter, I deconstruct the phallic power exerted by the alliance of patriarchy, capitalism and marketing. Still having trouble getting an intellectual grip on this complex phallic apparatus? Well, take a moment to envision the emaciated, drug-devastated body of the near-death Hank Williams or the grotesque, drug-devastated body of the near-death Elvis. See, now you understand completely. My story is about the twisted erotic allure of the mass-marketed, body of the tortured, self-martyring masculine artist and the never-fails, they'll-buy-it-every-time marketing myth of the tragic fall from grace that inscribes it. A lucrative patriarchal model of identity that reproduces itself with every turn of the capitalist-marketing-art regime.

Singing a Lac(k)anian tune

So back to the songs. The first lyric, beautifully punctuated by Willie Nelson's plaintive, life-weary voice, wails a familiar tale of unrequited manhood; a struggling flesh and blood man seeking to live up to an unreachable standard of a disembodied, omnipotent father figure. A Strict Father ideal that can never be met. You ceaselessly struggle to live up to this impossible, unflinching, uncompromising standard without reward or satisfaction except for the sheer sadomasochistic pleasure of your Sisyphean fate. Take it like a man you brave, stoic, noble son.

The second song, not so beautifully punctuated by Tom Waits's appropriately bileful growl, is much more in tune with my own feelings. It spews forth cynicism, it seethes with iconoclasm, it defiles the temples of patriarchal authority, and it defies all obsequiousness. Yet, this rebellious voice is not one that actually escapes or even subverts the patriarchal order. No, it is the purest expression of the deep desires produced by patriarchy: unencumbered autonomy, perpetual adolescence, never becoming so dominated, so hypocritical (just to survive), so beholding to others, so 'sold-out' to the system. Those are the very impulses that ensure those who sing this defiant tune will inevitably have their spirit tamed. They will become the dutiful son or the broken man or else they will go out in a blaze of glory. And sometimes, like Elvis and Hank, those who flame out will be forever canonised as masculine martyrs and become every marketer's wet dream.

In the heat of my passionate desire to expose the phallic functions of the cultural-art-marketing regime, I confess to having had a tawdry intellectual tryst with the prodigious poststructural, postcomprehensible, postFreudian, postpsychoanalytic auteur Jacques Lacan who really did it to Freud.[2] Lacan's (1977) obtusely obscure writings on why the phallus must always be veiled explains the carnal, homosocial allure of this always marketable tale of the tortured male artist whose greatest gift is the very thing that tragically drives him to self-destruction. That's right, the marketing of Art is a Lacanian affair.

Lacan's most famous idea is that the unconscious is a cultural construction structured like a language. In a direct contrast to Freud's primordial view of the unconscious (as a repository of libidinal energy), the Lacanian unconscious is said to emerge in concert with the child's acquisition of language. It is only within (and against) the prohibitions of this great Symbolic Order that there can be an unconscious of linguistically mediated, repressed and sublimated desire. The Symbolic Order encodes the 'always, already there' structures of patriarchal domination and that is why Julia Kristeva – in one damned audacious, fame acquiring, rhetorical move – rechristened Lacan's big concept the Law of the Father.

The mysterious power which is (mis)attributed to the phallus is that once you possess it, you can compete, fight and battle your way out of the Symbolic Order: climb to the top of the hierarchy where no one has any power over you. Of course, the patriarchal structure of the Symbolic Order guarantees that any claim to phallic status is always a tenuous one, under constant siege and challenge. The more you fight to get out of its grips, the deeper you become interpellated by its demands to compete perpetually and place yourself in a hierarchal ranking. The phallus (the symbol of omnipotent power) must always be veiled because it can never fulfil the ultimate 'will to power': that is, the power to construct an identity that lies outside the patriarchal order so that the phallus is no longer needed or desired. Even if you reach the top, your phallic dominance is an illusion because it is always subsumed within the Symbolic Order.

This 'lack' drives all the masculine (unconscious) psychodramas. To mask the fundamental lack at the heart of masculine identity, men unconsciously project the phallus on to someone who is in some sense bigger or more powerful. Once the impotence of that phallic object is revealed, the phallus is displaced onto a higher and higher symbolic plane that culminates in the myth of the metaphysical Great Father, who is always judging and ranking from above and whose never forthcoming approval represents the final, most deeply coveted phallus. Believe it or not, that is the life story for both Hank and Elvis.

This is not an interpretation of Brown's and Holbrook's struggle for the right position in the art of marketing

Yes, I have promised to write about the marketing of art using Elvis and Hank as the archetypes of tragic masculinity who go out in a self-martyring blaze of glory. And I will too, but first a few words from my sponsors (of sorts). By way of a segue, the marketing of art is dialectically related to the art of marketing, which is unconsciously mirrored by the aesthetic qualities of the marketing literature whose Lacanian subtexts become most apparent in marketing writings about marketing scholarship as a literary genre. The recent spat between Stephen Brown and Morris Holbrook encodes the very patriarchal dynamics that drive the myth of the tortured male artist and it exposes the ceaseless reproductive circuit between marketing, culture and art as manifested in marketing scholarship, which itself is a cultural product. Does my point seem opaque and veiled in unnecessary rhetorical circumlocutions? Perfect.

To those outside the interpretivist sect of marketing research, this rough discursive intercourse between Brown (1999, 2000) and Holbrook (2000) that unfolded in the hallowed pages of the *Journal of Marketing* may seem like another example of self-absorbed, self-imploding, intraparadigmatic warfare. Those of us in the sect, however, see it for what it really is. An incredibly titillating example of self-absorbed, self-imploding, intraparadigmatic warfare (remember that love is war) the likes of which has not been seen since Stephen Gould (1991) let it all hang out and Wallendorf and Brucks (1993) struck forth with their most incisive, razor-sharp castigations. (Brown and Holbrook should be glad that the women did not get involved. As Gould can attest, there are worse anxieties than those about being influenced).

In the name of the father

Here is the *Readers' Digest* summary. Brown (1999) straps on Harold Bloom's 'anxiety of influence' to do Holbrook's introspective corpus. His big theoretical thrust is that Holbrook's career has been driven by an unconscious desire to vanquish the legacy of his Oedipal figure, Theodore Levitt. Morris 'I ain't no Teddy Boy' Holbrook (2000) writes a ripping riposte charging that Brown has violated him repeatedly by misquoting, misinterpreting and misrepresenting everything he has ever done, written, intended, or unconsciously sublimated. He further charges that Brown is a 'preposterous hypocrite', a malicious 'backstabber' and a pale imitation of the fourteenth-century writer Giovanni Boccaccio (I know, what the fuck?).

Let me get to the Lacanian subtext. The passionate nature of this dialogue is clearly and unequivocally displayed by the exceptionally dispassionate tone of Brown's article. A fact that Holbrook points out with all due indignity when he writes, 'Stephen has chosen to analyze my work as though I were some sort of alien' (2000: 84).[3] Damn good point but the alien metaphor is slightly off the tropic mark. Holbrook then tellingly recounts how he and Brown have exchanged innumerable intimate correspondences (hey read the paper) and, after all this, his postmodern paramour turns around and gave him the ole 'wham, bam, thank you Morris-the-Catoptric'. In commenting on Holbrook's catty response, Brown (2000) demurely characterises his paper as an attempted 'homage to their [Levitt and Holbrook] superlative achievements'. He then goes on to confess that 'I ain't nothing but a hound dog' and says that Holbrook knew he liked to do it doggie style (hey read the paper) so he has nothing to apologise for. Brown declines any further debate on the grounds that he is but a poor, Irish, marketing acolyte who is no match for Holbrook, who he now names Morris the Immanent. I tell you straight, that is the biggest, boldest, most domineering, most penetrating, move of the whole phallic interchange. Let me explain.

In lieu of a Lacanian perspective, I would have been puzzled as to why Holbrook takes such umbrage to having his introspective writings (which have been greatly underappreciated if not ignored in the mainstream marketing literature) canonised by Brown. Seriously, why write a scathing rejoinder to a paper that proclaims you to be the most gifted, poetic, innovative, creative and immanent marketing academic of all time? And moreover does so by invoking the great myth of the tortured artist, suggesting that Holbrook's introspective *oeuvre* should be treated as great literature epitomising the Romantic struggle to forge a truly authentic style. Sure, Brown says that Holbrook's early efforts were a bit flawed and he makes a few other less than charitable interpretations. Yet, all these 'textual peccadilloes' are depicted as the little strands that Holbrook has woven into a fabric of inimitable genius. Let us not lose sight of the fact that Brown proclaims the mature Holbrook to have reached an artistic apogee that Levitt had never even dreamed of and anoints him the poet laureate of marketing. Of course, the act of naming and the power to name is exactly the issue.

Flat out and simple, this patriarchal quarrel is about who is on top. Brown inscribes Holbrook in his own discursive regime. He makes the big phallic power play by naming Holbrook marketing's artistic genius nonpareil and then claiming to reveal all his inner secrets, drives and foibles. 'Yes,' said Brown, 'Holbrook possesses the phallus and I shall unveil it.' Brown's phallic conceit is twofold. He avers that Holbrook's consciousness has been penetrated by his panoptic Bloomian gaze and he demands subservience to his newly erected Symbolic Order. You can understand why Holbrook would get testy at being so totalised and even why he would try to reclaim the phallus by trumping Brown at his own game of alliterative alchemy, diabolical diatribes and rancorous rhetorical riffing.

But Morris, you should have listened to that *femme feminist* Kristeva (1986): you can't use the Father's language to vanquish the Father. All that happens is you get more fully interpellated. You are not from the South, so you cannot truly understand that, in such trying times, one must always look to Elvis for guidance. Had you known, you would have found just the right, ironically reflexive words to subvert his Symbolic Order:

[FAMOUS ELVIS PRESLEY SONG][4]

I saw the light

True confessions

My retrospective analysis is an impressionistic narrative rather than a meticulously documented academic analysis. I have read many works written on Elvis and Hank, seen many documentaries on their lives, and I know their discographies by heart. But I am writing largely from the 'structure of feeling' that I gained by growing up as a Southern white trash male where Elvis and Hank infused my very being. In my household, the true holy trinity was Elvis, Hank and a local celebrity, hard drinking, professional wrestler and Pentecostal evangelist named Whitey Caldwell, who ended all his televised matches by belting out a stirring rendition of Hank's country gospel classic 'I Saw the Light'. Whitey – like Elvis and Hank – died a premature death, fatally knifed in a drunken bar room brawl. In Southern white trash culture, having the mind of a Christian and the heart of a sinner is the sure fire spark for any tragic male figure's final blaze of glory.

During my childhood days, I really never fully understood that Elvis or Hank were bigger than Whitey. I had yet to internalise the patriarchal duty to rank order. Whether wrestling some villainous opponent to the ground or handling venomous snakes in our Pentecostal church, Whitey seemed every bit as big and every bit as important as Elvis or Hank, he just couldn't sing as well. Eventually the innocent plane of my childhood perceptions become appropriately stratified. I came to understand that Whitey was a minor local celebrity unknown outside my hometown, and even there soon forgotten, and that Elvis and Hank were ELVIS and HANK. And just like Lacan said, once I knew that Symbolic Order, I also understood my Southern white trash place in the great social class hierarchy.

Much later on (after having battled my way up the socio-economic ladder by doing unnatural things like learning to pronounce Lacan in a way that didn't rhyme with bacon), I realised that Whitey had poached every aspect of his identity from these GREAT white trash masculine icons, like during the most impassioned moments of his charismatic preaching, when he would strike an Elvis pose – legs spread, hips gyrating, lips snarling – and boom out 'SAVE ME JEEEESUS!!' and then fall to his knees just like Elvis did at the end of a performance. It always scared the shit out of me (a lot more than the copperheads slithering around the church pews) and it electrified the whole damn congregation, who knew that was about as close to the Elvis magic as they would ever get.

As much as Whitey wanted it, he wasn't even close to possessing the phallus. He never could hit the key of Hank and his Elvis posturing was a piss poor facsimile. Whitey knew it too. That was the damning realisation that drove his drinking, and his fighting. And in the one fight he got into that wasn't a staged wrestling match, the poor guy got himself killed. I guess he went out in a blaze of glory but, poor ole Whitey, try as he might, he just couldn't burn that bright.

Only very recently have I come to understand finally and fully the deep significance of these tragic men to my own identity struggles. Sure, this whole narrative is couched as a PoMo reading of the patriarchal structuring of tragic masculinity as it relates to the *marketing of art*. But you know that is not what this chapter is really about. Its truth, its deepest secret, its darkest confession is this. For reasons that I could never really pin down before, Whitey always seemed more important to me than Hank or Elvis. Now I understand the deep unconscious explanation for this intense identification. It is this epiphany of self-realisation that I present to you.

I bear the psychic burdens of Southern white trash masculinity; Jesus is the archetypic original; Hank is the one true, authentic reproduction; Elvis the talented emulator of Hank's derivative sacredness; Whitey the talentless wannabe who badly imitated the emulation, and I am the dreadful simulation of Whitey's failed mimetic attempt. Only at the very end, could Whitey come to terms with being tragically incapable of imitating the tragic male artist who is emulating Jesus. Here, I come to terms with being tragically inept at being tragically incapable of imitating the tragic male artist who is emulating Jesus.

So, the real, true, genuine reason I went so far out of my way to antagonise Stephen and Morris with my malicious, mendacious, malodorous, malfeasance is that, like poor ole Whitey, I am fighting my first, only, and last bar room brawl. I am going out in a blaze of glory the only way I know how. This obscure forum might seem like a strange textual location for my tragically untragic tragic demise but, hey, I am but a bit player in marketing's great psychodrama, so what more fitting stage than a chapter in a book that almost no one will read? Whitey here I come.

Elvis the white trash king

You already know the story of Elvis. You know he was born into poverty down in Tupelo, Mississippi. You know all about the fateful move to Memphis where he learned to sing and play delta blues from street musicians. You know that he was just barely getting by working as a truck driver when he cut a demo for Sun Studios. You know that he sang a maudlin version of 'Old Shep' and a rockabilly take on Bill Monroe's 'Blue Moon of Kentucky' and that Colonel Tom Parker heard that special something in his voice. You know that he became a cultural phenomenon whose hips were too damn dangerous to show on the Ed Sullivan show. You know that his commercial juggernaut was derailed by a stint in the Army. You know that he returned a 'has-been' who years later made an improbable return to the cultural spotlight as a hulking, white jump-suited, faux karate kicking, Las Vegas conquering entertainer. You know that at the end of his strange journey he was a paranoid, monstrously overweight, recluse who thought he might just be Jesus incarnate. You know that Elvis was finally done in by his gluttonous consumption of drugs and fried peanut butter, banana, bacon, and mayonnaise sandwiches. And you know that he died crapping on the toilet. Now, let me tell you what you already know about Lacanian style.

Somehow, Colonel Tom saw this scrawny kid with that weird wail and recognised the future of rock 'n' roll before anyone even knew that rock 'n' roll had a future. A white boy that (sort of) sounded black was just the gold mine that Colonel Tom had been looking for. Elvis looked dangerous, sounded dangerous but everyone could see behind the rebel stance to the real 'backstage' identity that Colonel Tom put in place for mass market consumption: the good Christian mama's boy, who said 'yes sir' and 'yes mam'. All the parents who yelled those angry invectives about Elvis getting their daughters' panties all wet secretly hoped that their little darlings would grow up to marry a nice boy just like the 'real Elvis'.

Of course, Colonel Tom originally marketed Elvis as one of the million dollar quartet that raised the question of which prodigy would rise to the top of his hierarchy. Actually, Jerry Lee 'the Killer' Lewis took the early lead. Elvis never generated the sweaty impassioned, mind-of-a-Christian-heart-of-a-sinner mania the way Jerry Lee did. Just listen to 'Great Balls of Fire' and you will know who should have been the King. Jerry screwed up in a major way by marrying his 14-year-old cousin. Hell, Jerry Lee wasn't even rebelling. The self-righteous mainstream just couldn't understand that in Southern white trash culture, an unmarried 14-year-old is damn near a spinster and that every 14-year-old white trash girl (and all their white trash parents) wished to God that she could have been the cousin of Jerry Lee, the man who would be king. No matter, Jerry Lee incurred the wrath of the record buying public and then he got the bums rush by the powers that be in the music industry who sure as hell couldn't put up with a rebel poseur that got anyone really upset. As for Carl Perkins and Johnny Cash, well they were long on talent but short on looks and style.[5] Colonel Tom named Elvis the King and the rest is history.

Sooner or later, the greater patriarchal power structures that valorised Elvis as the walking, talking, gyrating, mass marketed icon of rebellious masculinity would demand public submission and sacrifice. You might think I am talking about Elvis's induction into the Army (where he played the dutiful soldier at every PR showcase). Sure military service is our culture's pre-eminent expression of patriarchal domination but Elvis didn't need to get drafted to understand his inherently subservient position in the grand patriarchal scheme. White trash men know their place and Elvis knew full well what it meant to be Colonel's Tom boy. No, the military didn't do nothing to Elvis that hadn't been done already. Whether Elvis played the rebel or the good soldier, he was always taking it like a man.

The timing of the Army gig was merely coincidental with a more profound shift in capitalist-marketing-art regime. When Elvis's career went on military hiatus, the music world was already looking for the next new thing. Social changes were rapidly diminishing the economic incentives to put a pretty white face on black culture. Elvis's sexed-up Al Jolson act just didn't have the marketing imperative it once did. The patriarch of Motown, Gordon Berry, figured out that if he dressed his acts up in non-threatening 'is-he-the-singer-or-the-waiter suits', or promoted a pale-skinned, straight-nosed babe like Diana Ross, his stable of black artists could be lucratively packaged for white consumption. Just when it looked like the Motown sound might become the future of rock 'n' roll, the great Anglocising British invasion occurred. The cutie-pie Beatles and those damned ugly Rolling Stones were its yin and yang, the Kinks and the Who its *sturm and drang*. Throw in Eric Clapton – the guitar god known to his fans as GOD – and the white trash boy from Memphis by way of Tupelo never had a chance.

Post-army Elvis returned to a popular culture that had passed him by. Except for some marginalised cultural pockets like the world of my childhood, Elvis was out-of-fashion. Colonel Tom tried to resuscitate Elvis's career by making him into a matinée idol. Poor Elvis spent most of the 1960s trapped in a series of laughably bad B-grade movies (though my mom took me to see every one), and his hits were few and far between (and nowhere as big as they once had been).

There was a critical moment during this period, 1968 to be exact, where Elvis began his break from Colonel Tom's control and started striking a blow against the system that had made him in every sense of the word. I am talking about an amazing prime-time television special that has acquired a legendary status over the ensuing thirty plus years. In the midst of the summer that marked the beginning of the end for the 'Love Generation', Elvis exploded into America's living room clad in full leather, hips gyrating and lips snarling. In a stunningly bold retro act of PoMo self-redefinition (what, you think Madonna started that?), Elvis rocked from the one fabricated identity he could wear like no other. With a swagger that looked just like authenticity, he blew the minds and the libidos of a culture that had forgotten what it felt like to be really turned on. You saw this special and you knew that no one else ever mattered. Hell, I thought Whitey might even rise from the grave. My mom swooned and damn near fainted three times. Then, the show was over and he was gone never to be seen again. Elvis the prodigal son went off looking for new clothes.

A new Elvis re-emerged in the early 1970s. This new, ever more corpulent Elvis, in all his garish grandeur, would become the true White Trash King. No longer a marketable commodity fashioned by Colonel Tom, Elvis stood regally on his own, true white trash royalty instantly recognised by his loyal subjects. Long live mythical Elvis; the Elvis who healed the sick with his mere touch; the Elvis whose consumer excesses and paranoid fantasies about alien abductions and political conspiracies resonated with something deep in the marginalised, culturally traumatised psyche of Southern white trash men; the Elvis who would be immortalised in myriad tacky velvet paintings; the Elvis who would be impersonated by so many that the simulations have become more real than Elvis himself; the Elvis who every right-thinking Southerner knows never really died and who will forever lurk in the dark corners of our collective consciousness; the Elvis who became a Jesus-like figure if only Jesus could have owned a fleet of pink Cadillacs and self-righteously shot out of television screens in hotels across the country.

Young Elvis 'took it like a man' and dutifully played the rebel. Colonel Tom crafted him into an easy-to-sell commodity. Mystical Elvis named himself and became a living work of art that had no place in the capitalist-marketing-art regime. Of course, mystical Elvis was marketed and promoted but suddenly these acts of commodification were on his ever more audacious, ever more eccentric terms. What right thinking marketer would ever envision that a sweaty, pushing 300 pounds, middle-age man bellowing 'I'm just a hunka hunka burnin love', between bites of fried ham, would outsell all those young, svelte, angelic voiced, generically attractive David Cassidy/Donnie Osmond clones who dominated the pop scene back in the 1970s. Mystical Elvis did it to the phallic order that had been turning out skinny-ass teen idols since ole blue eyes.

Elvis's commercial resurrection subverted the marketing-capitalist-art regime in ways that the system could profit from but not control because Elvis was willing to pay the price of going out of control. Elvis went out of control through his weight, his drug use, his materialistic excesses, his meglamanical fantasies. He became grotesque – a monstrous exaggeration of the lower bodily strata (e.g. Bakhtin 1984) – in a manner simply abhorrent to the aesthetic ideals propagated by the capitalist-marketing-art regime.

Through this indescribably grotesque, incredibly original, dangerously rebelli-ous identity, Elvis fully embodied the cultural domination and marginalisation of all Southern white trash men. He fashioned our long history of patriachal/cultural subjugation into a crown for his coronation. Through the holy body of Elvis, every cultural caricature of the Southern white trash masculinity was transmuted into a carnivalesque affront to the dominant culture. Elvis created his own Symbolic order through his sartorial travesties, the fleet of gaudy pink Cadillacs, the abom-inable decor of Graceland, his redneck entourage – the 'Memphis Mafia' – and the outlandish diet that engulfed every culinary artefact of white trash culture, often in one sitting.

You cannot live this large, this defiantly, without it taking a toll. Elvis thumbed his nose at the establishment, refused to take it like a man, and forged his own system of status, an 'Elvis world', which is home to many imitators but has only one King. And he paid the price with body and soul. Everyone says 'oh ain't it awful that Elvis died on the toilet, how undignified'. Hell no! No more fitting way for Elvis to go in his inimitable blaze of glory than crapping all over the place. The perfect epitaph for the grotesque King.

Brilliant and defiant as he was, Mystical Elvis, the one true King of the White Trash South, never did grab the phallus. He always remained an anxious mimesis, the next best thing for a dominated culture that would accept a substitute in desperation. I think what really did in Mystical Elvis was the haunting realisation that he was merely following a path that had already been blazed by one who burned brighter and faster. Mystical Elvis was the second coming of a more expansive legend, a more immeasurable talent, a grander genius, the true poet of the [white trash] people, someone much closer to the phallus, and ultimately a far more tragic figure. A man whose untimely though not unexpected demise in the *back of a Cadillac* down in Knoxville, Tennessee (my home town) on New Year's day 1953 was the day the music truly died.

Hank the white trash messiah

Anyone who has ever heard a scratchy acetate recording from Hank William's ironically entitled 'Health and Happiness Shows' or one of his live gigs on the Louisiana Hay ride knows that he could out sing, out honky tonk, out strut, out emote, any Rebel without poseur who has ever come down the pike. Ask any Southerner who is the father of rock 'n' roll and they will tell you Hank Williams damn straight. Listen to his 'Move it on Over' and you will understand those damn Yankees stole it and repackaged it as 'Rock around the Clock'. So, think about this. The capitalist-marketing-art regime had to put a pretty white face on black culture to mask its threat but it had to put a pasty, pudgy choir boy fuckin' Bill Haley face on Hank's subversive genius.

I am not sure how to best convey the scope of Hank's talent or his sacred place in Southern white trash culture. I could recite his mind-boggling song book from the well-known classics like 'Your Cheating Heart', 'I'm So Lonesome I Could Cry', 'Cold, Cold Heart', 'Hey Good Lookin', 'Tear in My Beer', 'Honky Tonkin' and 'Long Gone Lonesome Blues' to the more obscure but even more sublime gems like 'Lonely Blues from Waiting', 'A Mansion on the Hill' or 'Lost Highway'. But I think there is a better example to be gleaned from a recording he did under the pseudonym Luke the Drifter.

Back in the day, everyone knew that Luke was Hank but this branding strategy helped the juke-box crowd distinguish his popular songs from the social, political and religious sermons he dispensed as Luke the Drifter. The particular record I have in mind was released during Joe McCarthy's Red Scare. Ever the great Southern rebel, Luke/Hank coined a little ditty called 'No, No Joe' that called McCarthy for the buffoon he was and told him to shove it where the sun don't shine. When all the Hollywood and New York cultural elite were quaking in fear of being blacklisted, Hank gave McCarthy the musical finger and his label MGM went along with the plan simply because they figured the commie-hunting clan in Washington wouldn't dare fuck with Hank. And they were right. Tail Gunner Joe damn well knew he couldn't call the rednecks' beloved, honky tonk troubadour 'red' and survive the week.

By his mid-20s, Hank was in failing health with a degenerative back disease that left him in chronic, often incapacitating, pain. After becoming the 'biggest noise' in country music, he got fired from the Grand Ole Opry for his frequent no-shows and notorious drunken on-stage debacles (George Jones would pick up this self-destructive torch a few years later). Hank's legendary musical talent seems to have been only exceeded by his ability to drug himself into a complete stupor. Towards the end, his diet consisted mostly of injected pain killers, speed balls, barbiturates and booze. Hank was only 29 when he flamed out for good.

Mystical Elvis had to delude himself into thinking he was the Southern messiah. I can tell you, Hank was the real thing or at least the best damn reproduction Southern White Trash culture will ever get. Hank knew deep down that he was the chosen one and so he didn't have to do all that ostentatious 'I can heal the sick' posturing that the latter Elvis came to fancy (and all the many, Southern tele-evangelists who have mimetically followed in Elvis's wake). No, Hank did it in a humble, gentle and hell saintly way through his musical genius. In a radio inter-view, Hank was queried about how he wrote songs and his answer says it all 'I just sit down for a few minutes do a little thinking, and God writes them for me.' If anyone else said 'God writes my Songs', you would think he must either be a lunatic or laying on the Christian crap to sell more records to the bible thumpers. When Hank says it, you feel it is the truth.

Hank the messiah whose talent came straight from divine provenance. So, maybe he didn't possess the phallus but he sure as hell had first dibs. You think you have a personal relationship with God? When is the last time he wrote an 'I'm So Lonesome I Could Cry' for you? You know, had the phallus just been between God and Hank, I think everything would have been alright too, but, of course, it couldn't be. Hank got sacrificed on the cross of capitalism.

Whether it was hawking his records and songbooks on radio shows or playing the naive hayseed in all those cornball sketches with Minnie Pearl during his stint on the Grand Ole Opry, Hank had to continuously subjugate his genius to the capitalist-marketing-art regime. Hank had his own Colonel Tom, Roy Acuff – the legendary performer, songwriter and musical publishing magnate. Roy gave Hank his 'big break' in the business and constantly advised him on how to make his songs more commercial and even went so far as to rewrite some of Hanks lyrics and melodies. If you compare the original demos of Hank's songs with the 'Acuffed' versions that were eventually released, you will realise one thing: Roy screwed Hank's genius every chance he got.

Hank, the man whose songs came from GOD, could only get his message to the people by submitting to 'authorities' who had nowhere near his talent, nowhere near his public adulation, but who just happened to inhabit a more privileged position in capitalism's corridors of power. Hank rebelled by becoming increas-ingly undependable, unmanageable, unruly, unreachable and unconscious. Through all the self-destructive excesses, the hits kept coming. Try as he might, the divine inspiration – his great gift and great curse – just wouldn't be extin-guished unless Hank went out with it. The poet of the people became the ultimate tragic figure: the great white trash masculine martyr. Irony of ironies, he was never more marketable. Even Hank couldn't beat the Symbolic Order at its Own Game. Elvis would learn the same lesson less that twenty years later.

Rising outlaw

You knew that the business about this being my last paper because I am going out in a blaze of glory was a load of crock. And I knew that you knew that and that was the collective, wink-wink complicity needed to pull off a playful postmodern production. Here is the cool part. All the yahoos who didn't get the PoMo irony, man they're long, gone lonesome blues. Shhh . . . keep it down, they might hear.

Just between us, the whole Lacanian, 'I'll never possess the phallus', 'I'm so anxious about being influenced', tragic artist lament just doesn't sell anymore. So let us talk about Shelton Williams (a.k.a. Hank III), the son of Hank Williams Jr. and Hank's grandson. Now, there is no question about it, Shelton's daddy Hank Jr. has the anxiety of influence bad. Funny thing, though, anyone who has ever heard Hank Jr. knows one thing for damn sure: he ain't no chip off the ole block.

Hank III is a different case altogether. He is the atavistic throwback. He looks just like Hank, he sings just like Hank, he writes songs that have Hank's honky-tonk flair. Anxiety of Influence? Hell, he named himself Hank III to get the inevitable publicity and he never lets the record buying public forget that he is walking in granddaddy's fabled footsteps.[6] There are some subtle PoMo differences though. Hank III makes it known that he parties hard, drinks hard, just like Granddad (and Dad for that matter) but it is not because he is haunted by demons or killing deep emotional pain. Hank III plays the hard drinking/hard living role because that is what he has to do in order to simulate Hank: no more, no less. Hank III loves to sell out by playing the rebel and his promotional pictures always proudly display his very cool 'Risin' Outlaw' tattoo just right for the part. Hank III has a better hat, better boots and way better body than Hank. No doubt about it, Hank III embodies everything Whitey ever wanted to be: the perfect hybrid identity of rebellious/commodifiable Elvis and Hank the messiah. Unlike Whitey, Hank III knows that the art of simulation is all there is.

Of course, the art of simulation brings us right back to the aesthetics of marketing [I know, 'what the fuck?' Just go with me on this one okay?] and the seemingly contentious dialogue between my two dear friends Stephen and Morris. Here is what I really think about it. First off, I have no idea about the psychosocial dynamics that might be at work (or even if there are any) and I have no interest in trying to speak to such matters. I do want to comment on the significance of this exchange to any future efforts at cultivating the aesthetic dimensions of marketing research and the whole concept of the marketing literature as an artistic form.

The discord between Stephen and Morris reflects a core structural feature of the cultural institution of artistic production. Underneath all artists' fulminations that they don't give a damn about the critics or that the critics are untalented pariahs and underneath all the critics' self-important, self-righteous, deconstructive bravado lies an undeniable, unbreachable symbiotic interdependency. Without artists, there simply is no role for the art critic. Without critics to discuss, analyse, classify, debate, and yes even rate the work of art, the creative activities of the artist would not be culturally significant. The critic inscribes the artist's creation in a discursive matrix that is needed to valorise the work. Even the most damning review still places the creation and its producer within the hallowed cultural circuit of the 'art world'. It is only through this circuit of artistic criticism that the aesthetic product of the artist is semiotically distinguished from the profane world of the commodity maker. Sure, the art world and the world of commerce are interpenetrated and their demarcations are always shifting but this valorising discursive effect transcends that postmodern condition. The commodity form is always culturally valorised when treated as a work of art and artistic status is always threatened by the appearance of crass commodification.

This symbiotic interdependence creates an institutional dynamic that plays out like a love–hate relationship. Maybe critics and artists sometimes do hate each other genuinely, deeply and with feeling but make no mistake about it, their antagonisms are structurally determined. The art world needs this productive tension and it inscribes the conflict between critic and artist right into their very institutional positions through that inescapable mode of power that Foucault (1984) called subjectification. Artists act most like artists when they rail against being codified by critics even though critical recognition is essential to their cultural position. Critics act like most critics when they go out of their way to alienate and antagonise the very artists who justify their very institutional existence.

Outside of their institutionally situated, symbiotic interdependency, artists and critics would act like, well, marketing academics. So, to have marketing *literature*, we must have marketing critics. Stephen did some much needed ground-breaking work. Until his paper, the literature on marketing literature had been all artistic production. Our field simply had no disciplinary discourse for codifying the marketing artist as an artist and, hence, no way to legitimate the aesthetic enterprise. The only discursive grid of intelligibility previously available to marketing had been those sterile, soul numbing, creativity crushing, 'but is it science?' confabulations. Stephen's *JM* paper and the ensuing comments and countercomments have changed that forever.

If I were still pushing that homoerotic/Lacanian subtext gambit, I would say that Stephen is marketing's dominatrix of deconstruction because the art critic plays a strangely feminised role of dominance by placing the masculinised figure of the artist in a submissive position. Of course, the dominatrix only has power as long as her 'supplicant' agrees to play along and the same is true for the artist, who plays along by protesting the game but never dares leave it. So, Morris played the artist to perfection by bemoaning that his intentions had been distorted, his creations travestied, and his muse despoiled and Stephen responded in kind, just like a critic should.

Who knows where this might all lead? Perhaps the aesthetic genie is now finally out of the bottle. Perhaps we are now on the irreversible path that will someday lead to a special issue of *JMR* devoted to the literary criticism of marketing literature and where our conferences will be dominated by debates between the Bakhtinians and the Bloomians, the New Critics and the Deconstructionists, and of course, the Marketing Artists and their Critics.

As much as I relish the thought, I have a nagging suspicion that something is ever so slightly askew in this rhetorical play between Stephen and Morris. I concur with Stephen (Brown 2000) that Morris's response struck a modernist chord by arguing so vehemently for a correct interpretation of his work and his not so implicit privileging of authorial intent. Stephen is also right that no one understands this better than Morris. But Stephen all too well knows that disavowing authorial intention as the truth of the text does not make one a postmodernist. The Bloomian anxiety of influence thesis is an unabashedly modernist construction of the artist as a phallus-coveting, authenticity-seeking, tragic figure. Damn puzzled I was about these inexplicable modernist gaffes and then it dawned on me.

Stephen and Morris jointly (and maybe even unconsciously) constructed a wink-wink postmodern ironisation by simulating the modernist conflict between artist and critic. What a brilliantly subversive aesthetic turn. Just like Hank III's dead-ringer simulation of Hank, Stephen and Morris's ironic performance is almost indistinguishable from the real thing; in fact the only give-away is that the whole thing is too perfect to be anything but a simulation. We are talking the hyperreal sublime. Of course, appreciating such subtle forms of PoMo self-referential parody and catching the full irony of these postmodern aesthetes waxing so perfectly modernist is just, well, ask Doug Holt (1998), it is a cultural capital *thang* and marketing is in dire need of a few art history classes, if you get my drift. It is a tough quandary guys. You did it so well that no one can tell how well you did it and moreover, you cannot ever tell anyone what you were up to without wrecking the whole performance. Let us call it the Andy Kaufman effect. Stephen and Morris, you know what you need? A good critic.

Coda: a talk with the Lord

So, Willie Nelson dials up the Lord's private cell phone and says, 'Dear Lord, this is Willie, please let me be a man and I'll give it all that I can.' The Lord says, 'Damn, did Elvis give you this number? If I've told him once, I have told him a thousand times not to give this number out. Holy shit, sometimes he's as thick-headed as Moses. Let's see, you're the "Blue Eyes Crying in the Rain" guy right? Look Will, right now I'm kinda busy with Hank's grandson, Shelton. Get this, he calls himself Hank III. Jesus, what a pistol that kid is. But anyway, I'll keep you in mind if something opens up. And one more thing, don't call us, we'll call you.'

Notes

1 Ah, let me explain. You know all that PoMo stuff about writing self-referential text that reveal the background socio-economic and cultural conditions that have shaped the production of the text? Well, here is the straight dope. I had planned to use Willie Nelson's 'Let Me Be a Man' and Tom Waits's 'I Don't Wanna Grow Up' as lyrical openings for my discourse. Alas, this plan became hopelessly entangled in the legalities of copyright releases. And so it is that my artistic vision must be accommodated to the repressive hegemonic order of capitalist commodification and the impersonal bureaucratic order of patriachal authority. The title of the ole Moe Brandy hit song says it all: 'Hank Williams, You Wrote My Life'.

2 Lacan sought to consummate the earlier works of Freud. All the opaque Lacanian prose cannot fully mask that he lusted after the young, nubile, erudite, optimistic, mythos revealing Freud (1900) who wrote *The Interpretation of Dreams* with such Proustian flair. Read that book and you can understand why Lacan went so Oscar Wilde over him.

3 As a disinterested observer, I too find it quite despicable that Professor Brown would write about Professor Holbrook in terms suggesting that he is a disinterested observer and, thereby, masking their personal relationship. Such writers should never, ever, be trusted.

4 Yes, once again the oppressive patriarchal spectre of the musical-industrial complex demands capitulation (or a ridiculously huge tithe of cold hard cash). In a truly subversive act of defiance (Foucault's panopticon be damned), I am singing in my mind (one space that the iron hand of the music publishing industry cannot yet reach) the lyrics to Elvis's biggest post-Army hit, 'Suspicious Minds'. Go ahead, it is engrained in your consciousness too. So, sing it loud, sing it proud and you will know what I mean.

5 You got to really hand it to Johnny Cash though. He sure carved out a great career by 'taking it like a man'. Though he did not write a 'Boy Named Sue', his biggest hit perfectly captured the patriarchal dynamics of being named by the father and eventually accepting that fate.

6 So, maybe you're thinking that his infatuation with granddad must be masking some deep-seated anxiety about being like Daddy, Hank Jr. Yeah right, put yourself in Hank III's boots. You're a twenty-something guy; you want to be a big music star, and you want to have sex with lots of women. Which family member are you going to emulate?

The symbolic order and the imaginary

Bakhtin, M. (1984) *Rabelais and his World*, Bloomington: Indiana University Press.

Brown, S. (2000) 'Theodore Levitt, Morris Holbrook, and the anxiety of immanence', *Journal of Marketing* 64, January: 88–90.

—— (1999) 'Marketing and literature: the anxiety of academic influence', *Journal of Marketing* 63, January: 1–15.

—— (1998) *Postmodern Marketing 2: Telling Tales*, London: Thomson Business Press.

—— (1995) *Postmodern Marketing*, New York: Routledge.

Brown, S. (1997) Personal communication.

—— (1997a) Personal communication.

—— (1997b) Personal communication.

—— (1998) Personal communication.

—— (1998a) Personal communication.

—— (1998b) Personal communication.

—— (1998c) Personal communication.

—— (1998d) Personal communication.

—— (1999a) Personal communication.

—— (1999b) Personal communication.

—— (1999c) Personal communication.

—— (1999d) Polite but reproving note.

—— (1999e) Tersely worded admonishment.

—— (1999f) Stern warning to not proceed any further.

—— (1999g) Formal notice of legal action.

—— (2000) Ranting, raving, and cursing.

—— (2000a) Death threat.

—— (2000b) Ranting, raving, and cursing, followed by death threat.

—— (2000c) Ancient Celtic hex (to the effect of 'may Shelby Hunt review all your papers') followed by ranting, raving, and cursing, followed by death threat.

—— (2000d) An hysterical, graphic description of the painful, slow, gruesome death that awaits me.

—— (2000e) Elvis stamped postcard stating that a greater power has intervened on my behalf and that the Celtic hex has been lifted and I need no longer fear bodily harm (for the time being at least).

Foucault, M. (1984) *Power/Knowledge: Selected Interviews and Other Writings, 1972–1977*, C. Gordon (ed.), New York: Pantheon.

Freud, S. (1900) *Die Traumdeutung* (The Interpretation of Dreams), Vienna: Franz Deuticke.

Gould, S. (1991) 'The self-manipulation of my pervasive, perceived, vital energy through product use: an introspective-praxis perspective', *Journal of Consumer Research* 18, September: 194–207.

Hick, A. (1990) *Lacan for Dummies (Southern White Trash Edition)*, Nashville, TN: HeeHaw Press.

Hirschman, E.C. (2001) 'I was Elvis's secret teenage concubine because he promised that anything I ever wrote would be published in *JCR* and he was right!!', the subliminal message embedded in her 1995 Association for Consumer Research Fellows' presentation that can be heard when the audiotape is played in reverse. The subliminal message will be mysteriously transcribed and published in the *Journal of Consumer Research*.

Holbrook, M. B. (1995) *Consumer Research: Introspective Essays on the Study of Consumption*, Thousand Oaks, CA: Sage.

—— (2000) 'The anxiety of influence: ephebes, epées, posterity, and preposterity in the world of Stephen Brown', *Journal of Marketing* 64, January: 84–6.

—— (2001) 'Pounding out a jazz solo with my baseball bat on the head of that southern white trash bastard: a very bloody stereographic photo essay', manuscript destined to be simultaneously published in the *Journal of Marketing*, *Journal of Marketing Research* and *Journal of Consumer Research*.

—— (2002) 'A lyrical ode to an unrequited vendetta: an introspective reflection on why the spirit of Elvis should mind his own damn business', in S. Brown (ed.) *Postmodern Consumer Research: Someday We Will Get that Southern White Trash Bastard Because the Spirit of Elvis Won't Protect Him Forever*, London: Routledge.

Holt, D.B. (1998) 'Does cultural capital structure American consumption?', *Journal of Consumer Research* 25, June: 1–25.

Kristeva, J. (1986) *The Kristeva Reader* (ed. T. Moi), New York: Columbia University Press.

Lacan J. (1997) *Ecrits* (trans. Alan Sheridan), London: Tavistock.

Thompson, C.J. (2001) 'Hey, I was only kidding!: a Foucauldian analysis of the end of my career', unpublished, unemployed paper.

Wallendorf, M. and Brucks, M. (1993) 'Introspection in consumer research: implementation and implications,' *Journal of Consumer Research* 20, December: 339–59.

—— (1993a) 'Death to the introspecting infidels: implementation and implications', unpublished, unwritten, apocryphal paper.

—— (2002) 'Death to that southern white trash bastard: implementation and implications', *Journal of Consumer Research*, manuscript that will be in progress as soon as this book hits the press.

—— (2003) 'A market-oriented death to that southern white trash bastard: the most brutal implementations', *Journal of Marketing Research*, manuscript that will be in progress as soon as they read these references.

—— (2006) 'Sooner or later that southern white trash bastard is going to piss off Elvis and then we're gonna dialectically tack all over his skinny ass with an AK-47: implementation and implications', in S. Brown and S. Hunt (eds) *Postmodern Consumer Research: Someday We're Gonna Get that Southern White Trash Bastard Because the Spirit of Elvis Won't Protect Him Forever, Vol. 6*, London: Routledge.

Hirschman, E.C. (2003) 'A semiotic analysis of the television series I'll probably be watching when that southern white trash bastard gets it: The Monday Show', first of a seven-part analysis all to be published in the *Journal of Consumer Research*.

Hirschman, E.C. (2007) 'The semiotics of why you should never piss off Elvis's secret teenage concubine', in E.C. Hirschman, M.B. Holbrook, T. Levitt, M. Wallendorf, and S. Brown (eds) *Postmodern Consumer Research: We Finally Got that Southern White Trash Bastard!*, London: Routledge.

11 Suburban soundtracks

Hope J. Schau

It was a cool and dreary Southern California day. The sky was flirting with moisture, but opted for overcast gloom. I was oppressively bored sitting around staring at my computer screen with no sense of social connection. No one was home. E-mail was down. The walls of my student apartment were moving in on me and I felt claustrophobic. I briefly contemplated torching my very Bundy building and sitting down on the grass to watch it burn with a couple of wire hangers and a bag of marshmallows. I could almost smell the stained wood blazing and the warm, sticky marshmallows roasting to a delicious char brown. Precious.

Brazenly enjoying the scene of my own fictitious crime, I decided I would make a terrible arsonist. Bad career move. Reluctantly, I settled for an escape to the new suburban entertainment paradise down the freeway. Nursing my feelings of felonious inadequacy, I walked the six short steps from my front door to the littered parking lot. Pausing at the car, I gazed back at the mould-streaked stucco framing my bedroom window. I fantasised the flames engulfing my apartment and the smoke melting into the grey sky-like waves rolling onto shore. It was a strangely beautiful and liberating vision: all my academic aspirations and ambitions reduced to delicate flakes of ash scattered by gentle inland breezes. I took momentary refuge in the image. Empowering. A phone rang in a nearby apartment and the fantasy fled. I hoped the whole scene would look different in an hour or two.

Sitting in my car, I waded through music discs in the side panels and selected one to fit my mood: The Gin Blossoms' (1992) *New Miserable Experience*. I turned the key in the ignition and backed out of the spot. As I made my way out of the lot past the underutilised recycling bins and overflowing trash receptacles, the pressure lifted slightly off my chest and I breathed a bit easier. With increasing confidence that the day might be salvaged, I drove off campus by the Starbuck's I habitually inhabit. The patio area was full of people reading, philosophising, and intellectually one-upping each other. Piloting my hermetically sealed metal and plastic bubble, I floated down the suburban streets with 'Lost Horizons' spinning. The melody washed over me and I slid the volume high. I was alone with several thousand other solitary road warriors each creating their own suburban sound-tracks, as they drifted from place to place along wide asphalt streets trimmed with well manicured foliage. I imagined the experience to be significantly different depending on the tracks you played. Weaving in and out of the moderate traffic and onto the freeway, I let the melancholy music lead me. I read the exit signs until I found the one I needed, 'Irvine Center Drive'. I could see my destination clearly from the freeway: the Spectrum. It literally sparkles from the road as a metropolis of entertainment and consumption in an otherwise horizontal, concrete terrain.

Despite the sheer magnitude of the architecture, the Spectrum is not easily located once you are off the freeway. The parking lots that surround the central structures are a labyrinth of stop signs amidst a plethora of freshly painted parking stalls. Each building looks surprising like the next from ground level. Disoriented by the layout, I could not find an empty space to ditch the bubble. The air inside the car felt stale and the panic of suffocation set in again. I needed to leave the car as I had the apartment and my eyelids began to twitch in a distinctly pre-migraine manner. Desperately, I focused on the stereo. Risking the very real possibility of blowing out my feeble factory speakers, I turned up the music full tilt.

Dazed by the task of parking and confused by the winding trails that circled the buildings, I thought I saw a Minotaur out of the corner of my eye. It turned out to be a salesman type in Hagar pants, a short-sleeved shirt and a blue and red striped tie; a Minotaur would have been categorically better. Disappointed, I turned into the lot proper and snailed up and down the rows trolling for a spot. Finally, I saw the brake lights of a departing car and flipped on my blinker to claim the stall. Relieved, I shut down the music and the car in one motion. I stepped outside and tried to get my bearings. Damn, where the hell did I park? I could not quite decide which way to walk. I should have swung by and grabbed a cartographer on the way, but hindsight is a privileged perspective. Caressing the side panel of my car, I blew it a little kiss as I hesitantly started towards the pedestrian crossing. I thought I may never see my beloved Honda again. As a vehicle of my salvation it had served me well, but as a vestige of my current malaise it was a sweet sacrifice.

The crossing led to the velvet roped valet parking shack and then on to the main entrance of Mecca itself. Wandering through the neutral-coloured buildings with bright shiny signs, I found the enormous marquee of the Edward's Theater. Twenty-one screening rooms. The Megaplex. Amazingly, no films struck me as worthy of the hefty fee. Even Hollywood, the dream industry, was letting me down. With undaunting faith, I decided to meander through the servicescape a bit before I made up my mind what to do.

I walked past the plaza vendors with their odd wares displayed on cubicle carts: butterfly hair clips, glossy celebrity photos, novelty coffee mugs, and vintage Levi's. I surveyed the open air market with restless eyes. Lord, I needed redemption and was in a spending mood. My wallet felt heavy, yet absolutely nothing was appealing; no saviour for sale. What does it take to escape these days? How far do I need to drive?

Some pinnacle of entertainment and consumption this turned out to be. All hype, no substance. The Spectrum is Vegas without the sex, money and intrigue and Disneyland without the stylised animatrons. It is paradise for the overtly branded and currently trendy: Sketchers, Woody's, California Pizza Kitchen. I looked down at the Sketchers logo on my shoes, the red Woody's Girl shirt I was wearing, and recalled fondly the Thai Chicken Pizza from CPK in my fridge at home. I struggled to remember a time when corporate images did not inform my reflections and my mind was a blank. Twenty-something and relying on a commodified imagination. This is an alienation Marx could not have envisioned.

Looking for an overdue clue, I saw a huge triangular sign indicating that more phases of construction were underway. Apparently, there were themes informing this space, but they were somehow not communicated to me until I saw the board. Bad semiotics. Someone had not read their Silverman, nor their Baudrillard.

I circled the sign in disbelief. I wondered who wrote the copy as it so did not match my impression of the place. Corporate morons. Who the hell do they think they are fooling? Me?! Damn, I am a doctoral student in the Graduate School of Management; I cannot think this way, or I will be outed as a ideological traitor and a failed capitalist. Oh well, I have certainly been called worse. I cleared the sign and walked along a more narrow offshoot of the plaza. A coffee bar. Just what I needed.

Hobbling up to the counter, I ordered a tall Cafe Mocha with non-fat milk and no whipped cream. A guilt-free fix. Pure sugar and caffeine. I congratulated myself; I am nothing if not a proficient coffee drinker. It's a skill, right? I paid my small fortune and took my drug of choice with me to find a table outside in the hazy post-real California noir. Feeling like locusts would descend any moment, I sat down at a table with four chairs, which magnified my loneliness. I put my backpack/purse on the seat next to me to keep me company. Bad conversationalist. I should have called my husband to see if he could meet me here. He has made a second career out of managing my sanity in a true minimalist tradition. In typical me fashion, I had not thought ahead and there was no phone in sight. Just not my day, or perhaps all too much my day. Randy Newman may love LA, but Orange County in a fit of manic depression is anything but lovable. Damn my dissertation. This was all its fault. The migraine courting me the entire morning declared its intentions once again.

Just when I thought things couldn't get much worse, they did in a big way. Swaggering straight towards me was my ex-boyfriend in all his well-contrived glory. He still has a way of disrupting my respiratory pattern when he walks into a place, catches my eye, or smiles. I swear every time I see him I revert back to the 14-year-old girl who idolised him. It is a dangerous place that forces me to limit our interactions. I hate it when he appears without warning. I need forethought to focus and contextualise him. Unfortunately, unexpected run-ins with him and all sorts of folks who populate my past are hazards of hanging around the place I grew up. With nowhere to hide, I decided to grin and acknowledge him.

'Hey, Craig,' I said, trying to sound casual.

'Babe, what are *you* doing here?' He smiled broadly, pulled out one of the empty chairs at my table and sat down.

'Have a seat, man,' I laughed and motioned to the seat he had already confiscated. Craig looked at his feet awkwardly.

'Presumptuous, eh?' He moved his eyes up from the concrete slowly intending a seductive ambush. I looked away quickly before he caught my eye. It was his oldest trick and one I was determined not to fall for this time.

'Hyping up,' I said, pointing to my coffee in front of me. 'Besides, I live here. What are *you* doing here?' Last I knew he was in LA. I wondered what would make him slum down in the land of planned communities.

'Looking for work. I got laid off. Or maybe it was downsized.' He set a leather folder down on the table. He opened it and handed me a copy of his résumé. I looked it over and decided it could use a lot of revising. It was vaguely reminiscent of the triangular sign the corporate widget heads placed in the centre of the Spectrum. It bore no real resemblance to Craig, just as the sign did not seem to communicate the space; both were unkept promises. It appeared Craig had copied his résumé straight out of a book adding his name and some employment details Mad Lib style. I would not put it past him; Craig is hopelessly addicted to the easy road.

'Are you handing this out around town?' I tried not to sound too critical, but he picked up on the tone immediately.

'Shit, it sucks, huh?' Craig looked dead at me without his usual hint of lechery.

'I've seen better. You're selling yourself short here.' I gestured to one of the first items on his sheet. 'It's kinda sloppy.' I pointed out a couple of typos. 'You need to clean it up and pump it up with some personality. You're résumé needs to get you in the door. Face to face is your strong suit, Babe. This [pointing at the paper before me] doesn't really do it.' I had been to far too many résumé workshops. I even included resumé writing in a lower division management class that I taught a couple of summers ago.

'Really? I've peddled about thirty of them and so far no bites. Maybe that's why. I guess I could use some help. Are you offering?' Even his eyes were smiling. Craig was turning on the charm and I wished I had kept quiet.

'I could give you some ideas right now, I suppose.' I ran my hand across the top of my head pulling my hair back. My whole body screamed, 'retreat'. I breathed audibly through my mouth and picked up the résumé as if it were a brick.

'Thanks. I'm glad I ran into you today. Let me grab a coffee. I'll be right back.' Craig got up and went into the coffee bar. I watched him saunter away. His hair was past his shoulders and caught the light from the sky even on a crappy day.

Pity, he may even have to cut it depending on what industry he chose. Slightly amused, I smiled to myself. I had never known him with short hair and I could not get a visual on it at all. An IBM drone do? No. Maybe something spikey and two toned. More likely. In any case, I feared cutting his hair may prove fatal, as it had for Samson. Certainly, I did not wish that on him, but I *did* wish he had not appeared here.

I kicked myself in the foot under the table and hit my forehead with my fist. Some escape this turned out to be. I am stuck in hell with the devil himself. Craig had stated his case plenty of times that our status was solely my doing and completely alterable. He wore this option on his sleeve every time we met, taunting me. In my more honest moments, I considered the conscious efforts I made to resist my old self-destructive habits. Thankfully, when it came to choosing a life mate, I was clever enough to import one from Norway, combating the tendencies to fall in with Craig and the others shaped from the same So Cal mould. I continually pondered whether my current relationship was too healthy. I concluded my husband was much more solid than I deserved. His inexhaustible patience and his seemingly unconditional affection were completely unwarranted and, to my profound shame, seriously underappreciated. It is a cultural conundrum; I was raised to admire men like Craig, whose unapologetic self-absorption is read as an endearing quality, and whose fragile egos dutiful girlfriends painfully sustain. Reformed and stronger, I carefully insulate myself from my own consistently poor choices and *still* here Craig was flaunting his local charm and luring me towards the eternal wave.

I considered his résumé again. There were too many font styles and sizes giving it a disorganised printer test quality. I made a note for him to be more consistent. The air was moist and a little heavy in my lungs. Zipping up my jacket a few more inches, I scrawled some inclusions in the margins. Sipping coffee, I crossed out his entire objective section. Struggling to stay on task, I jotted down a more compelling and accurate opening emphasising his expertise in public relations. Satisfied, I set my pencil down.

Conjuring up an image of the fates mocking me from the faux Roman architecture, I stuck my tongue out at the nearest column. I named the less alluring attributes of Craig: his extreme egoism, his chemical dependence, his lack of emotional depth, his inability to manoeuvre in difficult situations, and his irreparable present tense orientation. I looked down at his résumé. 'FOOL', I heard the internal alarm from somewhere in my now vacant head. I concluded Craig is precisely the personification of the Gin Blossoms' 'Hey Jealousy' lyrics: 'You can trust me not to think/And not to sleep around/If you don't expect too much from me/You might not be let down.' This was certainly an old miserable experience in the new and commodified space of the Irvine Spectrum.

Of course, the problem is, and always will be, that I do expect much more. It is certainly not Craig's fault. He is a product of a social environment that defines masculinity as overt sexual domination and reveres the pigmented and the sun bleached. Personally, Craig was always supportive of the things I wanted to do, in his own, low-key, non-committal way, so long as it did not infringe on the pre-established gender roles we enacted daily. It is just that his agendas, when he has any, never match mine. The numerous times we have called it quits (an elusive figure as the phenomenon was deeply embedded in everyday practice) should in itself remind me of the implausibility of a steady union with Craig or anyone like him. He is the perfect lover in an uneventful, mundane existence, but the course of life is seldom calm and usually infused with stress and spectacular idio-syncrasies. Craig's calm is an artifice of his construction that does not hold in the sea of ambiguity and discomfort that ordinary people navigate each day.

Every time we separate he says, 'You know I love you, Babe.' Unfortunately, it is just never enough. Craig disrupts my respiratory process, but never permeates the darker more torturous places I often dwell. He is the relationship equivalent of a morphine drip; it feels so good while it lasts and it incapacitates us both as productive members of society. However, there is no gentle way down; the crash is nearly lethal. The very same hands that can make me feel so happy and safe can suddenly become menacing when his confidence falters. Like a Holodeck on *Star Trek*, he is an awesome illusion that cannot exist outside the projection param-eters. Still the lure is real and at times intense. He represents the romanticised ideal of my California upbringing, wrapped in a state of suspended present tense.

All my cerebral activity caused my head to pound. I took a long look around the Spectrum. Jesus, a place could not be more like Craig. People are not living life here, they are avoiding it. Consumers come seeking refuge in the transtemporal, transgeographical servicescape that can offer no lasting, tangible relief from the drudgery and material affects of ordinary life. I considered my own motives for hauling myself here and what promise it had offered me. I was looking for a retreat from the overwhelming oppression of daily life, the loneliness of working in a sequestered cyber environment, and the enormity of my dissertation project. I drove straight here. The Spectrum was constructed to be an opiate of the sub-urban masses and to distract the citizenry from the reality of its physical isolation from a cultural hub. The architecture was designed as an amalgam of pre-fabricated cultural representations juxtaposed in an uncritical, haphazard manner. I was falling into my familiar behaviour patterns that could only lead me to grief. No good can come from hiding out here. No good can come from hiding out with Craig.

'I got a decaf. I don't want to spoil my buzz.' Craig was back with a paper cup with a plastic lid.

'No, I guess not.' He was the same old Craig. Here he was hazed and looking for work. Charmed bastard. I knew he would probably land a better job than I could totally sober. I pushed the defaced résumé across the table to him with mounting contempt.

'Cool. Thanks, Babe.' He glanced at the paper and put it back into his folder. 'How's your dissertation coming?'

'Well, I came here to run away from it.' I smiled and sighed. It felt like an eternity had passed since I dreamed of torching my apartment.

'Wanna go for a drive? I got some great live Counting Crows tracks in my car. We could drive down the freeway and then along the beach. Oh Babe, it could be fun.' He spoke softly in a conspiratorial way. The words themselves were innocuous, but his tone exuded sensuality. I felt the familiar seduction beginning.

'Man, it sounds good, but I should get back to working on the dis, or I'll never have it done.' I wanted to go with him, hook up to the drip, and feel the burning sensation of the morphine before it sedated me. I longed for his cool mirage and the chimera of continual bliss. This time could be different from the thousands of others, right? I wanted to believe, but I know a fool's bet when I see it.

'You look great, Babe. Perpetual school must agree with you.' Craig took a more direct tack. No doubt he smelled opportunity and was plotting against me. He reached for my hand across the table. I knew intimately that he could make the wholesome art of hand holding salacious, especially if my hand ever made it to his lips. Perilous. He lifted his eyebrows quickly and sucked in his bottom lip. Understated lechery. Delicious. He knows me, which makes him a formidable opponent. Damn those eyes. I blinked and lost my respiratory rhythm. I gave his hand a pat and folded my hands safely on my own lap. Mercifully, the moment passed.

'What about Tina? Wasn't she moving in with you?' He was not the type to run around on the side, though he certainly tried to convince me it was an acceptable pastime. I was valuable to him for the same reason he was dangerous to me; I brought him back to those days when he was omnipotent. He was willing to settle for small doses, rather than go without. Poor Tina probably recognised his frailties and made the mistake of articulating them. She most likely asked him to be a man, not knowing he would not settle for less than god status.

'You know, "straight through indifference without a second look".' He shrugged. No trace of regret on his face.

Damn, he was on the same soundtrack. It was a Gin Blossoms' quote from the song '29'. How does he do that? Sorcery? I could not hide my amazement.

'What's up? Did I say something?' Craig looked genuinely disconcerted. I thought I saw a flicker of true emotion. He must have been closing in on the end of his buzz.

'No, I was just listening to *New Miserable Experience* on the way here. It sort of fits the day.' I leaned my elbows on the table and my chin on my folded hands. I changed the subject. 'This place is sort of creepy don't you think? It's so totally artificial. I don't even get what it is trying to signify.'

'I don't know, Babe. You're always over-thinking things. I kinda like it. It's like going back through history and travelling the globe on foot. Kinda warm and nostalgic.' He pointed toward the theatre. 'Have you been in there, Angel? Each theatre has it's own theme. You know, one is Egyptian, and so on. Over here it's gonna be like Spain. Kinda cool.' He paused. 'What this place really needs is Rainforest Cafe. I love that place. Man, it's like you're in the heart of the Amazon.'

'Really? I think it's weird. All these parodies of reality with no substance make me uncomfortable. I feel dislocated and off balance. Just makes me wanna bolt.'

'Aw Baby, you never could suspend your disbelief, even when you were a kid.' He was laughing out loud and shaking his head. I laughed with him.

'I guess that's why we never worked out.' I put the pencil back in my backpack and prepared to go.

'Damn Girl, that was cold.' Craig fell silent for a moment. 'I think we had the real thing. It's more real than anything I ever had before or since.'

'I don't doubt it.' I said, without censoring. He was hurt and I felt bad for being the cause.

'Ouch. Fuck, don't cut me like that, Babe.' His voice was breathy and tense.

'Look, I didn't mean that the way it sounded. I'm just bitchy today. Forget about it. OK?' I stood up to leave. He stood up too. Craig gave me a warm hug and kissed the top of my head. His arms lingered around me.

'Are you sure I can't talk you into a movie?' He motioned with his eyes towards the Megaplex.

'Absolutely sure. I have to leave while you are still resistible.' I smiled and wiggled out of his arms. He smiled too, letting go.

'You know I love you, Babe.' Craig brushed the hair off my shoulder and touched my cheek.

'I know you think so.' I paused. 'I gotta get home now. Send me the revised résumé on e-mail and I'll take another look.' I stepped backwards away from him. I dropped my coffee cup in the trash can. He nodded his head. At 32, he looked scarcely different than he had at 18.

I retraced my steps back through the plaza and past the valet shack. I used the crosswalk and started to hunt for my green Honda. Finally, I glimpsed it a few spaces down. Overcome by relief, I ran the last couple of steps to the driver's side. I sat down and sealed the bubble around me. It felt safe. I drove back to my apartment in silence. The city looked different without a superimposed beat. I saw my complex and thought only an hour ago I was a claustrophobic pyromaniac. Now my mania had brought me full circle and the walls of my apartment seemed warm and snug.

I locked the door behind me and dialled my husband's work number. He answered on the second ring. 'Hey, can you get away?' I asked. 'Nothing is going well today.'

12 Drove my Chevy to the levee

Stephen Brown

Hey, I've been to the States. I know the score. I've seen the movies. I've heard the songs. I've read the books. Driving irresponsibly is part of the American way of life. Next to Old Glory, Mom's apple pie, baseball, the Liberty Bell, body beautiful, handguns, alien abductions, mass murderers, wacko New Age religious cults, Jerry Seinfeld, Jay Leno, Larry King and eggs over easy, reckless driving is a major national pastime, a norm, an expectation, a duty, a goddamn constitutional *right*.

Well, all I can say is that they've never heard of the Auto Amendment in Salt Lake City. You want smokin' tires, screeching gears, hand-brake turns and flyaway hubcaps? Steer clear of Salt Lake City. You want to drive the wrong way down the freeway, like Mel Gibson in *Lethal Weapon 2*? Or go fender to fender with a bus like Eddie Murphy and Nick Nolte in *48 Hours*? Or lead the patrol cars a merry dance like Jake and Elmo in *The Blues Brothers*? Don't even think of it in SLC. The proximity of the Sundance Film Festival shouldn't fool you. Salt Lake City is not a driver-friendly kind of town. Or at least it's not very friendly to drivers like me.

Okay, I admit it, I'm not the best driver in the world. I'm not the most law-abiding member of the Automobile Association. I'm not unfamiliar with that invigorating state of mind colloquially known as Road Rage. I make a point of jumping every traffic light. I never stop at pedestrian crossings. I flit from lane to lane. I rarely if ever signal before I manoeuvre, let alone look in my mirror. I keep my headlights locked on full beam. I consider it my solemn duty to abuse other road users, especially old age pensioners, women, farmers and, above all, caravaneers (anyone, basically, who's smaller and slower than myself). Advanced driving test have I none.

Now, you may be wondering how a road hog like me has managed to keep his licence for so long. Surely maniacs such as myself are quickly identified by the authorities and the full force of the law is brought down upon their irresponsible heads. Not a bit of it. If you treat the plod with impunity, as I do. If you don't give a fig for their pathetic radar traps or roadside cameras, as I do. If you flout the Highway Code, as I do. If you flaunt your floutation, as I do, you can get away with it for years. As I have. My licence is clean. My conscience is clear. My number is up if this confession is ever used in evidence against me (it was extracted under duress, your honour, it's a stitch up, police brutality, free the Utah One!).

Anyway, to get back to what I was saying. I cannot deny that I have a bit of a reputation as a dangerous driver, a demented driver, a mad-bastard-shouldn't-be-allowed-on-the-road driver. I have been known to overtake on the outside of a bend, on the inside of a bend, on two wheels whilst drinking a cup of coffee and fiddling with the radio. In these circumstances, you'd think America would be the perfect place for me. America, the land of convoys, Caddys and car chases. America, the land of food, gas and lodging. America, the land of Jack Kerouac, Robert Pirsig and *Easy Rider*. America, the land of Henry Ford, hot rods and whitewalls. America, the land of opportunity, the land of the open road, the land of the free – well, the free gift at least.

I thought so too, until I got to Salt Lake City.

You know, I knew something was wrong, right from the start. The omens were bad, the signs discouraging, the auspices inauspicious. It wasn't the long, irritable line at the Hertz counter that bothered me. After all, airports are busy places and I'm living proof of the fact that lots of irate people hire cars (I'm the man, after all, who put the 'ire' into hire). Nor, for that matter, was I disconcerted by the strange look on the sales-clerk's face when she saw my Irish driving licence. Perhaps she'd heard about Ireland's infamous testing farrago of a couple of years back when there were so many applicants and so few testers that anyone who wanted a driving licence was given one – no questions asked. Nor, indeed, was I unsettled by the rental form I had to sign, with its never-ending list of disclaimers. Basically, it boiled down to the fact that if I hit anything or if anything hit me, I'd be held responsible for paying off America's national debt, the next phase of the space programme and underwriting Utah's state lottery until the middle of the next millennium.

No, the thing that set the premonitional alarm bells ringing was my inability to find the car. Russ, my mentor, host and marketing scholar extrordinaire, had met me on arrival and was waiting patiently outside the rental parking lot. I'd been informed that my blue compact was parked in space 13, line K. But could I find it? No I could not. As far as I could make out, the parking petered out at line J. After wandering around for ten bemused minutes and apologetically asking for guidance from an employee of a rival rental company, who was singularly unimpressed by my lame 'I've just arrived from Ireland' line, I eventually tracked the vehicle down. Line K, surprisingly enough, turned out to be immediately adjacent to line J and space 13 was right there between 12 and 14. Cunning devils, these Americans.

I got into the car, started it up and revved the mighty 1.1 litre engine. Hey, this isn't so bad. Wasn't it P.J. O'Rourke who said that the best performing cars in the world aren't the fuel-injected, air-cooled, 16-valved, souped-up behemoths of legend. They are hire cars. Boy, was I going to wring this baby out! But could I get its gear shift to move? No I could not. I depressed the button and tugged on the stick. I tugged on the stick and depressed the button. I depressed the stick and tugged on the button. To no avail. Even with both hands and all my admittedly negligible strength, I couldn't shift the shift. I was just about to go back to the counter and berate them for supplying me with a clapped out, seized–up auto when I saw the little shift-side sticker, 'Place Foot on Brake Before Engaging Drive'. Oh, so that's how you do it. Easy when you know how. Select R for reverse, wrong way round the lot, somehow find the exit and there's Russ still patiently waiting even though he's got a class in less than an hour. What a guy!

Exhausted from my transatlantic flight, soaked with sweat from wrestling with a recalcitrant gear shift and driving on the right-hand side of the road for the first time in my life in an unfamiliar car, in an unfamiliar city, in an unfamiliar automatic transmission, I find myself in the middle of an unfamiliar snow storm. Just take it slowly Stephen, get in behind Russ and everything will be all right. However, less than one minute after picking up my guide, I'm sitting at 75 miles per hour on an eight-lane interstate, in the middle of the rush hour with monstrous trucks whizzing past on either side and Russ's Audi a rapidly disappearing speck on the indistinct horizon. It's not like this in the movies.

We eventually get to the apartment after numerous twists, turns, near misses and panic attacks. I parked the car with my justly renowned expertise, approximately six feet from the curb, switched off the engine and slowly exhaled a huge sigh of relief. But could I get the key out of the ignition? No I could not. I tugged and I tugged. I turned it back and forward, to and fro, hither and yon, on and off. I watched Russ's expression slowly change from 'glad you could make it', through 'what have we let ourselves in for?', to 'who invited this cretin?' Then I realised that the gear shift was still in Drive. Cunning devils these Americans. They certainly make their autos idiot-proof. The difficulty arises with the idiots who don't know they're idiot-proof.

Remove key, release seat belt and open the door. A buzzer sounds. Christ, what is it now? Oh yes, the headlights are still switched on. Russ smiles wanly, shakes his head and scuttles off to class. I settle in. Nice apartment, nice view, nice to be here. Nice car – once you get used to it.

An hour or so later, after a much-needed shower and shave, I decide to stroll up to the department to check out the office I'll be occupying for the next couple of months. As I close the door behind me, I cast an affectionate glance in the direction of my frisky azure steed and notice a piece of paper tucked under the windscreen wiper. Bound to be a promotional flier for a local restaurant, club, dry cleaners or pizza delivery service. God, these American marketers don't waste much time, do they. Jesus H. Christ. A parking ticket! A parking ticket outside my own apartment. Within an hour of my arrival. What's going on here? It's only then that I notice I'm in a residents-only parking zone. But I am a resident! This can't be right, I say to Russ later on that day. He agrees and advises me to appeal the decision but, just to be on the safe side, recommends that I park on the grass verge for the meantime. Apparently the previous occupant had parked there without incident for the whole semester. Thanks Russ. What a guy!

The next day I have sufficiently recovered from my post-citation trauma to go downtown to appeal the decision, pick up a parking permit and change the car. I'd noticed that an oil pressure light kept coming on and, since the auto was going to be in my possession for some considerable time, I didn't want the engine to explode whilst I was driving through the desert, or whatever. So, I rang the downtown office of the rental company and the clerk said they had no more vehicles of my make but he'd personally drive out to the airport to pick up another. Now that's what I call customer service.

En route to City Hall, I remember thinking that driving on the right hand side of the road is much easier than I imagined it would be. It feels natural somehow. Maybe it's the driving position, maybe it's a deep-seated instinctive reaction to watching so many movies or maybe it's just that I spend so much time overtaking in the right-hand lane at home that it seems like the proper place to be. These happy thoughts are rudely interrupted when I spot a piece of paper flapping furiously under my wiper-blade. No! It can't be. Yes, it is. Another bloody traffic violation. This time for parking on the grass verge. My grass verge! Boy, was I going to give these people a piece of my mind.

I parked in the Hertz lot and marched a couple of blocks to City Hall. You know, if it wasn't for the traffic cops, Salt Lake City would be a really nice place. Unlike many American downtowns, it's clean, unthreatening and completely devoid of crazies, panhandlers, street-people and the like. I should have guessed. All the delinquents, miscreants, reprobates, cut-throats, muggers and bums in the State are ahead of me in the 'parking appeals' line. I had a choice of paying my fines – all major credit cards accepted – or waiting my turn. The officer dealing with the line didn't look like the kind of guy who'd be sympathetic to my pre-prepared 'I'm just off the boat from Ireland, give me a break amigo' speech. So, like any red-blooded white boy I promptly paid up for both violations. Hell, I'd have paid everyone's fine just to get out of there and back to the uxorious womb of the university. In retrospect, of course, I realise that the line undoubtedly comprised indigent actors, employed by the PD to put the fear of God into any Caucasian foolish enough to consider appealing a traffic violation. Cunning devils these Americans. Hollywood has a lot to answer for.

On the way back to the Hertz lot, I call into the parking permits office and, after having my Irish driving licence carefully scrutinised, conspiratorially informed that my name, address and misdemeanours were now on the police computer (only my driving misdemeanours, I hope!), and relieved of a substantial slice of folding money in return for a tiny windshield sticker, I am given a map of the university area with permissible parking places clearly marked. Would you credit it, the opposite side of my street is a commercial zone that is exempt from parking controls. Christ Almighty, I could have avoided all this hassle by parking across the way. Well, at least now I know. Once I pick up the replacement car, all my problems will be over.

The guy behind the Hertz counter is very pleasant, despite the fact that his unanticipated trip to the airport must have severely disrupted his schedule. Maybe he's on some kind of commission. Anyway, we complete the paperwork with good grace and I amble outside thinking that I'd finally managed to crack the American cultural code. I start up the engine and the oil pressure light comes on again. I don't believe this; not another defective hire car. It's been a difficult couple of days, my wallet is considerably lighter than it was and, easy-going kind of guy though I ordinarily am, my patience is wearing very, very thin. I storm back up to the counter and harangue the harassed clerk with a clichéd diatribe about Hertz not trying harder. Heroically maintaining his customer-friendly demeanour and resisting the temptation to tell me that it's Avis who try harder – well trained these people – he replies that the vehicle was perfectly all right when he drove it back from the airport. 'Well, it's not all right now,' I bark.

So we make our way out to the parking lot, where he gets in the car, turns the key and the oil pressure light comes on, thank God.

'You see what I mean,' I crow triumphantly.

'But sir,' he replies, surprisingly calmly considering the grief I'd given him, 'the light is meant to appear when you switch on. It tells you that the oil pressure gauge is working properly. Does it come on when you drive?'

'Er, no.'

'Did the oil pressure light on the previous car come on when you were driving?'

'Well, it might have flickered from time to time. They're not like this at home, you know. I've just arrived from Ireland . . . '

He hands me the key and walks away in silence. Hertz tries harder.

Still, at least my problems are finally behind me. I drive back to the apartment in my bright red chariot and park across the street. Russ calls by later to ask how my trip downtown had gone. I respond with a carefully manicured version of events – my stock is so low I couldn't possibly tell him the truth – and casually mention that I had to change the car. Oil pressure problems, you know how it is. Yes, I noticed you'd changed it, he replies. What a guy! How on earth did you know that? There's a red car across the street that's parked against the traffic and only an Irishman . . . Jeez, so it is. I'm pointing uphill, the rest are pointing downhill. Americans park with the traffic flow. You learn something new every day. It's not illegal is it, Russ? No, it's not illegal, just unusual.

Next day – April Fool's Day, of all days – I'm strolling home from the department full of the joys of spring in Salt Lake City. What a place. Clean, fresh, friendly and, er, law abiding. Hold on a minute. Something's missing. Jesus, my car has been stolen. Oh shit! What'll I do? There's bound to be a penalty clause about this in my rental agreement. The colour drains from my face at the thought of my entire salary, from here to retirement, being siphoned into some Hertzian sump. Foregoing my perfectly natural desire to dial 911 – if this isn't an emergency, I don't know what is – I check the phone book. Diverse police department services are listed: drugs, homicide, larceny, prostitution, public order offences. Christ, what sort of town is this? Non-violent crime, that must be it.

After responding to several computerised messages and associated touch-tone requests, a very amiable police officer finally answers my call. I explain that my car has gone.

'What's the licence plate number, sir?'

'I don't know.'

'What make of car is it?'

'Sorry officer, I'm not sure.'

'How old is it?'

'Um.'

'Do you know anything about your automobile, sir?'

'It's red, officer.'

'It's red?'

'I'm afraid I'm Irish officer, just arrived in town. This kind of thing has never happened to be before. It's a hire car and I don't know anything about it.'

'It's a what car?'

'A hire car.'

'A what?'

'A hire car. You know, Hertz, Avis, Budget, that kind of thing.'

'Oh, you mean a renl.'

'A what, officer?

'A renl.'

'A renl? What's a renl?'

'A renl – you know Hertz, Avis . . . '

'Oh, a rental. Yes, it's a rental, officer. A rental, that's what it is.'

'Let me see. Where do you live, sir? Oh yes, a red, 1996 Chevy, Licence Plate 6P9332G was towed from that street at 2.31p.m. this afternoon. Parking in a two-hour zone.'

My head is reeling by this stage due to a combination of relief and bewilderment. I want to kiss the duty officer. I want to raise two fingers to Hertz and their goddam rental agreement. I want to ask how on earth they managed to winkle the car out of that tight parking space (no I don't). I want to ask how on earth they knew I was parked there for more than two hours (damn, pointing the wrong way). Above all, I want to ask about this two-hour limit business. My map says you can park there at any time.

'Any time, sir, but only for two hours. Didn't you read the sign?'

'Er, where is the car, officer? How do I go about getting it back?'

'It's in the pound, sir.'

Not the pound, I think to myself. Sounds grim. Sounds hellish. Sounds like things are gonna get a lot worse before they get better. Anyway, I thank the officer for her help and ring the city impound lot to check that a red, 1996 Chevy, Licence Plate number 6P9332G is in their possession. The somewhat brusque impoundor informs me that it's there but I have to go to the central precinct and pay the fine before my vehicle can be released. The pound, it transpires, is on the opposite side of town and, sans car, it looks as though I'll have to hire a cab. I wonder if they take traveller's cheques? Should I ring Russ, or not? I've put him through so much already. He thinks I'm an idiot. He works so hard and I hate to interrupt his routine. 'Hi, Russ, you'll never guess what's happened . . . The precinct opens at 8 o'clock, apparently. So you'll call for me at ten before? What a guy!'

At 7 a.m. the following morning, I peek out from between the curtains and there it is. My car is back! My red Chevy is parked in front of the apartment. It was all an April Fool's Day joke. The best ever, bar none! How did you do it, Russ? Everyone was in on the act: the police, the pound, the people in the department. He even moved the car. Where did he hide it? How did he get into it? How did he start it? Who cares?! I rush outside, the sheer euphoria covering my semi-naked state. I check the car. It's not mine. It's another red Chevy parked there by chance. The bastard was towed, after all.

Russ ferries me down to the central precinct, feigning sympathy and trying to keep a straight face. He can't understand it. He's lived here for fifteen years and he's never had his car impounded. Boy, is he going to enjoy recounting the story of the dumb Irishman who visited Utah for a semester. The precinct, as you might expect, is just like it is in the cop shows (life imitating art or art imitating life, I wonder). Officer on high chair behind desk, bullet-proof glass, dregs of society in line ahead of me: violations, citations, fingerprinting, pimping, soliciting. God, I feel like a wimp with my pathetic impound problem. At least I'm not alone. The guy behind me had his boat towed and impounded. His fucking *boat* towed! It was attached to his pick-up at the time and they impounded that for good measure. We fall into conversation and it transpires that there's only one state in the Union where the police's propensity to tow is more pronounced than Utah. California, apparently. Guess where I'm going next? Got it in one.

I get to the head of the line and explain my misdemeanour to the officer. She strokes her computer a couple of times and says that there's no record of a new red Chevy in the pound. 'But I spoke to the impound people, officer.'

'Oh yeah?, they haven't told us. Come back in half an hour. Back of the line, buddy.'

Needless to say, Russ is on a roll by this stage as his after-dinner anecdote continues to develop apace. He doesn't seem to mind being kept from his research. He's going to dine out on this one for years to come. We just have time to check the cabinets and displays in the precinct's entrance hall – Rookie of the Month (ticketing Chevys a speciality, doubtless), Commendations for Public Spirited Citizens (so that's the shit who reported a mis-orientated, time-expired rental), Officers who have Fallen in the Line of Duty (Moloney, accidentally shot by one of his colleagues; nice to know we're in safe hands) – before rejoining the line. No out-of-work actors here, believe me.

Sixty dollars and a strange look at my Irish driving licence later, we're on our way to the city lot, official release form in hand. It's on the wrong side of the tracks and I *mean* the wrong side of the tracks. Russ has never been to this part of town before. I can see why. Trailer parks, satellite dishes, unkempt yards, piles of junk, potholes, pitbulls, flyovers and, eventually, impound lots. Christ, it's huge. Christ, it's full. Christ, I'm going to drive carefully in future. I knew my sins would find me out eventually but I never thought they'd find me out in America, of all places. God forgive me.

We pull up at a massive chain-link fence, behind which lurks a ramshackle 'office'. There are two signs on the fence. One announces that parked cars will be towed. Jeez, what a scam! You and a buddy arrive to collect an impounded auto. They tow the car while you're inside. You get another friend to take you and your first friend out to the lot. They tow his car too and so it goes on. Now I know why the lot is so full. This is the automotive equivalent of pyramid selling or a chain letter. Every automobile in Salt Lake City is here. The second sign is equally disconcerting, albeit much more dramatic. 'Do Not Touch the Fence', it says. Fuck me sideways, the fucker's electrified! But no, it's just automatic and, at the touch of a button from the bowels of the office, the impound portcullis retracts.

Russ waits in his Audi, ready to drive off at the first sign of a tow-truck, while I take care of business. My God, it's like David Lynch's worst nightmare. The in-bred troglodyte behind the counter is straight out of central casting, *Deliverance* division. Cross-eyed, purple teeth, scarlet neck, plaid shirt, oil-black blue jeans and bare feet. At least I think they're feet. I pass over the release form. He turns it round several times trying to work out which way is up.

'Red Chevy, boy?'

'Red Chevy,' I reply.

'Renl?'

'Renl.'

'Gotta see your licence, boy.'

The shit hits the fan. I try to explain that it's a European driving licence. He looks at me blankly.

'You know, Europe, a large land mass, way, way to the east.'

Nothing. Nada. No comprende.

'It's an Irish driving licence.'

'Now you're talkin', boy. I'm Irish!'

Of course you are. The seventh son of a seventh son, I'll be bound.

'We might be cousins,' he grunts, or was that a leer?

'Not kissing cousins,' I mutter, whilst nodding inanely.

Bosom buddies now — bit too bosom for my liking — he gives me precise instructions concerning the whereabouts of my Chevy, but to be honest they completely pass me by. I just want to get out of there before 'Duelling Banjos' strikes up from somewhere and he insists on a dance with his long-lost relative.

Throwing caution to the winds, St Russell risks joining me in a latter-day Mormon Trek though the gargantuan impound lot. The place is a sea of semi-crushed Continentals, burnt-out Buicks, mangled Mustangs, dented Dodges, fenderless Fords and long-abandoned pick-ups. It's an annex of the breaker's yard. It's Cadillac Ranch writ large. It's Auto Armageddon. Eventually, in the far corner, a speck of red. It's a Chevy. It's a renl. It's okay. It's undamaged. It's mine. Underneath the wiperblade, a note. 'Your car has been impounded . . . ' Tell me something I don't fucking know, you fucking fuckers!

Starts first time. Oil pressure light appears. Foot on brake. Into Drive. Drop Russ off at his Audi just as the tow truck arrives. Logo on the side says 'Bozo Tow'. It figures. Follow Russ back into town. Switch on the radio. 'Drove my Chevy to the levee but the levee was dry.' Don McLean. *American Pie*. What a guy!

13 A cultural biography of my Groucho glasses

Russell W. Belk

A short preface about life writing and academic research

There are multiple genres of writing about the self. We might place towards one end of the continuum those texts that make primarily academic claims, often written under a label of introspectionism. Towards the other end of this continuum we might position those postmodern texts that erase or purposefully confuse the distinction between fact and fiction. Within the study of consumer behaviour, examples of the former, introspective vein, include writings by Morris Holbrook (1995, 1996), Stephen Brown (1997) and Stephen Gould (1991). Consumption studies at the more postmodern end of this continuum are more numerous and include writings by Nick Hornby (1992, 1995), Nicholson Baker (1988), Don DeLillo (1984), Alain de Botton (1994) and John Vernon (1999). Predictably, those examples of life writing that have been positioned towards the academic end of this genre continuum have come under attack from the more priggish of our colleagues (e.g., Wallendorf and Brucks 1993). The issues involve positivist notions of objectivity and Truth versus interpretivist notions of subjectivity and truths.

Nevertheless, there is much to be learned about consumer behaviour from sources that depart from the narrower canons of academia. Such departures from the standard academic style offer us other ways of seeing (Berger 1972), other ways of knowing (Belk 1986, 1998). I have suggested that these alternative ways of understanding are more experiential, complete and emotional. To accomplish this, such writing must be more direct and more personal than most academic writing. As Torgovnick suggests, 'It makes the reader know some things about the writer – a fundamental condition . . . of any real act of communication' (1990: 26). Life writing is both a different way of knowing and a different way of telling. As Kadar defines it:

> Life writing as a critical practice, then, encourages (a) the reader to

> develop and foster his/her own self-consciousness in order to (b) humanize
> and make less abstract . . . the self-in-the-writing.
>
> (Kadar 1992:12)

A resulting effect is ideally to make our writing more interesting, engaging, and relevant, rather than the dry intellectualised scientese that fills our journals.

Montaigne (1957) concludes that the only valid form of autobiographical writing is questioning. By means of self-interrogation and elaboration, the writer learns about both the self and the world this self experiences. From the author's point of view, almost all our research and writing is in some sense self-reflexive. We draw on our own experiences and our own peculiar curiosities to choose what to investigate and the frameworks we bring to understanding it. Even when we study others who are as different as possible from us and even when we try as best we can to tease out the emic interpretations of our informants, it is still our own life worlds that help to frame our understandings and which we ultimately seek to illuminate (Cole 1992). The older tradition of authoritative authorless writing that was taken to define objectivity and science, is merely an attempted disguise for the imposition of personal subjectivity (Clifford and Marcus 1986; Geertz 1988; Marcus and Fischer 1986). So, in a very real sense, all our work is a very personal attempt to understand ourselves and our place in the world, even when the style of our writing seeks to hide the writer as much as possible.

The present chapter is one of several quite small efforts I have made in this direction. The story examines a continuing thread of personal relevance to me and my family involving a small consumer good.

The glasses

In examining my consumption behaviour, I find that while I am a rather reluctant acquirer, I am a tenacious keeper of possessions. While most likely related to some deep-seated childhood material insecurity, my inability to perform the necessary rituals of divestment (McCracken 1988) also seems to reflect a romanticism and nostalgia that has firmly embedded these objects in my extended self. As a case in point, consider an old pair of Groucho Marx glasses that currently lie in a drawer of the desk in my university office. You know the type: big black glass-less glasses with a large false nose, furry false eyebrows and a thick false moustache. They are a stock gag, a party prank, a cheap disguise offering a transparent transformation intended less to deceive than to lampoon the deception. This particular pair of Groucho glasses is missing both its earpieces. The adhesive that once held the right eyebrow to the rims gave way some time ago as well and a black fuzzy strip now lies like a dead caterpillar in the bottom of the drawer (see Plate 1). As their sad state of disrepair suggests, it is highly unlikely that I will ever use these glasses again. In truth I never did use these glasses. They were never capable of

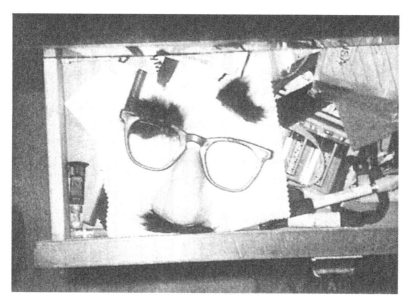

Plate 1 My Groucho glasses

correcting my vision and their potential utility as theatrical prop, clown mask, or impetus for humour is now greatly diminished. The fact that I continue to keep these glasses despite the highly overcrowded clutter and chaos of my office, seems only to testify to my obsessive packrat possessiveness. Yet I treasure these glasses far more than any of the more functional possessions in my office, including my beloved books.

I believe I can account for my love for these pitiful glasses. Their story may not only justify their closeted enshrinement in my desk drawer but, it may also offer a small insight into how other objects that have outlived their usefulness neverthe-less continue to resist the rubbish heap (Thompson 1979). In the following account I first recount what these specific glasses mean to me and how it is that they came to be in my drawer. Based on this case of possessiveness I seek insights into my more general possessive tendencies. And based on my own possessiveness I then speculate about certain aspects of possessiveness generally: what it may mean, how society tends to treat its occurrence, and how objects must survive a gauntlet of destructive urges in order to be deemed worthy of retention. Thus, with a pale parallel to Proust's madeleines and lime blossom tea, I wish to use these glasses both as lenses that allow a view of my own consumption history and as windows that may allow a partial view of the human material condition. Specifically, I wish to examine our tendency towards retaining that which is perfectly useless: the broken, battered, and bruised; the dirty dying debris; the whimsical, wistful and wonderful stuff that we accumulate in life.

Their story

As Igor Kopytoff (1986) has suggested, it may be insightful to anthropomorphise objects and to account for their lives as we do people's. From this perspective objects, like people, are born, live and die. The manner in which they do so and the nature of our personal relationships with these objects are of some consequence. It matters how they are gotten, given, disparaged, revered, used, kept, or discarded. For through these small ritual interactions with objects we may imbue them with meaning in our lives as well as imbue our own lives with meaning. An insightful recent example of constructing such object biographies is Thatcher Freund's (1993) reconstruction of the lives of three key pieces of antique furniture at the 1991 New York Winter Antiques Show: a blue blanket chest, a satinwood sofa table and an elaborate card table. In the cases of the objects Freund analyses, an individual craftsperson created these rare furnishings and they were once used as utilitarian furnishings before finding their way through numerous owners and dealers and into the great American antiques show where he first encountered them. In tracing their prior lives as well as their transformations of ownership during the show, Freund documents the ability of these objects to mystify and quicken the lives of their owners. The colossal sums these pieces command at the New York show affirms their apotheosis into heavenly objects of desire.

The life of my Groucho glasses is much more mundane. These are manufactured objects from an anonymous factory. They bear no mark of the company that made them, but it is a reasonable guess that they were stamped out by some small-scale plastics fabricator in a developing country in Asia with the design specifications having come from the United States. They were no doubt intended as 'novelties' from the start. The cultural translation specifying what Americans might find humorous, the historical origin of the first pair of Groucho glasses, and how it is that the face of that irreverent comedian Groucho Marx became an imitable cultural icon, would all be of interest to a full social history of Groucho glasses. But these aspects are outside of the scope of the present more limited cultural biography. This is instead a more personal biography of a particular pair of glasses.

The American purveyor of my Groucho glasses is a mail order novelty company in Seattle, Archie McPhee & Co. In their printed catalog they bill themselves as 'Outfitters of Popular Culture'. A sampling of their wares reads like a museum of gags, novelties, and camp cultural icons of post-World War Two America: bouncing phosphorescent eyeballs, lava lamps, rubber chickens, pink flamingos, boxing nun hand puppets, Elvis tattoos, Gumby, Pokey, and much more. My wife Kay is a frequent mail order patron of Archie McPhee, and the Groucho glasses are one of her acquisitions. Three or four years ago this particular pair of glasses entered my office as a surprise gift in a bag lunch Kay had packed for me. If Archie McPhee catalogues are full of delightful surprises, my lunches at the time were at least equally amazing and amusing. The Groucho glasses in that particular lunch brought me great delight. The surprise nature of the gift is one element that lends special meaning to the glasses. The selection and presentation of a commodity as a gift from a loved one helps to decommoditise (Kopytoff 1986) or sacralise (Belk *et al.*1989) the object. But this is the end of a more involved story of the investment of meaning in this pair of Groucho glasses.

The story starts in Philadelphia in 1973. My first teaching job was at Temple University there and this September we celebrated our daughter Amy's third birthday with a picnic on the banks of the Schulykill River. Our friends Bobbie (Barbara) and Pete joined us and we all presented Amy with some small birthday gifts. By pure coincidence Bobbie and Pete gave Amy a gift that we had also chosen: Groucho glasses! Amy was delighted (see Plate 2). Not only did she don her glasses, I picked up the extra pair and put them on. Everyone agreed that there was a striking family resemblance between us. This was the beginning of a

Plate 2 My daughter's third birthday party

family tradition of various costumes, masks, and disguises intended to amuse other family members and friends.

As with most family traditions, my wife Kay as senior female had the most to do with instituting and preserving this tradition. For many birthdays, each Halloween, some Christmases, and scattered no-occasion surprises throughout Amy's childhood in Pennsylvania, Illinois and Utah, both Kay and Amy would delight in new masks and disguises: dogs, trees, mice, bees, Yoda, E.T., reindeer, rabbits and many others. While this pattern was never explicitly discussed, times of joy in our household were also times of delight in costumed transformations of self. In her younger years our only child Amy was not unlike a doll or pet whom we dressed up as much for our own amusement as hers. But, like most children, Amy thoroughly enjoyed the practice of self-transformation through disguises and costumes. When she and her friends in Illinois came across a box full of old clothing discarded by the others' parents, for a time we were treated to a series of impromptu plays aided by these props. When Amy went to Brazil for a year as a junior in high school, Carnival offered a week of licence to abandon normal decorum and enact other selves. No doubt Amy's current collection of masks from around the world also has its roots in the informal family traditions begun with the duplicate Groucho glasses she received on her third birthday.

During 1991 and 1992 Kay and I spent a sabbatical year in Romania. The timing overlapped Amy's graduation from Rutgers University, so Kay returned to the United States to witness this milestone. I had teaching and research obligations in Romania and had to remain behind. Several weeks after Amy's graduation, I received a letter from Kay with some graduation pictures. She had told me on the telephone that the photos included a surprise. The initial pictures showed all of the typical regalia and stock poses: the college campus in its springtime splendour, lines of black-robed students, mortar boards and colourful tassels, proud relatives and beaming graduates. But then I found it. There was Amy in her cap and gown and Groucho glasses (see Plate 3). She had gone through graduation wearing them. She recalls that the President who presented her diploma said, 'Congratulations. Maybe now you can afford to get that nose job.' The photos were a treasure trove of happiness for me, although they caused great confusion among the Romanian friends to whom I showed them. Disguises to them belonged in the theatre, on Christmas Mummers, or to the *Securitate* (secret police). Karl Marx was more familiar than Groucho Marx. And why a young woman would ruin her appearance in this manner was unfathomable. So Amy's great graduation prank remains a family in-joke, requiring some knowledge of our family history and traditions in order to be fully appreciated.

Seven years later my wife and I found ourselves spending my sabbatical year in Zimbabwe as my daughter and her husband were about to have their only child, a granddaughter who would be named Zoe. Again I had teaching obligations and only my wife was able to fly back for the birth. But this time, thanks to advances in

Plate 3 My daughter's university graduation

electronics, we were able to receive e-mail photos in Zimbabwe, beginning with a sonar-gram of Zoe in Amy's womb. Thus, it was not long after the blessed event that I received another photo, this one of Zoe showing her unique family resemblance (see Plate 4).

Thus, when Kay put the Groucho glasses in my lunch bag a few years ago, she was not simply giving me a gag gift. These glasses are vivified and enlivened with a flood of family memories from the past twenty-five years of life with two (now three) delightfully demented women. Like Proust's madeleines and line blossom tea, they conjured up a flood of memories. Conjure is the right word, in that their effect is magical – resulting not in a magical transformation of self, but resulting instead in the magical recollection of family that they invoke. There is no more sacred and meaningful icon of our family than Groucho glasses. I would not be surprised if someone were someday buried in them.

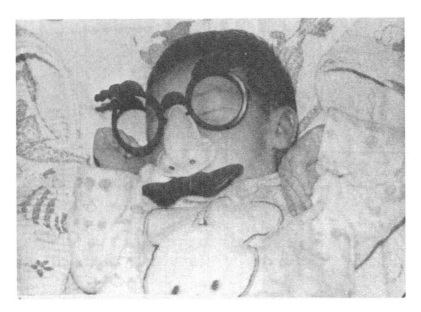

Plate 4 My grandaughter

Possessiveness: an appraisal

As I survey the other useless objects that clutter my home and office, I find that they too are most often small repositories with manifold meanings from my life and the lives of those around me. A pen, a pot, a picture of a perfect spot where one of us once travelled; these are not just tiny treasures that tell of life, nor souvenirs, nor emblems of status, they are the things that link us to the world and to each other. They evoke smiles and tears and recollections. If they are anchors to the past, evidences of nostalgic retentiveness (Belk 1991) and trivial objects lacking wider social importance, so be it.

Perhaps it is this unshared personal encoding of object meanings that makes society at large uneasy and quick to disparage the otherwise useless ephemera of our lives as junk, debris, and chaotic clutter. Lacking a readable code, such objects can act neither as cues to personality nor as signs of status. Rather, they appear as esoteric and indecipherable mementos. While Western society is willing to sanction some expression of individual idiosyncracy, when we cannot read what is being expressed we feel uncomfortable. We either feel that we have intruded or that we are being excluded from more narrowly shared meanings. Feelings of intrusion make for embarrassment, while feelings of exclusion make for resentment. Our reaction in the latter case is often to brand the owner of unfathomable objects as strange, weird or bizarre. At the extremes of possessiveness, we label the person as obsessed, a miser, a hoarder, a bag person, or simply crazy. As with all labels of abnormality and deviance, these judgements are socially constructed. But while the objects that comprise our private museums may be unlikely candidates for deification in our public museum temples and art gallery shrines, they are nevertheless powerful personal reliquaries from which we may derive feelings of connection, warmth, meaning and purpose in life.

Consider the alternative: a life devoid of all clutter and excess baggage; a life stripped to what is either functional, in some Bauhaus spirit of simplicity, or to what is merely expressive of our place in the social order. In both cases we would be living a life of impression management, designed to meet or manipulate someone else's expectations of us. In the extreme cases of both stripped-down functionality or pure status-seeking, a spouse who has become paralysed or terminally ill should be regarded as a liability. We should cut our losses and avoid cluttering our lives with this person, either by means of divorce or simple abandonment. But while some might be able to do this with a sick dog or a sick car, hopefully none of us would condone doing this with a sick mate, even in today's serial relationship society.

But is our lack of loyalty to an aged or decrepit car a matter of no consequence? Does the desire for the status of the new mean that we can discard with impunity the automobile that faithfully served us, that witnessed the human drama of our lives and that was perhaps once a vehicle of our fantasies – a source of autoeroticism? For several years I conducted interviews with the owners and restorers of automobiles entered in a *concours d'élégance* held on our university campus. Even within the ranks of these enthusiasts of old automobiles however, the social sanctions favoured status over personal meanings. Nearly everyone appreciated a well-restored Ferrari, Cobra, Jaguar, MG, Mustang, or Pierce Arrow. It mattered little if the owner had it since it was new or acquired it last year, although personal restoration skills were appreciated. But virtually no one appreciated two exhibitors. One was a woman with a well-worn 1960s Cadillac that had belonged to her deceased husband. She had made some small improvements to the car, but clearly the deep meaning of this car for her would be diminished rather than enhanced if it were restored to showroom condition. Similarly, one man exhibited a 1970s Subaru sedan and was working on restoring a 1980s Dodge Dart. He had bought the Subaru near the end of his college dating years and had 'moth-balled' it after a few thousand miles in order to preserve these memories and to preserve the car's 'all-original' condition (an important judging criterion in *concours*). The Dart had belonged to his father who had willed it to him when he died. Thus, while these cars rippled with personal meanings for their owners, they rankled the other competitors in the shows. It was especially galling for them when the lowly Subaru won its class over more exotic, but less original, cars.

None of this is to say that the ideal at either the personal or the public level should be to indiscriminately preserve anything and everything that has any association with people, places, and events that mean something. These days saving every greeting card we receive or paying money for a vial of Elvis' purported perspiration seems rightly excessive. The excesses of Victorian sentimentality in the home still strike us as suffocating. Keeping everything in an affluent materialistic society is impossible and undesirable. Keeping everything would also mean preserving bad memories as well as good. There may be some instances when status and sentimental attachments coincide, as with certain family heirlooms, like those whose lives Freund (1993) documents. But just as we regard the body of a deceased loved one as sacred and worthy of respect, ritual and reverence (as opposed to, say, being used as food), so should the attachment to and retention of possessions give us pause to appreciate the personal, familial, and private symbolism of useless objects. This is the lesson that my Groucho glasses have taught me. They have improbably helped me to see my life and what is important to me more clearly.

In Japan an unflawed tea cup is considered imperfect and of far less value than one with a blemish, nick or other minor flaw. I think the same is true with my Groucho glasses. I find greater meaning in these glasses in their present state of decay. For not only are such objects extensions of self for me, they are also a metaphor for self. Their less than perfect condition is like my own. Yet they still have deep meaning and can bring a smile within our family circle. I hope this is true of me as well. And perhaps it is their enigmatic imperfection that makes me appreciate them all the more. Their ability to function within an internal sign system rather than through a set of more widely readable, but superficial, properties is what gives them their true meaning for me.

References

Baker, N. (1988) The Mezzanine, New York: Vintage Books.

Belk, R. (1986) 'Art versus science as ways of generating knowledge about materialism', in D. Brinberg and R.J. Lutz (eds) Perspectives on Methodology in Consumer Research, New York: Springer-Verlag, 3–36.

—— (1991) 'Possessions and sense of past', in R.W. Belk (ed.) Highways and Buyways: Naturalistic Research from the Consumer Behavior Odyssey, Provo, UT: Association for Consumer Research, 114–30.

—— (1998) 'Multimedia consumer research', in B. Stern (ed.) Representation in Consumer Research, London: Routledge, 308–38.

—— Wallendorf, M. and Sherry, J.F., Jr. (1989) 'The sacred and the profane in consumer behavior: theodicy on the Odyssey', Journal of Consumer Research 16, June: 1–38.

Berger, J. (1972) Ways of Seeing, London: British Broadcasting Company and Penguin Books.

Botton, A. de (1994) The Romantic Movement: Sex, Shopping, and the Novel, London: Macmillan.

Brown, S. (1997) Postmodern Marketing Two: Telling Tales, London: Routledge.

Clifford, J. and Marcus, G. (eds) (1986) *Writing Ethnography: The Poetics and Politics of Ethnography*, Berkeley: University of California Press.

Cole, S. (1992) 'Anthropological lives: the reflexive tradition in a social science', in M. Kadar (ed.) *Essays in Life Writing*, Toronto: University of Toronto Press, 113–27.

DeLillo, D. (1984) *White Noise*, New York: Viking Penguin.

Freund, T. (1993) *Objects of Desire: The Lives of Antiques and Those Who Pursue Them*, New York: Pantheon.

Geertz, C. (1988) *Works and Lives: The Anthropologist as Author*, Stanford, CA: Stanford University Press.

Gould, S. (1991) 'The self-manipulation of my pervasive, perceived vital energy through product use: an introspective-praxis perspective', *Journal of Consumer Research* 18, September: 194–207.

Holbrook, M. (1995) *Consumer Research: Introspective Essays on the Study of Consumption*, Thousand Oaks, CA: Sage.

—— (1996) 'Romanticism, introspection, and the roots of experiential consumption: Morris the Epicurean', in R. Belk, N. Dholakia, and A. Venkatesh (eds) *Consumption and Marketing: Macro Dimensions*, Cincinnati, OH: South-Western, 20–82.

Hornby, N. (1992) *Fever Pitch*, London: Victor Gollancz.

—— (1995) *High Fidelity*, New York: Riverhead Books.

Kadar, M. (1992) 'Coming to terms: life writing – from genre to critical practice', in M. Kadar (ed.) *Essays in Life Writing*, Toronto: University of Toronto Press, 3–16.

Kopytoff, I. (1986) 'The cultural biography of things: commoditization as process', in A. Appadurai (ed.) *The Social Life of Things: Commodities in Cultural Perspective*, Cambridge: Cambridge University Press, 64–91.

Marcus, G.E. and Fischer, M. (1986) *Anthropology as Cultural Critique: An Experimental Moment in the Human Sciences*, Chicago: University of Chicago Press.

Montaigne, M. de (1957) *The Complete Essays of Montaigne* (trans. D. M. Frame), Stanford, CA: Stanford University Press.

McCracken, G. (1988) *Culture and Consumption: New Approaches to the Symbolic Character of Consumer Goods and Activities*, Bloomington, IN: Indiana University Press.

Thompson, M. (1979) *Rubbish Theory: The Creation and Destruction of Value*, Oxford: Oxford University Press.

Torgovnick, M. (1990) 'Experimental critical writing', *Profession* 90: 25–7.

Vernon, J. (1999) *A Book of Reasons*, New York: Houghton Mifflin.

Wallendorf, M. and Brucks, M. (1993) 'Introspection in consumer research: implementation and implications', *Journal of Consumer Research* 19, March: 489–504.

14 Burning in the bush of ghosts

Joel Watson

1

The edge of sanity is a familiar place. It's the place where he felt totally out of control of his life, mind and body in constant engagement. It's the conscience and unconscious levels of the mind living lives out of touch. This is the place where structure and form fall in on each other until they explode into a brilliant light, the light of absolution. Unable to reach out and touch, unable to cry out, unable to say the words, '*How long, how long?*'

The edge is the doorstep of death, the calm feeling of decisiveness, the peace of releasing all the pain, all the guilt and all the punishment. It's time and space folding towards infinity. But there, for the first time, exists clarity of purpose, and intention, the ability to carry out one final act of redemption. Being in the bowels of pain is a haunting and horrible place, filled with self-doubt and self-incrimination. The wounds grow exponentially with each act of self-hatred. The exile is self-imposed, the journey travelled with purpose, the horror magnified with the knowledge that the journey is travelled alone. The swirls of madness, presenting only one way out, one door to walk through.

The clarity of purpose belied the condition of his body and his mental state. Days of drugs and alcohol had made reality somewhat tolerable, had dulled enough of that pain to make it possible to get up in the morning. The mind needed to be clouded, the body punished, the self destroyed. There was no more room for feelings and emotions they had betrayed him, left him scared, angry and broken.

They went looking for the American Dream. Somewhere, somehow it been lost and it seemed the only quest left that seemed to have any worth. He travelled with John, in and out of consciousness, in and out of reality, through time and space. Neither sure nor concerned with what was real or fantasy, or if reality and fantasy existed at all or were just parts of one continuum.

John was both a brilliant and a removed person; the two parts each seeming to have a life apart from the other. He was tall and slightly built, almost wiry. His eyes were warm and piercing, they seemed to look into your soul, but would never reveal what they had found. He looked like he had not eaten in days yet he had the stature and face of a model. He was a beautiful man. Everything about him was long, his body, his gait, his speech, his flow. There were times when he seemed to glide rather than walk, arms, legs and voice flowing through time and space.

He and Dylan were both lost in a world that had become increasingly hard to understand. It was more than just confusion; it was a fundamental lack of under-standing of how the world worked. Confused about what they believed and what people told them they believed. This confusion ran deep into their beings, it was their being. It was worse than life having no meaning because at least then the search is over, there is no more ground to cover, and you can play or leave. But for John and Dylan life had some deep meaning hidden by the demons that walked the earth. The demons would not tell the truth. He and Dylan feed off of each other's inability to function in the mainstream. They had both fallen far from the beam and could not seem to catch up with it. They ran together drawing strength from their resistance to reality. John had the moral strength of ten men; he knew right from wrong and had deep and immovable values. It might have been this strong sense that forced him into a world of separation. How much time had been spent not achieving, not taking part in the texture of life? It was these qualities that made him a perfect companion for Dylan. Dylan was full of self-doubt, not sure if he was even worthy of his existence. He was sure that he was at his core a bad person one who was unable to see past his own selfish desires. John was a barometer, a way for Dylan to gauge the hopelessness of his own moral fibre. In a sense John was also a punishment, a constant reminder of what Dylan was not. They were at the same place in the world but with such different feelings of propriety. Yet they both were totally devoid of self-worth.

The American Dream seemed a perfect quest for these travellers, one last quest to play with, one last reason to live. For Dylan the journey was to be the last, one final attempt to solidify his belief that there was nothing to grasp at with his bloody and warm hands.

'Take my hands,' he begged her. 'Take them and hold them until I'm gone. I need to feel the contact; I need to know there is something real left for me to remember. I need to have one concrete moment to hold on to before I slip.' The demarcation between reality and fantasy had long been lost. The woman was not sure what he meant. She sensed a desperate urgency in his voice, but she didn't know how to help him. He scared her, as he held her hands so tightly they became blue. 'I'm not connected here, I can't feel your warmth, I can't feel your soul,' he said to her. She pulled away as his eyes became distant, focusing on a point in another world. The music was loud, swirling tighter and tighter, weaving around and around him. He was caught in the tornado and was lost. He reached out for her, in no particular direction, not really reaching for her but for some image of her that was imprinted on his mind from moments and lives before. She was now just an amalgam of all that came before her. That last attempt at contact had not saved him; he was spinning away caught in a spiral of sound that engulfed him. He was home. The spiral was a warm and comfortable place. It was the place he understood, the place where he was himself, the place where there was no fear, no threat of human contact, and no need for the touch. The motion was the feeling, the touch he could not get anywhere else. One final attempt to reach out, to feel, had failed, now he was back in the only place he really understood, a place where the conscious mind was not an asset, a place where life could happen without commitment or understanding. He had travelled her for the last time.

'I cannot see, I cannot hear, I cannot touch and feel, I need to understand. Help me find the healing place, the place where the demons can't project and edit my life. Give me the strength to search, give me a sign that my search is not in vain.' The thought screamed through Dylan's mind, crashing against the walls of denial.

'Yours is the path of darkness and despair, the road to self-indulgence and neglect. I can't walk your path, I won't let you lead me to your place of conceit, your palace of contentment.'

'Without you there is no me, without you there is no life. You define me, by all that you are and all that I am not. I have lost all but this; I can't feel you anymore. I can't feel me. I want to feel the touch, hear the love, live the passion, but I am encased in glass, in time. Please help me decide or let me go,' he whispered to no one. The girl was startled, she reached out instinctively to hold him, but he felt solid and cold as if he were a shell. He didn't react to her. There was nothing in his eyes, black holes where life had been only moments before. She held him, not sure what else to do. He looked to the sky. 'Thank you for letting me go, I'm tired and I need to move on, I need to start over, this body can't feel anymore.' He pulled away from her and moved quickly for the door, she didn't follow.

The night outside was thick. The music moved farther and farther away and the spiral finally stopped, finally peace. He could sense the night, the stars, the people but he could not feel them. His eyes showed him he was not alone but his senses could not register the experience in any way that he could understand. The world seemed to be going on all around him but not with him or in him. He had already left. He walked more slowly than usual, seeming to move without feeling the ground. He felt a sense of total peace, for the first time in years he knew exactly what to do. There was a direction, a hope to start over to achieve the feeling and understanding that this life had so lacked. In a rush of thought he knew how to stop the pain, to end the torture of not being able to feel. It just came to him in an instant while he was in the spiral. He had asked for help and he had gotten it – a way out, a way to break the glass. He was engulfed in a feeling of total calm. There was no more anxiety, no more tension, and no more pain.

2

A voice echoed from nowhere in particular. 'Each of us is on a journey through life. We are thrust into the spiral of existence and are constantly reaching for meaning and fulfilment. We all look hard for membership, be it to ourselves, a group, a family, we want to belong. We define and redefine through transitions in life. Our constant search is for who we are, what we can be. We desire to be self-contained yet loved, so we use marks and symbols to define ourselves. We acquire symbols that become metaphors for and help us understand belongingness, self-control, intimacy, courage, beliefs and love. We make these symbols part of ourselves. We assimilate them.' What was this, who was this? Dylan looked out at the ocean, but he couldn't see anybody. Then from behind, a shadow emerged. Dylan turned, expecting to see John, but it was a stranger. A tall, dark man appeared wearing only shorts. His body was covered with tattoos. His hair was half way down his back, long and curly. His skin tan but not worn, he seemed to glide towards Dylan. 'What are you doing out here in the starlight?' he asked. 'I followed you from the party, I thought you might be looking for something, that you might be trying to define your own transition. My body is covered with my transitions, with my pain and glory. Can you tell me about your pain, your glory?'

Dylan didn't know how to respond; he struggled to find words to describe what he was feeling.

As Dylan began to speak, anger ripped at him. He had given everything, love, faith, hope, energy and time, all that he could give, all that he knew, all that he was. He could feel his body and soul being torn away, with each passing moment another cut, no end in sight, helpless to stop the bleeding. This was dark, things had seemed surreal for a long time, but this had an air of horror about it, nothing would ever be the same again, all the work all the preparation and in a passing violent moment life had changed forever.

The spiral had been a place to rest for such a long time, a place where he could feel strong and content, a place that made it possible to be whole. What he hadn't realised until now was that the spiral was his life, it was where he was happy. The spiral was the only place that was tolerable, the only place where he could find the contact he so desired. Over and over he went there to be renewed but he would always come back. Now he felt it was time to go somewhere else, no more hiding in the spiral, no more coming back to the place of pain.

Why was love so hard to feel? He wanted desperately to love, to feel love. He had lost himself somewhere. He was a stranger. He could find nothing to hold onto. He found nothing to make him think that the spiral was a place where redemption was possible.

'I love you, but I cannot show you. The conflict in me is tearing me apart. I am ageing a thousand years every minute. I want to tell you, to show you, it's all

that life is for me, to give love and I can't find a way, I can't find a place, a time, a space.'

He explained to the stranger that Laine was the one who could save him and he could think but not talk to her. He loved her so deeply that it paralysed him. He wanted to give all of this to her but he wasn't able to fight the demons, he could not shake the loss, the pain. He knew she was the one shining moment in his life, but he feared he could not escape the spiral long enough to catch her, and he feared she could not wait.

She was the wind, the earth, the water and the stars. She walked in the room and he felt a sense of peace, a sense that everything would be all right, yet it was this feeling that scared him so. How could he hang onto one so beautiful, when he was so removed from life? He knew that the spiral would prevent him having the spiritual connection his soul needed to be free.

'My name is Gabriel,' the tattooed man said. 'I understand what you are saying, I have been some of the places you have been, and I have seen some of your transitions.' Gabriel went on to say, 'In times of transition our symbols help us understand and communicate the transition. My tattoos are metaphors for who I am and my place in the spiral. I believe this is true for many people. I believe that we try to navigate the spiral using many heuristics, one of which is consuming all that is around us. A key to understanding why we consume and what we consume is the notion that I borrowed from a man named Russ Belk. He said, "knowingly or unknowingly, intentionally or unintentionally we regard our possessions as parts of ourselves".[1] It has been argued by some that objects become a part of the self when we are able to exercise control over or possess the object.[2] Belk found that humans feel the most control and sense of possessiveness over their bodies and body parts.[3] Thus body alteration, such as my tattoos, becomes a powerful symbol in helping to define or redefine the self. Still others have found that in times of life transition the self-concept may become blurred and new sets of role identities may be adopted that put a person in flux.[4] Body alteration is then a catalyst to bring the body and self-concept into line with the new ideals.[5] I have talked to many people with tattoos and they usually view their tattoos as expressions of them, a way to transmit information about their uniqueness to others.'[6]

Dylan's head was spinning. He thought to himself, 'Who is this man, what is he saying to me, why is he talking to me?' Although Dylan was not in a great frame of mind, he realised that this man, this Gabriel, must have tapped into his pain, into his confusion, but he was talking in such real terms, like a grip on reality is what Dylan needed. But as Dylan began to fade into the spiral again, he thought reality was not exactly what he was looking for, but more a sense of belonging, fairness, a marginal sense of peace.

It was a strange feeling not needing any sense of reality to be happy, but it seemed to be working, working in such a way that the disjointed trip he was on seemed to make total sense. Sense out of unreality, that summed up his environment or to be more exact his world. As he travelled he was not focused on anything in particular except leaving his life behind, or more precisely, on permanent hold. As usual there was nothing in the way of closure to any part of what he had left. He wasn't employed, so that wasn't an issue, but there were people who cared for him that were left without an explanation, or in most cases not even being told he was leaving. This was his way, not the best way or the most caring way, but his way.

What was so strange about it was that he was a caring person. So much of what he did revolved around caring for others. So much of his life was dictated by how his actions would impact others. He wondered if his priorities, his philosophy, ever existed. He thought he had both but now he couldn't remember them. He sat puzzled for hours at a time dwelling on what he was guided by, what had led him to where he was. He couldn't find an answer. He figured he had caused a lot of pain and that he couldn't forgive.

How had he gotten here? Dylan just wanted to answer this one question. He no longer could worry about priorities or philosophy of life. These issues were unattainable, hidden in one of the closets in his mind. He just needed to know what brought him to this point. He didn't care what Gabriel was telling him, he didn't understand what Gabriel was saying. He thought to himself, 'Hate all that you have become, because it is destructive, you can destroy yourself, but if the destruction is reckless, you will destroy others. I have been reckless.'

He shouted, 'God forgive me because I've been reckless with my life. Reckless with the love that has been given, reckless with the pain I have wrought.' He began to walk off into the ocean. He then heard Gabriel's voice again.

'I can take you on another journey. There are people you must meet, people who understand transitions. People who understand love, hate, self . . . people who have been where you are now. Come with me for awhile, let's travel and see if we can find a reason to live outside the spiral.'

3

Dylan and John had no place to go. Their journey had ended in their minds. Gabriel's entrance into their lives was like that of a cherub sent to protect them from themselves. Gabriel took them both in and he said they could stay for as long as they wanted, or more to the point, as long as they needed. Gabriel lived downtown in a two-storey warehouse: all the space was his. The hum of the city was ever-present in the warehouse, because both storeys had huge windows on the street side of the space that allowed the outside world in. However, huge metal blinds made it possible to control how much of the city life could enter. John had made himself a home on the second level right in front of the windows, because he liked being able to watch the world from above without the world being able to touch him. Dylan, on the other hand, was downstairs with Gabriel. They had become constant companions, Gabriel trying to reach Dylan and keep him in the here and now and out of the spiral.

Gabriel gave Dylan a book to read. It was a book about tattoos, consuming and the human spirit. Gabriel said it was an introduction to living outside the spiral. As he read to himself certain things resonated:

> Permanent 'decorative forms' are associated with enduring constructs such as gender, life long group affiliations (clan, tribal) and cultural notions of beauty such as blocked feet, or nose alterations.[7] The notion of a permanent and voluntary choice to alter the body sets tattooing apart from most other consumption behaviors.
>
> Previous research indicates that life transitions triggered either by external forces or some change within an individual are a major motivation for obtaining a tattoo.[8] This motivation carries through research on other permanent forms of body alteration, most notably plastic surgery.[9] At times of transition, there may exist a sense of incompleteness that motivates a person to create or re-create parts of the self-concept and in the process of self-creation one uses consumption to shape the self.[10] During the time of transition, persons will begin to construct or recognize alternative possible selves and there may be non-permanent changes in dress, etc. When an alternative new self is found or invented, then permanent alterations may occur to solidify this new or altered self.[11]

Dylan was beginning to see what Gabriel was trying to tell him. The spiral represented transition. For Dylan and John, it was their way to cope with an ever-changing world. They embarked on their journey so long ago looking for the American Dream, but really they were looking for themselves.

Gabriel came through the door. 'Dylan,' he said, 'are you ready to find out about the symbols we put on our bodies? I have so many people for you and John to meet, so many that were caught in the spiral that found a way out by altering themselves as their lives were altered.'

'I guess we're ready. I don't think that anybody can help me understand what the hell this journey is, but I've got time, I'm not going anywhere.' John nodded his head in affirmation; he was ready to continue the journey. He said, 'We've been out of the spiral for a while, it doesn't seem real. I need to feel some sense of belongingness in this space.' With that cryptic remark, they began.

Gabriel said that for some, tattoos marked a significant stage in a relationship. For some, becoming marked was motivated by ascension to a new relationship or family, such as a gang, the tattoo symbolising membership. He said tattoos mark the transition from individual to member. For others, tattoos symbolise the extension of family through marriage. The tattoo unites the family heritage with the new marriage. For some there was an epiphany of understanding, a moment of clarification, a transition to a higher level of consciousness, the tattoo symbolising the power of knowledge. Transitions are not always propelled by positive events. For some, the moment that prompts one to alter their body is traumatic. The tattoo, in this case, becomes a memorial, a symbol of a life lived and its link to lives that must still be lived. In many cases, the transition was a rite of passage, being freed from internal or external bonds. The tattoo symbolised a coming of age; it was an expression of personal power and control. Altering the body was an expression of freedom. The symbol and the act expressed that freedom to each individual.

Gabriel went on and on with stories of people who had marked themselves. Dylan and John became more intrigued with each story with each reason. Gabriel told them both they would meet people who would tell their stories; stories about how marking their bodies helped them control their lives. Finally they arrived at an arts centre stuck in the middle of the warehouse district. They could hear music coming out of every crack in the building, a cacophony of voices rained onto the streets. The huge doors swung open and the three travellers were immediately assimilated into the mass. Gabriel moved quickly through the crowd with John and Dylan attached to him as if on a string. The music was loud, and the voices swirled around them like a torrent of energy.

4

With the same energy as he was using moving through the crowd, Gabriel abruptly stopped at a large red door. He swung the door open and all three entered the room. It was full of people talking but with much less urgency and the music was quiet, in the background. Gabriel quickly moved to a table at the far end of the room. He said to everyone there, 'These are my new friends Dylan and John, they need help, they need to hear your stories.' Dylan and John sat down and the people began to tell their stories. The first was Mary. She began, 'I wanted something that would represent my relationship to my husband. We had been married for about a year and I wanted to mark that event with something. I decided that a tattoo would be the best way for me to do this. I wanted something permanent that was important to me. I had a hard time deciding what would represent this, and then it came to me. We got married at my parent's house, and part of getting the house ready was taking care of a huge bed of Day Lilies. I would go up to the house every weekend and take care of the garden. It is what I think of when I think of our wedding, so it seemed the Lily was the perfect symbol for me.'[12]

As Mary's voice trailed off, Siobhan's voice picked right up as if it was the same person. Siobhan began, 'My marriage was only one year old as well when I sort of had a crisis of identity. It seemed that very quickly my life had become my married life, that the person I was before marriage had become tangled up with the unit my husband and I had become. I felt this urgent need to have a tie back to my life before marriage. I wasn't unhappy, but I was afraid of losing myself. I decided that marking myself was a way to help me preserve who I was. I decided that I would put a rose on my shoulder. The rose was the symbol of my sorority in college, a time where I felt very independent, in total control of myself.'[13]

Without a break Gabriel introduced the next three people. 'I want to introduce you to Ellie, Nick and Jesus, all three were or are members of gangs.' Ellie spoke first, 'I have a gang tattoo. I got it because I was a gangster. I got it the night I was chosen . . . ' She then went on, 'I keep it because I want to remember that life, that life that I want no part of . . . '[14]

'Hey man,' Jesus broke in, 'don't say nothin' bad about gangs. My gang is my family, my gang is my life.' Nick interrupted, 'I got my tattoo when I was initiated into the neighbourhood gang that was almost 25 years ago, I got no allegiance to that anymore, that isn't any part of my family.'[15]

Jesus jumped back in, 'My tattoo is "R13". Everyone in my neighborhood gang wears it. The "R" is for the first letter of the neighbourhood, (I'm) from. The "13" is for the 13th letter of the alphabet which is (M) which stands for Mexican, Murder, Mafia!'[16] Jesus thrust a fist into the air and headed off to the bar.

Kevin spoke next, '(I guess sort of like Jesus) I wanted something that echoed my family heritage and would be timeless. (The symbol) means from beginning to end. My girlfriend, now my wife and I wanted something that would create an enduring bond between us.'

Jesse was next. He stood up and lifted his shirt showing Dylan and John his back; on it was a huge tattoo covering his whole back. It said 'Woodson Pride', Woodson across the top of his back and pride across the bottom. 'This is my symbol to family. This is my family heritage. I am proud of my family, proud to be a Woodson. Both my older brothers have the same tattoo, and my two little brothers are asking when they can get theirs. I think the older brothers are all going to go with each of them and give them the tattoos for their 16th birthdays. That's family pride, you can't take it away from us. It is on us for good.'[17]

Gabriel spun away from Jesse and welcomed Bill and Ellen. Bill and Ellen were considerably older than the rest of the group. Gabriel introduced them and Bill began to tell his story. 'I got my tattoo just after Ellen got hers. This is a second marriage for both of us and I think, although the symbols of our tattoos are very personal, the fact that we both have them and the fact that we got them together, makes them a unifying feature for both of us. My tattoo is an Indian symbol, a bear and a feather with the point of the compass surrounding them. I didn't pick the tattoo, it picked me. The bear came to me in a dream. I was walking in the forest, but I was a ghost feeling detached from my surroundings. As I approached a clearing, a bear approached me and said that I was not whole, that my human form was only part of what I was. The bear explained that in my past life I had been a bear, a protector of nature, and that if I did not acknowledge this part of me, I would never be whole. The bear then walked into me, my form assimilating the bear. I was no longer a ghost, but a whole person, and I felt as one with the woods I was in. I woke up with that feeling, knowing that the bear was my symbol. The feather was a gift from my tattoo artist. He is a full-blooded Black Foot Indian. He had just finished the bear and we both looked and said something was missing. Just before I was able to speak, he said that I needed to have a hawk feather. The amazing thing was that was exactly what I was thinking about. I work in the medical profession, I'm a registered nurse and I do a lot of work on the reservation. In my travels I found a hawk feather, and the medicine man in the tribe told me that the hawk feather had much power and I should always keep it with me when I was performing medicine. The feather was what my tattoo needed, the feather and the bear together was me. Now whenever I make something or I include this symbol on it, it is my signature, it is me.'[18] Ellen explained that her tattoo was a tree, and it reminded her of her childhood and of the nature she loved to paint. She said, 'The tree is as much a part of me as my eyes or my hands, it speaks directly of my soul.'[19]

After Ellen and Bill, each of the others at the table told their stories. Lacy talked about empowerment. 'My tattoo is a stencil-like drawing of the Greek goddess Artemis, she is the symbol of independence. (I got the tattoo) after reading "The Mists of Avalon", I felt empowered.'[20]

Francie spoke of a spiritual awakening. '(My tattoo is) a monkey. I was born in the year of the monkey. I am a primatologist. The Hindu god "Hunaman" is an albino rhesus monkey who is said to be the "son of the wind and the embodiment of devotion", something I'd like to emulate. I had been thinking about it for several years. I was 28, and going through some sort to spiritual re-awakening. Everything became very clear, and I knew exactly what I wanted, and exactly where to put it!'[21]

Nancy was crying as she spoke. She told Dylan and John about her rose, 'One of my good friends came up missing. She was killed and her body was so mangled you couldn't really tell who she was. I got something I thought no one else would have, a Rose with a leaf in front and a heart behind it.'[22]

Then came Lauren, '(My tattoo) is the sign for the heart chanra, it enables you to see from the heart, to see beauty and truth. It reminds me where I want to come from, where and what kind of space I want to be in. I got the tattoo at a time in my life when I was just coming out and I was dealing with a lot of issues that didn't allow me to come from my heart. It stood as a symbol for me of everything I hold to be my own truth.'[23]

For Stacy it was independence, 'I got my tattoo spring break senior year in high school. I was finally free of my family, and of my adolescence.'[24]

'(My tattoo) is a Jaguar (surrounded) by yin/yang. It represents the ebb and flow of all things, gracefulness and strength,' Tina said, '(I got it) as a rite of passage, a recognition of self. (It) strengthened my own beliefs, values.'[25]

This went on for some time. Both Dylan and John could barely focus on what people were saying. They just stared at each other as they talked. It was like an AA meeting, everyone giving his or her testimonials. Dylan turned to John and whispered, 'What the hell is going on here, is this some kind of hellish dream? . . . ' John interrupted, 'These stories mean something to me, I understand what they are saying about their lives. I feel connected to these people and I don't even really know them.' Dylan looked at John with a blank stare. He thought to himself, 'John is reaching for something that isn't there, what the hell is going on?' Just as Dylan started to get up and tell John he was leaving, two more people arrived. They caught Dylan's eye, as he was about to talk to John. Liza was a tall, lithe woman, her deep brown eyes and black hair caused Dylan to stop in his tracks. Right behind her was Elija, his arms were covered with tattoos, and his waist-length brown hair hid what appeared to be a back full of symbols. This pair mesmerised Dylan and he sat back down. Gabriel quickly moved back across the bar and embraced Liza and Elija. He turned to John and Dylan and said, 'These are the two I wanted you to meet, Liza and Elija have seen the spiral and have broken free.' He turned to Liza and said, 'These are the two I told you about. Can you tell them about your journey?' Liza sat down next to John and began to speak:

> I had been considering a tattoo for a couple of years but felt reluctant to make a permanent mark, plus I was quite poor. When I had a good job finally and most of my debt was gone, I started taking more risks in general. It seemed natural to get the tattoo I'd always wanted to have.
>
> One night I was angry, driving fast late at night, when a beer ad came on the radio that mentioned the national UFO Museum in Portland, to which I had been planning a trip. The guy in the ad mentioned 'the key to the universe' several times. I thought about this 'key' and it occurred to me that it really didn't need to be an entry key. Maybe the real key to the universe is an ignition key. Yeah, an ignition key. Then, remembering the fury I'd been feeling, the reason I was driving fast to begin with, and I thought, 'yeah, I want the goddamn key to the universe. Steal it, crank it up, drive the universe real fast all night 'til it runs out of gas. Leave it trashed and abandoned on the side of the road.' The next morning I saw what the key to the universe would look like. So I drew it and tattooed it on my arm.
>
> I was a grownup, had just turned 30, and I was doing everything I could to stir up my life. It seemed a potent symbol at the age of 30 to finally mark this virgin skin I'd been keeping pristine all this time. And it was great. Once the artist made the first mark I felt absolutely freed. After 30 years, God didn't own my skin anymore.[26]

John was excited, he had heard enough. He told Gabriel, 'I think I know what you are saying Gabe, I think I know what I need to do.' Gabriel responded, 'Do you want to go now, do you know what mark is yours?' John rose and said, 'Yeah, I know. I don't want to wait any longer, lets move on, lets put it away.' Gabriel and a few of the others embraced John and then headed for the door. Gabriel looked back at Dylan, 'You stay here we'll be back soon, let Elija tell you his story. Maybe he can help you find your voice.' With that they were gone.

Dylan was a taken aback. He didn't know these people, he didn't know what the hell John was doing and he felt like Gabriel had left him to be consumed by some strange cult. He whipped his head around and barked at Elija, 'Who the hell are you, and how do you know Gabe . . . What does he mean, find my goddamn voice . . . ?'

Elija put his hand on Dylan's shoulder. His voice was calm and slow, 'Gabriel has told me a lot about you and John. He has told me he found you at the edge of the ocean. He told me he found you at the end of your journey. He told me he thought you were thinking the ocean was your place, the end of your journey. He told me all those things but here you are so you must think, or at least hope, that there is more to your journey, or at least that it has a different end.'

Dylan's head slumped to the table. He was tired of fighting, tired of putting up resistance. Without lifting his head, he told Elija, 'I don't know what I think anymore. Part of me is mad at Gabe for bringing me here, I had made up my mind, I knew what was right, the ocean was calling me and I was going home. Now I'm here and I don't know why. I fought so long to understand and now I am back where I started.'

Elija asked Dylan to look at him and listen for just a few more minutes. Dylan lifted his head and looked into Elija's eyes, he sensed someone who cared, but he didn't understand why this stranger would care.

Elija began to speak; 'My body is covered with my life, lots of memories. I have had the chapters of my life burned into my skin, to help me remember. The marks are a part of me, they are emblematic of my existence. You see pictures, but they are not just pictures, they are a part of me, almost like my experiences. My memories have come up to the surface of my skin. Not all the symbols are good, but all are a part of me.' Elija began to explain each of his 20 tattoos to Dylan. His stories started when he was 12, his stepfather kicked him out of the house and he had to live on the street, 'I felt I needed something to make me strong, something I could lean on. I got my first tattoo here on my upper right arm. It's the Phoenix, the bird that rises from the ashes. I felt that my world had just been blown apart, but I was determined to survive and conquer.'

Elija went on with his stories describing each tattoo in detail. Dylan's eyes were fixed on each as the tales unfolded. Elija had told his stories in chronological order except for one notable exception, that being the large tattoo on his stomach, he kept telling Dylan they would deal with that later. This tattoo was the most provocative of all. It said 'COSA NOSTRA' in big bold letters, stretching from his breast down to his waist. As the stories unfolded this symbol began to haunt

Dylan. He thought to himself, 'This gentle patient man doesn't seem like the type to have such a symbol on his body. With each story this tattoo seems more and more incongruent with the man in front of me.' Finally the end had come, there was only one story left to tell, one part of life yet to be discovered.

Elija began slowly, almost haltingly, to describe the tattoo that covered his stomach. 'There was a time in my life . . . a time when I had lost my way. I had become something that I am not proud of . . . something that my family was not proud of. I was a runner for the Mafia in New York. I did a lot of bad things . . . a lot of cruel things . . . a lot of things that the people above me would never do. That is how it works, you start in the gutter, and work your way up to being just a criminal. I got some sort of power out of being part of the "family", I don't understand it anymore.' As he pointed to the symbol on his stomach he said, 'I wanted this to tell the "family" about my commitment, and to tell the world who I was and what I was. The amazing thing is that it's the only tattoo I'm going to have removed. It will be like removing that part of myself, that part of my life. To me, just like each of the tattoos help make me who I am, I think that by removing this, it will help me remove that part of my life. I'm tired of being judged by this symbol, and I don't think of that as part of me anymore.'

'The "COSA NOSTRA" tattoo has caused me to think a lot about all my symbols. How each is a part of me, and how by removing them I can, in essence, remove parts of me that are no longer viable.'

'I think in navigating the spiral of life there are many transition periods. As we reach for the light, the light that represents happiness, contentment and solace we've got to conquer these transitions. Some of us mark ourselves to delineate the passage of these transitions acknowledging that the self must be defined and redefined at crucial moments. Navigating the spiral alone is futile, we need a way to help us navigate, to help us keep our sense of self.'[27]

Elija got up and reached out to touch Dylan's hand. 'I hope you find a way to define your journey, Dylan. It is in the search that we become who we are. It is the journey that frames us. Learn to love yourself, and let the journey help you grow.' With that Elija left the room.

Dylan's head was spinning, but not from being in the spiral. It was spinning from self-reflection. He sat there with his head on the table for some time, thinking about his life. Thinking about his travels with John. Thinking about John brought him out of the trance of self-reflection. His head jerked up from the table. No one was left in the room. He was alone. He got up quickly and went back into the club. It was almost empty. He didn't recognise anyone there. The only thought he had was to get back to Gabriel's and find John. He ran outside and started running up the street. His head was pounding; he had a strange sense of urgency. He had a gnawing feeling that John was in trouble. He kept running and running through the dawn of the new day.

5

Dylan finally found Gabriel's. He had been running for hours. Yet the sense of urgency that had overtaken him at the warehouse only grew as he tried to get to John. He burst into Gabe's and saw John lying on the couch.

John writhed in pain, the cross on his back seeming to carry him down some terrible dark street. Dylan didn't understand the cross on John's back, he didn't understand the pain in John's eyes. Finally he stared into those broken eyes and asked them why, why this mark, this symbol. John pulled a crumpled piece of paper out of the breast pocket of his jacket, which was stretched over the only chair in the room. He handed the paper to Dylan, without a word. Dylan began to read:

> Please wear this cross as a symbol of the cross I must bear for myself, for you, for us and for our unborn children. The cross is heavier from the unfulfilled promises, deeds not undertaken, achievements as yet not attained, effort and love not fully given. These weights can be removed, and the cross I give to you and the one I wear myself are symbols of the commitment, effort and love which I am giving and will always give to you. Please wear this cross now and forever, because it will be a sign if we are to survive as partners of the love and commitment that I have for you and us, and if we do not survive as partners it will be a reminder that in your life there was someone who recognised you as a beautiful person, who like the phoenix rose from the depths to fight for the love of another person and to do what ever was necessary to shower another with love. The cross is a symbol of devotion, and no matter how things turn out if you keep it with you, you will always know there was someone who loved you from the bottom of their heart and someone who committed all his energies to that love. I cannot change the past and the cross will be heavy with it for some time, I believe that there is a chance for us, I will give everything to find that chance. I still see my unborn children in your eyes, and my whole self is filled with love for you. Please let the cross symbolise that love and devotion, and even if we do not survive, let it remind you that I loved you with all my heart and that people can awaken and give all that they have for the love of another.

Dylan realised in an instant that this journey could lead only one place, the symbols bouncing, dancing and piercing their souls. Neither Dylan nor John had any strength left to fight for what they were, both bodies covered with life, with time, decisions and revisions. John got up from the bed and began to run out the door and into the street. 'I can't hear you anymore . . . ' John's voice trailed off into the hum of the streets. 'We started and we finished . . . ' his voiced trailed off further ' . . . alone'. Dylan wasn't even able to acknowledge this emotion by now.

He stared not off into the void like he had for some time, but he glared at the mark John had on his back. He thought about Jesus on the cross. 'Did John feel he was dying each day for my sins or his own? Did John even know about sin?' He yelled at John, 'Don't relinquish your life for mine, don't live for me or die for yourself.' He screamed at John, 'Don't you see we need to be saved, saved from this Goddamn journey, saved from the spiral, saved by death . . . I can't even see what we are anymore, I don't understand love . . . it's love that makes the spiral so enticing and so horrible. It's love that makes us what we are . . . ' John stopped running, sweat and rain running off his face, the fear and anger subsided in an instant, the moment of clarity he had been seeking. He turned to see Dylan slumped in the doorway his head in his hands. John walked quickly back towards Dylan; he could see his mouth moving but couldn't make out what he was saying. As he came upon him, Dylan's head did not move, he stayed motionless slumped in the doorway saying over and over again 'Why can't we just love, why can't we just love . . . ' John sat down next to him in the rain and put his arms around Dylan, and whispered to him, 'We can love, we can love each other and ourselves. That's a start not an end . . . '

Finis

Notes

1 Belk, R.W. (1988) 'Possessions and the extended self', *Journal of Consumer Research* 15, September: 139–68.
2 McClelland, D. (1951) *Personality*, New York: Holt, Rinehart &Winstons.
3 Belk (1988) op. cit.
4 Schouten, J.W. (1991) 'Selves in transition: symbolic consumption in personal rites of passage and identity reconstruction', *Journal of Consumer Research* 17, March: 412–25.
5 Schouten 1991 op. cit.
6 Sanders, C.R. (1988) 'Marks of mischief: becoming and being tattooed', *Journal Contemporary Ethnography* 16, 4: 395–431.
7 Sanders 1988 op. cit. Schouten 1991 op cit.
8 Watson, J.C. (1996) 'Why did you put that there?: gender, materialism and tattoo consumption', *Journal of Consumer Research* 10, December: 319–29.
9 Schouten 1991 op. cit.
10 Csikszentmihalyi, M. and Rochberg-Halton, E. (1981) *The Meaning of Things: Domestic Symbols and the Self*, New York: Cambridge University Press. Schouten, 1991. Op. cit Belk, 1988 op. cit.
11 Markus, H. and Narius, P. (1986) 'Possible selves', *American Psychologist* 41, 9: 954–69.
12 Female, married, 28 years old.
13 Female, married, 26 years old.
14 Female, single, 17 years old.
15 Male, married, 39 years old.
16 Male, married, 20 years old.
17 Male, single, 23 years old.

18 Male, married, 51 years old.
19 Female, married, 47 years old.
20 Female, single, 24 years old.
21 Female, single, 28 years old.
22 Female, married, 25 years old.
23 Female, single, 19 years old.
24 Female, single, 19 years old.
25 Female, married, 34 years old.
26 Female, single, 30 years old.
27 Male, single, 29 years old.

Conclusion

The Rime of the Ancient Marketer

Listen up while I tell 'e' a tale –
The Rime of the Ancient Marketer
'Tis a tale of woe that you should
    know
Told by a one eyed Pirater

'Twas on the good ship 'Enterprise'
We sailed the market seas
The work was tough, the seas were
    rough
Fanned by commercial breeze

We always flew a flag of peace
To fool the market place
But skull and cross bones 'twas our
    mark
Much to our disgrace

A Marketer? No, Marketeer
A pirate occupation
A buccaneer, a profiteer
'Twas me true vocation

Ah! Ah! Ah! me 'arties

Customers bring good fortune
So superstition says
But I'm no softie marketing man
Ya get for what ya pays!

'Twas what I told the customer
It were me opening shot

We lost her custom from that day
They blame *me*, rotten lot

As marketing man I paced the poop
A sword 'twas in me hand
What was left for me but end it all?
I was scorned throughout the land

Ah! Ah! Ah! me 'arties

Shame as a millstone wreathed me neck
Where medal should have hung
I did the job they bade me do
My praises should be sung

The consultant guru climbed the nest
To see what she could do
'Customer care! 'tis what ya need'
But we hadn't got a clue

'Customer care – what piffle and tosh'
The sales man spun his line
'Rig the sales, bring in the dosh
'Tis then we're doing fine'

Ah! Ah! Ah! me 'arties

Becalmed were we 'pon treacherous
    sea
The prospects looking grim
But I weren't in charge as Piercy agrees
So don't blame *me*, blame *them*

While the sun beat down upon our
  heads
The crew's moans did abound
The spectre of the customer
Lay heavy all around

Business, business everywhere
Nor any to be had
The whole of the crew had given their
  last
Things were looking bad

Ah! Ah! Ah! me 'arties

Coopers and Lybrand criticised me
Cranfield set the score
'Marketing's too good fer the likes of
  you'
So what was I there for?

Bosun and captain were finance men
So Doyle's research did tell
They steered the ship, *they* set the
  course
And *that* 'twas our death knell'

'Advertising 'tis all we need
To turn their heads our way
'Tis all that marketing really is
What need fer more?' quoth they

Ah! Ah! Ah! me 'arties

Professional qualifications?
For us there is no need
Knowing about the job's just a waste
Mathews and Redman concede

And as for background experience
Sales 'tis probably best
Or perhaps engineering will do just as
  well
So Plymouth's findings suggest

Even my marketing friends all agreed
The job we did was poor
So was concluded by Taylor and Co
Of this I shall say little more

Ah! Ah! Ah! me 'arties

If marketing's to be criticised
Where do the problems lie?
If I think real hard I can work it all out
Let me see, I can if I try

First, I know *not* what marketing is
Second, nor do they
Third of all, 'tis all so mixed up
That's why we lost our way

Now back on shore it all becomes
  clear —
The error of our ways —
If customers refuse to do what ya
  wants
Pretend to give 'em yer praise

Ah! Ah! Ah! me 'arties

And so the marketer told his tale
So spake he to the throng
Keep the customers happy me friends
They say ya can't go wrong

But all 'tis not plain sailing
When ya chart the market seas
When the going gets rough, ya gotta
  get tough
Or they'll bring ya to yer knees

Some hurl abuse at us marketing folks
They taunt us and they tease
But we're all out to lunch,
The expense account bunch

Ah! Ah! Ah! me 'arties

David Pickton

15 Beyond the pleasure principle: the death instinct of pioneer studies in marketing

Robert Grafton Small

This is the bow tie my father always wore.[34]
34. B. Small, St. Andrews University, England, at the *Advances in Consumer Research Conference*, Amsterdam 1993

(Antonides and Van Raaij 1998:72, 88)

All situations are inspired by an object, a fragment, a present obsession, never by an idea. Ideas come from everywhere, but they organize themselves around an objective surprise, a material *derive*, a detail. Analysis, like magic, plays on infinitesimal energies.

(Baudrillard 1996: 1–2)

Alessi's role is to mediate between the most interesting expressions of creativity of our times, and the dreams of the consumer. We like to lead where others follow. Some of our objects are so extraordinary no other manufacturer would consider making them; it is a risk to put them into production, but if the design feels right, I have no hesitation in going ahead. The possibilities of creativity are immense and we have no limit on what we can do.

(Alberto Alessi, quoted in Sweet 1998:7)

It is a truth universally acknowledged that a single-minded don in want of a good fortune, must be in possession of publications. As reader, writer, editor and reviewer, even as the keeper of those totemic texts openly displayed for their titles yet rarely looked into, an academic is pressed to be in print. How odd, then, to uncover a homonym, the cited semblance seemingly based on published work and reported speech but affirming, if anything, whatever was not in the originals, and without modish irony too. My paper at the Association for Consumer Research in Amsterdam did, indeed, revolve around a bow tie, albeit my grandfather's and one unworn by anybody until I took it on.[1]

This said, the signal pairing referred to by Antonides and Van Raaij (1998: 72) is very much their own and not my interpretation. At least it was not in 1992, when I visited the ACR as a representative of St Andrews, Scotland's oldest university, then and now, and never far enough from Fife to count as English. However. One of these apparently aberrant authors was also in attendance as a colloquium organiser, the other less obvious. I know – that is, I assumed I did – because I believed I was there as well, unravelling the ribbon of my inheritance, its silky significance trailing a long way after Robert Louis Stevenson: 'I thought I had rediscovered one of those truths which are revealed to savages and hid from political economists; at the least I had discovered a new pleasure for myself. And yet even while I was exulting in my solitude I became aware of a strange lack' (1984: 95).

With lesser prescience in mind, there are evident parallels here between my arguments among the Dutch about artefacts and culturally mediated understanding, and the broadcast misunderstandings of both my immediate and indirect audiences – Van Raaij and Antonides, respectively. Is this really what Derrida and Lévi-Strauss intended when they declared, independently, that writing must be invoked as a deliberately subversive stratagem to make speech present when it is absent (Champagne 1995: 6)? A plaint by Sokal and Bricmont (1998: 4–5) – techniques and philosophies of science are being misused to impress and intimidate the inexpert – might equally well apply, though their views of the world, and the world of their views, are beyond me. Others with a taste for alterities – de facto Snark hunters *du jour* – may venture the *mise en abyme*, the whole story, so to speak, of career academics at Erasmus whose conscious choice of illustrative text is not only an unconscious yet direct negation of what its author – I – was attempting to say (Grafton Small 1993: 44) but more importantly in these relativist times, far beyond the implicit limits of the sign system seemingly shared unproblematically with Van Raaij's convention, and in print with Antonides (Eco 1986: 184).

Leaving aside the knowing plays on ties and closure – so self-referential – as well as a brand-new, second-hand bow that embodies the presence of absence – the original owner is unremittingly dead – and the absence of presence – the lately acquired symbolic object will never contain the void of its own making, there are certain complex uncertainties emerging from an event that despite eye-witness accounts, meaning Van Raaij and Bamossy's (1993) and mine (Grafton Small 1993: 38–45), neither of us can recall without contradiction. Antonides and his accomplice have since put together a volume of work – I profess, they are professors – so at first sight, the scales are not balanced at all but seen to fall from our eyes. Yet the inaccuracies and small omissions that caught my attention remain, significant because in being published, they present the semblance of scholarship without representing readers' – our – more private concerns with its practice. So Van Raaij and partners' perspective on consumer behaviour in Europe becomes, briefly, an ethnography of authorship, an advertisement for themselves more in the manner of Norman Mailer, say, than the evocation of an earlier event presaged by Colette (1973) or herald Garfinkel (1984).

Denied and undead, in the spirit of Doc Daneeka's Dantean addendum to

Heller's record 'Catch', I am rendered a shadow in my own write – right? – a simulacrum among orders of symbols (Baudrillard 1993: 75). This, though, is the life of the intellect, where we unscroll screeds of script instead of saying what we otherwise might. Besides which, the urge – the urging – to publish, to supplement ourselves (Baudrillard 1993: 42–3), could hardly be more consuming or tragically, for those under sentence of serial reproduction, less current. As Zbigniew Herbert explains, we went Dutch then as well:

> the game, however, did not take place on an island especially leased for the purpose, but in a country where the cardinal virtues were caution, moderation and accountability. A system based on bourgeois calculation could not coexist with a system of financial phantasmagoria. The collision of the world of desires with everyday reality was inevitable, and as is usual in such cases, painful. It is worthwhile now to ponder in what way, in what places, and in what social framework the speculation in tulip bulbs took place. The answer closest to the truth would be: on the margin of normal economic life, in its darkest corners, so to say.
>
> (Herbert 1994: 52–3)

Yet these repetitions are no farce. From a further coining of the same concern – an assay of Baudelaire's 'Counterfeit Money' – Derrida notes that as long as we can count with and on cash to produce effects, as long as false tender passes for real, there is nothing between the two, but beyond this frame, with its finite possibilities of decision and judgement, other contexts are opened up and delimited in turn (1992: 153). What is the true referent of *'La fausse monnaie'* (Derrida 1992: 129)? Where is difference when currency becomes disembodied, in cheques, debit cards and so on? How – to whom – are we accountable here? Can anyone tell the tale of money and would you credit their account? More prosaically, I am troubled by the inverse: what are words worth – owed? – when they refer only to themselves? Equally, if reports of counterfeit coinage retail as readily as anything else, what are we trafficking in?

The Rotterdammers' rerouting – rewriting – of my one-way, far from singular, street means I shall never play Marlowe, much less the detached observer (Benjamin 1997: 66), the *flâneur* following Baudelaire's footfall, however faintly, through the byways of my autobiography. Admittedly, I was not Philip or Charles in the first place and only PC by accident. I am, though, from a society where Van Raaij and Antonides' (1998: 72, 88) quotation marks are commonly taken, by readers and writers alike, to track the traces of some prior circumstance or script, and footnotes or references to indicate statements, not assertions, of fact. Why should it occur to anyone, then, to see in a story the primacy of the unsaid and the contrary, to question something they have newly adopted in allaying an earlier uncertainty?[2] Psychologists may delight that I deny my father so – Sigmund *froideur*, no doubt – Sokal and Bricmont (1998: 93–4) seem bemused by the seminal indistinction. Doesn't reading inform their own research? It does their po-faced campaign against postmodern abuses of a privileged lexicon by unknowing and uncaring authors.

The same crusaders for truth also insist (Sokal and Bricmont 1998: 177) the natural sciences are no mere reservoir of metaphors ready to be plundered, nor the themes of a theory to be summarised in a few words – discontinuity, chaos, what have you – then analysed in a purely verbal manner. In their primal context, these terms have specific meanings that differ in subtle but crucial ways from our everyday understandings. As these nuances are not self-explanatory or self-evident, Evelyn Fox Keller's caution (Wolff 1990: 80) is crucial. We must recognise that despite the undeniable successes and the robust detachment displayed in scientific writings, these are chronicles of specific phenomena 'prescribed to meet particular interests and described in accordance with certain agreed-upon criteria of both reliability and utility'.

So, if bodies of knowledge or lines of argument are to be developed within a discipline – any discipline – meaning partial understandings at best, even among the expert, the knowing and aware, we are obliged to treat the results as text, as mutually inhabited and inhibiting symbolic systems (Derrida 1976: 13–14), culturally maintained and moderated to make the world manageable, whether we realise it or not. How Sokal and Bricmont would undo the misconceptions that result, or stem the proven semiotic slippage, is not overly apparent. Equally, the broader questions of why one aspect of objective research should be preferred over others, or the significance, the rewards, society in general attaches to the production of certain results including, ironically, constants we are told would remain so unobserved, are largely ignored (Wolff 1990: 77). What language animals (Steiner 1998: 85) like ourselves read into this silence, and these lacunae, will, of course, depend on our individual backgrounds, our previous exposure to academics, for better or worse, and our appreciation of their competing interests (Sokal and Bricmont 1998: 70) as well as their interest in competing.

Not that I am accusing Antonides *et al.* of scientism (Sokal and Bricmont 1998: 180–1) necessarily; crude empiricists may have another explanation for the failure to check a printed reference. More seriously, how should we accommodate Van Raaij's rendition – his participant observation – of the impossible? An unwitting phenomenology of the imagination or one which not only forgets itself but also forgets its own forgetting, a tale passed on like the gift of tobacco, to be consumed and enjoyed before disappearing in a puff of smoke (Derrida 1992: 14,107)? Perhaps not. These worthies do, however, demonstrate a like degree of naivety over the nature of relativism, witness Sokal and Bricmont's (1998: 182) value judgement on the value of acknowledging local values, though notably never in studying ourselves, thank you very much. The 'anthropologist is not principally concerned with knowing whether those beliefs are true or false; it is difficult to see what she would gain by dragging into her research her own aesthetic preferences'.

Call it fate, call it kismet: Hardy's (1940: 25) counter is fatal. 'The mathematician's patterns, like the painter's or the poet's, must be *beautiful* (original emphasis); the ideas, like the colours or the words, must fit together in a harmonious way. Beauty is the first test: there is no permanent place in the world for ugly mathematics.' This was written for a lay audience, precisely those whom Sokal and Bricmont presume to protect, yet closer to the madding crowd, Hardy expects incomplete and transient interpretations across a range of topics, especially among the adept in each one. Whatever the facts encoded in calculation or the truths revealed in verse, these are products of the cultural flux they enable and extend, experienced by people with ultimately personal perceptions of industrial order and iteration. Alternatively, as *Venus in Furs* (Sacher-Masoch 1989) implies, all analogies are equally elegant but some are more elegant than others . . .

Textures of representation and the realities of text become tangibly more elusive when we dip a toe into the undertoad of *autocritique* – the frog at your throat – where even authorial ambiguities and ambiguous authorship (Barthes 1995: 152–3) will not dam, damn, the Lying Dutchmen, nor ground them as Sokal and Bricmont (1998: 53–4) suppose, in some coherent correspondence, give or take, between the outside world and the image our senses provide of it. The instability of this stance is, paradoxically, perhaps best illustrated by George Steiner's (1998: 19) initially supportive insistence on discourse as far more than an autonomous game of self-referential validation and effacement. Meaning, the great man maintains, is as close-knit to circumstance, to material perceptions, however conjectural and impermanent these are, as is our body. Attempts at understanding, at 'reading well', at responsive reception are, at all times, historical, social and ideological. How, then, can you explain (Twigger 1997: 281) the startling popularity of Hunting World bags?

The question comes from a sensational trial in Japan, centred around a suave-looking and finally convicted salaryman murderer who was caught on camera carrying one whenever he entered the courthouse. Afterwards – he had first been called to bear witness – sales soared, rivalling even Louis Vuitton. But why would that seed nationwide popularity? Ultimately, Twigger concedes, any analysis runs into the sand, evaporates, leaving explanation to those who prefer comfort over the lesser truths of well-observed description and incoherence. Here, Steiner changes his testimony on the stand, as well as his standing in his own testimony,

> It took too long before I understood that the ephemeral, the fragmentary, the derisive, the self-ironising . . . the interactions between high and popular culture, notably via the film and television – now the commanding instruments of general sensibility and, it may be, of invention – had largely replaced the monumental pantheon. Influential as they are, deconstruction and

post-modernism are themselves only symptoms, bright bubbles at the surface
of a much deeper mutation.

(Steiner 1998: 156)

Burying himself symbolically, in a sarcophagus of his own inscription (1998:
153–71), Steiner suggests, as a bequest, it is our elemental perceptions of mortality and the related classical impulse in art and poetry to endure, to achieve
timelessness, which today are in radical question. Not, perish the thought, where
have we been since 'Ulysses' came to bloom. Equally, if 'the aim of all life is
death' (Freud 1967: 70), what does our investment in the illusory immortality of
print, or any other representation, imply for each and every understanding of
ourselves and our various places in whichever worlds we may come to know? The
problem is pervasive and put into most pungent perspective by Richard Lloyd
Parry's (1999) toothsome return to Borneo on the back of another war between
the Dayaks and hated settlers from the island of Madura. Previously, three months
behind mouthings of head-hunters and cannibalism, he had spent a week searching
for signs but found only a few skeletons in the jungle, some grisly pictures and a
handful of witnesses.

Afterwards, Lloyd Parry wrote a couple of lengthy pieces for newspapers and a
30-page magazine article – 20,000 words altogether – about failing to find a
severed head. Now, he is spoiled: 'In the past six days I have seen seven of them,
along with a severed ear, two arms, numerous pieces of heart and liver, and a
dismembered torso being cooked over a fire by the side of the road – and I find
myself at a loss over what to say' (Lloyd Parry 1999). Yet contrarily, our reporter
records his contradictory reactions: relief, a secret pride, at facing such horror
without being overcome by fear or nausea, and something close to shame in not
being more upset by these same sights, for gathering proofs nobody could ever
publish, particularly when their most devastating effect is a sense of profound,
terrible banality. Or bathmology as Barthes (1995: 67) brands the interplay of
degrees – first I write, then I write that *I write* - ensnaring every contemporary
discourse.

This running commentary in, and on, our own exchanges is also a way of life:
'all we need to do is change the focus of a remark, of a performance, of a body, in
order to reverse altogether the enjoyment we might have taken in it, the meaning
we might have given it' (Barthes 1995: 66). So the sought-after skull is a syn-
ecdoche supposing some less skeletal insight if, as Lloyd Parry perhaps believes
but leaves unsaid, there are experiences too grave for shallow scribes. Here,
though, across another abyss, Roland (Barthes 1995: 65) sounds a warning: thinking like this becomes infinitely corrosive when we tolerate only languages which
testify, however frivolously, to a power of dislocation. The ensuing tensions are
vital and unavoidable; even as we say what we must, we realise, in Parry's unprint-
able riposte, the denial of who knows how much more.

The future certainly is eroded by our common capacity to query the quotidian, at least that displacement, that denial of desire foretold by Freud (1967: 26–7) for in a moment of multiple realities, beyond the pleasure principle is now. From the assumption (Betsky 1999: 27) modern science would find its embodiment in a new kind of truth: the object of use that told us all what it was, we have learned knowingness, to bring a sense of self, and each other, into our consumption of generic products, promoting these first degree declarations as bases for the particular possibilities provided by our personal predictions and creativity. This bespoke-in-bulk, this sloughing of redundant meanings is a twin to those single-cell communities that find life in avoiding their own waste (Freud 1967: 86) and makes tolerable sense, even in Betsky's (1999: 27) utopia. Here, as pilgrims of the virtual worlds opened up by computerisation, we may unveil, among the strange blobs emerging from balletic robots and laser cutting machines, a 'beauty that reminds us both of how the thing was made, and of our own – and the maker's – hand and body'.

Such serial indeterminacy is hardly new, however. Long before Lloyd Parry's lapses over recapping Dayak decapitation, his bare-bones handling of head-hunting without skulls, Sottsass Associates (1988: 56) were insisting their collective diary was not really a catalogue of the objects, monuments and buildings they had brought into being, 'somehow to find our place in history', but the story of an indefinite profession, 'situated between that of the architect and the designer, between, as it were, the artist and the constructor, the intellectual and the craftsman, the businessman and the sandwich eater'. Unsure, then, of their own standing and certain only of its shifting, these adepts in contemporary aesthetics were, by 1980, dealing from a commercial footing with a similarly secured society.

Recalling Steiner's cairn to the classical impulse, and Italy's part in it, our latter-day Milanese (Sottsass Associates 1988: 56) lament their ignorance, unable even to recognise the names or remember the dates in TV quizzes they cannot complete.[4] For them amid this milieu, this culture, of compressed and fragmentary notions of time, where memories matter more than archives, life also seems to be a permanent nostalgia 'for what it isn't, for what it has never succeeded in being, for what it has always abandoned, for what, each day, it will never be again'. Caught up in, while giving currency to, these currents of all-consuming cross-talk, I find myself detached from the body of my work, that is, the work of my body, by an act of critical cannibalism. In the wake of Antonides and Van Raaij (1998: 72, 88), another for the long pig-dead Author, now dismembered – disremembered – and displaced.

This heedless – headless? – undoing amid a riot of reconstruction is how the mediaeval university was invented (Eco: 1986: 84), with the same carefree attitude today's vagabond clerks assume in destroying, transforming, it as part of our own Middle Ages, our new order of permanent transition and constant readjustment. Signally, for those who trade – don't we? – in these shifting standards of pleasure and preference, beauty and the best, the market's future, the future's markets, will be no less fraught: 'we are not anxious to "solve any problem" nor to satisfy any need, or even to "sell" (neither to big nor to small industry), we don't want to conclude anything, in fact we find conclusions depressing; we wish all our projects were the mothers and fathers of the next' (Sottsass Associates 1998: 57). In closure – endings are for others – and to offset some semblance of myself unwillingly erased under writing, a sign of Will Self (1999: Ackn.) written under erasure: 'In the same volume there's an interesting essay by Olivier Cohen which suggests that despite the fact he has met me personally, I still don't exist'.

Notes

1 *Two steps back, the paso doble*

> At a restaurant in Saragossa this month, two elderly women met to complete one of the last missions of the Spanish civil war. Ascension Zaborras, aged 90, took out an eight-sided box which her family had had made specially for this occasion and handed it to Isabel Vicente, aged 81.
>
> Inside was an envelope containing a neatly folded cream and maroon handkerchief. The handkerchief, so well preserved it still looks new, belonged to Lieutenant-Colonel Etelvino Vega, and the last time he held it was on November 15 1939 when guards at the Alicante Reformatory came to escort him to his execution.
>
> Though only 30 years old, he had been a commander on the Catalonian front. And when the Republic crumbled, its already exiled leadership chose him to go back to Spain to be military governor of its final bastion, Alicante. He was captured in the war's dying hours.
>
> As General Franco's forces marched him to the courtyard to face the firing squad, he asked if he could go back for a coat. Into a cellmate's pocket he tucked the cream and maroon handkerchief which his wife's mother had just given him. 'It's all I have. Give it to my wife', he said.
>
> (Hooper 1999)

2 *Measure for Measure*

It's a Friday, some time in summertime, and I've sought Shelter, sifting the second-hand clothes for short-sleeved shirts until – my hunt is over – a Jaeger *Sportsman* in pearl grey, with patch pockets. 'Pure Cotton', boasts the label inside the button-down collar. 'Made in Italy – S'. It's surprising how many things have my name on but don't fit me at all. Machine washable? Yes, says a tag off the side seam, and 54% Linen too. Four pounds, no haggling.

3 *Just potter . . .*

> Few things are more useful, more absolutely indispensable, than pots and plates and jugs. But at the same time few human beings concern themselves less with utility than do the collectors of fine porcelain and glazed earthenware. To say that these people have an appetite for beauty is not a sufficient explanation. The commonplace ugliness of the surroundings in which fine ceramics are so often

displayed is proof enough that what their owners crave is not beauty in all its manifestations, but only a special kind of beauty – the beauty of curved reflections, of softly lustrous glazes, of sleek smooth surfaces.

(Huxley 1979: 90)

4 *Walk like an Egyptian*

With an eye, maybe, to Henry Ford, the eponymous and oddly entrepreneurial Ettore (Sottsass Associates 1988: 56) once told us: 'All things considered, really, we don't know what history is.' Yet in 1981, he christened his newly composed design collective 'Memphis' – after an established trading and administrative centre of the Southern States, home to Elvis Presley, Sun Records' king, and the Mommy's Boy Mausoleum, or Memphis the ancient artistic and administrative centre of the Lower Kingdom, home to Ptah, a major god, long worshipped as the creative power? Memphis, from Milan and truly *avant-garde*, an idea so old its time has surely come again.

References

Antonides, G. and Van Raaij, W.F. (1998) *Consumer Behaviour: A European Perspective*, Chichester: John Wiley and Sons Ltd.

Barthes, R. (1995) *Roland Barthes*, London: Papermac/Macmillan Books.

Baudrillard, J. (1993) *Symbolic Exchange and Death*, London: Sage.

—— (1996) *Cool Memories II 1987–1990*, Durham: Duke University Press.

Benjamin, W. (1997) *Charles Baudelaire*, London: Verso.

Betsky, A. (1999) 'The art of production', *Blueprint* 160, April: 26–7.

Champagne, R.A. (1995) *Jacques Derrida*, New York: Twayne/Macmillan.

Colette (1973) *The Thousand and One Mornings*, London: Peter Owen.

Derrida, J. (1976) *Of Grammatology*, Baltimore: Johns Hopkins University Press.

—— (1992) *Given Time: 1. Counterfeit Money*, Chicago: University of Chicago Press.

Eco, U. (1986) *Faith in Fakes: Essays*, London: Secker & Warburg.

Freud, S. (1967) *Beyond the Pleasure Principle: The Pioneer Study of the Death Instinct in Man*, New York: Bantam Books.

Garfinkel, H. (1984) *Studies in Ethnomethodology*, Cambridge: Polity Press.

Grafton Small, R. (1993) 'Everyday life in a brand-new second-hand bow tie', *European Journal of Marketing* 27, 8: 38–45.

Hardy, G.H. (1940) *A Mathematician's Apology*, Cambridge: Cambridge University Press.

Herbert, Z. (1994) *Still Life with a Bridle: Essays and Apocryphas*, London: Vintage.

Hooper, J. (1999) *The Guardian*, March 22.

Huxley, A. (1979) *The Doors of Perception and Heaven and Hell*, St. Albans: Panther/ Granada Publishing.

Lloyd Parry, R. (1999) *The Independent*, March 25.

Sacher-Masoch, L. von (1989) *Venus in Furs*, New York: Blast Books.

Self, W. (1999) *Tough, Tough Toys for Tough, Tough Boys*, Harmondsworth: Penguin Books.

Sokal, A. and Bricmont, J. (1998) *Intellectual Impostures*, London: Profile Books.

Sottsass Associates (1998) *Sottsass Associates*, New York: Rizzoli International Publications.

Steiner, G. (1998) *Errata: An Examined Life*, London: Phoenix/Weidenfield & Nicolson.

Stevenson, R.L. (1948) *Travels with a Donkey in the Cevennes*, London: Falcon Press.

Sweet, F. (1998) *Alessi: Art and Reality*, London: Thames & Hudson.

Twigger, R. (1997) *Angry White Pyjamas*, London: Indigo/Cassell Group.

Van Raaij, W.F. and Bamossy, G.J. (eds.) (1993) *European Advances in Consumer Research*, Vol. 1, Rotterdam and Amsterdam: Association for Consumer Research.

Wolff, J. (1990) *Feminist Sentences: Esssays on Women and Culture*, Cambridge and Oxford: Polity Press/Basil Blackwell.

Index

Page numbers appearing in **bold** refer to tables, figures and plates.

For Product Safety Concerns and Information please contact our EU
representative GPSR@taylorandfrancis.com Taylor & Francis Verlag GmbH,
Kaufingerstraße 24, 80331 München, Germany

Printed and bound by CPI Group (UK) Ltd, Croydon, CR0 4YY
08/05/2025
01864357-0003